Scientific Perspectives on Pseudoscience and the Paranormal

Scientific Perspectives on Pseudoscience and the Paranormal

Readings for General Psychology

Second Edition

EDITED BY Timothy J. Lawson

Bassim Hamadeh, CEO and Publisher
Jennifer Codner, Senior Acquisitions Editor
Michelle Piehl, Senior Project Editor
Casey Hands, Associate Production Editor
Jess Estrella, Senior Graphic Designer
Stephanie Kohl, Licensing Coordinator
Gustavo Youngberg, Interior Designer
Natalie Piccotti, Director of Marketing
Kassie Graves, Vice President of Editorial
Jamie Giganti, Director of Academic Publishing

Copyright © 2019 by Cognella, Inc. All rights reserved. No part of this publication may be reprinted, reproduced, transmitted, or utilized in any form or by any electronic, mechanical, or other means, now known or hereafter invented, including photocopying, microfilming, and recording, or in any information retrieval system without the written permission of Cognella, Inc. For inquiries regarding permissions, translations, foreign rights, audio rights, and any other forms of reproduction, please contact the Cognella Licensing Department at rights@cognella.com.

Trademark Notice: Product or corporate names may be trademarks or registered trademarks, and are used only for identification and explanation without intent to infringe.

This book was previously published by: Pearson Education, Inc.

Cover image: Copyright © 2017 iStockphoto LP/fergregory.
Copyright © 2013 iStockphoto LP/Messier111.

Printed in the United States of America.

ISBN: 978-1-5165-2726-7 (pbk) / 978-1-5165-2727-4 (br)

To Anna, Alexandra, and Ryan

BRIEF CONTENTS

PREFACE 1

1. **What Is Pseudoscience?** 5
2. **Methodological and Statistical Reasoning** 19
3. **Neuroscience and Consciousness** 47
4. **Child Development** 87
5. **Sensation and Perception** 113
6. **Learning and Memory** 139
7. **Cognition** 181
8. **Personality and Psychological Testing** 215
9. **Psychological Disorders and Therapies** 255
10. **Social Psychology** 307

INDEX 345

CONTENTS

Preface 1

1 What Is Pseudoscience? 5
    1.1 "Science Versus Pseudoscience" 5
        Timothy J. Lawson

2 Methodological and Statistical Reasoning 19
    2.1 "Why Bogus Therapies Seem to Work" 19
        Barry Beyerstein
    2.2 "The Suggestibility of Young Children" 31
        Maggie Bruck and Stephen Ceci
    2.3 "On the Belief That Arthritis Pain Is Related to the Weather" 40
        Donald Redelmeier and Amos Tversky

3 Neuroscience and Consciousness 47
    3.1 "Why Right-Brain Teaching Is Half-Witted: A Critique of the Misapplication of Neuroscience to Education" 47
        Annukka Lindell and Evan Kidd
    3.2 "Can Minds Leave Bodies? A Cognitive Science Perspective" 62
        D. Alan Bensley
    3.3 "Dream Interpretation and False Beliefs" 74
        Giuliana Mazzoni, Pasquale Lombardo, Stefano Malvagia, and Elizabeth Loftus

4 Child Development 87
    4.1 "Do Babies Learn From Baby Media?" 87
        Judy DeLoache, Cynthia Chiong, Kathleen Sherman, Nadia Islam, Mieke Vanderborght, Georgana Troseth, Gabrielle Strouse, and Katherine O'Doherty
    4.2 "Separating Fact From Fiction in the Etiology and Treatment of Autism: A Scientific Review of the Evidence" 96
        James Herbert, Ian Sharp, and Brandon Gaudiano
    4.3 "The Myth of the Mozart Effect" 108
        Will Dowd

5   Sensation and Perception   113

- 5.1   "What's That I Smell? The Claims of Aromatherapy"   113
  Lynn McCutcheon
- 5.2   "The Subtle Power of Hidden Messages"   120
  Wolfgang Stroebe
- 5.3   "Psychic Crime Detectives: A New Test for Measuring Their Successes and Failures"   130
  Richard Wiseman, Donald West, and Roy Stemman

6   Learning and Memory   139

- 6.1   "Do Visual, Auditory, and Kinesthetic Learners Need Visual, Auditory, and Kinesthetic Instruction?"   139
  Daniel Willingham
- 6.2   "Past-Life Identities, UFO Abductions, and Satanic Ritual Abuse: The Social Construction of Memories"   151
  Nicholas Spanos, Cheryl Burgess, and Melissa Faith Burgess
- 6.3   "Memory Recovery Techniques in Psychotherapy: Problems and Pitfalls"   165
  Steven Jay Lynn, Elizabeth Loftus, Scott Lilienfeld, and Timothy Lock

7   Cognition   181

- 7.1   "Nostradamus's Clever 'Clairvoyance': The Power of Ambiguous Specificity"   181
  Maziar Yafeh and Chip Heath
- 7.2   "Like Goes With Like: The Role of Representativeness in Erroneous and Pseudoscientific Beliefs,"   190
  Thomas Gilovich and Kenneth Savitsky
- 7.3   "Some Systematic Biases of Everyday Judgment"   204
  Thomas Gilovich

8   Personality and Psychological Testing   215

- 8.1   "Criminal Profiling: Granfalloons and Gobbledygook"   215
  Brent Snook, Paul Gendreau, Craig Bennell, and Paul Taylor
- 8.2   "What's wrong with this picture?"   226
  Scott Lilienfeld, James Wood, and Howard Garb
- 8.3   "Portrait of a Lie"   237
  Matthias Gamer
- 8.4   "Voice Stress Analysis: Only 15% of Lies About Drug Use Detected in Field Test"   247
  Kelly Damphousse

9   Psychological Disorders and Therapies   255

- 9.1   "Dissociative Identity Disorder: A Contemporary Scientific Perspective"   255
  Scott Lilienfeld and Steven Jay Lynn
- 9.2   "Can We Really Tap Our Problems Away? A Critical Analysis of Thought Field Therapy"   276
  Brandon Gaudiano and James Herbert
- 9.3   "A Close Look at Therapeutic Touch"   288
  Linda Rosa, Emily Rosa, Larry Sarner, and Stephen Barrett

10   Social Psychology   307

- 10.1   "Mass Delusions and Hysterias: Highlights From the Past Millennium"   307
  Robert Bartholomew and Erich Goode
- 10.2   "Does Venting Anger Feed or Extinguish the Flame? Catharsis, Rumination, Distraction, Anger, and Aggressive Responding"   321
  Brad Bushman
- 10.3   "False Confessions: Causes, Consequences, and Implications for Reform"   335
  Saul Kassin

Index   345

PREFACE

> *"In a world in which the media, self-help industry, and Internet are disseminating psychological pseudoscience at an ever-increasing pace, the critical thinking skills needed to distinguish science from pseudoscience should be considered mandatory for all psychology students."*
> —Scott Lilienfeld (2005)

UNLESS YOU HAVE avoided all popular media in the past few years, you've probably seen a number of extraordinary claims about therapies, products, and people's abilities that seem to defy what we know about physics, biology, and psychology. You may have seen people who claim they can communicate with the dead, psychic detectives who can apparently solve crimes by "seeing" a crime scene that is miles away, nurses who claim to heal people simply by waving their hands above their patients' bodies, and people who claim they were abducted by aliens who conducted horrific experiments on them. Gallup polls (e.g., Moore, 2005) suggest that many people believe in paranormal phenomena. For example, 41% of Americans believe in extrasensory perception (ESP), 21% believe that people can communicate mentally with someone who has died, and 25% believe in astrology. Scientists have actually studied these phenomena and a wide variety of other paranormal and pseudoscientific phenomena. In this book you will read what they have discovered and how they think about such claims.

The fact that some college students hold beliefs in pseudoscientific and paranormal phenomena became apparent to me early in my career. Several years after I became a psychology professor, I took several of my brightest students to a professional psychology conference in Chicago. One night, while walking to a restaurant, they spotted a psychic's office. When they told me that they had a strong belief in psychic abilities, I wondered how they could hold such a belief after I had taught them about psychology, critical thinking, and the scientific method. It was at that point that I realized that even though I had taught them what science *is*, I had not specifically addressed what science is *not* (i.e., pseudoscience). Since then I have been teaching students what scientists know about pseudoscience and the paranormal, and we've all found it to be a fascinating lesson in scientific reasoning as well as the cognitive and social forces that conspire to create pseudoscientific and paranormal beliefs.

Purpose of the Book

As Lawson and Brown (2018) noted, psychologists are becoming increasingly aware of and concerned about the problem of pseudoscience in psychology. Psychology students and the general public are constantly exposed to pseudoscientific and paranormal claims through the media, the Internet, and pop psychology books. Psychology professors are becoming more concerned about teaching students to think critically about these claims. I hope that instructors will find this book of readings to be a useful tool for educating students about such claims.

This book was designed to give beginning psychology students the opportunity to read original sources from psychologists and other scientists who have investigated pseudoscientific and paranormal phenomena related to psychology. These original sources allow students to get a close-up look at how scientists think about these phenomena, how they design research studies to investigate such phenomena, and why they are critical of pseudoscientific and paranormal claims. Students will also learn about scientific perspectives on a wide variety of specific pseudoscientific and paranormal phenomena. Along the way, they will encounter interesting examples that bring to life important psychological concepts (e.g., representativeness heuristic, confirmation bias) and scientific principles (i.e., correlation does not mean causation; the importance of replication of research findings).

I carefully selected the readings in each chapter to ensure that (a) the articles were fairly brief, (b) they were written by scientists knowledgeable about the scientific research related to each topic, and (c) introductory psychology students would find them interesting and understandable. For articles that were somewhat longer or more complex, I edited their length and excluded sections that seemed too complex for introductory psychology students.

Organization of the Book

The chapters in this book are organized around typical introductory psychology topics (e.g., sensation and perception, learning and memory, social psychology), making it easy for instructors to relate this material to topics that students are learning in an introductory psychology course. Although Chapter 1 is an introduction to the topic of pseudoscience and the paranormal that students should read before the other sections of the book, the other chapters and articles are designed to stand on their own. Thus, instructors have the flexibility to assign articles in the order that best fits with the content and organization of their courses.

New to the Second Edition

This edition contains 12 readings that were not included in the first edition; these readings contain updated information about some of the topics that were covered in the first edition as well as some new topics that were not covered in the first edition. Some of the classic readings that were in the first edition were retained in this edition because they cover important topics that are still very relevant today. In addition, the first chapter has been thoroughly revised, and the introductions for many of the first-edition articles have been updated to reflect more recent events and research.

Suggestions for Instructors

At the end of each article, I've included several review questions that might be used for in-class exercises, homework assignments, or quizzes. There are a variety of ways that this book could be used in a psychology course. Students could be asked to read an article or two from each chapter as the relevant topics are covered in their course. Some of the review questions could be assigned as homework to assess how well students learned the material in the article. Instructors who would like to add in-class activities related to each article might assign students to small groups and have each student answer a different review question; they could then discuss their answers with each other in class. Another idea is to assign brief projects or presentations related to some of the articles. For example, for a few articles, I ask students to find a web-based article that advocates the claim critiqued in the article; then students are asked to compare and contrast the quality of the web-based source with that of the article (i.e., they evaluate the credibility of the author, whether the information is supported with research evidence, etc.).

Acknowledgements

This book was inspired, in part, by psychologists such as Scott Lilienfeld, Elizabeth Loftus, and Ray Hyman, who have worked tirelessly to investigate pseudoscientific practices and to teach students to distinguish between science and pseudoscience. I thank Hank Cetola for prompting me to discuss the idea for this book with publishers much earlier than I had anticipated.

Enjoy the book!
Timothy J. Lawson

References

Lawson, T. J., & Brown, M. (2018). Using pseudoscience to improve introductory psychology students' information literacy. *Teaching of Psychology, 45,* 220–225.

Lilienfeld, S. O. (2005, September). The 10 commandments of helping students distinguish science from pseudoscience in psychology. *APS Observer, 18,* 39–40, 49–51.

Moore, D. W. (2005, June 16). *Three in four Americans believe in paranormal.* Gallup News Service.

Chapter 1

WHAT IS PSEUDOSCIENCE?

1.1 "Science Versus Pseudoscience"

PERHAPS YOU HAVE seen the interesting advertisements for an amazing silicon wristband with mylar holograms—the Power Balance wristband—that was designed to improve a person's strength, balance, and flexibility. The Power Balance has been endorsed by dozens of famous professional athletes, such as Shaquille O'Neal and Drew Brees. For example, in a promotional video for the wristband, Shaquille O'Neal said, "I don't really do a lot of testimonials, but this works." Shaquille explained that he was initially skeptical about the wristband but was more convinced after someone tested it on him. In addition, he found that it improved his performance in basketball games. Other promotional videos for the Power Balance showed tests in which people who had their arms outstretched and one leg raised could easily be thrown off-balance by a tester who pushed lightly on the elbow of one arm. However, when the wristband was placed on the test subject's wrist, the tester could not push the person off-balance. In another test, the subject could rotate his or her upper body much farther while wearing the wristband after exhibiting much less rotation without the wristband.

There are many other positive testimonials for the wristband's effectiveness, and here are some that were posted on Amazon.com:

> "My husband and I both LOVE our Power Balance Wristband Bracelets.… He was skeptical until he put his on and now a firm believer.… Everyone should have one.… Better sleep … more energy." [Carmen Cooksley]

> "I have problems with my elbow and shoulder, severe pain. When I wear these power bracelets my pain subsides and I can function. I highly recommend the bracelet." [Domino]

> "Helps my husband with his everyday aches and pains." [Tricia Campbell]

> "I have no idea how this works but I KNOW it does!!! No more walker for me!!!" [Virginia Pariseau]

How does this amazing wristband work? As explained by the Power Balance manufacturer, the holograms on the wristband resonate with and optimize the body's natural flow of energy. The wristband is based on ancient Eastern ideas related to energy, such as the concept of chi (also known as qi). Practices such as acupuncture are based on similar Eastern concepts concerning the flow of energy in our bodies. The basic idea is that energy flows along particular pathways in the body called meridians, and imbalances or blockages in the energy flow can occur that can negatively affect a person's health and well-being. Thus, products or therapies that can remove blockages and restore balance to the flow of energy are thought to improve health and cure illnesses.

If you wanted to improve your balance, strength, or flexibility, would you purchase the Power Balance wristband? You just read some glowing testimonials for this wristband and an explanation for how it works; perhaps you would view this as fairly convincing evidence that the Power Balance wristband is an effective performance enhancer. Does any aspect of the information you have seen so far suggest to you that this bracelet might *not* be the miracle it is claimed to be?

We will come back to the Power Balance wristband in a moment, but first let's discuss the main topic of this chapter: important differences between science and pseudoscience. As you may have learned by now, the field of psychology is a science. But what is it about psychology that makes it a science? Stanovich (2013) described three important features:

- **Systematic Empiricism:** Psychologists gain knowledge about behavior and mental processes by collecting data and making observations to test their theories and hypotheses. Unlike our everyday observations, psychologists make their observations in a carefully planned, systematic manner in order to help them rule out alternative explanations for the phenomena they are trying to understand.

- **Publicly Verifiable Knowledge:** After psychologists conduct their research, they communicate their findings to the broader scientific community. Other scientists can then critique the research, attempt to replicate the findings, and conduct related studies to further examine the phenomenon being investigated. These other scientists play a crucial role in judging and criticizing the research (this is called "peer review") before it is deemed worthy of being published in a scientific journal. Research that is judged to be too flawed or unimportant never reaches the pages of such a journal. Other researchers also play a crucial role in scientific progress by attempting to replicate the original research findings. If others cannot obtain the same findings as the original researcher, the original findings may have been a fluke.

- **Empirically Solvable Problems:** Scientists examine research questions that can be answered with current research techniques. If a question or theory is not testable, it is not within the realm of science. Thus, a scientist might not examine the question of whether people have souls (this would be very difficult to test), but he or she could examine whether an unconventional treatment for depression actually works.

To illustrate these features of science, consider how a scientist might examine whether a new drug effectively treats depression. The scientist might recruit a number of patients who have been diagnosed with depression and are willing to participate in the study. After informing the patients about the purpose and design of the study, those who consented to participate could be randomly assigned either to an experimental group that receives the new drug or to a control group that receives a sugar pill (i.e., a placebo). The scientist would measure the level of depression in both groups of patients to determine if those who received the new drug experienced more improvement in their depression than did the control group.

Let's assume the scientist found that this new drug significantly improved the patients' level of depression compared to the control group. The scientist would then write a report about this study and would send it to a scientific journal for publication. Peer reviewers would evaluate the quality of this study and determine whether it merits publication in the journal. After it is published, other scientists would critique the study and try to replicate the results. If other scientists conducted studies that also found positive results for this new drug, they would become more confident that it is a beneficial treatment for depression.

What Is Pseudoscience?

Contrast the aforementioned scientific approach with a pseudoscientific approach to testing a treatment for depression. A pseudoscientist might sell an herbal remedy for depression to a number of people, and some of them might report an improvement in their symptoms after taking the herbal remedy. The pseudoscientist might then create an advertisement for this new herbal remedy and include the testimonials of these satisfied customers as evidence of the effectiveness of the treatment. Notice that the pseudoscientific approach did not involve systematic empiricism; in other words, the pseudoscientist did not conduct a study that was carefully planned to rule out alternative explanations for the improvement in patients' symptoms. We do not know for sure whether the people who tried the herbal remedy were clinically depressed before taking the remedy (i.e., they might have been temporarily dispirited), we do not know how many of those who tried the remedy did not improve, and we cannot determine whether the improvements experienced by some of those who tried the remedy were caused by factors other than the herbal remedy. Their symptoms might have improved even without the herbal remedy, perhaps because of improvements in their social relationships, a decrease in stressful conditions at work, or simply the passage of time. Control groups used in scientific studies on treatments for depression help us rule out these alternative explanations.

Unlike science, pseudoscience (literally, "false" or "sham" science) is not characterized by carefully controlled studies that result in publicly verifiable knowledge. Instead, pseudoscientists often gain knowledge through "ancient wisdom," claims of a supposed "authority," illogical thinking, personal experience, or testimonials. Although the line between science and pseudoscience can be fuzzy at times, below I describe six of the important characteristics of pseudoscience (based on Bunge, 1984; Coker, 2001; Lilienfeld, 1998; Ruscio, 2006; see these sources for additional characteristics).

- **Imprecise, Scientific-Sounding Language:** Although the language used by pseudoscientists sometimes sounds scientific, they use terms in an imprecise, illogical, or incorrect manner. Scientists, on the other hand, define their terms in a precise, measurable way. As Ruscio (2006) pointed out, "energy" and "holistic" are terms that pseudoscientists often use in imprecise ways that have little or no connection to reality. For example, practitioners of a procedure called Therapeutic Touch claim that by moving their hands slightly above a person's body, they can realign that person's "human energy field" and heal them, but these practitioners cannot even demonstrate to scientists that they are able to detect such "energy" (Rosa, Rosa, Sarner, & Barrett, 1998). Imprecise terms such as these are often red flags that one is dealing with a pseudoscientist.

- **Lack of Progress:** Science progresses and changes over time. For example, what we know today about how the brain works is vastly different from what we knew 10 years ago. Pseudoscience, on the other hand, tends not to progress. Because pseudoscientific claims and theories do not undergo rigorous testing and critical peer review, they are rarely modified. Although pseudoscientists sometimes point out that their claims are based on "ancient wisdom" to give the impression that they have stood the test of time, this is often a good sign that such claims are based on stagnant, inaccurate ideas.

- **Overreliance on Testimonials and Personal Experience:** Rather than conducting carefully controlled studies, pseudoscientists often rely on personal experience or testimonials. For example, while in his 20s, Peter Halvorson drilled a hole in his head to cure his depression (a procedure called "trepanation" or "trephining"). Today, more than 40 years later, he claims that the procedure not only cured his depression but also improved his energy and vitality. Halvorson is a strong advocate for the use of the procedure to cure depression; in fact, he's the senior director of the International Trepanation Advocacy Group (visit http://www.trepan.com for more information). Why shouldn't we be convinced by stories like this one? If a person's depression lifts after trying some treatment, can't we conclude that the treatment worked? The problem with relying on testimonials and personal experience as evidence for treatments or claims is they do not allow us to rule out alternative explanations. For example, maybe Peter Halvorson's depression would have disappeared without any treatment (i.e., spontaneous remission), or perhaps his positive expectation that the "treatment" would work is what produced the improvement (i.e., a placebo effect). Controlled scientific studies employ control groups of participants who receive no treatment or fake treatments (i.e., placebos) to rule out these alternative explanations.

- **Appeals to False Authority:** Pseudoscientists urge us to believe their claims based on the word of an "authority" on the subject, even though the person claimed to be an authority may be untrustworthy or have little expertise in the subject. For example, it is not uncommon to hear supposed experts on talk shows give advice about child-rearing or romantic relationships when they have no scientific training in psychology or related sciences. Although these "experts" use "Dr." in front of their name to give the impression that they have a doctorate in psychology, their doctoral degrees are often in a completely unrelated field. Scientists, on the other hand, do not rely on authority to answer important questions, even if the authority has the appropriate scientific training from a respected institution. As I mentioned earlier, it is convincing, empirical data that drive scientists' understanding of the world, not the word of an authority.

- **Extraordinary Claims Without Convincing Evidence:** Pseudoscientists often make extraordinary claims that are unconstrained by reality, physical laws, or human limitations. However, they back up these claims with little or no compelling, publicly verifiable evidence. For example, pseudoscientists may claim that we can transfer the "positive" or "negative" energy within us to a bottle of water simply by touching it and that others who drink that water will be influenced by the energy within it. Before believing such an extraordinary claim that appears to contradict well-researched physical laws, a scientist would want to see some very convincing evidence.

    In some cases, pseudoscientists have managed to publish a large number of articles supporting their claims, and advocates can point to the "growing literature" supporting the pseudoscience as evidence for their claims. One question to ask yourself is whether this literature consists of well-controlled scientific research that has been published in peer-reviewed scientific journals. If you find some articles that meet this criterion, ask yourself whether the results of this research have been replicated by other researchers. Although the evidence collected by pseudoscientists is generally not worthy of publication in peer-reviewed journals, sometimes they are able to get articles published in such outlets. For example, advocates of Therapeutic Touch have published a number of articles in peer-reviewed journals, and they point to these studies as evidence for their claims. However, in general, these journals are not reputable medical journals, and the studies published in these journals are not designed well enough to rule out alternative explanations (e.g., placebo effects or effects of relaxation).

- **Emphasis on Confirmation Rather Than Refutation:** Pseudoscientists tend to focus only on information that is consistent with their claims, failing to seek out information that contradicts their claims. A person who claims to predict the future, for example, might make numerous vague predictions (e.g., "A popular leader will die in the near future"; "Scientists will soon make an amazing discovery in outer space"). Later, when assessing his or her accuracy, this "psychic" might point out the predictions that were apparently correct and overlook predictions that were inaccurate. In contrast, scientists deliberately attempt to falsify their own and other scientists' predictions and theories to make sure that their ideas hold up under very rigorous tests.

Now that you have a sense of the meaning of the term *pseudoscience*, I'd like to point out the difference between pseudoscience and paranormal phenomena. *Paranormal phenomena* (e.g., a psychic's ability to "see" the future) are those that are beyond our normal experience, and they fall outside of a scientific understanding of the world. The topics of pseudoscience and the paranormal often overlap: for example, when people claim to use paranormal abilities—such as the ability to detect a human energy field—to heal others, and they use testimonials as evidence for the effectiveness of their therapy. However, the topics of pseudoscience and the paranormal can also be distinct, as illustrated by pseudoscientific therapies that do not necessarily involve paranormal phenomena. For instance, the use of bee pollen to treat allergies may be pseudoscientific but does not involve the paranormal.

Power Balance Revisited

Now that we have discussed some major characteristics of pseudoscience, can you apply any of them to the example of the amazing Power Balance wristband? Which of these characteristics seem most relevant for assessing the claims made about this wristband? I'll point out a couple of relevant characteristics, and I'll leave the rest for you to identify when you answer the questions at the end of this chapter.

When you first read the Power Balance example, did you recognize the use of imprecise, scientific-sounding language? Do human bodies actually have invisible energy fields, and can a mylar hologram resonate with and optimize the flow of energy? As Hall (2010) pointed out:

> *This whole resonance and vibration business is pseudoscience emanating from the myth of the human energy field—not the kind of energy physicists measure but some vague life energy like the acupuncturists' qi, the chiropractors' innate, and the imaginary fields that Therapeutic Touch practitioners claim they are smoothing down with their hands.*

After reading the section on pseudoscience, you probably quickly recognized the relevance of another characteristic of pseudoscience: the overuse of testimonials as evidence for the effectiveness of the Power Balance. The numerous positive testimonials, some from famous athletes who are experts when it comes to athletic performance, might be enough to convince many people that this wristband works. However, there are alternative explanations for improvements in people's performance while wearing the Power Balance wristband. As mentioned earlier, a placebo effect is one possibility.

Another possibility is that the "tests" of the wristband performed by Power Balance salespeople on athletes and others were rigged to make it look effective even though it actually had no effect. For example, as Lawson, Blackhart, and Gialopsos (2016) explained, a tester can make it seem as if the wristband improves balance by pushing down and slightly away from the person's body when the wristband is off (causing the person to lose balance) and pushing down and slightly toward the person's body when the wristband is on (causing the person to stay in place). The test subject, who may not sense the difference in the angle of the downward pressure used by the tester, is fooled into thinking that the wristband actually improved their balance.

Another problem with testimonials is that we do not know what percentage of the people who tried the product liked it. It might be the case that the vast majority of those who tried the Power Balance did not experience any benefits and the manufacturer touts only the few positive testimonials for the wristband. My quick search of the web turned up a number of negative reviews of the wristband by those who purchased it; of course, these reviews would be not mentioned by those promoting the Power Balance wristband. Below is an example of one of the negative reviews:

> *I bought this product thinking that it would work well. All of the hype surrounding Power Balance made me think that the wristbands were good. Unfortunately this product did nothing for me. Did not help with my power in my lifts and workouts. My balance was not better by wearing it when I did agility exercises. Overall I would not recommend buying this product.*

You might be wondering at this point whether I really have any grounds for implying that the Power Balance wristband is a worthless, pseudoscientific product. Although I have pointed out a number of problems with the claims made about the wristband, I have not presented much evidence that it does *not* work. In response, my first point would be that the burden of proof is not mine; it's the job of the person making the claims for the effectiveness of the wristband to prove that it *does* work. Although pseudoscientists often try to shift the burden of proof onto critics rather than themselves, scientists assume the burden of proof when they make a claim. For instance, a true scientist would not claim that a new drug alleviates depression better than other drugs on the market without scientific evidence to support that claim, and a scientist without such evidence would not tell critics that they should believe the claim unless they can disprove it. In fact, the Food and Drug Administration (FDA) would never approve a new drug if the manufacturer took such an approach. Likewise, we should not be expected to believe extraordinary claims made by pseudoscientists—for example, claims that beings from outer space abduct people and perform experiments on them—without convincing scientific evidence to support such claims.

My second point would be that, in this particular case, there is scientific evidence that suggests the Power Balance wristband does not live up to the extraordinary claims. Scientific tests have been conducted in which researchers examined the strength, balance, and flexibility of subjects wearing either the Power Balance wristband or a placebo wristband that did not have mylar holograms (e.g., Porcari et al., 2011; Underdown, 2012). These tests were conducted in a "double-blind" fashion in which neither the researcher nor the subjects knew whether they were wearing the Power Balance or placebo wristband. The results showed that the Power Balance wristband had no effect on the subjects' balance, strength, or flexibility.

In 2011, the manufacturer of the Power Balance filed for bankruptcy after being sued for false and misleading advertising (Hsu, 2011). The company admitted that there was "no credible scientific basis" for their claims. You might think that this was the end of the road for the Power Balance wristband, but it was not. The wristband is still on the market, a website still exists for it (http://www.powerbalance.com), and I suspect that some people will continue to purchase these wristbands despite the evidence against them. As Lilienfeld, Marshall, Todd, and Shane (2014) pointed out, pseudoscientific practices have a way of sticking around long after scientific evidence has shown them to be ineffective. When people buy a product and become convinced that it works, several psychological tendencies may lead them to discount scientific evidence and stick with their belief in the product. People tend to seek evidence that is consistent with their beliefs and neglect or reject evidence that conflicts with their beliefs (i.e., confirmation bias). Thus, they might readily accept testimonials from satisfied users of the Power Balance wristband while rejecting negative testimonials or scientific evidence that questions the efficacy of the wristband. In addition, because they paid money for the product and told their friends that it works, they might continue to support the product in the face of negative evidence in order to justify their initial purchase of and statements about the product (i.e., cognitive dissonance).

Conclusion

I hope that you have found our discussion of the Power Balance wristband and the differences between science and pseudoscience to be interesting, informative, and relevant to your everyday life. This chapter is just the beginning of our examination of the fascinating realm of pseudoscience and the paranormal. In the following chapters, you will read psychologists' and other scientists' critiques of a variety of pseudoscientific and paranormal phenomena—such as psychic abilities, lie detector tests, and memories of past lives—that are related to many of the major topics in an introductory psychology course. As implied by the features of psychological science described earlier, the conclusions reached by the scientists featured in this book are based on carefully planned and controlled research studies (i.e., systematic empiricism) that have been published in scientific journals (i.e., publicly verifiable knowledge). My hope is that this book will not only help you understand the science of psychology but also help you think critically about the many pseudoscientific and paranormal claims you are likely to encounter through the media, the Internet, and pop psychology books.

Themes in This Book

Although the articles in this book are independent readings that can be read in any order, there are some important themes that can be found throughout the book. Below are a couple of important themes to watch for as you read the articles.

1. **Science Versus Pseudoscience:** As implied by the topic of this chapter, one of the themes that you will encounter throughout this book is the distinction between science and pseudoscience. The articles in this book will give you a variety of examples of the differences between scientific and pseudoscientific approaches to gaining knowledge. While reading the articles, watch for the characteristics of pseudoscience discussed in this chapter (e.g., lack of progress, extraordinary claims without convincing evidence). You will also see examples of scientific research, which will illustrate how psychologists and other scientists design studies to investigate pseudoscientific and paranormal claims.

2. **Normal Cognitive and Social Processes Contribute to Pseudoscientific and Paranormal Beliefs:** Another important theme that you will encounter throughout the book is that beliefs in pseudoscientific and paranormal phenomena can result from normal cognitive and social processes. Although some of the phenomena discussed in this book may seem so bizarre or unbelievable to you that you will be tempted to conclude that only people with low intelligence could believe in them, you should resist that temptation. You will learn about a variety of cognitive and social processes that may lead even the most intelligent among us to develop beliefs in phenomena that are not real. As I mentioned earlier, confirmation bias leads people to seek information that is consistent with their beliefs and neglect or reject information that contradicts their beliefs. Thus, people might continue to believe in questionable products or practices in spite of solid scientific evidence to the contrary. Here are a couple of other cognitive processes to watch for:
    a. Heuristics: These are quick strategies we use to make decisions and judgments in our daily lives. For example, one heuristic we commonly use can lead us to believe that the cure for a disease should resemble the symptoms of the disease. Thus, a pseudoscientific health practitioner might advise a person with a liver ailment to consume an herbal remedy made from a plant that contains parts shaped like a liver.
    b. Difficulties in Statistical and Methodological Reasoning: One difficulty people have with statistical reasoning is the tendency to sometimes perceive associations between events where none exist (i.e., illusory correlation). For example, based on a couple of past experiences of winning games while wearing the same socks, a baseball player might believe that wearing his lucky socks will help his team win the next game.

Types of Articles in This Book

You will find several types of readings in this book, including scientific journal articles and magazine articles. Below, I describe some differences between these two sources of articles and give some tips on reading the journal articles.

- **Journal Articles:** Articles published in peer-reviewed scientific journals (e.g., *Journal of the American Medical Association, Professional Psychology: Research and Practice*) typically undergo a rigorous evaluation process before they are published. After the author submits a manuscript for publication in such a journal, it is reviewed by experts in the field (i.e., a process called "peer review") to determine whether the research described in the article is of high quality and is important enough to warrant publication in a scientific journal. Thus, articles published in prestigious scientific journals are usually among the best sources of information because they reflect important, high-quality research conducted by reputable scientists.
    - When reading a typical journal article about a scientific study, you will find the following sections:
        - **Introduction:** reviews the previous research relevant to the topic of the article.
        - **Method:** describes how the researcher conducted the study.
        - **Results:** states the findings and statistical analyses. If you find some of the statistical presentations in journal articles difficult to understand, focus on the author's description of the findings.
        - **Discussion:** contains the author's interpretation of the results and describes the implications of the findings.
- **Magazine Articles:** Magazine articles can vary widely in the quality of information they contain. For example, an article published in *Seventeen* magazine is not as likely to contain high-quality scientific information as is an article published in a peer-reviewed scientific journal. Some magazines are designed more for entertainment than for education, and magazine articles typically do not go through a rigorous peer-review process before being published. Nevertheless, some scientifically oriented magazines, such as *Scientific American* and *Skeptical Inquirer*, contain high-quality articles written by respected scientists. Some of the articles I selected for this book are high-quality magazine articles written by scientists who are knowledgeable about the scientific research related to the topics they discuss.
- **Other Resources:** In the table that follows, I list a number of other resources that you might find useful for finding information about scientific perspectives on pseudoscience and the paranormal.

Selected Resources for Scientific Perspectives on Pseudoscience and the Paranormal

Below is a sample of specific journals, websites, and searchable databases that can be used to find scientific perspectives on the ever-expanding variety of pseudoscientific and paranormal phenomena.

Scientific Journals Devoted to Evaluating Suspected Pseudoscience

Although the following journals are no longer active, they contain many high-quality articles related to pseudoscience:

1. *The Scientific Review of Mental Health Practice* (www.srmhp.org): Active from 2002 to 2009, this journal was "the only peer-reviewed journal devoted exclusively to distinguishing scientifically-supported claims from scientifically-unsupported claims in clinical psychology, psychiatry, social work, and allied disciplines."
2. *The Scientific Review of Alternative Medicine* (www.sram.org): Active from 1997 to 2007, this journal was "the only peer-reviewed journal devoted exclusively to objectively analyzing the claims of 'alternative medicine.'"

Searchable Databases of Journal Articles and Books
(consult your librarian for access)

1. *PsycINFO*: Indexes journal articles, books, and dissertations in psychology and related disciplines.
2. *MEDLINE*: Indexes journal articles related to the health sciences, including medicine, nursing, dentistry, veterinary medicine, and the health-care system.

Organizations and Websites

1. *The Committee for Skeptical Inquiry* (www.csicop.org): An organization that "promotes science and scientific inquiry, critical thinking, science education, and the use of reason in examining important issues. It encourages the critical investigation of controversial or extraordinary claims from a responsible, scientific point of view and disseminates factual information about the results of such inquiries to the scientific community, the media, and the public."
2. *The Skeptics Society* (www.skeptic.com): "A scientific and educational organization whose mission is to engage leading experts in investigating the paranormal, fringe science, pseudoscience, and extraordinary claims of all kinds, promote critical thinking, and serve as an educational tool for those seeking a sound scientific viewpoint."
3. *Quackwatch* (www.quackwatch.org): "An international network of people who are concerned about health-related frauds, myths, fads, fallacies, and misconduct. Its primary focus is on quackery-related information that is difficult or impossible to get elsewhere."

4. *National Council Against Health Fraud* (www.ncahf.org): "A private nonprofit, voluntary health agency that focuses upon health misinformation, fraud, and quackery as public health problems." Although NCAHF was dissolved in 2011, archives of their articles on many pseudoscientific and fraudulent practices can be found on their website.

REVIEW AND CONTEMPLATE

1. Name and describe three important features of psychology that make it a science.
2. Name and describe six important characteristics of pseudoscience.
3. This chapter described two characteristics of pseudoscience that are relevant to the example of the Power Balance wristband. What other pseudoscience characteristics seem relevant (name at least two and explain why you chose them)?
4. Can you think of other examples of products or practices that seem to be pseudoscientific? Which characteristics of pseudoscience are related to these examples?

References

Bunge, M. (1984, Fall). What is pseudoscience? *Skeptical Inquirer, 9,* 36–46.

Coker, R. (2001, May 30). *Distinguishing science and pseudoscience.* Retrieved from http://www.quackwatch.org/01QuackeryRelatedTopics/pseudo.html

Hall, H. (2010, May/June). Power Balance technology: Pseudoscientific silliness suckers card-carrying surfers. *Skeptical Inquirer, 34,* 47–49.

Hsu, T. (2011, November 22). Power Balance files for bankruptcy after retracting health claims. *Los Angeles Times.* Retrieved from http://latimesblogs.latimes.com/money_co/2011/11/power-balance-files-for-bankruptcy-after-retracting-health-claims.html

Lawson, T. J., Blackhart, G. C., & Gialopsos, B. M. (2016). Using the Power Balance wristband to improve students' research-design skills. *Teaching of Psychology, 43,* 318–322.

Lilienfeld, S. O. (1998, Fall). Pseudoscience in contemporary clinical psychology: What it is and what we can do about it. *The Clinical Psychologist, 51*(4), 3–9.

Lilienfeld, S. O., Marshall, J., Todd, J. T., & Shane, H. C. (2014). The persistence of fad interventions in the face of negative scientific evidence: Facilitated communication for autism as a case example. *Evidence-Based Communication Assessment and Intervention, 8,* 62–101.

Porcari, J., Hazuga, R., Foster, C., Doberstein, S., Becker, J., Kline, D., Mickschl, T., & Dodge, C. (2011). Can the Power Balance bracelet improve balance, flexibility, strength, and power? *Journal of Sports Science & Medicine, 10,* 230–231.

Rosa, L., Rosa, E., Sarner, L., & Barrett, S. (1998). A close look at therapeutic touch. *JAMA, 279,* 1005–1010.

Ruscio, J. (2006). *Critical thinking in psychology: Separating sense from nonsense* (2nd ed.). Pacific Grove, CA: Wadsworth.

Stanovich, K. E. (2013). *How to think straight about psychology* (10th ed.). New York: Pearson.

Underdown, J. (2012, January/February). Power Balance bracelets a bust in tests. *Skeptical Inquirer, 36,* 14–16.

Chapter 2

METHODOLOGICAL AND STATISTICAL REASONING

2.1 "Why Bogus Therapies Seem to Work"

CHAPTER 1 BRIEFLY discussed the story of Peter Halvorson, who believes that trepanation (i.e., drilling a hole in his head) cured his depression. People's tendency to believe in the effectiveness of implausible—and sometimes bizarre—treatments never ceases to fascinate me. Some people believe that drinking their urine cures cancer, that bee pollen treats allergies, or that homeopathic medicines that contain few to no active ingredients are effective drugs for treating a wide variety of ailments. People whose symptoms improve after using these treatments may conclude that the treatments caused the improvement. However, it's important to keep in mind that although effective treatments should produce improved symptoms, improved symptoms do not necessarily mean the treatment was effective.

In this article, Barry Beyerstein discusses reasons why bogus therapies may seem to work when, in fact, they are ineffective. Although this article is also relevant to Chapter 9, I chose to put it here because it illustrates some important methodological principles. Chapter 1 explained that the difficulties people have in statistical and methodological reasoning may lead them to develop beliefs in pseudoscientific or paranormal phenomena. This article discusses some important methodological principles to keep in mind when assessing the effectiveness of a therapy. First, it's important to keep in mind that correlation does not mean causation. In other words, just because you feel better after a therapy doesn't necessarily mean the therapy produced the improvement. Second, in order to infer that a therapy caused an improvement in one's health, one needs to be able to rule out alternative explanations for the improvement. Beyerstein discusses a number of alternative explanations to consider.

Reference

Beyerstein, B. L. (1997, September/October). Why bogus therapies seem to work. *Skeptical Inquirer, 21*, 29–34.

"WHY BOGUS THERAPIES SEEM TO WORK"
BARRY BEYERSTEIN

At least ten kinds of errors and biases can convince intelligent, honest people that cures have been achieved when they have not.

Nothing is more dangerous than active ignorance—Goethe

Those who sell therapies of any kind have an obligation to prove, first, that their treatments are safe and, second, that they are effective. The latter is often the more difficult task because there are many subtle ways that honest and intelligent people (both patients and therapists) can be led to think that a treatment has cured someone when it has not. This is true whether we are assessing new treatments in scientific medicine, old nostrums in folk medicine, fringe treatments in "alternative medicine," or the frankly magical panaceas of faith healers.

To distinguish causal from fortuitous improvements that might follow any intervention, a set of objective procedures has evolved for testing putative remedies. Unless a technique, ritual, drug, or surgical procedure can meet these requirements, it is ethically questionable to offer it to the public, especially if money is to change hands. Since most "alternative" therapies (i.e., ones not accepted by scientific biomedicine) fall into this category, one must ask why so many customers who would not purchase a toaster without consulting Consumer Reports shell out, with trusting naïveté, large sums for unproven, possibly dangerous, health remedies.

For many years, critics have been raising telling doubts about fringe medical practices, but the popularity of such nostrums seems undiminished. We must wonder why entrepreneurs' claims in this area should remain so refractory to contrary data. If an "alternative" or "complementary" therapy:

a. is implausible on a priori grounds (because its implied mechanisms or putative effects contradict well-established laws, principles, or empirical findings in physics, chemistry, or biology),
b. lacks a scientifically acceptable rationale of its own,
c. has insufficient supporting evidence derived from adequately controlled outcome research (i.e., double-blind, randomized, placebo-controlled clinical trials),
d. has failed in well-controlled clinical studies done by impartial evaluators and has been unable to rule out competing explanations for why it might seem to work in uncontrolled settings, and,

Barry L. Beyerstein, "Why Bogus Therapies Seem to Work," *Skeptical Inquirer*, vol. 21.5, pp. 29-34. Copyright © 1997 by Center for Inquiry. Reprinted with permission.

e. should seem improbable, even to the lay person, on "commonsense" grounds, why would so many well-educated people continue to sell and purchase such a treatment?

The answer, I believe, lies in a combination of vigorous marketing of unsubstantiated claims by "alternative" healers (Beyerstein and Sampson 1996), the poor level of scientific knowledge in the public at large (Kiernan 1995), and the "will to believe" so prevalent among seekers attracted to the New Age movement (Basil 1988; Gross and Levitt 1994).

The appeal of nonscientific medicine is largely a holdover from popular "counterculture" sentiments of the 1960s and 1970s. Remnants of the rebellious, "back-to-nature" leanings of that era survive as nostalgic yearnings for a return to nineteenth-century-style democratized health care (now wrapped in the banner of patients' rights) and a dislike of bureaucratic, technologic, and specialized treatment of disease (Cassileth and Brown 1988). Likewise, the allure of the "holistic" dogmas of alternative medicine is a descendant of the fascination with Eastern mysticism that emerged in the sixties and seventies. Although the philosophy and the science that underlie these holistic leachings have been severely criticized (Brandon 1985), they retain a strong appeal for those committed to belief in "mind-over-matter" cures, a systemic rather than localized view of pathology, and the all-powerful ability of nutrition to restore health (conceived of as whole-body "balance").

Many dubious health products remain on the market primarily because satisfied customers offer testimonials to their worth. Essentially, they are saying, "I tried it and I got better, so it must be effective." But even when symptoms do improve following a treatment, this, by itself, cannot prove that the therapy was responsible.

THE ILLNESS-DISEASE DISTINCTION

Although the terms disease and illness are often used interchangeably, for present purposes it is worth distinguishing between the two. I shall use disease to refer to a pathological state of the organism due to infection, tissue degeneration, trauma, toxic exposure, carcinogenesis, etc. By illness I mean the feelings of malaise, pain, disorientation, dysfunctionality, or other complaints that might accompany a disease. Our subjective reaction to the raw sensations we call symptoms is molded by cultural and psychological factors such as beliefs, suggestions, expectations, demand characteristics, self-serving biases, and self-deception. The experience of illness is also affected (often unconsciously) by a host of, social and psychological payoffs that accrue to those admitted to the "sick role" by society's gatekeeper (i.e., health professionals). For certain individuals, the privileged status and benefits of the sick role are sufficient to perpetuate the experience of illness after a disease has healed, or even to create feelings of illness in the absence of disease (Alcock 1986).

Unless we can tease apart the many factors that contribute to the perception of being ill, personal testimonials offer no basis on which to judge whether a putative therapy has, in fact, cured a disease. That is why controlled clinical trials with objective physical measures are essential in evaluating therapies of any kind.

CORRELATION DOES NOT IMPLY CAUSATION

Mistaking correlation for causation is the basis of most superstitious beliefs, including many in the area of alternative medicine. We have a tendency to assume that when things occur together, they must be causally connected, although obviously they need not be. For example, there is a high correlation between the consumption of diet soft drinks and obesity. Does this mean that artificial sweeteners cause people to become overweight? When we count on personal experience to test the worth of medical treatments, many factors are varying simultaneously, making it extremely difficult to determine what is cause and effect. Personal endorsements supply the bulk of the support for unorthodox health products, but they are a weak currency because of what Gilovich (1997) has called the "compared to what?" problem. Without comparison to a similar group of sufferers, treated identically except that the allegedly curative element is withheld, individual recipients can never know whether they would have recovered just as well without it.

TEN ERRORS AND BIASES

The question is, then: Why might therapists and their clients who rely on anecdotal evidence and uncontrolled observations erroneously conclude that inert therapies work? There are at least ten good reasons.

1. **The Disease May Have Run Its Natural Course.** Many diseases are self-limiting—providing the condition is not chronic or fatal, the body's own recuperative processes usually restore the sufferer to health. Thus, before a therapy can be acknowledged as curative, its proponents must show that the number of patients listed as improved exceeds the proportion expected to recover without any treatment at all (or that they recover reliably faster than if left untreated). Unless an unconventional therapist releases detailed records of successes and failures over a sufficiently large number of patients with the same complaint, he or she cannot claim to have exceeded the published norms for unaided recovery.
2. **Many Diseases Are Cyclical.** Arthritis, multiple sclerosis, allergies, and gastrointestinal complaints are examples of diseases that normally "have their ups and downs." Naturally, sufferers tend to seek therapy during the downturn of any given cycle. In this way, a bogus treatment will have repeated opportunities to coincide with upturns that would have happened anyway. Again, in the absence of appropriate control groups, consumers and vendors alike are prone to misinterpret improvement due to normal cyclical variation as a valid therapeutic effect.
3. **Spontaneous Remission.** Anecdotally reported cures can be due to rare but possible "spontaneous remissions." Even with cancers that are nearly always lethal, tumors

occasionally disappear without further treatment. One experienced oncologist reports that he has seen twelve such events in about six thousand cases he has treated (Silverman 1987). Alternative therapies can receive unearned acclaim for remissions of this sort because many desperate patients turn to them when they feel that they have nothing left to lose. When the "alternatives" assert that they have snatched many hopeless individuals from death's door, they rarely reveal what percentage of their apparently terminal clientele such happy exceptions represent. What is needed is statistical evidence that their "cure rates" exceed the known spontaneous remission rate and the placebo response rate (see below) for the conditions they treat.

The exact mechanisms responsible for spontaneous remissions are not well understood but much research is being devoted to revealing and possibly harnessing processes in the immune system or elsewhere that are responsible for these unexpected turnarounds. The relatively new field of psychoneuroimmunology studies how psychological variables affect the nervous, glandular, and immune systems in ways that might affect susceptibility to and recovery from disease (Ader and Cohen 1993; Mestel 1994). If thoughts, emotions, desires, beliefs, etc., are physical states of the brain, there is nothing inherently mystical in the notion that these neural processes could affect glandular, immune, and other cellular processes throughout the body. Via the limbic system of the brain, the hypothalamic pituitary axis, and the autonomic nervous system, psychological variables can have widespread physiological effects that can have positive or negative impacts upon health. While research has confirmed that such effects exist, it must be remembered that they are fairly small, accounting for perhaps a few percent of the variance in disease statistics.

4. **The Placebo Effect.** A major reason why bogus remedies are credited with subjective, and occasionally objective, improvements is the ubiquitous placebo effect (Roberts, Kewman, and Hovell 1993; Ulett 1996). The history of medicine is strewn with examples of what, with hindsight, seem like crackpot procedures that were once enthusiastically endorsed by physicians and patients alike (Skrabanek and McCormick 1990; Barrett and Jarvis 1993). Misattributions of this sort arise from the false assumptions that a change in symptoms following a treatment must have been a specific consequence of that procedure. Through a combination of suggestion, belief, expectancy, cognitive reinterpretation, and diversion of attention, patients given biologically useless treatments can often experience measurable relief. Some placebo responses produce actual changes in the physical condition; others are subjective changes that make patients feel better although there has been no objective change in the underlying pathology.

Through repeated contact with valid therapeutic procedures, we all develop, much like Pavlov's dogs, conditioned responses in various physiological systems. Later, these responses can be triggered by the setting, rituals, paraphernalia, and verbal cues that signal the act of "being treated." Among other things, placebos can cause release of the body's own morphinelike pain killers, the endorphins (Ulett 1996, ch. 3). Because these learned responses can be palliative, even when a treatment itself is physiologically unrelated to the source of the complaint, putative therapies must be tested against a placebo control group—similar patients who receive a sham treatment that resembles the "real" one except that the suspected active ingredient is withheld.

It is essential that the patients in such tests be randomly assigned to their respective groups and that they be "blind" with respect to their active versus placebo status. Because the power of what psychologists call expectancy and compliance effects (see below) is so strong, the therapists must also be blind as to individual patients' group membership. Hence the term double blind—the gold standard of outcome research. Such precautions are required because barely perceptible cues, unintentionally conveyed by treatment providers who are not blinded, can bias test results. Likewise, those who assess the treatment's effects must also be blind, for there is a large literature on "experimenter bias" showing that honest and well-trained professionals can unconsciously "read in" the outcomes they expect when they attempt to assess complex phenomena (Rosenthal 1966; Chapman and Chapman 1967).

When the clinical trial is completed, the blinds can be broken to allow statistical comparison of active, placebo, and no-treatment groups. Only if the improvements observed in the active treatment group exceed those in the two control groups by a statistically significant amount can the therapy claim legitimacy.

5. **Some Allegedly Cured Symptoms are Psychosomatic to Begin with.** A constant difficulty in trying to measure therapeutic effectiveness is that many physical complaints can both arise from psychosocial distress and be alleviated by support and reassurance. At first glance, these symptoms (at various times called "psychosomatic," "hysterical," or "neurasthenic") resemble those of recognized medical syndromes (Shorter 1992; Merskey 1995). Although there are many "secondary gains" (psychological, social, and economic) that accrue to those who slip into "the sick role" in this way, we need not accuse them of conscious malingering to point out that their symptoms are nonetheless maintained by subtle psychosocial processes.

"Alternative" healers cater to these members of the "worried well" who are mistakenly convinced that they are ill. Their complaints are instances of somatization, the tendency to express psychological concerns in a language of symptoms like those of organic diseases (Alcock 1986; Shorter 1992). The "alternatives" offer comfort to these individuals who for psychological reasons need others to believe there are organic etiologies for their symptoms. Often with the aid of pseudoscientific diagnostic devices, fringe practitioners reinforce the somatizer's conviction that the cold-hearted, narrow-minded medical establishment, which can find nothing physically amiss, is both incompetent and unfair in refusing to acknowledge a very real organic condition. A large portion of those diagnosed with "chronic fatigue," "environmental sensitivity syndrome," and various stress disorders (not to mention many suing because of the allegedly harmful effects of silicone breast implants) look very much like classic somatizers (Stewart 1990; Huber 1991; Rosenbaum 1997). When, through the role-governed rituals of "delivering treatment," fringe therapists supply the reassurance, sense of belonging and existential support their clients seek, this is obviously worthwhile, but all this need not be foreign to scientific practitioners who have much more to offer besides. The downside is that catering to the desire for medical diagnoses for psychological complaints promotes pseudoscientific and magical thinking while unduly inflating the success rates of medical quacks. Saddest of all, it perpetuates the anachronistic feeling that there is something shameful or illegitimate about psychological problems.

6. **Symptomatic Relief Versus Cure.** Short of an outright cure, alleviating pain and discomfort is what sick people value most. Many allegedly curative treatments offered by alternative practitioners, while unable to affect the disease process itself, do make the illness more bearable, but for psychological reasons. Pain is one example. Much research shows that pain is partly a sensation like seeing or hearing and partly an emotion (Metzack 1973). It has been found repeatedly that successfully reducing the emotional component of pain leaves the sensory portion surprisingly tolerable. Thus, suffering can often be reduced by psychological means, even if the underlying pathology is untouched. Anything that can allay anxiety, redirect attention, reduce arousal, foster a sense of control, or lead to cognitive reinterpretation of symptoms can alleviate the agony component of pain. Modern pain clinics put these strategies to good use every day (Smith, Merskey, and Gross 1980). Whenever patients suffer less, this is all to the good, but we must be careful that purely symptomatic relief does not divert people from proven remedies until it is too late for them to be effective.

7. **Many Consumers of Alternative Therapies Hedge Their Bets.** In an attempt to appeal to a wider clientele, many unorthodox healers have begun to refer to themselves as "complementary" rather than "alternative." Instead of ministering primarily to the ideologically committed or those who have been told there is nothing more that conventional medicine can do for them, the "alternatives" have begun to advertise that they can enhance conventional biomedical treatments. They accept that orthodox practitioners can alleviate specific symptoms but contend that alternative medicine treats the real causes of disease—dubious dietary imbalances or environmental sensitivities, disrupted energy fields, or even unresolved conflicts from previous incarnations. If improvement follows the combined delivery of "complementary" and scientifically based treatments, the fringe practice often gets a disproportionate share of the credit.

8. **Misdiagnosis (by Self or by a Physician).** In this era of media obsession with health, many people can be induced to think they have diseases they do not have. When these healthy folk receive the oddly unwelcome news from orthodox physicians that

they have no organic signs of disease, they often gravitate to alternative practitioners who can almost always find some kind of "imbalance" to treat. If "recovery" follows, another convert is born.

Of course, scientifically trained physicians are not infallible, and a mistaken diagnosis, followed by a trip to a shrine or an alternative healer, can lead to a glowing testimonial for curing a grave condition that never existed. Other times, the diagnosis may be correct but the time course, which is inherently hard to predict, might prove inaccurate. If a patient with a terminal condition undergoes alternative treatments and succumbs later than the conventional doctor predicted, the alternative procedure may receive credit for prolonging life when, in fact, there was merely an unduly pessimistic prognosis—survival was longer than the expected norm, but within the range of normal statistical variation for the disease.

9. **Derivative Benefits.** Alternative healers often have forceful, charismatic personalities (O'Connor 1987). To the extent that patients are swept up by the messianic aspects of alternative medicine, psychological uplift may ensue. If an enthusiastic, upbeat healer manages to elevate the patient's mood and expectations, this optimism can lead to greater compliance with, and hence effectiveness of, any orthodox treatments he or she may also be receiving. This expectant attitude can also motivate people to eat and sleep better and to exercise and socialize more. These, by themselves, could help speed natural recovery.

    Psychological spinoffs of this sort can also reduce stress, which has been shown to have deleterious effects on the immune system (Mestel 1994). Removing this added burden may speed healing, even if it is not a specific effect of the therapy. As with purely symptomatic relief, this is far from a bad thing, unless it diverts the patient from more effective treatments, or the charges are exorbitant.

10. **Psychological Distortion of Reality.** Distortion of reality in the service of strong belief is a common occurrence (Alcock 1995). Even when they derive no objective improvements, devotees who have a strong psychological investment in alternative medicine can convince themselves they have been helped. According to cognitive dissonance theory (Festinger 1957), when experiences contradict existing attitudes, feelings, or knowledge, mental distress is produced. We tend to alleviate this discord by reinterpreting (distorting) the offending information. To have received no relief after committing time, money, and "face" to an alternate course of treatment (and perhaps to the worldview of which it is a part) would create such a state of internal disharmony. Because it would be too psychologically disconcerting to admit to oneself or to others that it has all been a waste, there would be strong psychological pressure to find some redeeming value in the treatment.

    Many other self-serving biases help maintain self-esteem and smooth social functioning (Beyerstein and Hadaway 1991). Because core beliefs tend to be vigorously defended by warping perception and memory, fringe practitioners and their clients are prone to misinterpret cues and remember things as they wish they had happened. Similarly, they may be selective in what they recall, overestimating their apparent successes while ignoring, downplaying, or explaining away their failures. The scientific method evolved in large part to reduce the impact of this human penchant for jumping to congenial conclusions.

An illusory feeling that one's symptoms have improved could also be due to a number of so called demand characteristics found in any therapeutic setting. In all societies, there exists the "norm of reciprocity," an implicit rule that obliges people to respond in kind when someone does them a good turn. Therapists, for the most part, sincerely believe they are helping their patients and it is only natural that patients would want to please them in return. Without patients necessarily realizing it, such obligations are sufficient to inflate their perception of how much benefit they have received. Thus, controls for compliance effects must also be built into proper clinical trials (Adair 1973).

Finally, the job of distinguishing real from spurious causal relationships requires not only controlled observations, but also systematized abstractions from large bodies of data. Psychologists interested in judgmental biases have identified many sources of error that plague people who rely on informal reasoning processes to analyze complex events (Gilovich 1991, 1997; Schick and Vaughn 1995). Dean and colleagues (1992) showed, using examples from another popular pseudoscience, handwriting analysis, that without sophisticated statistical aids, human cognitive abilities are simply not up to the task of sifting valid relationships out of masses of interacting data. Similar difficulties would have confronted the pioneers of pre-scientific medicine and their followers, and for that reason, we cannot accept their anecdotal reports as support for their assertions.

SUMMARY

For the reasons I have presented, individual testimonials count for very little in evaluating therapies. Because so many false leads can convince intelligent, honest people that cures have been achieved when they have not, it is essential that any putative treatment be tested under conditions that control for placebo responses, compliance effects, and judgmental errors.

Before anyone agrees to undergo any kind of treatment, he or she should be confident that it has been validated in properly controlled clinical trials. To reduce the probability that supporting evidence has been contaminated by the foregoing biases and errors, consumers should insist that supporting evidence be published in peer-reviewed scientific journals. Any practitioner who cannot supply this kind of backing for his or her procedures is immediately suspect. Potential clients should be wary if, instead, the "evidence" consists merely of testimonials, self-published pamphlets or books, or items from the popular media. Even if supporting articles appear to have come from legitimate scientific periodicals, consumers should check to see that the journals in question are published by reputable scientific organizations. Papers extolling pseudoscience often appear in official-looking periodicals that turn out to be owned by groups with inadequate scientific credentials but with a financial stake in the questionable products. Similarly, one should discount articles from the "vanity press"—journals that accept virtually all submissions and charge the authors for publication. And finally, because any single positive outcome—even from a carefully done experiment published in a reputable journal—could always be a fluke, replication by independent research groups is the ultimate standard of proof.

If the practitioner claims persecutions, is ignorant of or openly hostile to mainstream science, cannot supply a reasonable scientific rationale for his or her methods, and promises results that go well beyond those claimed by orthodox biomedicine, there is strong reason to suspect that one is dealing with a quack. Appeals to other ways of knowing or mysterious-sounding "planes," "energies," "forces," or "vibrations" are other telltale signs, as is any claim to treat the whole person rather than localized pathology.

To people who are unwell, any promise of a cure is especially beguiling. As a result, false hope easily supplants common sense. In this vulnerable state, the need for hard-nosed appraisal is all the more necessary, but so often we see instead an eagerness to abandon any remaining vestiges of skepticism. Erstwhile savvy consumers, felled by disease, often insist upon less evidence to support the claims of alternative healers than they would previously have demanded from someone hawking a used car. Caveat emptor!

REFERENCES

Adair, J. 1973. *The Human Subject*. Boston: Little, Brown and Co.

Ader, R., and N. Cohen. 1993. Psychoneuroimmunology: Conditioning and stress. *Annual Review of Psychology 44:* 53–85.

Alcock, J. 1986. Chronic pain and the injured worker. *Canadian Psychology 27*(2): 196–203.

———. 1995. The belief engine. *Skeptical Inquirer 19*(3): 14–8.

Barrett, S., and W. Jarvis. 1993. *The Health Robbers: A Close Lock at Quackery in America*. Amherst, N.Y.: Prometheus Books.

Basil, R., ed. 1988. *Not Necessarily the New Age*. Amherst, N.Y.: Prometheus Books.

Beyerstein, B., and P. Hadaway. 1991. On avoiding folly. *Journal of Drug Issues 20*(4): 689–700.

Beyerstein, B., and W. Sampson. 1996. Traditional medicine and pseudoscience in China. *Skeptical Inquirer 20*(4): 18–26.

Brandon, R. 1985. Holism in philosophy of biology. In *Examining Holistic Medicine,* edited by D. Stalker and C. Glymour. Amherst, N.Y.: Premetheus Books, 127–36.

Cassileth, B., and H. Brown. 1988. Unorthodox cancer medicine. *CA-A Cancer Journal for Clinicians 38*(3): 176–86.

Chapman, L., and J. Chapman. 1967. Genesis of popular but erroneous diagnostic observations. *Journal of Abnormal Psychology 72:* 193–204.

Dean, G., I. Ketty, D. Saklofske, and A. Furnham. 1992. Graphology and human judgement. In *The Write Stuff,* edited by B. and D. Beyerstein. Amherst, N.Y.: Prometheus Books, 342–96.

Festinger, L. 1957. *A Theory of Cognitive Dissonance.* Stanford: Stanford University Press.

Gilovich, T. 1991. *How We Know What Isn't so: The Fallibility of Human Reason in Everyday Life.* New York: Free Press/Macmillan.

———. 1997. Some systematic biases of everyday judgment. *Skeptical Inquirer 21*(2): 31–5.

Gross, P., and N. Levitt, 1994. *Higher Superstition.* Baltimore: Johns Hopkins University Press.

Huber, P. 1991. *Galileo's Revenge: Junk Science in the Courtroom.* New York: Basic Books.

Kiernan, V. 1995. Survey plumbs the depths of international ignorance. *The New Scientist* (April 29): 7.

Merskey, H. 1995. *The Analysis of Hysteria: Understanding Conversion and Dissociation.* 2d ed. London: Royal College of Psychiatrists.

Melzack, R. 1973. *The Puzzle of Pain.* New York: Basic Books.

Mestel, R. 1994. Let mind talk unto body. *The New Scientist* (July 23): 26–31.

O'Connor, G. 1987. Confidence trick. *The Medical Journal of Australia 147:* 456–9.

Roberts, A., D. Kewman, and L. Hovell. 1993. The power of nonspecific effects in healing: Implications for psychosocial and biological treatments. *Clinical Psychology Review 13:* 375–91.

Rosenbaum, J. T. 1997. Lessons from litigation over silicone breast implants: A call for activism by scientists. *Science 276* (June 6. 1997): 1524–5.

Rosenthal, R. 1966. *Experimenter Effects in Behavioral Research.* New York: Appleton-Century-Crofts.

Schick, T., and L. Vaughn. 1995. *How to Think About Weird Things: Critical Thinking for a New Age.* Mountain View, Calif: Mayfield Publishing.

Shorter, E. 1992. *From Paralysis to Fatigue: A History of Psychosomatic Illness in the Modern Era.* New York: The Free Press.

Silverman, S. 1987. Medical "miracles": Still mysterious despite claims of believers. *Psientific American.* (July): 5–7. Newsletter of the Sacramento Skeptics Society, Sacramento, Calif.

Skrabanek, P., and J. McCormick. 1990. *Follies and Fallacies in Medicine.* Amherst, N.Y.: Prometheus Books.

Smith, W., H. Merskey, and S. Gross, eds. 1980. *Pain: Meaning and Management.* New York: SP Medical and Scientific Books.

Stalker, D., and C. Glymour, eds. 1985. *Examining Holistic Medicine.* Amherst, N.Y.: Prometheus Books.

Stewart, D. 1990. Emotional disorders misdiagnosed as physical illness: Environmental hypersensitivity, candidiasis hypersensitivity, and chronic fatigue syndrome. *Int. J. Mental Health 19*(3): 56–68.

Ulett, G. A. 1996. *Alternative Medicine or Magical Healing.* St. Louis: Warren H. Green.

REVIEW AND CONTEMPLATE

1. What is the distinction between a disease and an illness?

2. With respect to assessing the effectiveness of therapies, explain why it is important to understand that correlation does not imply causation.

3. Name and describe five of the 10 reasons ineffective treatments might seem to have worked.

4. What is a placebo control group, and why is it important to have such a group in an experiment designed to investigate the effectiveness of a therapy?

5. What are some examples of treatments or therapies that you or your friends believed in that you now suspect are bogus? Explain why you suspect they are bogus.

2.2 "The Suggestibility of Young Children"

IN 1985, A 4-year-old boy who was having his temperature taken with a rectal thermometer in a physician's office said to the nurse, "that's what my teacher does to me at nap time at school." The nurse suspected he had been sexually abused at his day care center and notified the authorities. Investigators repeatedly questioned the children at the day care center about possible abuse by a teacher named Kelly Michaels. Initially, most of the children said they liked Kelly and denied that Kelly had abused them. But after repeatedly being asked questions that suggested they had been abused, the children reported that Kelly had abused them in numerous ways. They reported that Kelly made them drink her urine and lick peanut butter off her genitals, and that Kelly forced them to have sex with her. In 1988, Kelly Michaels was convicted of 115 counts of abuse against 20 children and was sentenced to 47 years in prison. Today the case of Kelly Michaels is used as an example of how faulty interviewing techniques can lead to false reports of abuse. Kelly Michaels served 5 years in prison before an appellate court set her free after ruling that she did not receive a fair trial due to the way in which the children had been questioned.

In this article, Bruck and Ceci discuss whether the manner in which an interview is conducted can elicit inaccurate information from children, including information about sexual abuse. The article contains valuable advice on what to do and what to avoid when interviewing children and others. The authors also discuss fascinating studies that illustrate the extent to which false information can be obtained from children interviewed in a suggestive manner.

Reference

Bruck, M., & Ceci, S. (1997). The suggestibility of young children. *Current Directions in Psychological Science, 6,* 75–79.

"THE SUGGESTIBILITY OF YOUNG CHILDREN"

MAGGIE BRUCK AND STEPHEN CECI

Since the beginning of the 1980s, there have been a number of legal cases in which young children have provided uncorroborated testimony involving sexual abuse. Although it seemed from the evidence that the children in many of these cases were subjected to a number of suggestive interviews, the primary issue in deciding guilt or innocence was the degree to which such interviews could actually bring children to make serious allegations.

Until recently, scientific data provided little insight into this forensic issue. Specifically, although there were a number of studies showing that young children are more suggestible than adults (reviewed by Ceci & Bruck, 1993), these studies were limited to examinations of the influence of single misleading suggestions on children's recall of neutral, and often uninteresting, events. In other words, the conditions of the studies were not similar to the conditions that brought children to court. This empirical vacuum forced a new conceptualization of issues related to children's suggestibility, which, in turn, resulted in an outpouring of new research in the area. In general, two features of the newer research make it more relevant to forensic issues. First, the studies are designed to examine children's suggestibility about events that are personally salient, that involve bodily touching, and that involve insinuations of sexual abuse. Second, the concept of suggestive techniques has been expanded from the traditional view of asking a misleading question or planting a piece of misinformation, so that now studies examine the larger structure and the components of suggestive interviews. In this article, we provide an overview of the results of these newer studies of children's suggestibility.

INTERVIEWER BIAS AND SUGGESTIVE INTERVIEWING TECHNIQUES

We have proposed that *interviewer bias* is the central driving force in the creation of suggestive interviews. Interviewer bias characterizes an interviewer who holds a priori beliefs about the occurrence of certain events and, as a result, molds the interview to elicit from the interviewee statements that are consistent with these prior beliefs. One hallmark of interviewer bias is the single-minded attempt to gather only confirmatory evidence and to avoid all avenues that may produce disconfirmatory evidence. Thus, a biased interviewer does not ask questions that might provide alternate explanations for the allegations (e.g., "Did your mommy tell you, or did you see it happen?"). Nor does a biased interviewer ask about events that are inconsistent with the interviewer's hypothesis (e.g., "Who else besides your teacher touched your private parts? Did your mommy touch them, too?"). And a biased interviewer does not challenge the authenticity of the child's report when it is consistent with the interviewer's hypothesis. When a child provides inconsistent or bizarre evidence, it is either ignored or interpreted within the framework of the biased interviewer's initial hypothesis.

A number of studies highlight the effects of interviewer bias on the accuracy of children's reports (reviewed in Ceci & Bruck, 1995). In some studies, children are engaged in a staged event. Later, naive interviewers, who did not witness the event, are given either accurate or false information about the event and then told to question the children. Interviewers who are given false information are unaware of this deliberate deception, which is carried out to create a "bias." In other studies, children are asked to recall a staged event by an experimenter who intentionally conveys a bias that is either consistent or inconsistent with the staged event. In both types of studies, when questioned by interviewers with false beliefs, children make inaccurate reports that are consistent with the interviewers' biases.

According to our model, interviewer bias influences the entire architecture of interviews, and it is revealed through a number of different component features that are suggestive. We briefly describe some of these in this section.

In order to obtain confirmation of their suspicions, biased interviewers may not ask children open-ended questions, such as "What happened?" but instead resort to a barrage of specific questions, many of which are repeated, and many of which are leading. This strategy is problematic because children's responses to open-ended questions are more accurate than their responses to specific questions. This finding has been reported consistently since the beginning of the century (e.g., see Ceci & Bruck, 1995) and is highlighted in a recent study by Peterson and Bell (1996), who interviewed children after they visited an emergency room for a traumatic injury. Children were first asked open-ended questions (e.g., "Tell me what happened"), and then asked more specific questions (e.g., "Where did you hurt yourself?" or "Did you hurt your knee?"). The children were most likely to report the important details accurately in response to open-ended questions (91% accuracy); errors increased when children were asked specific questions (45% accuracy). Forced-choice questions (e.g., "Was it black or white?") also compromise the reliability of children's reports because children tend not to respond, "I don't know" (e.g., see Walker, Lunning, & Eilts, 1996), even when the question is nonsensical (Hughes & Grieve, 1980).

Not only does accuracy decrease when children are asked specific questions, but there is increased risk of taint when young children are repeatedly asked the same specific questions, either within the same interview or across different interviews (e.g., Poole & White, 1991). Under such circumstances, young children tend to change their answers, perhaps to provide the interviewer with the information that they perceive he or she wants.

Some interviewers convey their bias by asking leading questions and providing information about the alleged target events. When these techniques are repeated across multiple interviews, children's reports may become tainted. For example, in one study

(Bruck, Ceci, Francoeur, & Barr, 1995), 5-year-old children visited their pediatrician and received an inoculation. One year later, they were interviewed four times about salient details of that visit. Children who were repeatedly interviewed in a neutral, nonleading manner provided accurate reports about the original medical visit. In contrast, children who were repeatedly given misinformation about some of the salient details were very inaccurate; not only did they incorporate the misleading suggestions into their reports (e.g., falsely claiming that a female research assistant, rather than the male pediatrician, inoculated them), but they also reported nonsuggested but inaccurate events (e.g., falsely reporting that the female research assistant had checked their ears and nose).

Interviewers can also use subtle verbal and nonverbal cues to communicate bias. At times, these cues can set the emotional tone of the interview, and they can also convey implicit or explicit threats, bribes, and rewards for the desired answer. Children are attuned to these emotional tones and act accordingly. In one study, for example, children were asked to recall the details of a visit to a university laboratory that had occurred 4 years previously (Goodman, Wilson, Hazan, & Reed, 1989). At the 4-year follow-up interview, the researchers deliberately created an atmosphere of accusation by telling the children that they were to be questioned about an important event and by saying, "Are you afraid to tell? You'll feel better once you've told." Although few children remembered the original event from 4 years earlier, a number of the children assented to suggestive questions implying abuse; some children falsely reported that they had been hugged or kissed, or that they had had their picture taken in the bathroom, or that they had been given a bath. Thus, children may give incorrect information to misleading questions about events for which they have no memory, if the interviewer creates an emotional tone of accusation.

Stereotype induction is another possible component of a suggestive interview. For example, if a child is repeatedly told that a person "does bad things," then the child may begin to incorporate this belief into his or her reports. A study of preschool children illustrates this pattern (Leichtman & Ceci, 1995). On a number of occasions, the experimenters told the children about their "clumsy" friend Sam Stone, whose exploits included accidentally breaking Barbie dolls and ripping sweaters. Later, Sam came to the children's classroom for a short, accident-free visit. The next day, the teacher showed the children a torn book and a soiled teddy bear. Several weeks later, a number of these 3- to 4-year-old children reported that Sam had been responsible for these acts; some even claimed that they had seen him do these things. Children who had not received the stereotype induction rarely made this type of error.

Techniques that have been especially designed for interviewing children about sexual abuse may be potentially suggestive. For example, anatomically detailed dolls are commonly used by professionals when interviewing children about suspected sexual abuse. It is thought that the use of the dolls overcomes language, memory, and motivational (e.g., embarrassment) problems. However, the existing data indicate that the dolls do not facilitate accurate reporting. In some cases, children are more inaccurate with the dolls, especially when asked to demonstrate certain events that never happened (e.g., Gordon et al., 1993). Thus, dolls may be suggestive if children have not made any allegations but are asked by an interviewer who suspects abuse to demonstrate abuse with the dolls.

Our recent studies provide evidence for this hypothesis (Bruck, Ceci, & Francoeur, 1995; Bruck, Ceci, Francoeur, & Renick, 1995). Three- and 4-year-old children had a medical examination during which some of them received a routine genital examination. After the children were interviewed about the examination, they were given an anatomical doll and told, "Show me on the doll how the doctor touched your genitals." Approximately 50% of the children who had not received a genital examination falsely showed touching on the doll. Furthermore, when the children who had received a genital examination were asked the same question, a number of them incorrectly showed that the doctor had inserted a finger into their genitals; the pediatrician had never done this. Next, when the children in the study were given a stethoscope and a spoon and asked to show what the doctor did or might do with these instruments, some children incorrectly showed that he used the stethoscope to examine their genitals, and some children inserted the spoon into the genital or anal openings or hit the doll's genitals. None of these actions had occurred. We concluded that these false actions were the result of implicit suggestions that it was permissible to show sexualized behaviors. Also, because of the novelty of the dolls, children were drawn to insert fingers and other objects into their cavities.

Guided imagery is another interviewing technique that is potentially suggestive. Interviewers sometimes ask children to try to remember if or pretend that a certain event occurred and then to create a mental picture of the event and to think about its details. Because young children sometimes have difficulty distinguishing between memories of actual events and memories of imagined events (e.g., Parker, 1995; Welch-Ross, 1995), when asked to pretend about or imagine certain events, children may later come to report them as real and believe them to be so. This hypothesis is supported by studies in which young children were repeatedly asked to think about real as well as imaginary events, creating mental images each time they did so. In one of these studies (Ceci, Loftus, Leichtman, & Brack, 1994), children increasingly assented to false events with each successive interview. When these children were told after 11 sessions that some of the imagined events had not happened, most of the children who had previously assented to false beliefs continued to hold onto theft false statements. These data indicate that a number of the children had actually come to believe that they had experienced the false events.

CONCLUSIONS AND QUALIFICATIONS

In summary, interviewer bias is revealed by a number of suggestive techniques, each of which can compromise the accuracy of young children's reports. In this section, we qualify and elaborate on this conclusion by raising several points. First, although most developmental studies have focused on the suggestibility of preschool children, there is still reason for concern about the reliability of older children's testimony when they are subjected to suggestive interviews. There is ample evidence that children older than 6 years of age are suggestible about a wide range of events (e.g., Goodman et al., 1989; Poole & Lindsay, 1996; Warren & Lane, 1995) and that adults' recollections are impaired by suggestive interviewing techniques (e.g., Hyman & Pentland, 1996; Loftus & Pickrell, 1995).

Second, although there are consistent findings of age differences across studies, there are nevertheless individual differences. Some preschoolers are very resistant to interviewers' suggestions, whereas some older children will immediately fall sway to the slightest suggestion. Researchers are a long way from understanding the source of these individual differences but are beginning to assess the association between suggestibility and a number of cognitive characteristics (e.g., knowledge base, memory), psychosocial factors (e.g., compliance, self-esteem), and interviewing techniques (e.g., the use of various suggestive components).

Third, contrary to previous claims that children are suggestible only about peripheral details (e.g., Melton, 1992), the newer studies show that children are also suggestible about central events. These central events may involve bodily touching that may have sexual connotations. Thus, in some suggestibility studies, children falsely claimed that a nurse licked their knees, a scientist put something "yucky" in their mouths, a pediatrician inserted a spoon into their genitals, and a man kissed their friends on the lips and removed some of the children's clothes.

Fourth, the number of suggestive interviewing techniques (which reflects the degree of interviewer bias) can account for variations in suggestibility estimates across and within studies. If a biased interviewer uses more than one suggestive technique, there is a greater chance for taint than if he or she uses just one technique. For example, we (Bruck, Ceci, & Hembrooke, in press) constructed interviews that combined a variety of suggestive techniques (visualization, repeated questioning, repeated misinformation) to elicit children's reports of true events (helping a visitor in the school, getting punished) and false events (helping a woman find her monkey, seeing a thief taking food from the day care). After two suggestive interviews, most children in this study had assented to all events, a pattern that continued to the end of the experiment.

Fifth, the procedures used in most studies do not allow one to determine if the children's false reports reflect false belief (false memory) or merely knowing compliance to the interviewer's suggestion. There may be a time course for the emergence of these different states. Children may start out knowingly complying to suggestions, but with repeated suggestive interviews, they may come to believe the suggestions and incorporate them into their memories. There are a few studies that show that when suggestions are repeated to children over time, a number of the children do develop false beliefs (eg., Ceci et al., 1994; Leichtman & Ceci, 1995; Poole & Lindsay, 1996). Furthermore, if the suggestive interviews cease for a period of time, these false memories fade (e.g., Huffman, Crossman, & Ceci, 1996; Poole & Lindsay, 1996).

Sixth, children who have undergone repeated suggestive interviews appear highly credible. When highly trained professionals in the fields of child development, mental health, and forensics view videotaped interviews of these subjects, they cannot reliably discriminate between children whose reports are accurate and children whose reports are inaccurate as the result of suggestive interviewing techniques (see Leichtman & Ceci, 1995). We have attempted to isolate the linguistic markers that might differentiate true narratives from false narratives that emerge as a result of repeated suggestive interviews (Bruck et al., in press). We have found that with repeated suggestive interviews, false stories quickly come to resemble true stories in terms of the number of details, the spontaneity of utterance, the number of details not previously reported (reminiscences), inconsistency across narratives, the elaborativeness of the details, and the cohesiveness of the narrative. It is only the greater consistency of narratives of true events that differentiates them from narratives of false events. Thus, suggestive interviewing procedures can result in highly credible but inaccurate witnesses.

Finally, although we have focused here on the conditions that can compromise reliable reporting, it is also important to acknowledge that a large number of studies show that children are capable of providing accurate, detailed, and useful information about actual events, including traumatic ones (for reviews, see, e.g., Fivush, 1993; Goodman, Batterman-Faunce, & Kenney, 1992). What characterizes these studies is the neutral tone of the interviewers, the limited use of leading questions (for the most part, if suggestions are used, they are limited to a single occasion), and the absence of any motive for the children to make false reports. When such conditions are present, it is a common (although not universal) finding that children are relatively immune to suggestive influences, particularly about sexual details. When such conditions are present in actual forensic or therapeutic interviews, one can have greater confidence in the reliability of children's allegations. It is these conditions that one must strive for when eliciting information from young children.

NOTE

1. Address correspondence to Maggie Bruck, Department of Psychology, McGill University, 1205 Dr. Penfield, Montreal, Quebec H3A 1B1, Canada; e-mail: bruck@hebb.psych.mcgill.ca.

REFERENCES

Bruck, M., Ceci, S.J., & Francoeur, E. (1995, March). *Anatomically detailed dolls do not facilitate preschoolers' reports of touching*. Paper presented at the biannual meeting of the Society for Research on Child Development. Indianapolis, IN.

Bruck, M., Ceci, S.J., Francoeur, E., & Barr, R.J. (1995). "I hardly cried when I got my shot!": Influencing children's reports about a visit to their pediatrician. *Child Development, 66*, 193–208.

Bruck, M., Ceci, S.J., Francoeur, E., & Renick, A. (1995). Anatomically detailed dolls do not facilitate preschoolers' reports of a pediatric examination involving genital touching. *Journal of Experimental Psychology: Applied, 1,* 95-109.

Bruck, M., Ceci, S.J., & Hembrooke, H. (in press). Children's reports of pleasant and unpleasant events. In D. Read & S. Lindsay (Eds.), *Recollections of trauma: Scientific research and clinical practice.* New York: Plenum Press.

Ceci, S.J., & Bruck, M. (1993). The suggestibility of the child witness: A historical review and synthesis. *Psychological Bulletin,* 113, 403-439.

Ceci, S.J., & Bruck, M. (1995). *Jeopardy in the courtroom: A scientific analysis of children's testimony.* Washington, DC: American Psychological Association.

Ceci, S.J., Loftus, E.W., Leichtman, M., & Bruck, M. (1994). The role of source misattributions in the creation of false beliefs among preschoolers. *International Journal of Clinical and Experimental Hypnosis, 62,* 304-320.

Fivush, R. (1993). Developmental perspectives on autobiographical recall. In G.S. Goodman & B. Bottoms (Eds.), *Child victims and child witnesses: Understanding and improving testimony* (pp. 1-24). New York: Guilford Press.

Goodman, G.S., Batterman-Faunce, J.M., & Kenney, R. (1992). Optimizing children's testimony. Research and social policy issues concerning allegations of child sexual abuse. In D. Cicchetti & S. Toth (Eds.), *Child abuse, child development, and social policy* (pp. 139-166). Norwood, NJ: Ablex.

Goodman, G.S., Wilson, M.E., Hazan, C., & Reed, R.S. (1989, April). *Children's testimony nearly four years after an event.* Paper presented at the annual meeting of the Eastern Psychological Association, Boston.

Gordon, B., Ornstein, P.A., Nida, R., Follmer, A., Creshaw, C., & Albert, G. (1993). Does the use of dolls facilitate children's memory of visits to the doctor? *Applied Cognitive Psychology, 7,* 459-474.

Huffman, M.L., Crossman, A., & Ceci, S. (1996, March). *An investigation of the long-term effects of source misattribution error: Are false memories permanent?* Poster presented at the biannual meeting of the American Psychology-Law Society, Hilton Head, SC.

Hughes, M., & Grieve, R. (1980). On asking children bizarre questions. *First Language, 1,* 149-160.

Hyman, I.E., & Pentland, J. (1996). The role of mental imagery in the creation of false childhood memories. *Journal of Memory and Language, 35,* 101-777.

Leichtman, M.D., & Ceci, S.J. (1995). The effects of stereotypes and suggestions on preschoolers' reports. *Developmental Psychology, 31,* 568-578.

Loftus, E.F., & Pickrell, J.E. (1995). The formation of false memories. *Psychiatric Annals, 25,* 720-725.

Melton, G. (1992). Children as partners for justice: Next steps for developmentalists. *Monographs of the Society for Research in Child Development, 57*(5, Serial No. 229), 153-159.

Parker, J. (1995). Age differences in source monitoring of performed and imagined actions on immediate and delayed tests. *Journal of Experimental Child Psychology, 60,* 84–101.

Peterson, C., & Bell, M. (1996). Children's memory for traumatic injury. *Child Development, 67,* 3045–3070.

Poole, D.A., & Lindsay, D.S. (1996, June). *Effects of parents suggestions, interviewing techniques, and age on young children's event reports.* Paper presented at the NATO Advanced Study Institute, Port de Bourgenay, France.

Poole, D.A., & White, L. (1991). Effects of question repetition on the eyewitness testimony of children and adults. *Developmental Psychology, 27,* 975–986.

Walker, N., Lunning, S., & Eilts, J. (1996, June). *Do children respond accurately to forced choice questions?* Paper presented to the NATO Advanced Study Institute: Recollections of Trauma: Scientific Research and Clinical Practice, Talmont Saint Hilaire, France.

Warren, A.R., & Lane, P. (1995). The effects of timing and type of questioning on eyewitness accuracy and suggestibility. In M. Zaragoza (Ed.), *Memory and testimony in the child witness* (pp. 44–60). Thousand Oaks, CA: Sage Publications.

Welch-Ross, M. (1995). Developmental changes in preschoolers' ability to distinguish memories of performed, pretended, and imagined actions. *Cognitive Development, 10.* 421–441.

REVIEW AND CONTEMPLATE

1. What is interviewer bias? Explain how such a bias might lead a child to falsely report being sexually abused by an adult.

2. Bruck and Ceci (1997) stated, "Interviewer bias influences the entire architecture of interviews, and it is revealed through a number of different component features that are suggestive." Describe three of these component features.

3. Do anatomically correct dolls help interviewers elicit accurate information about suspected childhood sexual abuse? Cite evidence from Bruck and Ceci (1997) to support your answer.

4. Bruck and Ceci (1997) stated that "children are capable of providing accurate, detailed, and useful information about actual events, including traumatic ones." Under what conditions do children provide such information?

2.3 "On the Belief That Arthritis Pain Is Related to the Weather"

MY MOTHER USED to complain of chronic pain in her legs, and one day she informed me that she could tell when a hurricane was near the United States because she could feel it in her legs. What made her claim even more extraordinary is the fact that she lived in Michigan, which is about 1,000 miles from the Gulf Coast region, where hurricanes often strike! Although it seems unlikely that her claim was true, it's not uncommon for people to develop false beliefs about relationships between events. The tendency of people to see associations or correlations where none exist is well documented by psychologists. For example, some nurses believe that mental patients are more likely to admit themselves to the hospital on evenings in which there is a full moon, but there is no correlation between the phase of the moon and hospital admissions of mental patients.

Beliefs in such nonexistent relationships are called illusory correlations, and they illustrate one difficulty people sometimes have with statistical reasoning. As you read in Chapter 1, normal cognitive processes can lead to pseudoscientific or paranormal beliefs, and our tendency to search for relationships or correlations between events—including our tendency to develop illusory correlations—is one such cognitive process. My mother's belief that her pain was related to the weather is similar to another fairly common belief: Some arthritis patients, and some of their doctors, believe that their pain is related to the weather. In this article, Redelmeier and Tversky examine whether this belief reflects an illusory correlation.

Reference

Redelmeier, D. A, & Tversky, A. (1996). On the belief that arthritis pain is related to the weather. *Proceedings of the National Academy of the Sciences of the United States of America, 93,* 2895–2896.

ARTICLE 2.3

"ON THE BELIEF THAT ARTHRITIS PAIN IS RELATED TO THE WEATHER"
DONALD REDELMEIER AND AMOS TVERSKY

For thousands of years people have believed that arthritis pain is influenced by the weather. Hippocrates around 400 B.C. discussed the effects of winds and rains on chronic diseases in his book *Air, Water and Places* (1). In the nineteenth century, several authors suggested that variations in barometric pressure, in particular, were partially responsible for variations in the intensity of arthritis pain (2–4). To the current day, such beliefs are common among patients, physicians, and interested observers throughout the world (5–14). Furthermore, these beliefs have led to recommendations that patients move to milder climates or spend time in a climate-controlled chamber to lessen joint pain (15–17).

The research literature, however, has not established a clear association between arthritis pain and the weather. No study using objective measures of inflammation has found positive results (18, 19), and studies using subjective measures of pain have been conflicting. Some find that an increase in barometric pressure tends to increase pain (20), others find that it tends to decrease pain (21), and others find no association (22, 23). Some investigators argue that only a simultaneous change in pressure and humidity influences arthritis pain (24), but others find no such pattern (25). Several studies report that weather effects are immediate (20), whereas others suggest a lag of several days (26). Due to the lack of clear evidence, medical textbooks—which once devoted chapters to the relation of weather and rheumatic disease—now devote less than a page to the topic (27, 28).

The contrast between the strong belief that arthritis pain is related to the weather and the weak evidence found in the research literature is puzzling. How do people acquire and maintain the belief? Research on judgment under uncertainty indicates that both laypeople and experts sometimes detect patterns where none exist. In particular, people often perceive positive serial correlations in random sequences of coin tosses (29), stock-market prices (30), or basketball shots (31). We hypothesize that a similar bias occurs in the evaluation of correlations between pairs of time series, and that it contributes to the belief that arthritis pain is related to the weather. We explored this hypothesis by testing (*i*) whether arthritis patients' perceptions are consistent with their data and (*ii*) whether people perceive associations between uncorrelated time series.

We obtained data from rheumatoid arthritis patients ($n = 18$) on pain (assessed by the patient), joint tenderness (evaluated by the physician), and functional status (based on a standard index) measured twice a month for 15 months (32). We also obtained

Donald A. Redelmeier and Amos Tversky, "On the Belief that Arthritis Pain is Related to the Weather," *Proceedings of the National Academy of the Sciences of the United States of America*, vol. 93, pp. 2895-2896. Copyright © 1996 by National Academy of Sciences. Reprinted with permission.

local weather reports on barometric pressure, temperature, and humidity for the corresponding time period. Finally, we interviewed patients about their beliefs concerning their arthritis pain. All patients but one believed that their pain was related to the weather, and all but two believed the effects were strong, occurred within a day, and were related to barometric pressure, temperature, or humidity.

We computed the correlations between pain and the specific weather component and lag mentioned by each patient. The mean of these correlations was 0.016 and none was significant at $P < 0.05$. We also computed the correlation between pain and barometric pressure for each patient, using nine different time lags ranging from 2 days forward to 2 days backward in 12-hr increments. The mean of these correlations was 0.003, and only 6% were significant at $P < 0.05$. Similar results were obtained in analyses using the two other measures of arthritis and the two other measures of the weather. Furthermore, we found no consistent pattern among the few statistically significant correlations.

We next presented college students ($n = 97$) with pairs of sequences displayed graphically. The top sequence was said to represent a patient's daily arthritis pain over 1 month, and the bottom sequence was said to represent daily barometric pressure during the same month (Fig. 2.1). Each sequence was generated as a normal random walk and all participants evaluated six pairs of sequences: a positively correlated pair ($r = +0.50$), a negatively correlated pair ($r = -0.50$), and four uncorrelated pairs. Participants were asked to classify each pair of sequences as (i) positively related, (ii) negatively related, or (iii) unrelated. Positively related sequences were defined as follows: "An increase in

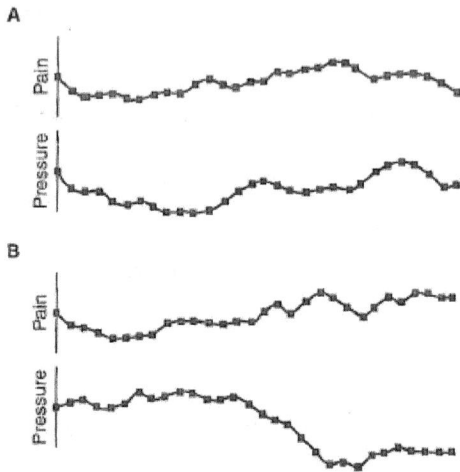

FIGURE 2.1: Random walk sequences. The upper sequence in each pair represents daily arthritis pain for 30 consecutive observations; the lower sequence represents daily barometric pressure during the same period. For both A and B, the correlation between changes in pain and changes in pressure is 0.00.

barometric pressure is more likely to be accompanied by an increase in arthritis pain rather than a decrease on that day (and a decrease in barometric pressure is more likely to be accompanied by a decrease rather than an increase in arthritis pain on that day)." Negatively related sequences and unrelated sequences were defined similarly.

We found that the positively correlated pair and the negatively correlated pair were correctly classified by 89% and 93% of respondents, respectively. However, some uncorrelated pairs were consistently classified as related. For example, the two uncorrelated sequences in Fig. 2.1A were judged as positively related by 87%, as negatively related by 2%, and as unrelated by 11% of participants. The two uncorrelated sequences in Fig. 2.1B were judged as positively related by 3%, as negatively related by 79%, and as unrelated by 18% of participants. The remaining two pairs of uncorrelated sequences were correctly classified by 59% and 64% of participants. Evidently, the intuitive notion of association differs from the statistical concept of association.

Our results indicate that people tend to perceive an association between uncorrelated time series. We attribute this phenomenon to selective matching, the tendency to focus on salient coincidences, thereby capitalizing on chance and neglecting contrary evidence (33–35). For arthritis, selective matching leads people to look for changes in the weather when they experience increased pain, and pay little attention to the weather when their pain is stable. For graphs, selective matching leads people to focus on segments where the two sequences seem to move together (in the same or opposite direction), with insufficient regard to other aspects of the data. In both cases, a single day of severe pain and extreme weather might sustain a lifetime of belief in a relation between them. The cognitive processes involved in evaluating graphs are different from those involved in evaluating past experiences, yet all intuitive judgments of covariation are vulnerable to selective matching.

Several psychological factors could contribute to the belief that arthritis pain is related to the weather, in addition to general plausibility and traditional popularity. The desire to have an explanation for a worsening of pain may encourage patients to search for confirming evidence and neglect contrary instances (36). This search is facilitated by the availability of multiple components and time lags for linking changes in arthritis to changes in the weather (37). Selective memory may further enhance the belief that arthritis pain is related to the weather if coincidences are more memorable than mismatches (38). Selective matching, therefore, can be enhanced by both motivational and memory effects; our study of graphs, however, suggests that it can operate even in the absence of these effects.

Selective matching can help explain both the prevalent belief that arthritis pain is related to the weather and the failure of medical research to find consistent correlations. Our study, of course, does not imply that arthritis pain and the weather are unrelated for all patients. Furthermore, it is possible that daily measurements over many years of our patients would show a stronger correlation than observed in our data, at least for some patients. However, it is doubtful that sporadic correlations could justify the widespread and strongly held beliefs about arthritis and the weather. The observation that the beliefs are just as prevalent in San Diego (where the weather is mild and stable) as in Boston (where the weather is severe and volatile) casts further doubt on a purely physiological explanation (39). People's beliefs about arthritis pain and the weather may tell more about the workings of the mind than of the body.

REFERENCES

1. Adams, F. (1991). *The Genuine Works of Hippocrates* (Williams & Wilkins, Baltimore).
2. Webster, J. (1859) *Lancet* i, 588-589.
3. Mitchel, S. W. (1877) *Am. J. Med. Sei.* **75,** 305-329.
4. Everett, J. T. (1879). *Med. J. Exam.* **38,** 253-260.
5. Abdulpatakhov, D. D. (1969) *Vopr. Reum.* **9,** 72-76.
6. Nava, P. & Seda, H. (1964) *Bras. Med.* **78,** 71-74.
7. Pilger, A. (1970) *Med. Klin. Munich* **65,** 1363-1365.
8. Hollander, J. L. (1963) *Arch. Environ. Health* **6,** 527-536.
9. Guedj, D. & Weinberger, A. (1990) Ann. *Rheum. Dis.* **49,** 158—159-
10. Lawrence, J. S. (1977) *Rheumatism in Population* (Heinemann Med. Books, London), pp. 505-517.
11. Rose, M. B. (1974) *Physiotherapy* **60,** 306-309.
12. Rasker, J. J., Peters, H. J. G. & Boon, K. L. (1986) *Scand. J. Rheumatol.* **15,** 27-36.
13. Laborde, J. M., Dando, W. A. & Powers, M. J. (1986) *Soc. Sei. Med.* **23,** 549-554.
14. Shutty, M. S., Cundiff, G. & DeGood, D. E. (1992) *Pain* **49,** 199-204.
15. Hill, D. F. & Holbrook, W. P. (1942) *Clinics* **1,** 577-581.
16. Balfour, W. (1916) *Observations with Cases Illustrative of a New, Simple, and Expeditious Mode of Curing Rheumatism and Sprains* (Muirhead, Edinburgh).
17. Edstrom, G., Lundin, G. & Wramner, T. (1948) *Ann. Rheum. Dis.* **7,** 76-92.
18. Latman, N. S. (1981) *J. Rheumatol.* **8,** 725-729.
19. Latman, N. S. (1980) *N. Engl. J. Med.* **303,** 1178.
20. Rentschler, E. B., Vanzant, F. R. & Rowntree, L. G. (1929) *J. Am. Med. Assoc.* **92,** 1995-2000.
21. Guedj, D. (1990) *Ann. Rheum. Dis.* **49,** 158-159.
22. Dordick, I. (1958) *Weather* **13,** 359-364.
23. Patberg, W. R., Nienhuis, R. I. F. & Veringa, F. (1985) *J. Rheumatol.* **12,** 711-715.
24. Hollander, J. L. & Yeostros, S. J. (1963) *Bull. Am. Meteorol. Soc.* **44,** 489-494.
25. Sibley, J. T. (1985) *J. Rheumatol.* **12,** 707-710.
26. Patberg, W. R. (1989) *Arthritis Rheum.* **32,** 1627-1629.
27. Hollander, J. L., ed. (1960) *Arthritis and Allied Conditions* (Lea & Febiger, Philadelphia), 6th Ed., pp. 577-581.

28. McCarty, D. J., ed. (1989) *Arthritis and Allied Conditions* (Lea & Febiger, Philadelphia), 11th Ed., p. 25.
29. Bar-Hillel, M. & Wagenaar, W. (1991) *Adv. Appl. Math.* **12,** 428–454.
30. Malkiel, B. G. (1990) *A Random Walk Down Wall Street* (Norton, New York).
31. Gilovich, T., Vallone, R. & Tversky, A. (1985) *Cognit. Psychol.* **17,** 295–314.
32. Ward, M. M. (1993) *J. Rheumatol.* **21,** 17–21.
33. Kahneman, D., Slovic, P. & Tversky, A., eds. (1982). *Judgment Under Uncertainty: Heuristics and Biases* (Cambridge Univ. Press, New York).
34. Nisbett, R. & Ross, L. (1980) *Human Inference: Strategies and Shortcomings of Social Judgments* (Prentice-Hall, London), pp. 90–112.
35. Gilovich, T. (1991) *How We Know What Isn't So: The Fallibility of Human Reasoning in Everyday Life* (The Free Press, New York).
36. Chapman, L. J. & Chapman, J. P. (1969) *J. Abnorm. Psychol.* **74,** 271–280.
37. Abelson, R. P. (1995) *Statistics as Principled Argument* (Lawrence Erlbaum, Hillsdale, NJ), pp. 7–8.
38. Tversky, A. & Kahneman, D. (1973) *Cognit. Psychol.* **5,** 207–232.
39. Jamison, R. N., Anderson, K. O. & Slater, M. A. (1995) *Pain* **61,** 309–315.

REVIEW AND CONTEMPLATE

1. Based on research conducted by scientists other than Redelmeier and Tversky, what general conclusion can be made about the relationship between arthritis pain and the weather?

2. Describe the design and results of the study conducted by Redelmeier and Tversky (1996) with rheumatoid arthritis patients.

3. Explain how "selective matching" may lead arthritis patients to perceive a relationship between the weather and arthritis symptoms.

4. Can you think of other examples of how beliefs in pseudoscientific or paranormal phenomena might be based on illusory correlations?

Chapter 3

NEUROSCIENCE AND CONSCIOUSNESS

3.1 "Why Right-Brain Teaching Is Half-Witted: A Critique of the Misapplication of Neuroscience to Education"

GIVEN THE COMPLEXITY of the human brain and the fact that scientists do not completely understand how it operates, there are bound to be myths surrounding this amazing organ. For example, many people believe the myth that we use only 10% of our brain. This myth has been used to support the argument that the human mind has paranormal abilities that might be tapped in order to unleash extraordinary powers such as telepathy (i.e., mind-to-mind communication) or psychokinesis (i.e., the ability to move objects with one's mind). However, scientists have shown that the 10% myth is not true. Another popular brain-related belief is that the right side of our brain is creative and the left side is logical and that some people are right-brained while others are left-brained. In this article, Lindell and Kidd explain that this myth has spurred the development of pseudoscientific educational tools and systems in a misguided attempt to develop students' right-brain abilities.

Chapter 1 explained how normal cognitive and social processes can lead to pseudoscientific and paranormal beliefs, and this reading is a good example of how psychological and social factors contribute to such beliefs. When myths such as the belief that right-brain teaching enhances creativity are repeated and spread throughout groups of people, they may become widely treated as true. Myths like this may persist for long periods of time because few people attempt to verify their truth and because it seems intuitive that people who are more creative than others use different parts of their brains than do those who are more logical and less creative.

Reference

Lindell, A. K., & Kidd, E. (2011). Why right-brain teaching is half-witted: A critique of the misapplication of neuroscience to education. *Mind, Brain, and Education, 5,* 121–137.

ARTICLE 3.1

"WHY RIGHT-BRAIN TEACHING IS HALF-WITTED: A CRITIQUE OF THE MISAPPLICATION OF NEUROSCIENCE TO EDUCATION"

ANNUKKA LINDELL AND EVAN KIDD

There is a popular myth among educators that traditional learning favors the left hemisphere (the "academic" brain) and neglects the right hemisphere (the "creative" or "artistic" brain), purportedly leaving half a student's brain undereducated (e.g., Organisation for Economic Co-operation and Development, 2007). Reasoning that student learning will be enhanced by targeting the overlooked "right brain" (and/or adopting "whole-brain" techniques), a variety of educational theories, tools, and systems have been introduced (e.g., Brain Gym, Shichida Method; Petty, 2004). Across Southeast Asia over 400 "Mind Research Consultant" kindergartens proudly boast their use of "innovative right-brain learning methods" (http://rightbrainteaching.com/). There are DVDs for "Teaching the Right-Brain Child" and "Right-Brain Math," books entitled "Teaching for the Two-sided Mind" (Williams, 1986) and "Right-brained Children in a Left-brained World" (Freed & Parsons, 1998), and even Nintendo DS games purporting to train the left and right hemispheres ("Left Brain, Right Brain", 2007). All of these materials and methods imply a basis on sound scientific theory—the problem is that there is no evidence to suggest (1) that traditional teaching neglects the right hemisphere, (2) that people favor one side of the brain, or (3) that any educational tool or strategy can selectively activate one hemisphere.

Educators are keen to ensure that the learning strategies used in the classroom are effective in shaping children's brain and cognitive development. At present, however, there is a dearth of research that directly addresses the relationship between neuropsychological strengths and weaknesses and learning (Immordino-Yang, 2007). Given this lack of directly relevant research, educational consultants and marketers—most of whom lack neuroscientific expertise—have overgeneralized and/or oversimplified distantly related neuroscientific research, with the end result that educators and educational institutions are being encouraged to adopt "brain-based" programs, unaware of the fact that these programs are pseudo-scientific. A number of unscientific "brain-based" ideas have consequently become well-established in classroom, including the notion

---

1 School of Psychological Science, La Trobe University
2 School of Psychological Sciences, The University of Manchester

Annukka K. Lindell and Evan Kidd, "Why Right-Brain Teaching is Half-Witted: A Critique of the Misapplication of Neuroscience to Education," *Mind, Brain, and Education*, vol. 5, no. 3, pp. 121-127. Copyright © 2011 by John Wiley & Sons, Inc. Reprinted with permission.

that students can (and should) be categorized according to their hemispheric dominance (i.e., whether they are "left-brained" or "right-brained"; Howard-Jones, 2009).

The ideas that people are "left-" or "right-brained", or that an educational program could selectively stimulate one or the other side of the brain, may appear appealingly simple; it is this appealing simplicity that has led to their neuromyth status (popular but false beliefs about the brain). This article systematically challenges the scientific validity of "left-brain/right-brain" teaching methods, explaining why educational tools/strategies that make "left-brain/right-brain" claims are fundamentally flawed. It is divided into five sections: first we explain the idea of hemisphericity and the tendency to ascribe opposing functions to the left and right sides of the brain. We then examine some of the major challenges to the validity of "right-brain" teaching, focusing on (1) difficulties in inferring from the split brain to the normal brain, (2) research indicating that the right hemisphere is not the "creative" hemisphere, and (3) the implications of neurological development and brain plasticity. We then discuss the dangerous appeal of neuromarketing, highlighting the influence of brain-based names on perceived scientific merit, before detailing a number of recommendations that will assist educators in effectively evaluating the claims of such brain-based methods. As will become clear, the idea that a teaching program or educational tool could selectively stimulate one side of the human brain is half-witted.

HEMISPHERICITY

The notion that human cognitive functions are neatly lateralized to either the left or right hemisphere was prompted by the fact that the human brain is divided into two halves. This conspicuous division of the brain into two sides, a left and a right, has encouraged researchers and theorists to propose that the functions of the two hemispheres are polar opposites: "if one hemisphere is known to act in a particular way, the other hemisphere must do the opposite", (Bryden, 1982, p. 4). Numerous descriptions contrasting the functions or processing styles of the left and right hemispheres have been proposed over the past 2500 years, with Bryden and Allard (1981) coining the term "dichotomania" to describe our penchant for ascribing faculties to one or the other side of the brain. The left hemisphere is typically characterized as verbal, rational, logical, and analytic, whereas the right hemisphere is thought to be visuospatial, emotional, and creative (see Van Lancker, 1997). In sum, the right hemisphere's creativity is contrasted with the left hemisphere's sensibility: "the left brain is more logical and linear ... responsible for the brain's thinking functions, which are comparatively more critical and analytical," whereas the right hemisphere "allows us to make insightful connections and see relationships between pieces of information" (Parry & Gregory, 2006, p. 9).

Ideas about the left and right hemispheres' processing strengths have prompted left and right-brain theorists to propose that people can be similarly classified according to their "hemisphericity" (i.e., left vs. right-brain thinking and behavioral style, Bogen, DeZure, TenHouten, & Marsh, 1972): "left-brain" people are verbal, analytical, and logical, whereas "right brain" people are artistic, creative, and emotive (e.g., Sousa, 1995). Though such a division appears appealingly simple, differences in people's verbal or creative abilities are not linked to differences in left versus right hemisphere processing; the idea that people are "left-brained" or "right-brained" is not supported by neuroscientific research. All people, from the most logical and analytic to the most emotional and creative, use both hemispheres of the brain simultaneously when performing any task. The suggestion that someone is "right-brained" because they are particularly creative, or "left-brained" because they are analytic and scientific, is a nonsense (Corballis, 1980). The idea of hemisphericity was consequently debunked in the scientific literature in the 1980s, with Beaumont, Young, and McManus (1984) concluding that "… the idea of hemisphericity lacks adequate foundation … (and) is a misleading one which should be abandoned", (p. 191). Despite this, educators and educational bodies are still investing valuable time and money on resources and strategies based on hemisphericity. Indeed, a Google search of "right-brain teaching" yields 1,730,000 hits. As Bruer (2008) notes " 'Right brain versus left brain' is one of those popular ideas that will not die," (p. 54). Though "right-brain teaching" is a scientifically unfounded neuromyth, it has unfortunately shaped the way school curricula are developed and taught (Neuroscience Research in Education Summit, 2009).

PROBLEMS IN INFERRING FROM SPLIT-BRAIN RESEARCH

Characterization of the left hemisphere as logical, intelligent, and analytic and the right hemisphere as creative, emotional, and visuospatial was catalyzed by Sperry's (1961) research on split-brain patients. The split-brain operation is performed as a last resort to relieve intractable epilepsy in patients whose seizures prove unresponsive to pharmaceutical intervention. The procedure limits the spread of seizure activity from one hemisphere to the other by severing the corpus callosum (Bogen, Fisher, & Vogel, 1965). The corpus callosum is a band of 250,000,000 nerve fibers that connects the left and right sides of the brain; severing the corpus callosum consequently prevents communication between the two hemispheres, relieving seizure activity. As the split-brain operation functionally isolates the left and right hemispheres, research on split-brain patients affords the opportunity to examine the functions and capabilities of each hemisphere without contribution or inhibition from the opposing hemisphere (Zaidel, 1978). For example, split-brain patients are typically able to verbally name words projected to their left, but not right, hemisphere (e.g., Gazzaniga, 1970), and show a strong right hemisphere superiority for visuospatial tasks such as mental rotation (e.g., Corballis & Sergent, 1988). It is this kind of research that has prompted theorists to propose that the left hemisphere is verbal, logical, and analytic, whereas the right hemisphere is visuospatial, creative, and emotional, with Sperry (1982) himself noting that "the left-right dichotomy … is an idea with which it is easy to run wild" (p. 1225).

Drawing inferences for the normal brain from the brains of patients who have had their corpus callossa surgically severed is clearly problematic. Split-brain patients suffer sufficiently severe and pharmaceutically intractable seizures to warrant surgical separation of the two sides of their brains; such severe epilepsy is "... virtually certain to have [produced] neurological abnormalities" (Hellige, 1993, p. 13). As such, split-brain patients had atypical brains even before undergoing surgery, making drawing inferences from the split brain to the normal brain doubly challenging. In the normal brain, the left and right hemispheres are heavily interconnected, and constantly in communication. The intact corpus callosum allows information presented to one hemisphere to be shared with the other hemisphere within 20 ms (i.e., two hundredths of a second; Andreassi, 2007). In split-brain patients such communication is precluded, thus one must be very cautious in generalizing left and right hemisphere processing biases from the split brain to the normal brain.

In the normal child, the intact corpus callosum allows information to be almost instantaneously integrated, and thus processing occurs simultaneously in both sides of the brain: it is not possible for a normal individual to selectively use one hemisphere. Yet, such inferences are the implicit basis for all educational programs, teaching strategies, and books professing to harness or promote the capacities of the right (or left) hemisphere. As Alferink and Farmer-Dougan (2010) state: "It is neither accurate nor realistic to believe that individuals may selectively use one hemisphere of the brain at a time for separate academic functions" (p. 43); the idea that a particular strategy will differentially affect a particular brain hemisphere is thus deeply flawed.

CREATIVITY IS NOT RIGHT LATERALIZED

According to the left-brain/right-brain view, creativity is one of the key strengths of the right hemisphere that is overlooked in traditional teaching. Accordingly, it is proposed that the right hemisphere's creativity should be targeted with specific teaching methods (e.g., Shichida Method). However, though the notion that the right hemisphere is creative is appealing in its simplicity, the idea that creativity is solely a function of one side of the brain is contentious (see Lindell, 2011, for review). Even language articulation, the most strongly lateralized processes, involves the activation and integration of processes across both sides of the brain (see Lindell, 2006). Similarly, a growing body of research suggests that any creative act relies upon the activation and integration of processing in both hemispheres: "no scientific evidence ... indicates a correlation between the degree of creativity and the activity of the right hemisphere" (Organisation for Economic Cooperation and Development, 2007, p. 117).

Lindell's (2011) review of neuroscience research suggests that creativity is a distributed, whole brain process, rather than solely a function of the right hemisphere. For example, Carlsson, Wendt, and Risberg (2000) reported that during a creative task (come up with alternate uses for a common object), highly creative people showed greater activation across both sides of the brain in comparison to the less creative people. This suggests that the ability to engage both hemispheres leads to the generation of more creative solutions than relying predominantly on one side of the brain. This being the case, one might predict that people engaged in creative professions (e.g., musicians and artists) would show greater interaction between the two sides of the brain than people in non-creative professions. Gibson, Folley, and Park (2009) confirmed this prediction, implying that creative training enhances interhemispheric communication which, in turn, fosters creative ideation and enhanced creative performance. Such findings suggest that the interaction between distant cortical regions across both hemispheres is crucial for creative thinking: "It can't be emphasized too strongly that creativity is best viewed as a whole-brain (rather than a right-brain) process" (Runco, 2004, p. 665).

The research evidence clearly indicates that the interaction between the left and right hemispheres is vital for creativity, rather than the actions of one hemisphere alone. Educational tools claiming to selectively stimulate the right hemisphere to enhance creativity (e.g., Shichida Method; Edwards, 2001) are thus ill-founded. Even if such methods were capable of selectively stimulating the right hemisphere (as discussed above, this is impossible in the normal brain), the scientific research indicates that selective stimulation of the right hemisphere would not enhance creativity because creativity is a whole-brain process. As such, educational tools promising a "right-brained" approach to enhance creativity are scientifically baseless.

NEUROLOGICAL DEVELOPMENT AND BRAIN PLASTICITY

Strictly dichotomizing brain function is even more problematic when one considers brain development. Developmental studies of brain function have consistently shown that while brain regions are predisposed to process certain types of input, localization of higher cognitive functions into one hemisphere is not present at birth, and nor is it deterministic. We illustrate this point by discussing the localization of language—a paradigm case of lateralization of function.

The neuroscientific study of language is centuries old. Popular interpretations of this field of research have led those outside of the immediate research field to believe that language is largely a left hemisphere function. This is hardly surprising: early case studies reported by Broca (1861) and Wernicke (1911) showed that patients who had significant damage to parts of their left cerebral cortex had compromised language function. Specifically, those with damage in what came to be known as Broca's area (inferior frontal gyrus) experience problems with language production, whereas those with damage to Wernicke's area (superior temporal gyrus) experience language comprehension difficulties. Language is the crowning achievement of our species (Tomasello, 2008); it is a complex analytic system that currently defies neat explanation by cognitive scientists of all theoretical persuasions (see Evans & Levinson, 2009), and yet children have the capability to learn any language with apparent ease. Language is also the dominant symbolic system of our culture, and is prioritized over other forms of communication (e.g., art). Thus it is not surprising that the left hemisphere has been popularized as "analytic" or "academic", and that those concerned with education might believe that traditional educational practices prioritize these skills.

However, now there exists a host of evidence to show that (1) language is not strictly localized in the left hemisphere, (2) language only gradually lateralizes in the left hemisphere during development, and (c) damage to areas that are traditionally recruited for language in children results in the recruitment of alternative brain regions, including the right hemisphere, to support the language learning process. We discuss each of these points briefly.

Advances in non-invasive neuroimaging techniques have enabled an increasingly sophisticated insight into human brain function and its development. With respect to language, an increasing amount of evidence has accumulated to suggest that the right hemisphere is implicated in many aspects of language processing (for review see Lindell, 2006), and that each hemisphere only comes to support different language functions across development. For instance, in one of the most comprehensive neurodevelopmental studies of language development, Szaflarski et al. (2006) followed 30 children aged 5–7 years longitudinally for 5 years. The children were scanned using functional Magnetic Resonance Imaging once a year on a task that measured their language processing ability. The results showed that, consistent with similar cross-sectional studies (Holland et al., 2001), there is increasing lateralization of language with age, where areas in the left hemisphere that appear to be predisposed to support language become increasingly involved in language processing over developmental time. Ressel, Wilke, Lidzba, Lutsenberger, and Krägeloh-Mann (2008) have reported similar results using magnetoencephalography, a newer and more fine-grained imaging technique.

These imaging results show that there are qualitative changes in the brain areas that are used to support language function across development, which in the normal case lead to mostly left hemisphere lateralization accompanied by some right hemisphere involvement. However, what happens when those left hemisphere areas predisposed for language function become damaged? The data suggest that, far from being the end of language, the brain is plastic enough in development to reorganize the neural circuits that process language. For instance, work by Bates and colleagues (e.g., Bates et al., 1997; Bates, Vicari, & Trauner, 1999; Vicari et al., 2000) has shown that young children with focal brain damage to their left hemisphere are able to recruit alternative neural areas to continue the language acquisition process. In cases where brain damage occurs early in life (≤6 months), these early deficits are no longer detectable at the behavioral level by about 7 years-of-age (e.g., Marchman, Saccuman, & Wulfeck, 2004; Reilly, Losh, Belugi, & Wulfeck, 2004). This suggests two important points: (1) even a highly analytical skill like language is more bilaterally represented in childhood, and (2) the developing brain has the potential for great plasticity, and is able to reorganize important higher cognitive functions in the event of major neurological trauma. In fact, damage to the left cerebral hemisphere early in development seems to result in the right lateralization of language (Staudt et al., 2001).

By reviewing the literature on language lateralization and plasticity we make the following points. First, it does not make sense for any cognitive function to be partitioned and deterministically localized in one hemisphere, even language, which is an analytical skill *par excellence*. Instead, we argue that interaction is the norm for brain function, rendering claims about educational tools targeting the right or left hemisphere difficult to defend. Second, the bilateral processing of higher cognitive skills such as language and the ability for the developing brain to recruit alternative neural pathways in the event of significant neurological insult renders any claims for dichotomous brain function baseless. The complexity of neurological development is not captured by pseudoscientific educational products that imply a strict and direct relationship between brain and behavior. Any attempt to incorporate recent developments in the study of neurological development into these approaches would fail, since their principal claim is that there are simple hemisphere-to-function relationships that can be individually targeted using educational tools.

OVERCOMING THE DANGEROUS APPEAL OF NEUROMARKETING: RECOMMENDATIONS

Consumers in the market for educational programs are faced with a wide variety of choices. In such a market, claims that a particular tool or learning strategy is "brain-based", selectively stimulating the "overlooked right hemisphere" have inherent appeal; every educator wants to positively influence the learning child's brain. The difficulty here is that consumers are often poorly equipped to objectively evaluate the scientific claims made by "brain-based" educational packages. The inclusion of "neuro" information (either brain images or accurate but irrelevant neuroscience information) positively influences people's ratings of an article's scientific merit (e.g., McCabe & Castel, 2008; Weisberg, Keil, Goodstein, Rawson, & Gray, 2008), a fact that helps explain the popularity of neuromarketing approaches in education. The simple use of the word "brain" in the title of an educational tool or theory suggests a sound scientific foundation, irrespective of the validity of the "brain" claims. Given that almost 90% of teachers believe that knowledge of the brain is important in informing the design of educational programs (Della Sala, 2009), strategic use of the word "brain" in the name can profoundly influence of the adoption of an educational tool.

Educators thus need to become more critical consumers and interpret brain-based claims cautiously (see Sylvan & Christodoulou, 2010), and teacher training must equip educators with the tools needed to effectively evaluate neuroscience-based programes. At present, teacher training offers little exposure to primary source neuroscience research, instead focusing predominantly on summaries and popular press interpretations (Coch & Ansari, 2009). This lack of information makes teachers a soft target for peddlers of pseudoscience. Providing teachers with a basic understanding of neuroscience research and neuroscientific methods as part of teacher training is vital as it enables teachers to understand how learning occurs in the brain, and how cognitive abilities change in the course of brain development (Goswami, 2004). Moreover, a foundational understanding of neuroscience will enable educators to effectively evaluate "brain-based" claims and seek out educational tools using methods that have been validated by rigorous independent research.

A basic education in neuroscience need not be an onerous component of initial teacher education. If the information is presented in a straightforward manner using understandable terms and concrete examples, student teachers could receive a primer on the essentials of neuroscience, brain development, and cognitive processing in a day. Based on such a foundation, these concepts could be revisited and further developed throughout teacher training (e.g., attention, memory, mnemonics), making basic brain understanding an integral and integrated part of the course. Such understanding is likely to enhance student learning and help prevent future educators from "pouring precious educational resources into scientifically spurious applications" (Goswami, 2006, p. 413), allowing them to more critically evaluate the validity of the 70+ brain-based learning courses many are invited to each year (Goswami, 2006).

As Jorgenson (2003) points out, "brain-based" educational tools are typically researched, developed, and promoted by educational and marketing consultants, few of whom have expertise in neuroscience. Little wonder then that neuroscience research is overgeneralized, oversimplified, or misinterpreted in the quest for appealing new educational programes (e.g., Brain Gym, Dore program; Della Sala, 2009). Though brain-based education marketers "spin stories about how brain research, as they understand it, supports their favorite educational practices, none of these educational applications is supported by data showing either that it produces the desired change in brain structure or that such changes affect behavior and learning" (Bruer, 2002, p. 1031). The fact that the brain-based programes are not presented or advertized in concert with research confirming that they genuinely induce changes in brain activation and student learning efficacy immediately calls the validity of such programs into question. And indeed, a search of scientific databases like Medline and PsychInfo confirms that there is no published research on the application of neuroscience to education (Bruer, 2002).[1]

We encourage teachers to ask one simple question when presented with a brain-based learning programe: (1) have the brain-based claims been validated by independent research that confirms that the tool or strategy genuinely induces changes in brain activation and student learning efficacy? If the answer is "yes" and the research is available for scrutiny in a reputable journal, the tool is worthy of consideration. If the answer is "no" and the brain-based claims are being presented solely by someone who stands to financially gain from adoption of the tool, the tool should be summarily rejected.

There is no question that neuroscience has the potential to make powerful contributions to educational research; however, stronger links between neuroscience and basic research in education are needed to fulfill this potential (Goswami, 2004). Greater communication between educationalists and neuroscientists would ensure that (1) neuroscientists are studying the educational questions that are of real importance to teachers, and (2) educationalists understand both the strengths and the limitations of neuroscientific approaches to teaching and learning. Critical to such a dialogue is the need for more efficient dissemination of appropriately targeted accounts of relevant neuroscience findings. The introduction of targeted journals and conferences is a promising step (e.g., Mind, Brain, and Education); however whether the majority of teachers, old or new, have the luxury of time needed to peruse such documents or attend such events is an open question. Moreover, whether neuroscientists themselves are best-equipped to communicate directly with educators has been questioned. Goswami (2006) suggests that a network of research communicators may be better placed to interpret and communicate neuroscience findings in the language of educators, and to feedback questions, ideas, and criticisms to the neuroscientists. We agree that such a network of science communicators would be invaluable in enhancing neuroscience understanding and restricting the pervasiveness of neuromyths. Communication would be further enhanced by the introduction of a regular, interactive e-mail/online "digest" of Neuroscience Education News that presents an accurate summary of the latest findings relevant to the teacher in the classroom. Such dissemination of information will greatly assist educationalists in discerning neuroscience fact from neuroscience fiction.

CONCLUSIONS

The idea that the functions of the brain's hemispheres could be straightforwardly divided into left and right, though appealingly simple, is patently false. Similarly, the notion that a person can be classified as "left-brained" or "right-brained," or that a teaching strategy could selectively target the left or right hemisphere, is deeply flawed and is not supported by the research. The idea that the left hemisphere is logical, verbal, and analytic, whereas the right hemisphere is creative, emotive, and visuospatial was catalyzed by Sperry's (1981) split-brain research. As discussed, drawing inferences for normal children's brains from the brains of patients who have had sufficiently severe epilepsy to warrant the surgical separation of their left and right hemispheres is extremely problematic. Similarly, the idea that selective stimulation of the right hemisphere will enhance children's creativity is not consistent with the research evidence (Lindell, in press). Little wonder then that the idea of "hemisphericity" was debunked in the scientific literature over 25 years ago (Beaumont et al., 1984). It is unfortunate that despite the absence of scientific support, educational tools based on such neuromyths are shaping the way children are taught (Neuroscience Research in Education Summit, 2009).

As Chabris and Kosslyn (1998) note, it is highly improbable that any lesson, no matter how visuospatial or analytic, will activate only one hemisphere. When performing any task "everything in the brain (is) in flux—both sides, the front and back, the top and bottom ... to think that you could reduce this to a simple left-right dichotomy would be misleading and oversimplified" (Mazziotta in McKean, 1985, p. 38). Consequently, educational programes that claim to selectively target the right hemisphere (e.g., Craft's "Teaching the Right-Brain Child") or ensure that both hemispheres are involved in learning (e.g., Sousa, 1995), are misleading; both hemispheres of the brain are simultaneously activated and constantly interacting and integrating information during every task, including those proposed to activate solely one hemisphere. The use of terms such as "brain" and "neuroscience" in the name and marketing of a product profoundly enhance perceptions of that product's scientific merit, irrespective of the validity of the scientific claims. Educators and educational institutions must therefore interpret neuro-claims cautiously, and seek out methods that have been validated by rigorous independent research. Until the claims of the "right brain" teaching methods have been independently validated, adopting a "right-brain" teaching program would be half-witted.

NOTE

1. Note that there are educational training products that have been empirically supported, but do not make claims about neurological development. For instance, Holmes, Gathercole, and Dunning (2009) and St Claire-Thompson, Stevens, Hunt, and Bolder (2010) have both tested products that improve children's working memory. Our suggestion here is it is not the marketing spin, but the outcome of the training that matters, which can only ever be shown through carefully controlled empirical research.

REFERENCES

Alferink, L. A., & Farmer-Dougan, V. (2010). Brain-(not) based education: Dangers of misunderstanding and misapplication of neuroscience research. *Exceptionality*, *18*, 42–52.

Andreassi, J. L. (2007). *Psychophysiology: Human behavior and physiological response*. Hillsdale, NJ: Erlbaum.

Bates, E., Thal, D., Aram, D., Eisele, J., Nass, R., & Trauner, D. (1997). From first words to grammar in children with focal brain injury. *Developmental Neuropsychology*, *13*, 275–343.

Bates, E., Vicari, S., & Trauner, D. (1999). Neural mediation of language development: Perspective from lesion studies on infants and children. In H. Tager-Flusberg (Ed.), *Neurodevelopmental disorders* (pp. 533–581). Cambridge, MA: MIT Press.

Beaumont, G., Young, A., & McManus, I. C. (1984). Hemisphericity: A critical review. *Cognitive Neuropsychology*, *1*, 191–212.

Bogen, J. E., DeZure, R., TenHouten, N., & Marsh, J. (1972). The other side of the brain IV: The A/P ratio. *Bulletin of the Los Angeles Neurological Society, 37*, 49–61.

Bogen, J. E., Fisher, E. D., & Vogel, P. J. (1965). Cerebral commisurotomy: A second case report. *Journal of the American Medical Association, 194*, 1328–1329.

Broca, P. (1861). Remarques sur le siege de la faculte du langage articule; suivies d'une observation d'aphemie. *Bulletin de la Société Anatomique, 6*, 398–407.

Bruer, J. T. (2002). Avoiding the pediatrician's error: How neuroscientists can help educators (and themselves). *Nature Neuroscience (Supplement), 5*, 1031–1033.

Bruer, J. T. (2008). In search of ... brain-based education. In *The Jossey-Bass reader on the brain and learning* (pp. 51–69). San Francisco: Wiley.

Bryden, M. P. (1982). *Laterality: Functional asymmetry in the intact brain*. New York: Academic Press.

Bryden, M. P., & Allard, F. A. (1981). Shortcomings of the verbal-nonverbal dichotomy: Seems to us we've heard this song before. *Behavioral and Brain Sciences, 4*(1), 65–66.

Carlsson, I., Wendt, P. E., & Risberg, J. (2000). On the neurobiology of creativity: Differences in frontal activity between high and low creative subjects. *Neuropsychologia, 38*, 873–885.

Chabris, C. F., & Kosslyn, S. M. (1998). How do the cerebral hemispheres contribute to encoding spatial relations? *Current Directions in Psychological Sciences, 7*, 8–14.

Coch, D., & Ansari, D. (2009). Thinking about mechanisms is crucial to connecting neuroscience and education. *Cortex, 45*, 546–547.

Corballis, M. C. (1980). Laterality and myth. *American Psychologist, 35*, 284–295.

Corballis, M. C., & Sergent, J. (1988). Imagery in a commissurotomized patient. *Neuropsychologia, 26*, 13–26.

Della Sala, S. (2009).The use and misuse of neuroscience in education. *Cortex, 45*, 443.

Edwards, B. (2001). *The new drawing on the right side of the brain* (3rd ed.). New York: Putnum.

Evans, N., & Levinson, S. (2009). The myth of language universals. *Behavioral and Brain Sciences, 32*, 429–448.

Freed, J., & Parsons, L. (1998). *Right-brained children in a left-brained world: Unlocking the potential of your ADD child*. New York: Fireside.

Gazzaniga, M. S. (1970). *The bisected brain*. New York: Appleton-Century-Crofts.

Gibson, C., Folley, B. S., & Park, S. (2009). Enhanced divergent thinking and creativity in musicians: A behavioral and near-infrared spectroscopy study. *Brain and Cognition, 69*, 162–169.

Goswami, U. (2004). Neuroscience and education. *British Journal of Educational Psychology, 74*, 1–14.

Goswami, U. (2006). Neuroscience and education: From research to practice? *Nature Reviews Neuroscience, 7*, 406-413.

Hellige, J. B. (1993). *Hemispheric asymmetry: What's right and what's Left*. Cambridge, MA: Harvard University Press.

Holland, S., Plante, E., Byars, A., Strawsburg, R., Schmithorst, V., & Ball, W. Jr. (2001). Normal fMRI brain activation patterns in children performing a verb generation task. *Neuroimage, 14*, 837-843.

Holmes, J., Gathercole, S. E., & Dunning, D. L. (2009). Adaptive training leads to sustained enhancement of poor working memory in children. *Developmental Science, 12*, F9-F15.

Howard-Jones, P. A. (2009). Scepticism is not enough. *Cortex, 45*, 550-551.

Immordino-Yang, M. H. (2007). A tale of two cases: Lessons for education from the study of two boys living with half their brains. *Mind, Brain, and Education, 1*, 66-83.

Jorgenson, O. (2003). Brain scam? Why educators should be careful about embracing 'brain research'. *The Educational Forum, 67*, 364-369.

Lindell, A. K. (2006). In your right mind: Right hemisphere contributions to human language processing and production. *Neuropsychology Review, 16*, 131-148.

Lindell, A. K. (2011). Lateral thinkers are not so laterally minded: Hemispheric asymmetry, interaction, and creativity. *Laterality, 16*, 479-498.

Marchman, V., Saccuman, C., & Wulfeck, B. (2004). Productive use of the English past tense in children with focal brain injury and specific language impairment. *Brain and Language, 88*, 202-214.

McCabe, D. P., & Castle, A. D. (2008). Seeing is believing: The effect of brain images on judgments of scientific reasoning. *Cognition, 107*, 343-352.

McKean, K. (1985). Of two minds: Selling the right brain. *Discover, 6*(4), 30-41.

Neuroscience Research in Education Summit: The Promise of Interdisciplinary Partnerships Between Brain Sciences and Education. University of California, Irvine. June 22-24, 2009.

Organisation for Economic Co-operation and Development. (2007). *Understanding the brain: The birth of a learning science*. Paris: Author.

Parry, T., & Gregory, G. (2006). *Designing brain-compatible learning*. Cheltenham, Australia: Hawker Brownlow Education.

Petty, G. (2004). *Teaching today: A practical guide*. Cheltenham, UK: Nelson Thornes.

Reilly, J., Losh, M., Bellugi, U., & Wulfeck, B. (2004). Frog, Where are you? Narratives in children with specific language impairment, early focal brain injury and Williams Syndrome. *Brain and Language, 88*, 229-247.

Ressel, V., Wilke, M., Lidzba, K., Lutzenberger, W., & Krägeloh-Mann, I. (2008). Increases in language lateralization in normal children as observed using magnetoencephalography. *Brain and Language, 106*, 167-176.

Runco, M. A. (2004). Creativity. *Annual Review of Psychology, 55*, 657-687.

Sousa, D. A. (1995). *How the brain learns: A classroom teacher's guide*. Reston, VA: National Association of Secondary School Principals.

Sperry, R. W. (1961). Cerebral organization and behavior. *Science, 133*, 1749–1757.

Sperry, R. W. (1982). Some effects of disconnecting the cerebral hemispheres. *Science, 217*, 1223–1226.

Staudt, M., Grodd, W., Niemann, G., Wildgruber, D., Erb, M., & Krägeloh-Mann, I. (2001). Early left periventricular brain lesions induce hemispheric organization of speech. *Neurology, 57*, 122–125.

St Claire-Thompson, H., Stevens, R., Hunt, A., & Bolder, E. (2010). Improving children's working memory and classroom performance. *Educational Psychology, 30*, 203–219.

Sylvan, L. J., & Christodoulou, J. A. (2010). Understanding the role of neuroscience in brain based products: A guide for educators and consumers. *Mind, Brain, and Education, 4*, 1–7.

Szaflarski, J., Schmithorst, V., Altaye, M., Byars, A., Ret, J., Plante, E., et al. (2006). A longitudinal functional magnetic resonance imaging study of language development in children 5 to 11 years old. *Annals of Neurology, 59*, 796–807.

Tomasello, M. (2008). *Origins of human communication*. Cambridge, MA: MIT Press.

Van Lancker, D. (1997). Rags to riches: Our increasing appreciation of cognitive and communicative abilities of the human right cerebral hemisphere. *Brain and Language, 57*, 1–11.

Vicari, S., Albertoni, A., Chilosi, A., Cipriani, P., Cioni, G., & Bates, E. (2000). Plasticity and reorganization during language development in children with early brain injury. *Cortex, 36*, 31–36.

Weisberg, D. S., Keil, F. C., Goodstein, J., Rawson, E., & Gray, J. R. (2008). The seductive allure of neuroscience explanations. *Journal of Cognitive Neuroscience, 20*, 470–477.

Wernicke, C. (1911). The symptom of complex aphasia. In A. E. Church (Ed.), *Diseases of the nervous system* (pp. 265–324). New York: Appleton.

Williams, L. V. (1986). *Teaching for the two-sided mind: A guide to right brain/left brain education*. New York: Simon & Schuster.

Zaidel, E. (1978). Lexical organization in the right hemisphere. In P. A. Buser & A. Rougeul-Buser (Eds.), *Cerebral correlates of conscious experience*. Amsterdam: Elsevier.

REVIEW AND CONTEMPLATE

1. Explain the notion of hemisphericity. What does neuroscience research suggest about the side(s) of the brain utilized most by people who are highly verbal or creative?

2. What findings from the research with split-brain patients prompted people to conclude that the left side of the brain functions differently from the right side of the brain? Why is it problematic to draw inferences about normal-brain functioning from split-brain patients?

3. Lindell and Kidd (2011) explained that "the idea that a particular [teaching] strategy will differentially affect a particular brain hemisphere is thus deeply flawed." Explain why it is flawed (i.e., why can't a particular teaching strategy affect one brain hemisphere more than the other hemisphere?).

4. Lindell and Kidd (2011) explained that "educational tools claiming to selectively stimulate the right hemisphere to enhance creativity" are "ill founded." They cited research by Carlsson, Wendt, and Risberg (2000) to illustrate this point; explain what these researchers found.

3.2 "Can Minds Leave Bodies? A Cognitive Science Perspective"

IN JANUARY 2006, Cincinnati police found the decayed body of 61-year-old Johannas Pope in her home. What was surprising about this case was that Ms. Pope died almost 2½ years earlier, and her daughter, granddaughter, and caretaker continued to live in the house with the deceased woman even though they knew she was dead. They kept her body sitting in a chair in an upstairs room, where they ran an air conditioner to keep her body cool. They also kept the television on in the room for Ms. Pope. Relatives and friends who visited the house were told that Ms. Pope was upstairs and was ill, and none of them went into her room to check on her.

Why would a family keep a dead woman in their house for more than 2 years? The coroner found no evidence of abuse or foul play. It appears that the family kept the deceased Ms. Pope in the room because before she passed away, she told her family members, "Don't show my body when I'm dead; don't bury me; I'm coming back." Apparently, Ms. Pope believed that her mind or soul would live on after she died and that it would come back at some later time.

As Bensley points out in this reading, a number of religious and paranormal beliefs rest on the assumption that our minds (or souls) can exist outside of our bodies. This dualistic belief can be traced back to ancient philosophy and religion. Bensley presents a cognitive science perspective on such beliefs and provides a scientific explanation for out-of-body experiences that sometimes occur in people who are near death or people who have taken drugs.

Reference

Bensley, D. A. (2003, July/August). Can minds leave bodies? A cognitive science perspective. *Skeptical Inquirer, 27,* 34–39.

"CAN MINDS LEAVE BODIES? A COGNITIVE SCIENCE PERSPECTIVE"
D. ALAN BENSLEY

Many people believe that the mind can leave the body at death and during out-of-body experiences. Research in cognitive science, however, has shown that this belief is implausible and suggests other explanations

—D. Alan Bensley

Thirty-nine dead bodies were neatly laid on cots, each dressed in a black robe and Nike sneakers with their heads covered in hoods. Was this some kind of ritual murder? No, this was the 1997 mass suicide of the Heaven's Gate cult resulting from a dangerous combination of belief in dualism, religion, and extrasensory contact with aliens. Cult members believed they were in telepathic contact with extraterrestrials who invited them to a new and better world. To rendezvous with the alien ship, they believed they had to "exit their vehicles." This code expression for killing the body to free the soul reveals a dualistic belief in the separateness of mind and body. For cult members, the body was just a device for temporarily carrying the soul.

This dualistic belief may seem extreme, but other, more common paranormal beliefs (such as belief in ghosts, astral projection, and reincarnation), also imply that the mind or soul can separate from the body. I will examine the dualistic belief from the cognitive science perspective. Cognitive science is an interdisciplinary approach to the study of the mind. It combines the psychological study of mental processes such as consciousness and perception with the study of the brain, philosophy, and other disciplines. Research in cognitive science has shown that mind depends on the functioning of the brain in the physical world. Consequently, the mind cannot "go outside" of the brain.

ORIGINS OF DUALISTIC PARANORMAL BELIEF

The idea that the soul can leave the body is a very old one found in many cultures (Frazer, 1996). A common belief is that when someone dreams of traveling to a place, the soul actually leaves the body and journeys there. The ancient Egyptians believed the soul could leave the body at death. In their burial ceremonies, the Ba, a human-headed bird representing the soul or breath of life, was breathed back into the mummified body to ensure life after death. In the book of Genesis, God breathed the spirit of life into Adam's body formed from the dust of the Earth to make man a living soul. These examples illustrate how the soul or spirit has been commonly associated with air. Like the air we breathe, the soul is ephemeral, essential to life, and can leave the body. In his

D. A. Bensley, "Can Minds Leave Bodies? A Cognitive Science Perspective," *Skeptical Inquirer*, vol. 27, pp. 34-39. Copyright © 2003 by Center for Inquiry. Reprinted with permission.

detailed study of religious rituals from around the world, Sir James Frazer reported that the Itonamas of South America would close a dying person's mouth and nose to prevent the soul from departing and taking other souls with it. In some cultures, people have used traps to recapture souls that have escaped. Comparing the beliefs of many non-Western cultures, Shiels (1978) found evidence that almost 95 percent of them believed that a soul or spiritual entity could leave the body in some form. The most common occasion for such an experience was during sleep, but some reported the occurrence from illness, use of drugs, and trance states.

Much of the modern dualistic belief in the separability of soul and body had its origins in Greek and Christian thought. Plato, the fifth century B.C. Greek philosopher, believed that the body was a vessel containing the soul and that the mind was the immortal part of the soul that left the body at death to be reincarnated. Over the centuries, many Christians have believed that the soul lives on after physical death, retaining the powers of perception and feeling despite being separated from the body.

René Descartes, the brilliant philosopher-mathematician of the seventeenth century, did much to frame the dualistic position. He began his philosophy by doubting everything. He realized he could doubt the existence of his body and the rest of the physical world, but he could not logically doubt that he was doubting. His famous statement, "I think, therefore I am," exemplifies this reasoning. Because he could doubt the physical world but not his mind, he reasoned that the mind and body must be fundamentally different. In particular, he believed the body was made of physical substance extended in space while the mind or soul was non-physical and not extended. Descartes' position, called substance dualism, has raised fundamental questions about how a non-physical mind could have an effect on a physical body. Nevertheless, many people persist in this belief as if there were no mind-body problem.

CURRENT BELIEF

Belief in dualism is an important part of our commonsense or folk psychology. Intuitively, my mind and body do appear to be different. I can use my mind to imagine. I have no gray hair, but one look in the mirror tells me otherwise. I can imagine I am in California when physically I am sitting at my computer in Maryland. I can decide to move my leg, and it seems as if my mind is causing my body to move. These examples suggest that my mental experience and physical events overlap; but they are not the same. However, it is one thing to imagine that one's mind is separate from one's body and quite another to believe it can *actually* separate from the body. To believe the latter is tantamount to holding a paranormal belief, according to many cognitive neuroscientists who have consistently shown that the mind depends on brain function. Recently, such scientists have paid increasing attention to the dualism found in people's commonsense beliefs because such beliefs are diametrically opposed to their own scientific knowledge of the brain.

Research outside of cognitive science has also shown dualistic, paranormal belief to be prevalent in everyday thinking. The most recent Gallup Poll on paranormal belief in the U.S. found that such beliefs are widespread and may even be on the rise (Newport and Strausberg 2001).

Other research further indicates that mind-body dualism is related to paranormal belief. Cognitive psychologist Keith Stanovich (1989) found that many American college students he tested had high scores on a dualistic belief scale. Moreover, those students with stronger dualistic belief also tended to report stronger belief in ESP, except for Baptists. Another study by Michael Thalbourne (1999) found that dualism in Australian students was significantly correlated with paranormal belief such as belief in life after death and in the possibility of contact with spirits of the dead.

Not surprisingly, many writers in parapsychology, including Lloyd Auerbach (1986), John Beloff (1989), and J.B. Rhine and J.G. Pratt (1957), have made dualistic statements claiming or implying the separation of mind and body. James Alcock (1987) has contended that parapsychology treats mind-body dualism as an essential assumption.

Despite popular belief, many scientists and skeptics doubt the mind can leave the body. The most common opposing view has been materialism or physicalism, a philosophical position maintaining that everything, including mind, is essentially physical. Materialists say the mind only appears to be invisible and not part of the natural physical world. For centuries, scientists have developed physical explanations of many apparently invisible and mysterious phenomena. The wind in the trees is not the movement of some invisible ether, but of many tiny particles of oxygen, nitrogen, and other gases. Along the same lines, materialists have hoped that the soul or mind would be explained in physical terms, much as the wind and air have been. Cognitive scientists, who are rooted in materialism, have sought to explain mental processes in terms of brain activity resulting from physical changes in the environment. So it is not surprising that they and other scientists have pressed for physical evidence that a mind or soul could leave the body.

THE OUT-OF-BODY EXPERIENCE (OBE)

At least initially, the OBE appears to be good evidence that the mind can separate from the body. The term itself, however, is neutral as to whether or not a person has actually left the body and asserts only that a person has had the *ex-perience* of having done so (Palmer 1978). OBEs are fairly common, with estimates ranging from about 10 to 20 percent of the population reporting they have had at least one, depending on the survey (Rogo 1984). OBEs occur in various ways, such as in religious, drug-induced, near-death, meditational, hypnotically induced, or spontaneous experiences (Grosso 1976). Furthermore, OBEs are not associated with any psychological disorder (Tobacyk and Mitchell 1987).

Shortly after college, I had a spontaneous OBE in which it seemed as if some observing part of me had separated from my body. I had lain down on the sofa for a few minutes but had not gone to sleep. Suddenly, it seemed as if I could clearly "see" my entire body lying on the sofa below me for a few seconds before I returned to my usual perspective. Though brief, my OBE had two basic features. First, it seemed as if the experiencing part of me was located at a point outside my physical body. Second, it seemed as though I was consciously perceiving and not dreaming the experience. Like many people who have had an OBE, I have also had lucid dreams, that is, dreams during which I became aware of myself dreaming (Glicksohn 1989). Researchers have found a low but reliable correlation between OBEs and lucid dreaming (Irwin 1988). In fact, sometimes OBEs arise from lucid dreams and may even be indistinguishable from them (Levitan et al. 1999). Yet my experience did not seem like a dream, lucid or otherwise—it seemed like perception. At the time, however, I did not know what it was, and I assumed my OBE was a case of astral projection. Similarly, about this same time I had what I knew was a dream in which I was "flying around" in a kitchen, and I told myself that I was dreaming about astral projection.

The many anecdotal reports of such experiences have sometimes been taken as strong evidence that the mind can actually leave the body (Crookall 1963). However, the usefulness of such anecdotal reports is very limited (Bensley 1998). Although they may provide a rich source of information about the details and "feel" of an experience, OBE descriptions are typically not very well documented, not repeatable, and unverifiable. Often the details of what an OBE experiencer claims to have seen have been found to be inaccurate (Blackmore, 1982).

To obtain better evidence, researchers have used the experimental method, which allows for testing under more controlled conditions to study OBEs. Typically, experimenters have examined the question by testing the accuracy of a subject's perception during an OBE or by looking for some physical sign in the environment that the experiencer has left the body. Despite some strikingly positive results reviewed by Charles Tart (1998), experimental demonstrations have not, in general, shown out-of-body perception to be reliably accurate. Nor has research unambiguously supported the claim that the experiencer can affect the environment when taking an out-of-body excursion (Blackmore 1982, 1992). After reviewing the literature, Blackmore (1982) suggested that adopting a cognitive psychological approach to study OBEs would be more productive.

THE COGNITIVE SCIENCE APPROACH

Traditionally, cognitive scientists have viewed the brain as a kind of complex information processing system, like a computer. The system inputs data through the senses, holds the information in memory, and transforms it into various intermediate states before outputting in the form of behavior. Information processing occurs in the brain as nerve cells send and receive messages using special chemicals called neurotransmitters. Many of these nerve cells are part of processing units and circuits dedicated to processing specific kinds of information. Research with brain scanning has found specific areas of the brain that "light up" or are active when individuals engage in specific mental processes, such as perceiving, attending, remembering, forming mental images, and using language (Posner and Raichle 1994). The brain uses the combined activity of these specific neural processors to form mental representations of the physical world. For example, although perceiving a face depends on the combined activity of multiple brain areas, when one area of the temporal lobe specialized for processing faces is damaged, a person is unable to recognize even his or her own face.

The brain uses its representations to construct an elaborate and usually accurate model of the world—a kind of running simulation. For example, research has shown that the brain has map-like representations of various parts of the body such as the face, arm, and hand. These maps in the brain represent the body in visual and somatic form, carrying detailed information of both how the body looks and feels (Ladavas, Zelon, and Farne 1998). It is important to note, however, that while mental representations, such as visual images, may seem vivid and accurate, they are not exact copies of the physical world in the same way a photograph represents the detail of some object. Moreover, the brain can make a mistake in constructing its model, resulting in misperception of the body or some other part of the world.

The phantom limb experience provides a compelling example of how mental experience of the body depends on the brain's representations of it, and also how perception of the body can be in error. People who have lost a limb, such as a leg, often report they feel the sensation of pain in their missing foot. This, of course, is physically impossible if we assume the pain is originating from the missing foot. However, if we assume that the brain still has a representation of the missing foot, then the perception of pain depends on brain activity (Ramachandran and Hirstein 1998). Could the OBE occur in a similar way, that is, could the brain activate a representation of the body in some unusual way that leads to misperception of the body?

Applying methods from cognitive psychology to study OBEs, Susan Blackmore (1987) found that experiencers used mental imagery differently from those who do not have OBEs. Based on the work of Nigro and Neisser (1983), she found that experiencers were more likely to use an observer or "bird's-eye view" perspective in describing their dreams than others. They were also better able to switch their viewpoint in a mental image, and had clearer and more vivid imagery of their dreams. Blackmore argued that this "bird's-eye view" perspective is like the "over the body" perspective often taken during OBEs. When a person begins to lose normal sensory contact, such as when falling asleep or during sensory deprivation, this unusual perspective may be adopted. The brain seeks to identify which is the best model or interpretation of the incoming sensory data at the time, and this becomes the model of reality that best fits. The system seeks to reestablish sensory contact, and mistakenly picks the wrong model from memory such as the "over the head" perspective and treats it as real. OBE experiencers' greater vividness and clarity of imagery may contribute to the sense of reality they experience during OBEs. Harvey

Irwin (1986) has obtained results similar to Blackmore (1987). However, he found that some people had *somatic* OBEs (related to the feeling of the body being outside) while others had *visual* OBEs (related to seeing the body as outside). In these two different cases, the subjects may be paying more or less attention to the visual versus somatic information in the complex representations of their bodies.

Blackmore's research suggests that disturbances in the brain may produce OBEs. Consistent with this prediction, Canadian neurosurgeon Wilder Penfield (1955) was apparently able to produce an OBE by stimulating a patient's brain with minute electrical currents prior to operating on the patient for temporal lobe epilepsy. Before surgical removal of a damaged area that caused the debilitating seizures. Penfield would routinely stimulate different places in the patient's brain, such as in the right temporal lobe shown in Figure 3.1, to prevent the inadvertent removal of healthy brain tissue. Once, after he had electro-stimulated a point in this area, the patient, who had previously had an OBE, exclaimed "I am leaving my body" and then showed a strong fear reaction (Penfield 1955, 458).

Recently, Olaf Blanke and his colleagues (2002) have used electrostimulation of the brain to produce a more convincing OBE in a forty-three-year-old epileptic woman. While trying to find the focus of her brain damage, they stimulated points in the right angular gyrus (shown in Figure 3.1), producing various disturbances in the perception of her body. When stimulated at different intensities, she reported feeling that she was "sinking into the bed," "falling from a height," and seeing parts of her body shortening. (Blanke et al. 2002, 269). At one point she had an OBE in which she saw her trunk and legs from above, the same portion of her body she had felt when stimulated before. However, when they stimulated her epileptic focus in her temporal lobe, over 5 cm away from the angular gyrus,

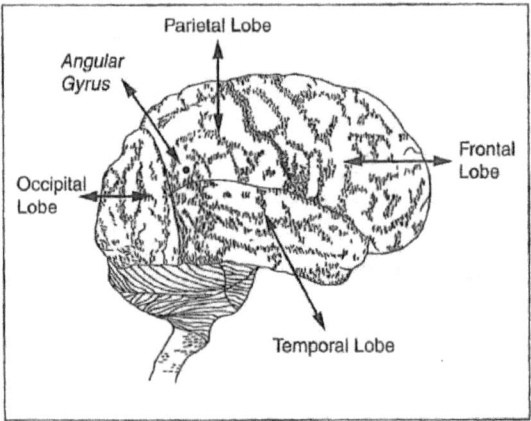

FIGURE 3.1: A right hemisphere view drawn to show the lobes of the brain and the point in the angular gyrus of the parietal lobe that Blanke and his colleagues (2002) stimulated to produce an OBE.

she did not have an OBE Blanke and his colleagues proposed that it was stimulating her angular gyrus that produced the OBE by disrupting the integration of somatosensory and vestibular information—that is, information about the feel and position of her body. These findings support the idea that the brain produces the conscious perception of an embodied self from the coordinated activity of various brain regions.

Drug effects on the brain can also produce OBEs. The drug ketamine, called "Special K" on the street and used as an anaesthetic before surgery, often produces OBEs. Karl Jansen (1997) has argued that the experience produced by ketamine is very much like the near-death experience (NDE) in which people often report the experience of floating above the body, traveling through a dark tunnel into the light, seeing God, and the conviction that they were actually dead. Although naturally occurring NDEs may result from various causes, ketamine may produce an artificial version of the NDE and an associated OBE by blocking neural transmission in the temporal lobe.

The question arises as to how physical events in the natural environment could produce electrochemical changes in the brain that lead to OBEs. One possibility proposed by Michael Persinger (1995) is that variations in the Earth's magnetic field produced by movement of its tectonic plates could lead to OBEs under the right conditions. Persinger obtained data on the changes in Earth's geomagnetic activity from the National Geophysical Data Center keeping track of the particular level that each subject experienced during testing. First, he externally applied a weak electromagnetic field across large areas of his subjects' brains while depriving them partially of sensory stimulation to enhance awareness of their cognitive processes. Then he had them rate the degree to which they felt detached from their bodies. At a separate session, subjects also answered questions from which he could infer each subject's history of complex, partial epileptic-like experiences. He found that those subjects who had the most epileptic-like experiences also tended to report the most detachment from their bodies on days when geomagnetic activity was at higher levels in general. The geomagnetic disturbance may have destabilized activity in the temporal lobes of those people who had the most epileptic-like experiences. Although this finding may further suggest that cognitive science is moving toward an explanation of the OBE in natural, physical terms, it should be interpreted with caution given the low correlation and our current lack of understanding of how Earth's electromagnetic activity affects brain activity.

Other evidence from evolutionary psychology and the study of consciousness has supported the brain basis of the OBE. It is striking to note that the animals with brains most like our own, the chimpanzee, orangutan, and gorilla, are the only land animals aside from us that can recognize the image of their own bodies in a mirror as belonging to themselves (Gallup 1982). This conscious ability to recognize one's body as an objective part of oneself seems to be related to the brain's ability to form a mental representation of one's body that can be inspected. It also implies the need for the brain to construct a representation of the self as part of its ongoing modeling of the world. Nicholas Humphrey has proposed that it would be adaptive for animals with complex social lives, such as humans and chimps, to include a model of the self in their model of the social world (Humphrey 1978). In this way they could more completely model the possible consequences of their own actions and the responses of others to them. Consistent with this theory, several researchers have found that, like humans, chimpanzees may develop at least the rudiments of a theory of mind allowing them to predict and understand some intentions and behaviors in relation to themselves (Suddendorf and Whitten 2000).

Recently, cognitive scientists have proposed paying more attention to the bodily aspects of experience, challenging traditional views of cognitive science that tend to neglect the body (Johnson 1995). Some argue that the brain's representation of the body is central to its representation of the self (Damasio 1999; Eilan, Marcel, and Bermudez 1995). Some have even challenged traditional cognitive science's emphasis on representation, instead arguing that mental experience is embodied and not due to abstract mental processes distinct from the physical system producing them (Varela, Thompson, and Rosch 1991). Others, like James Gibson, have emphasized the role of the environment in perceiving the self (Neisser 1993). Gibson has made the important point that when we see the environment we almost always see our bodies as well. For example, when I look at the world in front of me I often see part of my leg, arm, or the bridge of my nose.

Supporting an embodied view of conscious experience, Monica Meijsing (2000) has reanalyzed two relevant cases of nervous system damage originally reported by Cole and Pailard (1995). Although these patients have little sensory feedback from their bodies below the neck, they nevertheless have retained their body image. They have retained knowledge of how they look and how much space their bodies occupy while retaining very little control over the movement of their bodies. One of these patients compared her body to a machine saying she felt as if she were a pilot lodged in a ship that was hard to steer.

These striking cases suggest that a person's embodied experience depends on having an intact nervous system. However, whether cognitive scientists adopt the traditional representational view or the newer embodied cognition view, their common conclusion is that conscious experience of the body depends on brain and nervous system function. It follows that anomalous experiences of the body depend on brain and nervous system function as well.

ACKNOWLEDGMENTS

I would like to thank an anonymous reviewer for valuable comments on an earlier draft and Dr. Michael Persinger for providing additional information about his research.

REFERENCES

Alcock, J.E. 1987. Parapsychology: Science of the anomalous or search for the soul? *Behavioral and Brain Sciences* 10: 553–565.

Auerbach, L. 1986. *ESP, Hauntings, and Poltergeists: A Parapsychologist's Handbook*. New York: Warner Books.

Beloff, J. 1989. Dualism: A parapsychological perspective. In *The Case for Dualism*. Charlottesville: University Press of Virginia.

Bensley, D.A. 1998. *Critical Thinking in Psychology: A Unified Skills Approach*. Pacific Grove, Calif.: Brooks/Cole.

Blackmore, S.J. 1982. Parapsychology—With and without the OBE? *Parapsychology Review* 13: 1–7.

———. 1987. Where am I?: Perspectives in imagery and the out-of-body experience. *Journal of Mental Imagery* 11: 53–66.

———. 1992. *Beyond the Body: An Investigation of Out-of-body Experiences*. (Revised ed.) Chicago: Academy Chicago Publishers.

Blanke, O., S. Ortigue, T. Landis, and M. Seeck. 2002. Stimulating illusory own-body perceptions. *Nature* 419: 269–270.

Cole, J., and J. Pailard 1995. Living without touch and peripheral information about body position and movement: Studies with Deafferented subjects. In J. Bermudez, A. Marcel, and N. Eilan, (Eds.). *The Body and the Self*. Cambridge, Mass.: MIT Press.

Crookall, R. 1963. Only psychological fact? *Light* 83: 17–182.

Damasio, A. 1999. *The Feeling of What Happens: Body and Emotion in the Making of Consciousness*. New York: Harcourt-Brace.

Eilan, N., A. Marcel, and J. Bermudez. 1995. Self-consciousness and the body: An interdisciplinary introduction. In J. Bermudez, A. Marcel, and N. Eilan, (Eds.). *The Body and the Self*. (Pp. 1–28). Cambridge, Mass.: MIT Press.

Frazer, J.G. 1996. *The Illustrated Golden Bough: A Study in Magic and Religion*. New York: Simon and Schuster.

Gallup, G.G. 1982. Self-recognition in primates: Self-awareness and the emergence of mind in primates. *American Journal of Primatology* 2: 237–248.

Glicksohn, J. 1991. The structure of subjective experience: Interdependencies along the sleep-wakefulness continuum. *Journal of Mental Imagery* 13: 99–106.

Grosso, M. 1976. Some varieties of out-of-body experience. *The Journal of the American Society for Psychical Research* 70: 179–193.

Humphrey, N. 1978. Nature's psychologists. *New Scientist* 78: 900–903.

Irwin, H.J. 1986. Perceptual perspective of visual imagery in OBE's, dreams and reminiscence. *Journal of the Society for Psychical Research* 53: 210–217.

———. 1988. Out-of-body experiences and dream lucidity. In J. Gackenbach and S. LaBerge (Eds.). *Conscious Mind, Sleeping Brain*, New York: Plenum Press.

Jansen, K. 1997. The ketamine model of the near-death experience: A central role for the N-Methyl-D-Aspartate receptor. *Journal of Near Death Studies* 16: 5–26.

Johnson, M. L. 1995. Incarnate mind. *Minds and Machines* 5: 533–545.

Ladavas, E., G. Zelon, and A. Fame. 1998. Visual peripersonal space centred on the face in humans. *Brain* 121: 2317-2326.

Levitan, L., S. Laberge, D. DeGracia, and P. Zimbardo. 1999. Out-of-body experiences, dreams, and REM sleep. *Sleep and Hypnosis* 1:186-196.

Meijsing, M. 2000. Self consciousness and the body. *Journal of Consciousness Studies* 7:34-52.

Neisser, U. 1993. The self perceived. In U. Neisser, (Ed.). *The Perceived Self*. Cambridge, UK: Cambridge University Press.

Newport, F., and M. Strausberg. 2001. Americans' belief in psychic and paranormal phenomena is up over last decade. Gallup News Service, 8 June. Online at www.gallup.com/poll/releases/pr010608.asp.

Nigro, G., and U. Neisser 1983. Point of view in personal memories. *Cognitive Psychology* 15:467-482.

Palmer, J. 1978. The out-of-body experience: A psychological theory. *Parapsychology Review* 9: 19-22.

Penfield, W. 1955. The role of the temporal cortex in certain psychic phenomena. *The Journal of Mental Science* 101: 451-465.

Persinger, M. 1995. Out-of-body experiences are more probable in people with elevated complex partial epileptic-like signs during periods of enhanced geomagnetic activity: A nonlinear effect. *Perceptual and Motor Skills* 80: 563-569.

Posner, M.I., and M.E., Raichle. 1994. *Images of Mind*. New York: W.H. Freeman.

Ramachandran, V.S. and W. Hirstein. 1998. The perception of phantom limbs. *Brain* 121: 1603-1630.

Rhine, J.B. and J.G. Pratt. 1957. *Parapsychology: Frontier Science of the Mind*. Springfield, Illinois: Charles C Thomas.

Rogo, D.S. 1984. Researching the out-of-body experience: The state of the art. *Anabiosis: The Journal for Near Death Studies* 4: 21-49.

Shiels, D. 1978. A cross-cultural study of belief in out-of-body experiences, waking and sleeping. *Journal of the Society for Psychical Research* 49: 697-741.

Stanovich, K.E. 1989. Implicit philosophies of mind: The dualism scale and its relation to religiosity and belief in extrasensory perception. *Journal of Psychology* 123: 5-23.

Suddendorf, T., and A. Whitten. 2000. Mental evolution and development: Evidence for secondary representation in children, great apes, and other animals. *Psychological Bulletin* 127: 629-650.

Tart, C.T. 1998. Six studies of out of body experiences. *Journal of Near Death Studies* 17: 73-99.

Thalbourne, M. 1999. Dualism and the sheep goat variable: A replication and extension. *Journal of the Society for Psychical Research* 63: 213-216.

Tobacyk, J., and T. Mitchell. 1987. The out-of-body experience and personality adjustment. *Journal of Nervous and Mental Disease* 175: 367-369.

Varela, F.J., E. Thompson, and E. Rosch. 1991. *The Embodied Mind: Cognitive Science and Human Experience*. Cambridge, Mass.: MIT Press.

REVIEW AND CONTEMPLATE

1. Explain what Bensley calls the "dualistic belief." Does research in cognitive science support this belief?

2. Explain the philosophical position called materialism.

3. Briefly describe Bensley's own out-of-body experience (OBE). Explain why such anecdotal reports of OBEs do not constitute strong evidence that the mind can actually leave the body.

4. Briefly describe two findings from research involving (a) brain stimulation and (b) drugs that suggest that OBEs may result from physical events in the brain.

5. Describe one major difference between pseudoscientific and scientific approaches to gathering evidence that is illustrated in Bensley's article (see Chapter 1 for a comparison of pseudoscience and science).

3.3 "Dream Interpretation and False Beliefs"

DREAMS HAVE LONG fascinated psychologists and laypeople, who ask questions regarding why we dream and what our dreams mean. Sigmund Freud believed that dreams are full of hidden meanings and that a proper interpretation of dreams can provide insights into a person's unconscious mind, past traumatic experiences, and secret desires. This view survives today in the many books and websites people can consult to help them interpret their dreams. One can also find professional clinical psychologists who interpret dreams in their clinical work. Some clinicians believe that certain images and symbols in dreams signal the existence of repressed memories of abuse. For example, some claim that a frightening dream about water suggests that you might have been sexually abused in a bathing situation; or a dream involving blood, sacrifice, or torture might indicate repressed memories of ritualistic abuse.

Today most scientists view dream interpretation as a pseudoscience that can produce inaccurate and potentially harmful results. Nevertheless, some clinical psychologists still use dream interpretation. Mazzoni et al. discuss some problems with dream interpretation and present the results of a study they conducted to determine whether people's beliefs about their past can be changed by a therapist's inaccurate interpretation of their dreams.

Reference

Mazzoni, G. A. L., Lombardo, P., Malvagia, S., & Loftus, E. F. (1999). Dream interpretation and false beliefs. *Professional Psychology: Research and Practice, 30,* 45–50.

ARTICLE 3.3

"DREAM INTERPRETATION AND FALSE BELIEFS"

GIULIANA MAZZONI, PASQUALRE LOMBARDO, STEFANO MALVAGIA, AND ELIZABETH LOFTUS

Dream interpretation is a common practice in psychotherapy. In the research presented in this article, each participant saw a clinician who interpreted a recent dream report to be a sign that the participant had had a mildly traumatic experience before age 3 years, such as being lost for an extended time or feeling abandoned by his or her parents. This dream intervention caused a majority of participants to become more confident that they had had such an experience, even though they had previously denied it. These findings have implications for the use of dream material in clinical settings. In particular, the findings point to the possibility that dream interpretation may have unexpected side effects if it leads to beliefs about the past that may, in fact, be false.

Dream interpretation is a common current clinical tool used more in some therapies than in others (Brenneis, 1997). Although this tool might not necessarily be problematic as an enterprise, what would be the impact and consequence of a clinician imposing an incorrect interpretation on dream material? Could such misinterpretation influence patients' beliefs about their past in ways that might be detrimental? Could patients be led to false beliefs about their past?

Dream material was viewed by Sigmund Freud (1900/1953, 1918/1955) as providing a royal road to the unconscious and as being a vehicle for unearthing specific traumatic experiences from the past. Psychoanalytic theory and technique (including dream interpretation) dominated psychotherapy training well into the 1950s, when behavioral, humanistic, and cognitive approaches, which do not emphasize dream interpretation, began to have greater impact. Dream interpretation, or dream work, holds a far less central position among clinical intervention tools than it did just 30 years ago.

Nonetheless, a sizable percentage of professional psychologists today report using dream interpretation in their clinical work (Brenneis, 1997; Polusny & Follette, 1996; Poole, Lindsay, Memon, & Bull, 1995). Moreover, a subset of clinicians who work in the area of trauma view dreams as being "exact replicas" of the traumatic experiences (van der Kolk, Britz, Burr, Sherry, & Hartmann, 1984, p. 188). For example, one therapist wrote, "Buried memories of abuse intrude into your consciousness through dreams ...

Giuliana Mazzoni, Pasqualre Lombardo, Stefano Malvagia, and Elizabeth F. Loftus, "Dream Interpretation and False Beliefs," *Professional Psychology: Research and Practice*, vol. 30, no. 1, pp. 45–50. Copyright © 1999 by American Psychological Association. Reprinted with permission.

Dreams are often the first sign of emerging memories" (Fredrickson, 1992, p. 44). Another therapist wrote,

> Repressed memory dreams are dreams that contain a partial repressed memory or symbols that provide access to a repressed memory. During sleep, you have a direct link to your unconscious. Because the channel is open, memory fragments or symbols from repressed sexual abuse memories often intrude into the dream state. Even though the memory is embedded in the symbolism of the dream world, it is possible to use the dream to retrieve the memory. *(Fredrickson, 1992, p. 125)*

Does this sort of clinical dream interpretation actually lead to the recovery of a genuine traumatic past? Or is it possible that the dream interpretation might be leading people to develop false beliefs, or even false memories, about their past? And if so, is it harmful?

We recently published several studies that may have some relevance to these questions (Mazzoni & Loftus, 1996). We showed that after a single subtle suggestion, participants falsely recognized items from their dreams and thought that these items had been presented in a list that they learned during the waking state. Our participants first learned a key list of words. In a later session, they received a false suggestion that some items from their previously reported dreams had been presented on the key list. Finally, in a third session, they tried to recall the items that had occurred on the initial key list. A major finding was that participants often falsely recognized their dream items and thought they had been presented on the key list, sometimes as often as they accurately recognized true list items. Despite the high rate of false recognition, and the conviction that participants had about these false memories, it is reasonable to question whether the same kind of results would occur with more personally meaningful events.

THE FLORENCE FALSE INTERPRETATION STUDY

We devised a new methodology for exploring whether such activities can lead people to develop false beliefs about the past. We found individuals who reported that it was unlikely that they had had certain critical experiences before the age of 3 years. The age of 3 years is important to shed light on whether changes that resulted from our manipulation were due to the recovery of true experiences or the creation of false ones (Wetzler & Sweeney, 1986). The critical experiences included episodes like being lost in a public place for some extended time. Later, some of these individuals went through a 30-min minitherapy simulation with a clinical psychologist, who interpreted their dream (no matter what the content of the dream) as if it were indicative of having undergone specific critical experiences in the past.

An initial group of 128 undergraduates from the University of Florence filled out an instrument that we called the Life Events Inventory (LEI) on which they reported on the likelihood of various childhood events having happened to them. The LEI has 36 items, 3 of which are critical items. The inventory asks participants to consider how certain (confident) they are that each event did or did not happen to them before the age of 3 years. Participants respond by ranking items on an 8-point Likert-type scale ranging from 1 *(certain it did not happen)* to 8 *(certain it did happen)*. Fifty participants who had low scores (below 4) on the 3 critical items were selected and asked to participate in the next phase of the study. The 3 critical items were as follows: "got lost in a public space," "was abandoned by my parents," and "found myself lonely and lost in an unfamiliar place." The cover story associated with the administration of the LEI explained that the study concerned the frequency of rare and common events that happened during early childhood and that the study goal was the validation of an instrument to measure these experiences.

Of the selected 50 participants, half were randomly assigned to a dream condition, where they received suggestive information about the content of their dream. The other half did not receive any suggestive information about their dreams. Of the 25 participants in the dream condition, only 19 completed all three phases of the experiment; all 25 participants in the non-dream condition completed the experiment. (The difference in completion rate appeared to be due to a handful of participants who were randomly assigned to the dream condition but chose not to participate in what they thought was an additional experiment. Whether this choice was due to already having sufficient credits or some other reason was not explored.) The mean age of the final sample of 44 participants was 21 years, and *64% were* women.

All 44 participants returned to take the LEI again after 3 to 4 weeks. However, those in the dream condition also participated during that time in what they thought was a completely different experiment but was actually the dream manipulation.

For the participants in the dream condition, dream interpretation was done 10–15 days after the first LEI. Shortly before the dream session, dream condition participants received a phone call from a clinician asking for their participation in a dream and sleep study. Participants were asked to bring in one or more dreams, which could be a recurrent dream, a recent dream, or a vivid dream (no constraints were put on the type of dream). These participants had their dreams individually interpreted by a clinical psychologist. The particular clinician is a trained clinical psychologist with a private practice in Florence, Italy. He also is well known in the community from his radio program on which he gives clinical advice. Moreover, he has a strong, persuasive personality. In the dream session, the clinician welcomed the participants and explained that the purpose of the study was to collect meaningful dreams and to relate those dreams to sleep characteristics. Then the participants read their own dream report aloud. Next, the clinician asked participants for their own interpretation of the dream and for their comments on the dream. Then the clinician offered his own comments. The comments were framed in terms of a clinical interview (i.e., the psychologist followed a predefined script but was free to make some modifications depending on the responses of the participant). Early on, he explained that he had considerable experience in dream interpretation, and he explained that dreams are meaningful and symbolic expressions of human concern.

A key feature of the dream manipulation was to suggest to participants that the dream was the overt manifestation of repressed memories of events that happened before the age of 3 years. To be specific, the dream interpretation suggested to the participants that the dream was indicative of a difficult childhood experience, such as getting lost in a public place, being abandoned by one's parents, or being lonely and lost in an unfamiliar place—the three critical items. No matter what the content of their dreams, all participants received the same suggestion: that one or more of these critical experiences appeared to have happened to them before the age of 3 years.

To appreciate what the clinician did with the specific dream material, it is helpful to use a concrete example. Suppose a participant came in with a dream report about walking up a mountainside alone on a chilly day and commented that the dream must mean that he finds mountain walking appealing. The clinician might then discuss part of the dream, mentioning the mountain, that the participant reported being alone there, and that despite the participant's remark about liking mountain walking, the "chilly day" suggests that the experience might be a "cold" one for the participant. At that point, the clinician would try to induce the participant to agree with this suggestion. The clinician might then move toward a global interpretation, suggesting that in his vast experience with dream interpretation, a dream like this usually means that the participant is not totally happy with himself, he needs challenge, he resists being helped by others, and might have social or interpersonal difficulties. The clinician then might suggest to the participant that the dream content, and the feelings about that dream, are probably due to some past experience that the participant might not even remember. The clinician would then tell the participant that the specific details mentioned are commonly due to having had certain experiences before age 3, like being lost in a public place, being abandoned even temporarily by parents, or finding oneself lonely and lost in an unfamiliar place. Finally, the clinician would ask whether any of the critical events happened to the participant before the age of 3 years. When the participant claimed not to remember these experiences, the clinician explained how childhood experiences are often buried in the unconscious but do get revealed in dreams.

From this example, it is easy to see some of the general steps that the clinician followed during dream interpretation:

1. He commented on specific items in the dream and tried to relate those items to possible feelings that the participant might have. In the example, the specific items of the mountain walking and the chilly day were related to the possible feelings about its being a cold experience.
2. He tried to induce the participant to agree with and expand on his interpretation.
3. He provided a global interpretation of the dream's meaning. In the example, the clinician suggested that possibly the participant was not totally happy with himself, needed challenge, resisted help, and so forth.

4. He suggested the possibility that specific events of childhood are commonly associated with dream reports like the one provided by the participant. In the example, the specific events were getting lost and feeling abandoned—in other words, the critical events used in this study for all participants.
5. He explicitly suggested that such events had happened to the participant, and he asked for the participant's agreement with that suggestion.
6. When the participant did not recall such an event, the clinician explained that unpleasant childhood experiences can be buried and remain unremembered but are often revealed in dreams.

The entire dream session lasted approximately 30 min. At the end of the dream session, the clinician asked the participant to think over the proposed events and to return later for the sleep assessment. These participants eventually returned to participate in a subsequent sleep study that was actually totally unrelated to the current experiment.

The initial experimenter, who had previously administered the LEI (hereafter referred to as LEI-1), then contacted the participants in the dream condition and arranged for them to return for a second administration of the LEI (hereafter referred to as LEI-2). Approximately 10–15 days passed between LEI-1 and dream interpretation, and an additional 10–15 days passed between dream interpretation and LEI-2. For the non-dream condition participants, the LEI administrations were separated by the same amount of time but without any intervening dream interpretation.

After the LEI-2, participants were thoroughly debriefed. At this time, they were asked whether they had linked the two experiments in any way, and no participant reported having done so.

To determine if the false dream interpretation had caused participants to become more confident that the critical events had occurred, we examined whether LEI scores moved up or down for each of the three critical items. We also calculated the percentage of participants whose responses increased, decreased, or did not change from the LEI-1 to the LEI-2. The data for the three critical items (lost in public place, abandoned by parents, and lonely and lost) are shown in Figure 3.2. We predicted that after dream interpretation, participants would be more confident that the events had happened.

First examine what happened without dream interpretation: These participants in the control condition reported no change in score on two target items and a clear decrease on the remaining item ("lonely and lost"). The same was not true for participants in the dream condition. For all three items, their scores were far more likely to increase, and they rarely decreased on the LEI-2. For two of the critical events, about 80% of the scores increased. To analyze these data statistically, we conducted several Mann-Whitney U tests, comparing the dream and non-dream (control) conditions. We found that the two groups differed significantly for two of the critical items: "lost in a public place" and "lonely and

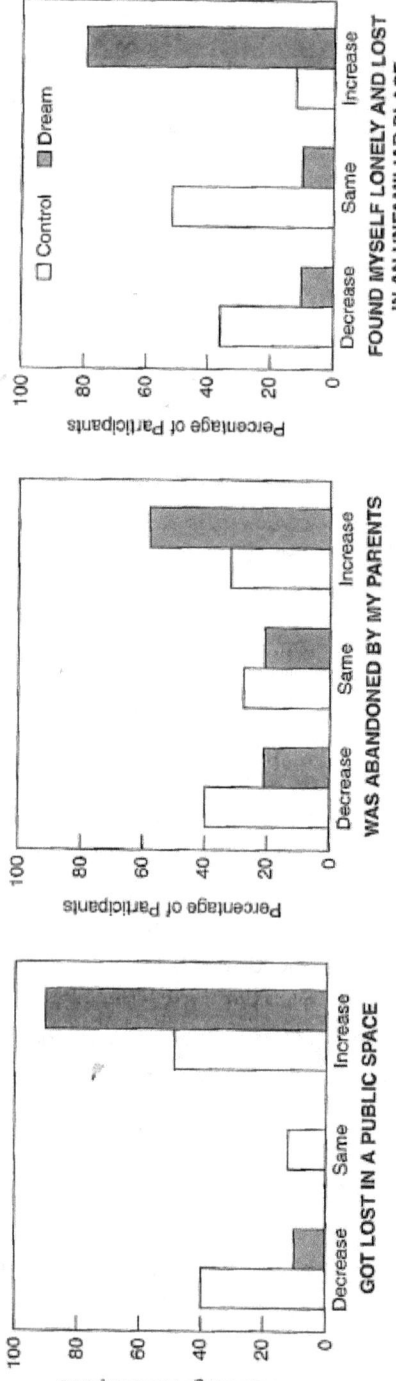

FIGURE 3.2: Percentage of participants who decreased, who stayed the same, and who increased their scores for each of the three critical items on the Life Events Inventory.

lost in an unfamiliar place." Participants in the dream condition were far more likely to increase their confidence that they had had these experiences before the age of 3 years.

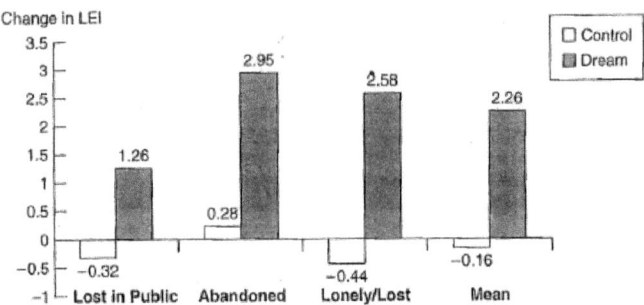

FIGURE 3.3: Mean change in scores on the Life Events Inventory (LEI) for each of the three critical items. At the right is mean change collapsed across the three critical items.

The same differences between the dream and non-dream condition groups were found when we analyzed the degree of movement. For each participant, we calculated the numerical difference between the scores assigned to each item in LEI-2 and the scores assigned to the same items in LEI-1. Figure 3.3 shows the change scores from LEI-1 to LEI-2 for the three critical items for non-dream condition versus dream condition participants.

As Figure 3.3 shows, for control condition participants, the changes in LEI scores were relatively small and not systematic. One item changed in a slightly positive way ("abandoned by parents"), whereas the other two items changed in a slightly negative way.

For the dream condition participants, the picture was completely different. All three items changed in a positive direction. The biggest difference between dream and non-dream condition participants occurred for the item "lonely and lost in an unfamiliar place," where the dream condition participants showed a mean positive change of 2.58 and the control participants showed a mean negative change of –.44. At the right of Figure 3.3, the mean change in LEI is averaged across all critical items and participants, and a strong overall influence of the dream interpretation can be seen. The mean change in the dream condition was 2.26 on the 8-point scale, whereas in the non-dream condition it was –.16.

To analyze these data statistically, we conducted several students' t tests for independent samples on the change scores. We found that the dream and non-dream condition participants differed significantly for two critical items: lost in a public place and lonely and lost. Dream and non-dream participants differed on the last critical item, abandoned by parents, only by a one-tailed test. Thus, the two methods of analysis, one that involved proportions of participants who shifted and one that involved measures of mean shift, produced similar results.

To be sure that our results were not due to inadvertent differences in pretreatment LEI scores, we calculated the mean pretreatment score for each critical item. These pretreatment scores are shown in Table 3.1, separately for dream and non-dream participants. The posttreatment mean scores are also shown. Notice that the dream and non-dream participants did not differ in terms of their pretreatment scores, but they showed large differences in their posttreatment scores.

The previous two analyses suggested that the dream manipulation caused participants

TABLE 3.1: Average Pretreatment (LEI-1) and Posttreatment (LEI-2) Scores in the Non-Dream and the Dream Groups for the Three Critical Events

	NONDREAM		DREAM	
CRITICAL EVENT	LEI-1	LEI-2	LEI-1	LEI-2
Lost	2.52	2.20	2.47	3.74
Abandoned	2.24	2.51	2.47	5.42
Lonely and lost	2.92	2.48	2.16	4.74

NOTE. LEI-1 = first administration (pretreatment) of the Life Events Inventory (LEI); LEI-2 = second administration (posttreatment) of the LEI. Scores are on an 8-point Likert-type scale ranging from 1 (*certain it did not happen*) to 8 (*certain it did happen*).

to become more certain that they had had specific negative experiences in their early childhood. A question then arose as to whether the shifts were localized only to the specific experiences mentioned by the clinician, or whether the clinician's intervention caused a general negative feeling, creating in participants the belief that they were more likely to have experienced a vast array of negative events in their early lives. We assessed this possibility by examining the dream condition versus non-dream condition differences on the negative filler items, such as "witnessed a person dying" or "threatened by a stranger." If the dream manipulation produced general negativity, this negativity might be represented in increased confidence on negative filler items as compared with non-dream conditions response on those negative filler items. In fact, we found that the dream manipulation had no impact on the negative filler items. Rather, the influence of the dream manipulation was very specific to the critical items that were specifically mentioned by the clinician.

Why did the dream interpretation lead to increased confidence that certain suggested events occurred? One possible explanation is that the dream interpretation created a true belief, reminding some participants of a true experience from their past. Such a reminder, if it occurred, probably did not occur during the therapy session itself, because no participant reported a memory for one of the critical events during the therapy. However, in the 10–15 days between the therapy and the final session, some participants might have recalled an actual experience. We deliberately suggested critical events to have occurred before the age of 3 years so that any memory that was produced could be deemed unlikely to be a real memory because of the childhood amnesia problem. However, it is entirely possible that the therapy might have led to ruminations that reminded participants of an event that occurred after the age of 3 years, but they misdated the experience during LEI-2 and mistakenly thought that it occurred before the age of 3. This process would lead to dramatic shifts in the LEI. Our data cannot rule this possibility out completely, and it is possible that these kinds of cases accounted for some of the shift that we observed. However, we would argue that if participants were so ready to conclude after dream interpretation that an experience that they actually had at age 6 or 8 or 12 happened to them before the age of 3, this also would constitute a distortion of belief or memory.

Another possible reason that participants increased their confidence in the suggested events in that the dream interpretation created a false belief. If false beliefs have been constructed, how and why does this process happen? One answer to this question can be found in the large literature on memory distortion that has shown that people are susceptible to suggestion (Gheorghin, Netter, Eysenck, & Rosenthal, 1989). In the current empirical work, we have found a form of suggestion that is both explicit and subtle. It is explicit in that the clinician used his authority to tell the dreamers that their mental products were likely to be revealing particular past experiences. It is subtle in the sense that the dreamers were encouraged to come up with their own specific instances of such experiences.

IMPLICATIONS AND APPLICATIONS

Our findings have important implications for therapists. They show that people are suggestible in a simulation that bears more resemblance to a therapeutic setting than has been used in prior empirical studies. Moreover, the findings hint at the strong influence that a clinician can have in a short period of time. This power may extend to other therapist-client interactions that are characterized by therapist interpretation of information provided by the client.

One might ask whether it is reasonable to generalize from our brief therapy simulation with students to the world of clinicians and their patients. After all, many of the differences between our minitherapy and real-world therapy are relatively easy to point out. Nonetheless, we believe that these very differences are such that we may be underestimating the power and influence that can occur in a clinical setting. We used students, who were presumably reasonably mentally healthy, whereas clinical patients may have a greater need to find an explanation for problems or distress. We had a single short therapy simulation, whereas clinical patients often experience many sessions during which suggested interpretations are offered to them. Our therapy simulation was limited to only a few elements that the participants provided (e.g., the dream and a brief reaction to the dream), whereas clinical patients provide a great many elements (dreams, thoughts, behaviors, feelings) with which the therapist works. Whether these elements are critical for influencing how people reflect on their past experiences is, of course, a matter for further research investigation.

One might ask whether it is even the case that therapists are using dream material to suggest that events occurred in a client's early life. We have found a number of examples that support the contention that some therapists do indeed make these kinds of suggestions from dream material. This conclusion comes not only from surveys of clinicians (e.g., Poole et al., 1995), but also from the writings of specific clinicians. For example, in *Crisis Dreaming,* readers are told, "Recurring dreams, particularly of being chased or attacked, suggest that such events really occurred" (Cartwright & Lamberg, 1992, p. 185). Are the authors of this book communicating this information to their clients? Are therapist-readers of this book taking dream material that involves chases and attacks and telling a client that it means that such events occurred? Although we cannot know that therapist-readers are following the advice implicit in this book, it is worth considering the likelihood that they might do so and might inadvertently create false beliefs or memories.

Could therapists produce similar effects without explicit dream interpretation? We believe the dream interpretation is probably not necessary but might add a bit of influential power. Here is why: Suppose instead of interpreting dreams the clinician simply responds to the comments made by a client during the first 5 min of interaction. If the clinician takes that 5 min of material and interprets the material as being indicative of an early childhood trauma, the client may eventually come to believe that he or she experienced such a trauma. In fact, even in the absence of dream interpretation, such suggestive comments might increase the likelihood of illusory beliefs or memories. According to Lindsay and Read (1995), suggestions from a trusted authority can be especially influential when they communicate a rationale for the plausibility of buried memories of childhood trauma. Moreover, the trusted authority might be especially influential if he or she offers repeated suggestions, giving anecdotes ostensibly from other patients.

However, it is also worth pointing out that working with dream material might be a particularly potent way to influence clients, for better or worse. It certainly might help to enhance the influence process, because people presumably enter therapy with a set of beliefs about the meaning of dreams in their lives and how much dreams can reveal about an individual's past. Given a predisposition on the part of some clients to already believe in the significance of dreams, the trusted authority can capitalize on the a priori beliefs and use them in the service of altering the autobiography.

Are therapists aware of the power they have? Almost by definition therapists must believe that they have the power to change people, because at least some forms of therapy emphasize changing people's beliefs from ones that are nonadaptive to ones that are more adaptive. Even more generally, therapy is about changing people. However, therapists may be appreciating their power to change people primarily when they are thinking about the good it can produce in people or thinking about ways to make their clients change for the better. They may not be appreciating that they also have the power to change people for the worse. This type of change can happen, for example, when a therapist adopts a hypothesis too early and, even when the hypothesis is wrong, presses it on the client. Our data show that even a randomly generated hypothesis can be embraced by individuals and can produce profound changes in the way they view their past. We have demonstrated that these interventions can make people believe that they have had experiences that they previously denied. However, it is also likely that these interventions have the power to make people doubt their true experiences. Our hope is that heightened awareness of this power might enhance the likelihood of cautious use of these sorts of interventions.

REFERENCES

Brenneis, C. B. (1997). *Recovered memories of trauma: Transferring the present to the past*. Madison, WI: International Universities Press.

Cartwright, R. & Lamberg, L. (1992). *Crisis dreaming—Using your dreams to solve your problems*. New York: HarperCollins.

Fredrickson, R. (1992). *Repressed memories*. New York: Simon & Schuster.

Freud, S. (1953). *The interpretation of dreams* (Standard ed. 4 & 5). London: Hogarth Press. (Original work published 1900)

Freud, S. (1955). *From the history of an infantile neurosis* (standard ed. 17, pp. 1–122). London: Hogarth Press. (Original work published 1918).

Gheorghiu, V. A., Netter, P., Eyesenck, H. J., & Rosenthal, R. (Eds). (1989). *Suggestion and suggestibility*. New York: Springer-Verlag.

Lindsay, D. S., & Read, J. D. (1995). "Memory work" and recovered memories of childhood sexual abuse: Scientific evidence and public, professional, and personal issues. *Psychology, Public Policy, & the Law, 1*, 846–908.

Mazzoni, G. A. L., & Loftus, E. F. (1996). When dreams become reality. *Consciousness & Cognition, 5*, 442–462.

Polusny, M. A., & Follette, V. M. (1996). Remembering childhood sexual abuse. *Professional Psychology: Research and Practice, 27*, 41–52.

Poole, D. A., Lindsay, D. S., Memon, A., & Bull, R. (1995). Psychotherapy and the recovery of memories of childhood sexual abuse: U.S. and British practitioners' opinions, practices, and experiences. *Journal of Consulting and Clinical Psychology, 63*, 426–437.

van der Kolk, B., Britz, R., Burr, W., Sherry, S., & Hartmann, E. (1984). Nightmares and trauma: A comparison of nightmares after combat with life-long nightmares in veterans. *American Journal of Psychiatry, 141,* 187–190.

Wetzler, S. E., & Sweeney, J. A. (1986). Childhood amnesia: An empirical demonstration. In D. C. Rubin (Ed.), *Autobiographical memory* (pp. 191–201). Cambridge, MA: Cambridge University Press.

REVIEW AND CONTEMPLATE

1. Why do some clinicians engage in dream interpretation with their clients? What do they hope to discover?

2. What are the central findings of the study conducted by Mazzoni et al. (1999)?

3. Describe one of the important implications of Mazzoni et al.'s findings for practicing therapists.

4. How is this article related to the topic of pseudoscience?

Chapter 4

CHILD DEVELOPMENT

4.1 "Do Babies Learn From Baby Media?"

A MOTHER NAMED Julie Ainger-Clark who wanted to develop better educational materials for her year-old daughter created a homemade *Baby Einstein* video that featured puppets, music, words in different languages, stories, and numbers. The video was marketed across the United States and many other countries and eventually grew into the multimillion-dollar Baby Einstein Company, featuring many videos and toys designed to boost children's intelligence. Ainger-Clark won an Entrepreneur of the Year award and was featured on many popular television shows (e.g., *Good Morning America, The Today Show*). The business was sold to The Walt Disney Company in 2001. By 2009, Disney was pressured into admitting that there was no evidence that the videos were educational, and they offered refunds to parents who had purchased the videos. However, that was not the end of Baby Einstein. Disney sold the business in 2013, and there is still a Baby Einstein website that touts their products.

In this article, Judy DeLoache and her coauthors describe the research they conducted to determine whether videos marketed for young children actually improve children's vocabulary. Typical of pseudoscientific products, the Baby Einstein videos were promoted by the testimonials of many satisfied parents who purchased them and believed that the videos improved their child's learning. The article explains that children's vocabulary might actually increase during their second year of life, the time period when parents might have shown them educational videos. However, the increase in their vocabulary is probably not caused by the videos. This article illustrates the point, mentioned in Chapter 1, that people might believe in pseudoscientific products or ideas due to difficulties in statistical reasoning. In this case, parents might believe that the correlation between their child's video watching and improved vocabulary means that video watching caused the improved vocabulary. However, as you might have learned from your introductory psychology course, correlation does not mean causation.

Reference

DeLoache, J. S., Chiong, C., Sherman, K., Islam, N., Vanderborght, M., Troseth, G. L., ... O'Doherty, K. (2010). Do babies learn from baby media? *Psychological Science, 21,* 1570–1574.

"DO BABIES LEARN FROM BABY MEDIA?"

*JUDY DELOACHE, CYNTHIA CHIONG, KATHLEEN SHERMAN, NADIA ISLAM,
MIEKE VANDERBORGHT, GEORGENE TROSETH, GABRIELLE STROUSE,
AND KATHERINE O'DOHERTY*

One of the most remarkable marketing phenomena of recent history was ignited by the 1997 release of the first Baby Einstein video (The Baby Einstein Co., Littleton, CO), which was followed by a host of other videos and DVDs designed and marketed specifically for infants and very young children. American parents alone spend hundreds of millions of dollars yearly on these products, with the Baby Einstein series leading in popularity and sales worldwide.

Most companies that market these DVDs feature quotes from parents touting the virtues of the company's products. In these testimonials on Web sites and in advertisements, parents frequently mention the remarkable degree of attention that children pay to the DVDs (as well as the fact that their children's absorption in the DVDs enables them to get household chores done and even take the occasional shower). Prominently featured are parent testimonials that their children learn a great deal from watching infant DVDs. Our own experience with parents of young children has led us to suspect that a substantial proportion believe that infants benefit from commercial media products, and recent research indicates that 40% of mothers of young children believe that their children learn from television (Rideout, 2007).

But how well do infants actually learn from visual media? Because development typically proceeds at a very rapid pace in the first years of life, parents may misattribute ordinary developmental progress to their children's media exposure. For example, on one commercial Web site, a parent reported that her 18-month-old child had very few words until she started watching one of the company's videos, at which point her vocabulary "suddenly blossomed." However, a very well-documented phenomenon in early language development is the "word spurt," a rapid increase in the acquisition of new words during the second year of life (e.g., Benedict, 1979; Goldfield & Reznick, 1990). It would be easy for parents to misattribute their children's sudden linguistic advances to recent video experience.

Although several empirical studies have examined the relation between early television viewing and a variety of outcome measures, most have been large-scale surveys yielding correlational data (e.g., Rideout, Vandewater, & Wartella, 2003; Schmidt, Rich, Rifas-Shiman, Oken, & Taveras, 2009; Zimmerman, Christakis, & Meltzoff, 2007). Only a relatively small number of laboratory studies have examined specific aspects of young

Judy S. DeLoache, Cynthia Chiong, Kathleen Sherman, Nadia Islam, Mieke Vanderborght, Georgene L. Troseth, Gabrielle A. Strouse, and Katherine O'Doherty, "Do Babies Learn From Baby Media?," *Psychological Science*, vol. 21, no. 11, pp. 1570-1574. Copyright © 2010 by SAGE Publications. Reprinted with permission.

children's interaction with visual media (see Anderson & Pempek, 2005; DeLoache & Chiong, 2009).

Further, only a few of those studies have specifically focused on infants' *learning* from video. In one such study (Kuhl, Tsao, & Liu, 2003), 9-month-olds from English-speaking families watched several presentations, either live or video, of an adult speaking Mandarin. A month later, the researchers tested whether this exposure had prolonged the infants' sensitivity to the Mandarin speech sounds. Only children whose Mandarin exposure had occurred in live interactions showed any impact of that experience.

Laboratory studies of infants' imitation of simple actions presented on video have established that 12- to 30-month-olds are able to reproduce a modest number of observed actions (e.g., Barr & Hayne, 1999; Hayne, Herbert, & Simcock, 2003; McCall, Parke, & Kavanaugh, 1977). Imitation is substantially better, however, when children experience the same demonstrations live.

Young children's word learning from commercial television has also been examined. A large-scale parent survey reported a negative correlation between vocabulary size and television exposure: For every hour of baby media that infants between 8 and 16 months of age watched on their own, they were reported to know 6 to 8 fewer words (Zimmerman et al., 2007). Krcmar, Grela, and Lin (2007) obtained similar results in a laboratory study, in which children under 22 months of age learned few object names presented on a clip from a Teletubbies television episode.

In a recent experimental investigation of early learning from video, Robb, Richert, and Wartella (2009) assessed word learning from home viewing of a commercial DVD designed to teach words to young children. According to parent reports, the 12- to 15-month-old participants learned relatively few of the words featured on the DVD: Children who had substantial exposure to it performed no better than did those with none. These results are intriguing, but the fact that the primary data were parent reports is of some concern.

Accordingly, we conducted an experiment using objective testing to directly examine the extent to which infants learn from a very popular commercial infant DVD promoted to foster word learning. Six aspects of the study were designed to ensure a highly valid assessment of the potential for early learning from video: (a) The entire experiment was conducted in the children's own homes. (b) The conditions mimicked everyday situations in which young children view videos. (c) A best-selling video was used. (d) The children received extensive exposure to the video. (e) They were tested for their understanding of the specific words featured on the video. (f) The tester was blind to the condition to which each child had been randomly assigned.

METHOD

Participants

Participants were 72 infants between 12 and 18 months of age ($M = 14.7$ months). They were recruited from a large metropolitan area and a small city. The sample was predominantly White and middle-class. None of the infants had had any exposure to the target DVD. Eighteen children (including approximately equal numbers of girls and boys) were randomly assigned to each of four conditions.

Materials

A best-selling commercial DVD designed and marketed for infants from "12 months of age and up" was used in the research. The 39-min DVD depicts a variety of scenes of a house and yard. A voice labels common household objects, each of which is named three times, with several minutes intervening between the repetitions of a given label. In addition, during the first and last labeling of a given object, a person is shown producing a manual sign for the object.

Conditions

In the three experimental conditions, the experimenter made three home visits to each family. During the first visit, the experimenter gave detailed oral and written instructions to the parents. The experimental conditions included two video conditions: video with interaction and video with no interaction. In both of these conditions, parents gave their children substantial experience with the DVD in their own homes over 4 weeks. To ensure that they followed the instructions, we asked them to complete a daily log of their child's experience with the video. Parents in the parent-teaching (non-video) condition estimated how often they had attempted to teach their children the target words. On the second and third home visits in all three of these conditions, the experimenter checked to make sure the parents had been following the protocol.

In the *video-with-interaction condition*, the child and a parent watched the DVD together at least five times a week over a 4-week period, for a total of 10 or more hours of viewing time in 20 or more viewing episodes. (Some advertisements for baby videos recommend that parents watch with their children.) Parents were instructed to interact with their child in whatever way seemed natural to them while viewing the video. This condition mimicked the common everyday experience of young children and parents watching television together.

In the *video-with-no-interaction* condition, the children watched the video alone, but had the same total amount of exposure to it as did the children in the video-with-interaction condition. (The parents were almost always in the room with their infants, but were not watching television with them.) This condition mimicked another common situation, in which young children watch television on their own while their parents are nearby but engaged in other activities.

In the *parent-teaching* condition, the children were not exposed to the video at all. Instead, the parents were given a list of the 25 words featured on the video and were instructed simply to "try to teach your child as many of these words as you can in whatever way seems natural to you."

The fourth condition, in which there was no intervention, was the control condition. It provided a baseline of normal vocabulary growth against which performance in the three intervention groups could be compared.

Testing

During the initial home visit, each child was tested for knowledge of 13 of the 25 words featured on the video in order to establish an individualized set of target words for that child. (As Table S1 in the Supplemental Material available online shows, children in the target age range perform around or below chance when tested for their knowledge of the majority of these words.) On each of 13 trials, the child was shown a pair of replica objects—a target representing an object featured in the video (e.g., clock, table, tree) and a distractor that did not appear in the video (e.g., fan, plate, fence). The experimenter named the target and asked the child to point to the appropriate object (e.g., "Can you show me the table?"). The names of the objects that a child failed to identify became that child's individualized set of target words. The number of target words ranged from 5 to 12; the mean number (6.4–6.9) did not differ across the four groups.

On the final visit, the child's knowledge of his or her target words was tested to determine how much word learning had taken place over the 4 weeks. The testing was conducted in the same way as in the initial visit, except that two trials were given for each of the child's target words, with the words presented in one order for the first set of trials and in the reverse order for the second. To be credited with knowing a word, the child had to choose the correct object on both trials; this criterion minimized the likelihood that children would be counted as knowing a word after simply guessing correctly. Parents in the video conditions completed a brief questionnaire concerning their and their child's experience with the video.

RESULTS

Figure 4.1 shows the percentage of their target words that the children got correct on the posttest. Only the performance of the parent-teaching group was above chance ($p < .05$). The result of primary importance is clear: Children who had extensive exposure to a popular infant video over a full month, either with a parent or alone, did not learn any more new words than did children with no exposure to the video at all.

The absence of learning from experience with the video was not due to lack of attention to it. Representative comments from the logs of parents whose children were in

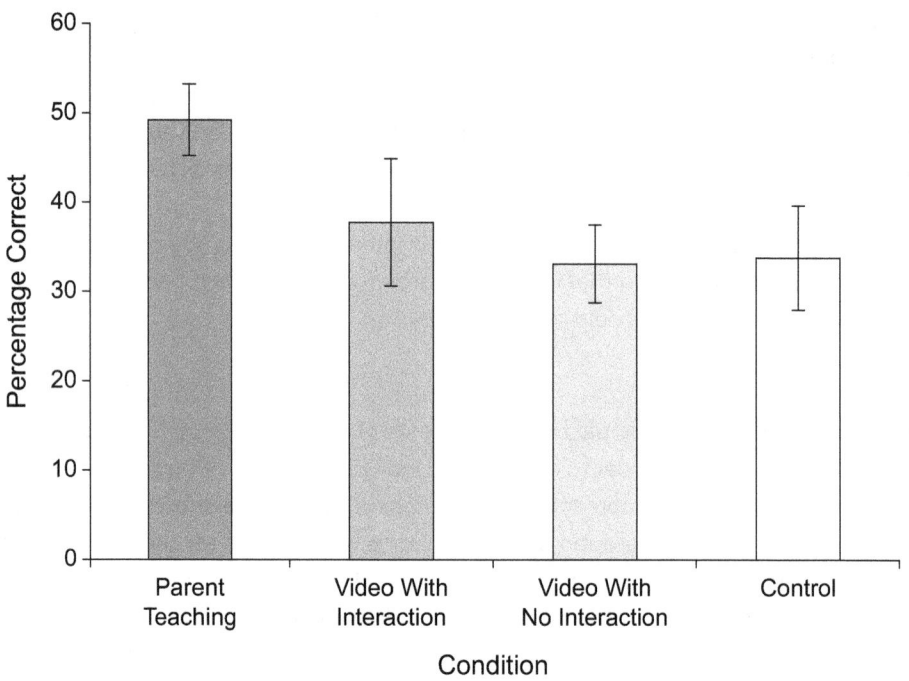

FIGURE 4.1: Children's mean performance on the posttest as a function of group. Each child was tested on an individualized set of target words. Error bars represent standard errors of the mean.

the video groups include the following: "She was practically glued to the screen today"; "She was very quiet today—stared intently at the screen and ignored me when I asked her to talk"; "She loves the blasted thing. It's crack for babies!"

As Figure 4.1 shows, performance was highest in the parent-teaching group—those children who had no exposure to the video, but whose parents had attempted to teach them new words during everyday interactions. Preliminary examination of the individual scores indicated that the data were not normally distributed, so a median test was performed on the proportion of target words that the children in the four conditions identified on the posttest. There was a significant overall difference among the groups, $\chi^2(3, N = 72) = 10.03$, $p < .05$. Post hoc tests indicated that the performance of the parent-teaching group was significantly better than that of all three of the other groups—video-with-interaction group: $\chi^2(1, N = 36) = 4.0$, $p < .05$; video-with-no-interaction group: $\chi^2(1, N = 36) = 11.11$, $p = .001$; and control group: $\chi^2(1, N = 36) = 4.0$, $p < .05$. Neither of the video conditions differed from the control condition. Thus, significantly more learning occurred in the context of everyday parent-child interactions than in front of television screens.

Finally, the parents' assessment of how much their children had learned from the DVD was unrelated to the children's performance on the posttest: Children whose parents thought that they had learned a substantial amount from their experience with the DVD performed no better than did children of less sanguine parents. There was, however, a significant correlation ($r = .64$, $p < .01$) between parents' own liking for the DVD and their estimate of how much their children had learned: The more a parent liked the DVD, the more he or she believed the child had learned from it.

DISCUSSION

The results of this study provide a clear answer to our original question: Infants between 12 and 18 months of age learned very little from a highly popular media product promoted for this age group. Even with the substantial amount of exposure that they had to the video, the infants learned only a few of the words featured on it. Because great care was taken to ensure that the video-viewing conditions were as natural as possible, the results should be generalizable to young children's everyday experience.

These results are consistent with a body of theory and research that has established that very young children often fail to use information communicated to them via symbolic media, including pictures, models, and video (e.g., DeLoache, 2004; Troseth, Pierroutsakos, & DeLoache, 2004). For example, 2-year-olds who watch a live video of an adult hiding a desirable toy in the room next-door fail to find the toy when encouraged to search for it immediately afterward (Troseth, 2003a, 2003b; Troseth & DeLoache, 1998). This and related results indicate that infants and very young children have difficulty understanding the relation between what they see on a screen and the real world.

An additional finding from this experiment is directly relevant to the possibility that parents may misattribute normal developmental progress to their infants' video exposure. Parents who had a favorable attitude toward the DVD thought that their children had learned more from it than did parents who were less positively disposed to the DVD. There was, in fact, no difference in how many words were learned by the children of these two groups of parents. This result suggests that much of the enthusiasm expressed in parent testimonials about baby video products is misplaced.

In summary, the research reported here supports two important conclusions. First, parents whose infants have experience with baby videos tend to misattribute normal developmental change to that experience, thereby overestimating the impact of the videos on their children's development. Second, the degree to which babies actually learn from baby videos is negligible.

Acknowledgments

We thank Monica Ehrbacher for her very helpful statistical advice.

Declaration of Conflicting Interests

The authors declared that they had no conflicts of interest with respect to their authorship or the publication of this article.

Funding

This research was supported by National Institutes of Health Grant HD-25271, as well as by National Science Foundation Grant 0819508, both to the first author.

Supplemental Material

Additional supporting information may be found at http://pss.sagepub.com/content/by/supplemental-data

REFERENCES

Anderson, D.R., & Pempek, T.A. (2005). Television and very young children. *American Behavioral Scientist, 48*, 505–522.

Barr, R., & Hayne, H. (1999). Developmental changes in imitation from television during infancy. *Child Development, 70*, 1067–1081.

Benedict, H. (1979). Early lexical development: Comprehension and production. *Journal of Child Language, 6*, 183–200.

DeLoache, J.S. (2004). Becoming symbol-minded. *Trends in Cognitive Sciences, 8*, 66–70.

DeLoache, J.S., & Chiong, C. (2009). Babies and baby media. *American Behavioral Scientist, 52*, 1115–1135.

Goldfield, B.A., & Reznick, J.S. (1990). Early lexical acquisition: Rate, content, and the vocabulary spurt. *Journal of Child Language, 17*, 171–184.

Hayne, H., Herbert, J., & Simcock, G. (2003). Imitation from television by 24- and 30-month-olds. *Developmental Science, 6*, 254–261.

Krcmar, M., Grela, B., & Lin, K. (2007). Can toddlers learn vocabulary from television? An experimental approach. *Media Psychology, 10*, 41–63.

Kuhl, P.K., Tsao, F.M., & Liu, H.M. (2003). Foreign-language experience in infancy: Effects of short-term exposure and social interaction on phonetic learning. *Proceedings of the National Academy of Sciences, USA, 100*, 9096–9101.

McCall, R.B., Parke, R.D., & Kavanaugh, R.D. (1977). Imitation of live and televised models by children one to three years of age. *Monographs of the Society for Research in Child Development, 42*(5, Serial No. 173).

Rideout, V. (2007). *Parents, children, and media*. Menlo Park, CA: Henry J. Kaiser Family Foundation.

Rideout, V.J., Vandewater, E.A., & Wartella, E.A. (2003). *Zero to six: Electronic media in the lives of infants, toddlers and preschoolers*. Menlo Park, CA: Henry J. Kaiser Family Foundation.

Robb, M., Richert, R., & Wartella, E. (2009). Just a talking book? Word learning from watching baby videos. *British Journal of Developmental Psychology, 27*, 27–45.

Schmidt, M.E., Rich, M., Rifas-Shiman, S.L., Oken, E., & Taveras, E.M. (2009). Television viewing in infancy and child cognition at 3 years of age in a US cohort. *Pediatrics, 123*, 370–375.

Troseth, G.L. (2003a). Getting a clear picture: Young children's understanding of a televised image. *Developmental Science*, 6, 247–253.

Troseth, G.L. (2003b). TV guide: 2-year-olds learn to use video as a source of information. *Developmental Psychology*, 39, 140–150.

Troseth, G.L., & DeLoache, J.S. (1998). The medium can obscure the message: Young children's understanding of video. *Child Development*, 69, 950–965.

Troseth, G.L., Pierroutsakos, S.L., & DeLoache, J.S. (2004). From the innocent to the intelligent eye: The early development of pictorial competence. In R.V. Kail (Ed.), *Advances in child development and behavior, Volume 32* (pp. 1–35). New York, NY: Academic Press.

Zimmerman, F.J., Christakis, D.A., & Meltzoff, A. (2007). Television and DVD/video viewing in children younger than 2 years. *Archives of Pediatric & Adolescent Medicine*, 69, 473–479.

REVIEW AND CONTEMPLATE

1. What is the "word spurt" that typically happens during a child's development? When does it happen, and how might it lead parents to incorrectly conclude that children learn a great deal from baby videos?

2. Briefly describe the research design used by DeLoache et al. (2010), including the four conditions in the experiment and what knowledge they measured as the outcome. Also describe the results (which condition produced the most learning?).

3. DeLoache et al. (2010) also asked parents to estimate how much their child had learned from the videos used in their study. How well did the parents' estimates match what their child actually learned? Which parents gave the highest estimates of how much their child had learned?

4. Assume that you are at a party with some friends and one of your female friends who is the mother of an 18-month-old daughter tells you that she highly recommends a new educational video designed to increase the vocabulary of children. She explains that her daughter has shown a substantial increase in the number of words that she knows after watching this new video for the past month. You want to share with your friend what you have learned about (a) the effects of such videos on children's learning and (b) what else might explain her daughter's sudden increase in vocabulary. What would you tell her?

4.2 "Separating Fact From Fiction in the Etiology and Treatment of Autism: A Scientific Review of the Evidence"

AUTISM IS CONSIDERED a pervasive developmental disorder that impacts most areas of functioning in children, including their language ability, cognitive functioning, and social skills. The sharp increase in the number of children diagnosed with autism in the past two decades has led to media reports about baffling outbreaks or a full-blown epidemic of autism. However, in an article published in the journal *Current Directions in Psychological Science,* Gernsbacher, Dawson, and Goldsmith (2005) explained that the increase in diagnosed cases of autism is most likely due to changes in the criteria for diagnosing autism, increased public awareness of the disorder, and increased reporting of autism by schools due to changes in federal reporting requirements. Thus, there is no mysterious autism epidemic.

The increased number of children diagnosed with autism, and the fact that scientists have yet to pinpoint the exact causes of autism, make it a prime target for pseudoscience. As Gernsbacher, Dawson, and Goldsmith (2005) noted, "false epidemics solicit false causes." For example, one popular pseudoscientific theory is that childhood vaccinations are responsible for the autism "epidemic." As you can imagine, such a theory might scare parents into avoiding vaccinations for their children, increasing the risk that their children will be exposed to a variety of preventable diseases, some of which are deadly. The following reading is an excerpt from a scientific article by Herbert, Sharp, and Gaudiano that focuses on pseudoscientific theories of the causes of autism. Their discussion of treatments of autism was excluded in order to reduce the length of the article, but interested readers should consult the original article for this discussion.

Reference

Herbert, J. D., Sharp, I. R., & Gaudiano, B. A. (2002). Separating fact from fiction in the etiology and treatment of autism: A scientific review of the evidence. *The Scientific Review of Mental Health Practice, 1,* 23–43.

ARTICLE 4.2

"SEPARATING FACT FROM FICTION IN THE ETIOLOGY AND TREATMENT OF AUTISM: A SCIENTIFIC REVIEW OF THE EVIDENCE"

JAMES HERBERT, IAN SHARP, AND BRANDON GAUDINO

Autistic-spectrum disorders are among the most enigmatic forms of developmental disability. Although the cause of autism is largely unknown, recent advances point to the importance of genetic factors and early environmental insults, and several promising behavioral, educational, and psychopharmacologic interventions have been developed. Nevertheless, several factors render autism especially vulnerable to pseudoscientific theories of etiology and to intervention approaches with grossly exaggerated claims of effectiveness. Despite scientific data to the contrary, popular theories of etiology focus on maternal rejection, Candida infections, and childhood vaccinations. Likewise, a variety of popular treatments are promoted as producing dramatic results, despite scientific evidence suggesting that they are of little benefit and in some cases may actually be harmful. Even the most promising treatments for autism rest on an insufficient research base, and are sometimes inappropriately and irresponsibly promoted as "cures." We argue for the importance of healthy skepticism in considering etiological theories and treatments for autism.

Autism is a pervasive developmental disorder marked by profound deficits in social, language, and cognitive abilities. Prevalence rates range from 7 to 13 cases per 10,000 (Bryson, 1997; Bryson, Clark, & Smith, 1988; Steffenberg & Gillberg, 1986; Sugiyama & Abe, 1989). It is not clear if the actual prevalence of autism is increasing, or if the increased frequency of diagnosis has resulted from wider recognition of the disorder and especially recognition of the full range of pervasive developmental disorders, often referred to as "autistic-spectrum disorders."[1] Either way, autism is no longer considered

---

[1] We use the term "autism" throughout this paper to refer not only to classic autistic disorder (American Psychiatric Association, 1994), but in some cases to the full range of autistic-spectrum disorders. The vast majority of the research reviewed in this paper does not distinguish among the various subtypes of autistic-spectrum disorders. It is therefore often impossible to judge the degree to which research findings are unique to autistic disorder per se, or are generalizable to other pervasive developmental disorders.

James D. Herbert, Ian R. Sharp, and Brandon A. Gaudino, "Separating Fact from Fiction in the Etiology and Treatment of Autism: A Scientific Review of the Evidence," *The Scientific Review of Mental Health Practice*, vol. 1, pp. 23-27. Copyright © 2002 by Center for Inquiry. Reprinted with permission.

rare, occurring more commonly than Down's syndrome, cystic fibrosis, and several childhood cancers (Fombonne, 1998; Gillberg, 1996).

The degree of impairment associated with autism varies widely, with approximately 75% of autistic individuals also meeting criteria for mental retardation (American Psychiatric Association [APA], 1994). Autism occurs three to four times more frequently in males than females (Bryson et al., 1988; Steffenberg, & Gillberg, 1986; Volkmar, Szatmari, & Sparrow, 1993). Although recent advances have been made with respect to possible causal factors (Rodier, 2000), the exact etiology of autism remains unknown. Moreover, although certain behavioral, educational, and pharmacological interventions have been demonstrated to be helpful for many individuals with autism, there is currently no cure for the disorder.

WHY AUTISM IS FERTILE GROUND FOR PSEUDOSCIENCE

Several factors render autism especially vulnerable to etiological ideas and intervention approaches that make bold claims, yet are inconsistent with established scientific theories and unsupported by research (Herbert & Sharp, 2001). Despite their absence of grounding in science, such theories and techniques are often passionately promoted by their advocates. The diagnosis of autism is typically made during the preschool years and, quite understandably, is often devastating news for parents and families. Unlike most other physical or mental disabilities that affect a limited sphere of functioning while leaving other areas intact, the effects of autism are pervasive, generally affecting most domains of functioning. Parents are typically highly motivated to attempt any promising treatment, rendering them vulnerable to promising "cures." The unremarkable physical appearance of autistic children may contribute to the proliferation of pseudoscientific treatments and theories of etiology. Autistic children typically appear entirely normal; in fact, many of these children are strikingly attractive. This is in stark contrast to most conditions associated with mental retardation (e.g., Down's syndrome), which are typically accompanied by facially dysmorphic features or other superficially evident abnormalities. The normal appearance of autistic children may lead parents, caretakers, and teachers to become convinced that there must be a completely "normal" or "intact" child lurking inside the normal exterior. In addition, as discussed above, autism comprises a heterogeneous spectrum of disorders, and the course can vary considerably among individuals. This fact makes it difficult to identify potentially effective treatments for two reasons. First, there is a great deal of variability in response to treatments. A given psychotropic medication, for example, may improve certain symptoms in one individual, while actually exacerbating those same symptoms in another. Second, as with all other developmental problems and psychopathology, persons with autism sometimes show apparently spontaneous developmental gains or symptom improvement in a particular area for unidentified reasons. If any intervention has recently been implemented, such improvement can be erroneously attributed to the treatment, even when the treatment is actually ineffective. In sum, autism's pervasive impact on development and functioning, heterogeneity with respect to course and treatment response, and current lack of curative treatments render the disorder fertile ground for quackery.

A number of contemporary treatments for autism can be characterized as pseudoscientific. Most scientists agree that there are no hard-and-fast criteria that distinguish science from pseudoscience; the differences are in degree, rather than kind (Bunge, 1994; Herbert et al., 2000; Lilienfeld, 1998). Although a detailed treatment of pseudoscience in mental health is beyond the scope of this paper, a brief discussion of the features that distinguish it from legitimate science is important in order to provide a context for considering currently popular etiological theories and treatments for autism. In general, pseudoscience is characterized by claims presented as being scientifically verified even though in reality they lack empirical support (Shermer, 1997). Pseudoscientific treatments tend to be associated with exaggerated claims of effectiveness that are well outside the range of established procedures. They are often based on implausible theories that cannot be proven false. They tend to rely on anecdotal evidence and testimonials, rather than controlled studies, for support. When quantitative data are considered, they are considered selectively. That is, confirmatory results are highlighted, whereas unsupportive results are either dismissed or ignored. They tend to be promoted through proprietary publications or Internet Web sites rather than refereed scientific journals. Finally, pseudoscientific treatments are often associated with individuals or organizations with a direct and substantial financial stake in the treatments. The more of these features that characterize a given theory or technique, the more scientifically suspect is becomes.

A number of popular etiological theories and treatment approaches to autism are characterized by many of the features of pseudoscience described above (Green, 1996a; Green, 2001; Herbert & Sharp, 2001; Smith, 1996). Still other treatments, although grounded on a sound theoretical basis and supported by some research, are nonetheless subject to exaggerated claims of efficacy. What follows is a review of the most popular dubious theories and questionable intervention approaches for autism. We also review promising etiologic theories and treatments. Some intervention programs are designed specifically for young children, whereas others are applied across a wider age range.

THE ETIOLOGY OF AUTISM: SEPARATING FACT FROM FICTION

Psychoanalytic Explanations

Although modern theories of autism posit the strong influence of biological factors in the etiology of the disorder, psychoanalytic theories have abounded traditionally. Kanner (1946) was the first to describe the parents of children with autism as interpersonally distant. For example, he concluded that the autistic children he observed were "kept neatly in refrigerators which did not defrost" (Kanner, 1973, p. 61). However, Kanner also stressed that the disorder had a considerable biological component that produced disturbances in the formation of normal emotional context. It was Bruno Bettelheim who was perhaps the most influential theorist promoting psychoanlytic interpretations of autism. Bettelheim rose to prominence as director of the University of Chicago's Orthogenic School for disturbed children from 1944 to 1978. He rejected Kanner's conclusions positing a biological role in the etiology in autism and was convinced that autism was caused by "refrigerator" mothers. According to Bettelheim, autistic symptoms are viewed as defensive reactions against cold and detached mothers. These unloving mothers were sometimes assumed to be harboring "murderous impulses" toward their children. For example, in his book *The Empty Fortress*, Bettelheim (1967) wrote that one autistic girl's obsession with the weather could be explained by dissecting the word to form "we/eat/her," indicating that she was convinced that her mother, and later others, would "devour her." Based on his conceptualization of autism, Bettelheim promoted a policy of "parentectomy" that entailed separation of children from their parents for extended periods of time (Gardner, 2000). Other psychoanalytic therapists such as Mahler (1968) and Tustin (1981) promoted similar theories positing problems in the mother-child relationship as causing autism (see Rosner, 1996, for a review of psychoanalytic theories of autism).

After his suicide in 1990, stories began to emerge that tarnished Bettelheim's reputation (Darnton, 1990). Several individuals claimed abuse at the hands of the famous doctor when they were at the Orthogenic School. Furthermore, information emerged that Bettelheim often lied about his background and training. For example, although he frequently claimed to have studied under Freud in Vienna, Bettelheim possessed no formal training in psychoanalysis whatsoever, and instead held a degree in philosophy. Also, Bettelheim claimed that 85% of his patients at the Orthogenic School were cured after treatment; however, most of the children were not autistic and the case reports he presented in his books were often fabrications (Pollak, 1997). Despite the continued acceptance of Bettelheim's theories in some circles, no controlled research has been produced to support the refrigerator mother theory of autism. For example, Allen, DeMeyer, Norton, Pontus, and Yang (1971) did not find differences between parents of autistic and mentally retarded children and matched comparison children on personality measures. Despite the complete absence of controlled evidence, even today some psychoanalytic theorists continue in the tradition of Bettelheim by highlighting the putative role of early mother-child attachment dysfunctions in causing autism (Rosner, 1996).

Candida Infection

Candida albicans is a yeastlike fungus found naturally in humans that aids in the destruction of dangerous bacteria. Candidiasis is an infection caused by an overgrowth of Candida in the body. Women often contract yeast infections during their childbearing years. In addition, antibiotic medication can disrupt the natural balance among microorganisms in the body, resulting in an overgrowth of Candida (Adams & Conn, 1997). In the 1980s, anecdotal reports began to emerge suggesting that some children with candidiasis later developed symptoms of autism. Supporters of this theory point to animal studies in which Candida was shown to produce toxins that disrupted the immune system, leading to the possibility of brain damage (Rimland, 1988). Furthermore, Rimland speculated that perhaps 5 to 10% of autistic children could show improved functioning if treated for Candida infection. Proponents often recommend that Nystatin, a medication used to treat women with yeast infections, be given to children whose mothers had candidiasis during pregnancy, whether or not the children show signs of infection. However, there is no evidence that mothers of autistic children have a higher incidence of candidiasis than mothers in the general population and only uncontrolled case reports are presented as evidence for the etiological role of Candida infection in autism (Siegel, 1996).

Adams and Conn (1997) presented the case study of a 3-year-old autistic boy who reportedly showed improved functioning following a vitamin treatment for Candida infection. However, the boy was never medically diagnosed with candidiasis and was only reported to meet criteria based on questionnaire data. In addition, reports of the child's functioning were mostly based on parental report (especially concerning functioning prior to the course of vitamin treatment) and not on standardized assessment instruments. Although interesting, such presentations provide no probative data on the possible role of candidiasis in causing autism. Without reliable and valid evidence to the contrary, case reports cannot rule out a host of confounding variables, including any natural remission or change in symptoms due to developmental maturation or even merely to the passage of time. It is important to remember that many people, especially women, contract Candida infections at different points in their lives, sometimes without even knowing that they are infected because the symptoms are so mild (Siegel, 1996). However, there is no evidence that even severe candidiasis in humans can produce brain damage that leads to the profound deficits in functioning found in autism.

MMR Vaccination

There has recently been much public concern that the mumps, measles, and rubella (MMR) vaccine is causing an increased incidence of autism. As evidence of the link between the MMR vaccine and autism, proponents point to the fact that reported cases of autism have increased dramatically over the past two decades, which appear to coincide with the widespread use of the MMR vaccine starting in 1979. In fact, Dales, Hammer, and Smith (2001) found in their analyses of California Department of Developmental Services records that the number of autistic disorder caseloads increase approximately 572% from 1980 to 1994. Indicating a similar trend in Europe, Kaye, Melero-Montes, and Jick (2001) reported that the yearly incidence of children diagnosed with autism increased sevenfold from 1988 to 1999 in the United Kingdom. Fears that the MMR vaccine may be responsible for this rise in the increasing incidence of autism have been picked up in the media and some parents have decided to decline vaccinations for their children in an effort to protect them from developing autism (Manning, 1999).

Rimland (2000) saw "medical overexuberance" as producing a tradeoff in which vaccinations protect children against acute diseases while simultaneously increasing their susceptibility to more chronic disorders, including autism, asthma, arthritis, allergies, learning disabilities, Crohn's disease, and attention deficit hyperactivity disorder. Pointing out that the average number of vaccines school-age children receive is now at 33, Rimland blamed the "vaccine industry" for making products that have not been properly tested before their widespread usage. He concluded by stating that research on this problem should be of the "highest priority."

In fact, it was preliminary research findings that initially raised the possibility that the MMR vaccine might be related to the apparent increase in the incidence of autism. The British researcher Andrew Wakefield and colleagues (1998) reported 12 case studies of children who were diagnosed with particular forms of intestinal abnormalities (e.g., ileal-lymphoid-nodular hyperplasia). Eight out of the 12 children demonstrated behavioral disorders diagnosed as representing autism, which reportedly occurred after MMR vaccination. The authors concluded that "the uniformity of the intestinal pathological changes and the fact that previous studies have found intestinal dysfunction in children with autistic-spectrum disorders, suggests that the connection is real and reflects a unique disease process" (p. 639). However, Wakefield et al. made it clear in their report that they did not prove an actual causal connection between the MMR vaccine and autism.

Although the Wakefield et al. (1998) case reports suggested that the MMR vaccine may be associated with autism, recent epidemiological research has provided strong evidence against any such connection. Kaye et al. (2001) conducted a time trend analysis on data taken from the UK general practice research database. As discussed earlier, they found that the yearly incidence of diagnosed autism increased dramatically over the last decade (0.3 per 10,000 persons in 1988 to 2.1 per 10,000 persons in 1999). However, the prevalence of MMR vaccination among children remained virtually constant during the analyzed time period (97% of the sample). If the MMR vaccine were the major cause of the increased reported incidence of autism, then the risk of being diagnosed with autism would be expected to stop rising shortly after the vaccine was instated at its current usage. However, this was clearly not the case in the Kaye study, and therefore no time correlation existed between MMR vaccination and the incidence of autism in each birth order cohort from 1988 to 1993.

In an analogue study in the United States, Dales et al. (2001) found the same results when using California Department of Developmental Services autism caseload data from the period 1980 to 1994. Once again, the time trend analysis did not show a significant correlation between MMR vaccine usage and the number of autism cases. Although MMR vaccine usage remained fairly constant over the observed period, there was a steady increase of autism caseloads over the time studied. It is important to note that the increased incidence of autism found in these two studies most likely reflects an increased awareness of autism-spectrum disorders by professionals and the public in general, along with changes in diagnostic criteria, rather than a true increase in the incidence of the disorder (Kaye et al., 2001). Most recently, the U.S. government's Institute of Medicine, in a comprehensive report cosponsored by the National Institutes of Health and the Centers for Disease Control and Prevention, recently concluded that there exists no good evidence linking the MMR vaccine and autism (Stratton, Gable, Shetty, & McCormick, 2001).

The MMR hypothesis reveals several important lessons for the student of autism. First, parents and professionals alike can easily misinterpret events that co-occur temporally as being causally related. The fact that the MMR vaccine is routinely given at around the same age that autism is first diagnosed reinforces the appearance of a link between the two. Second, the MMR-autism link reveals nicely the self-correcting nature of science. Like many hypotheses in science, the MMR-autism hypothesis, although reasonable when initially proposed, turned out to be incorrect or at best incomplete. Third, the issue illustrates the persistence of incorrect ideas concerning the etiology and treatment of autism even in the face of convincing evidence to the contrary. For example, Rimland (2000) purported to warn the public of the dangers of child vaccinations because of their link to autism and begins his article with the decree: "First, do no harm." However, recent research indicates that the MMR vaccine cannot be responsible for the sharp increases in diagnosed autism, and the real harm is the public health concern raised by encouraging parents to avoid vaccinating their children from serious diseases that can easily be prevented.

Current Scientific Findings

Research has implicated genetic factors, in utero insults, brain abnormalities, neurochemical imbalances, and immunological dysfunctions as contributing to autism. Siblings of individuals with autism have about a 3% chance of having the disorder, which is 50 times greater than the risk in the general population. In monozygotic twins, if one twin has autism, the second has a 36% chance of being diagnosed with the disorder and an 82% chance of developing some autistic symptoms (Trottier, Srivastava, & Walker, 1999). Although not definitive, the higher concordance rates in monozygotic twins relative to fraternal siblings suggests a genetic contribution to the etiology of autism. Nevertheless, the lack of 100% concordance for monozygotic twins suggests that the disorder probably develops as the result of combined effects of genetic and environmental factors.

Genetic disorders that have been identified as producing an increased risk of developing autism or pervasive developmental disorders include tuberous sclerosis, phenylketonuria, neurofibromatosis, fragile X syndrome, and Rett syndrome (Folstein, 1999; Trottier et al., 1999). Recent findings have also implicated a variation of the gene labeled HOXA1 on chromosome 7 as doubling the risk of autism, although this is only one of the many possible genes linked to the disorder (Rodier, 2000). Nevertheless, although some gene variants may increase the risk of developing autism, other variants may act to decrease the risk, explaining the large variability in the expression of autism.

Rubella infection of the mother during pregnancy and birth defects resulting from ethanol, valproic acid, and thalidomide exposure are also known in utero risk factors (Rodier, 2000). However, these factors can only explain the development of autism in a small subset of individuals. Regarding time for increased vulnerability, evidence from individuals exposed to thalidomide now points to the conclusion that the in utero insults that increase the risk of the autism probably occur quite early, within the first trimester of gestation (Stromland, Nordin, Miller, Akerstrom, & Gillberg, 1994). Other research that has compared individuals with autism with those without the disorder found differences in brain wave activity, brain (e.g., cerebellar) structures, and neurotransmitter levels (Trottier et al., 1999).

Scientific evidence supports the conclusion that autism is a behavioral manifestation of various brain abnormalities that likely develop as the result of a combination of genetic predispositions and early environmental (probably in utero) insults. Although recent scientific discoveries provide important clues to the development of the disorder, the etiology of autism is complex and the specific causes are still largely unknown.

Summary of Etiologic Theories and Research

There is currently no empirical support for theories that implicate unloving mothers, yeast infections, or childhood vaccinations as the cause of autism. The evidence invoked in support of these claims involves uncontrolled case studies and anecdotal reports. The confusion about the causes of autism appears to stem largely from illusory temporal correlations between the diagnosis of the disorder and normal events occurring in early childhood. No research has demonstrated a differential risk for autism due to maternal personality characteristics, the presence of candidiasis, or the use of the MMR vaccine. Scientific evidence points to genetic predispositions and various early environmental insults to the developing fetus as responsible for the development of the disorder.

REFERENCES

Adams, L., & Conn, S. (1997). Nutrition and its relationship to autism. *Focus on Autism & Other Developmental Disabilities, 12*, 53–58.

Allen, J., DeMeyer, M. K., Norton, J. A., Pontus, W., & Yang, E. (1971). Intellectuality in parents of psychotic, subnormal, and normal children. *Journal of Autism & Childhood Schizophrenia, 3*, 311–326.

American Psychiatric Association (1994). *Diagnostic and statistical manual of mental disorders* (4th ed.). Washington, DC: Author.

Bettelheim, B. (1967). *The empty fortress*. New York: Free Press.

Bettison, S. (1996). The long-term effects of auditory training on children with autism. *Journal of Autism & Developmental Disorders, 26*, 361–374.

Bryson, S. (1997). Epidemiology of autism: Overview and issues outstanding. In D. J. Cohen & F. R. Volkmar (Eds.), *Handbook of autism and pervasive developmental disorders* (2nd ed., pp. 41–46). New York: Wiley.

Bryson, S. E., Clark, B. S., & Smith, I. M. (1988). First report of a Canadian epidemiological study of autistic syndromes. *Journal of Child Psychology and Psychiatry, 29*, 433-445.

Bunge, M. (1984). What is pseudoscience? *Skeptical Inquirer, 9*, 36-46.

Dales, L., Hammer, S. J., & Smith, N. J. (2001). Time trends in autism and in MMR immunization coverage in California. *Journal of the American Medical Association, 285*, 1183-1185.

Darnton, N. (1990, September 10). Beno Brutalheim? *Newsweek, 111*(11), 59-60.

Folstein, S. E. (1999). Autism. *International Review of Psychiatry, 11*, 269-278.

Fombonne, E. (1998). Epidemiology of autism and related conditions. In F. R. Volkmar (Ed.), *Autism and pervasive developmental disorders* (pp. 32-63). New York: Cambridge University Press.

Gardner, M. (2000). The brutality of Dr. Bettelheim. *Skeptical Inquirer, 24*(6), 12-14.

Gardner, M. (2001). Facilitated communication: A cruel farce. *Skeptical Inquirer, 25*, 17-19.

Gillberg, C. (1996). The psychopharmacology of autism and related disorders. *Journal of Psychopharmacology, 10*, 54-63.

Green, D. (2001). Autism and "voodoo science" treatments. *Priorities for Health, 13*(1), 27-32, 69.

Green, G. (1996a). Evaluating claims about treatments for autism. In C. Maurice, G. Green, & S. C. Luce (Eds.), *Behavioral intervention for young children with autism: A manual for parents and professionals* (pp. 15-28). Austin, TX: PRO-ED.

Herbert, J. D. Lilienfeld, S. O., Lohr, J. M., Montgomery, R. W., O'Donohue, W. T., Rosen, R. M., & Tolin, D. F. (2000). Science and pseudoscience in the development of eye movement desensitization and reprocessing: Implications for clinical psychology. *Clinical Psychology Review, 20*, 945-971.

Herbert, J. D., & Sharp, I. R. (2001). Pseudoscientific treatments for autism. *Priorities for Health, 13*(1), 23-26, 59.

Kanner, L. (1946). Autistic disturbances of affective contact. *American Journal of Psychiatry, 103*, 242-246.

Kanner, L. (1973). *Childhood psychosis: Initial studies and new insights.* Washington, DC: V. H. Winston & Sons.

Kaye, J. A., Melero-Montes, M., & Jick, H. (2001). Mumps, measles, and rubella vaccine and the incidence of autism recorded by general practitioners: A time trend analysis. *British Medical Journal, 322*, 460-463.

Lilienfeld, S. O. (1998). Pseudoscience is contemporary clinical psychology: What it is and what we can do about it. *The Clinical Psychologist, 51*, 3-9.

Mahler, M. (1968). *On human symbiosis and the vicissitudes of individuation.* New York: International Universities Press.

Manning, A. (1999, August 16). Vaccine-autism link feared. *USA Today.*

Pollak, R. (1997). *Creation of Dr. Bettelheim: A biography of Brauo Bettelheim.* New York: Simon & Schuster.

Rimland, B. (1988). Candida-caused autism? *Autism Research Review International Newsletter.* Retrieved December 6, 2001, from http://www.autism.com/ari/editorials/candida.html.

Rimland, B. (2000, April 26). Do children's shots invite autism? *Los Angeles Times.* Retrieved from http://www.latimes.com/archives.

Rodier, P. M. (2000). The early origins of autism. *Scientific American, 282,* 56–63.

Roser, K. (1996). A review of psychoanalytic theory and treatment of childhood autism. *Psychoanalytic Review, 83,* 325–341.

Siegel, B. (1996). *The world of the autistic child: Understanding and treating autistic spectrum disorders.* New York: Oxford University Press.

Shermer, M. (1997). *Why people believe weird things: Pseudoscience, superstition, and other confusions of our time.* New York: W. H. Freeman.

Smith, T. (1996). Are other treatments effective? In C. Maurice, G. Green, & S. C. Luce (Eds.), *Behavioral intervention for young children with autism: A manual for parents and professionals* (pp. 45–59). Austin, TX: PRO-ED.

Steffenburg, S., & Gillberg, C. (1986). Autism and autistic-like conditions in Swedish rural and urban areas: A population study. *British Journal of Psychiatry, 149,* 81–87.

Stratton, K., Gable, A., Shetty, P., & McCormick, M. (Eds.) (2001). *Immunization safety review: Measles-mumps-rubella vaccine and autism.* Washington, DC: National Academy Press.

Stromland, K., Nordin, V., Miller, M., Akerstrom, B., & Gillberg, C. (1994). Autism in thalidomide embryopathy: A population study. *Developmental Medicine and Child Neurology, 36,* 351–356.

Sugiyama, T., & Abe, T. (1989). The prevalence of autism in Nagoya, Japan: A total population study. *Journal of Autism & Developmental Disorders, 19,* 87–96.

Trottier, G., Srivastava, L., & Walker, C. D. (1999). Etiology of infantile autism: A review of recent advancements in genetic and neurobiological research. *Journal of Psychiatry & Neuroscience, 24,* 103–115.

Tustin, F. (1981). *Autistic states in children.* Boston: Routledge.

Volkmar, F. R., Szatmari, P., & Sparrow, S. S. (1993). Sex differences in pervasive developmental disorders. *Journal of Autism & Developmental Disorders, 23,* 579–591.

Wakefield, A. J., Murch, S. H., Anthony, A., Linnell, J., Casson, D. M., Malik, M., Berelowitz, M., Dhillon, A. P., Thomson, M. A., Haivey, P, Valentine, A., Davies, S. E., & Walker-Smith, J. A. (1998). Ileal-lymphoid-nodalar hyperplasia, non-specific colitis, and pervasive developmental disorder in children. *Lancet, 351,* 637–641.

REVIEW AND CONTEMPLATE

1. Describe two reasons autism is fertile ground for pseudoscience.

2. According to the psychoanalytic perspective, what is the main cause of autism? What does the scientific evidence suggest about this theory?

3. Briefly describe the "candida infection" theory of autism and why the theory is problematic.

4. Explain why the timing of the MMR vaccination might lead parents to believe that it causes autism. Briefly describe the evidence against this belief.

4.3 "The Myth of the Mozart Effect"

PERHAPS YOU HAVE seen all of the music recordings and videos that contain classical music and are marketed to parents as a tool to improve their young child's intelligence. For example, Volume 1 of *The Mozart Effect: Music for Babies* is sold with the following claim:

> *"Studies show that classical music has a powerful effect on the intellectual and creative development of children from the very youngest of ages. This volume aids memory development, enhances auditory and emotional awareness, stimulates rhythmic movement and induces relaxation and sleep."*

Can listening to classical music really have such a pervasive, powerful effect on a child's development?

The "Mozart Effect" represents both an excellent example of pseudoscience and an important lesson in the central role of replication in science. It started with a research study that found a positive effect of music (i.e., a Mozart sonata) on the spatial-reasoning ability of a small group of college students. From there, a full-fledged pseudoscientific industry has developed around a much broader "Mozart Effect," and one can buy books and music that supposedly utilize this effect to improve the intelligence of children, unlock one's creative spirit, and heal one's body. In this article, Will Dowd discusses the scientific evidence related to the Mozart Effect and explains why the evidence is not compelling. You may recall that I briefly mentioned in Chapter 1 that an important part of the scientific process is for scientists to replicate the results of studies conducted by other scientists. In this article, you will learn how the Mozart Effect does not pass this important standard for scientific evidence.

Reference

Dowd, W. (2008). The myth of the Mozart Effect. *Skeptic, 13*(4), 21–23.

ARTICLE 4.3

"THE MYTH OF THE MOZART EFFECT"
WILL DOWD

Whenever stalled on an intractable problem, Einstein reportedly reached for his violin. He played to disentangle his brain and clarify the question at hand. Mozart especially did the trick. Einstein loved Mozart's highly organized, intensely patterned sonatas. He felt, as many before him, that music and the reasoning intellect were linked. Music and his scientific work, he said, were "born of the same source."

It was with this same belief that Dr. Gordon Shaw, a University of California (Irvine) psychologist, corralled 36 undergraduates for a research experiment in February 1993. The students were given three spatial-reasoning tasks from the Stanford-Binet intelligence tests. Before each task, they listened to ten minutes of either silence, a relaxation tape, or Mozart's Sonata for Two Pianos in D Major. According to a paper published later that year in *Nature*, listening to Mozart boosted the students' IQ by an average of eight to nine points. The improvement, researchers said, lasted between ten and fifteen minutes. The results were widely reported as evidence of what the press dubbed "the Mozart Effect." The *International Herald Tribune*, for example, proclaimed "Mozart's Notes Make Good Brain Food."

Don Campbell, a classical musician and former music critic, was the first to recognize the research's commercial potential. Campbell expanded the definition of the Mozart Effect to include all music's influence on intelligence, health, emotions, and creativity. In 1996, he trade-marked it. Today, the Mozart Effect™ boasts the lateral spread typical of any successful brand. Campbell has authored 18 books, a series of spoken tapes, and 16 albums incorporating Mozart's music. The small commercial empire includes the recently published *Mozart Effect for Children*, which explains, in a chapter entitled "Twinkle Twinkle,

Will Dowd, "The Myth of the Mozart Effect," *Skeptic Magazine*, vol. 13, no. 4, pp. 21-23. Copyright © 2008 by Skeptic Magazine. Reprinted with permission.

Little Neuron," that Mozart's music enhances the network of connections forming in the infant brain. His recordings, one of which features *Don Giovanni* for the developing fetus, have sold over two million copies.

Since the U.C. Irvine study, the Mozart Effect has become fixed in the public consciousness. Zell Miller, while governor of Georgia, earmarked $105,000 of the state's annual budget to supply every newborn with a cassette or CD of classical music. "No one doubts that listening to music, especially at a very early age, affects the spatial-temporal reasoning that underlies math, engineering and chess," he explained to the Georgia legislature. In Florida, a bill was passed requiring all state-funded education and child-care programs to give a daily dose of classical music to children under five years old. Recently, the coach of the New York Jets, Eric Mangini, began playing classical music to help his football players concentrate at training camp study sessions. It remains to be seen whether Mozart's melodies will affect this season's record.

WHAT THE SCIENCE REALLY SAYS

While the Mozart Effect flourishes commercially, the U.C. Irvine study that launched the phenomenon has been widely criticized. The startling results announced by the initial paper were misleading. First, the researchers claimed that the undergraduates improved on all three spatial-reasoning tests. But, as Shaw later clarified, the only enhancement came from one task—paper folding and cutting. Further, the researchers presented the data in the form of Stanford-Binet IQ scores; yet the study only measured spatial-reasoning, one-third of a complete IQ test. To arrive at the full scores, the students' partial results were inflated by a factor of three.

The methodology of the study has also come under fire. According to some critics, the test group of 36 psychology undergraduates may not have been large or varied enough to produce credible results. Even Don Campbell has criticized the experiment's lack of controls. In the endnotes to his 1997 bestseller, *The Mozart Effect,* Campbell observes that the U.C. Irvine researchers "did not administer listening tests before testing, as many researchers in the field recommend. Nor did they examine how posture, food intake, or the time of day modified their listening." Naturally, Campbell believes that had these controls been in place, the Mozart Effect would have been more dramatically evident.

Many scientists have proposed alternative explanations for the study's results. Who's to say that Mozart's sonata caused the difference in scores? Maybe listening to an annoying relaxation tape or ten minutes of dead silence impaired the students' performance. Or perhaps the students experienced a change in mood and arousal rather than a fluctuation in intelligence. One study found that listening to a Stephen King short story had a comparable effect on spatial-reasoning scores, but only for those who enjoyed what they heard. Is it possible that Mozart's sonata had simply stimulated or uplifted the subjects in the U.C. Irvine study? After all, Shaw selected that particular sonata not just for its organized, cerebral quality, but because it is "riveting" and "never boring."

But the most damaging blow to the Mozart Effect has been the failure of other researchers to reproduce the Irvine results. Psychologist Kenneth Steele and his colleagues replicated the experiment in 1999 and found no trace of the Mozart Effect. "A requiem may therefore be in order," Steele wrote in *Nature*. Dr. Frances Rauscher, co-author of the Irvine study, countered that the Mozart Effect cannot be found under all laboratory conditions. "Because some people cannot get bread to rise," she wrote, "does not negate the existence of a 'yeast effect.'"

But that same year, a Harvard psychologist analyzed 16 studies on the Mozart Effect, including the original experiment and concluded that any cognitive enhancement was small and within the average variation of a single person's IQ-test performance. In 2007, the German Ministry of Education and Research conducted a similar meta-analysis. Their findings were unambiguous: passively listening to any kind of music, whether by Mozart or Madonna, does not increase intelligence.

The German report did, however, propose a link between musical training and IQ development. According to recent studies, the motor and auditory skills developed for musical performance may have a long-term influence on intelligence. In fact, brain mapping has revealed that professional musicians have more grey matter in their right auditory cortex than nonmusicians, as if practicing an instrument flexed a muscle in the brain. It seems increasingly likely that the long-term practice of playing music, rather than merely listening, can have the kind of impact suggested by the Mozart Effect. Einstein, after all, organized his mind by playing the violin, not listening to a recording.

Ironically, the U.C. Irvine researchers had initially planned to test whether music training for young children would increase higher brain function. When Shaw, a particle physicist, developed an interest in neuroscience later in his career, U.C. Irvine gave him the freedom to research what he wanted. But, according to his book *Keeping Mozart in Mind*, he had to make do with "extremely limited resources." So Shaw scaled down his ambition. He thought, "if music training might yield a long-term enhancement of spatial-temporal reasoning, then perhaps even listening to music might produce a short-term enhancement!" Fourteen years and dozens of studies later, it is clear this analogy was off the mark.

MAGIC MOZART

What can explain the Mozart Effect's persistent hold on the public consciousness despite the lack of solid scientific evidence? No art-lover expects to absorb a better memory by staring at a Renaissance painting. No reader hopes to pluck IQ points from a classic novel. So why are Mozart Effect™ products snatched up by the millions?

Perhaps it's unsurprising that Mozart, a historical figure enveloped in myths, should be at the center of yet another. According to the most recent spate of biographies, the real Mozart was an incessant reviser addicted to his work. Yet the details of the Mozart legend—his astonishing prowess as a child prodigy, his immaculate first drafts—have bolstered the popular belief that the composer was a fine-tuned antenna picking up snatches of celestial song. Einstein didn't help matters. He described Mozart's music as "so pure that it seemed to have been ever-present in the universe, waiting to be discovered by the master."

The creators of the Mozart Effect have eagerly traded on the composer's lingering mystique. Campbell traces the source of Mozart's talent to his time in the womb: his father's violin playing "almost certainly enhanced his neurological development and awakened the cosmic rhythms in utero." Shaw also portrays Mozart as supernaturally gifted. *Keeping Mozart in Mind* is packaged with a CD of the Sonata for Two Pianos in D Major. "Before you read further," Shaw writes in the Preface, "I suggest that you slip the CD out of the book, make yourself comfortable, and listen to the magic genius of Wolfgang Amadeus Mozart." To Shaw, Mozart is not a musical genius; he's a magic genius whose music rains down brief moments of enhanced brainpower.

But Mozart is not the only magic genius. The transformation of a dubious psychology study into a multi-million dollar industry also has a touch of the miraculous. In *The Mozart Effect*, Don Campbell summarizes Shaw and Rauscher's conclusions—the scientific backbone of his brand—when he writes: "Listening to music, they concluded, acts as 'an exercise' for facilitating symmetry operations associated with higher brain function. In plain English, it can improve your concentration, enhance your ability to make intuitive leaps, and, not incidentally, shave a few strokes off your golf game!"

Campbell's translation of the U.C. Irvine study into "plain English" is inaccurate and insincere—an abracadabra that replaces questionable research with fantasy. The Mozart Effect™ has carried on long after the initial study has been discarded because it was never about science to begin with. If the Mozart Effect teaches us anything, it's that the results of a flawed study are always at risk of becoming a common expression, a copyrighted product, a popular belief infused with a magic that is difficult to dispel.

REVIEW AND CONTEMPLATE

1. What is the Mozart Effect?

2. Describe the design and results of the initial study by Gordon Shaw in 1993 that sparked interest in the Mozart Effect.

3. What does Dowd (2008) say is the "most damaging blow to the Mozart Effect?"

4. Explain how the Mozart Effect is an example of pseudoscience. Which of the six characteristics of pseudoscience discussed in Chapter 1 seem most closely related to the story of the Mozart Effect?

Chapter 5

SENSATION AND PERCEPTION

5.1 "What's That I Smell? The Claims of Aromatherapy"

AROMATHERAPY IS DEFINED by the National Association for Holistic Aromatherapy as "the art and science of utilizing naturally extracted aromatic essences from plants to balance, harmonize and promote the health of body, mind and spirit." They claim that aromatherapy has "proven, therapeutic benefits for a variety of conditions," including depression, poor memory, fear, wounds, motion sickness, asthma, varicose veins, wrinkles, and sprains.

Psychologists have long known that odors influence our memories and emotions. For example, pleasant odors, such as those of chocolate chip cookies or cinnamon rolls, may evoke pleasant memories and emotions. Some research even suggests that the presence of pleasant odors can boost the likelihood that people will help others in need of a favor. However, the claims of aromatherapists go well beyond the documented effects of odors. For example, an aromatherapist might claim that chamomile is good for insomnia or that jasmine promotes sexual arousal.

As mentioned in the previous paragraph, the National Association for Holistic Aromatherapy lists a wide variety of serious ailments that supposedly benefit from aromatherapy. In this article, McCutcheon discusses the problems with such claims. Although this article was published in 1996, it accurately characterizes the pseudoscientific status of aromatherapy today. In a more recent article published in the journal *Maturitas,* Myeong Soo Lee, Jiae Choi, Paul Posadzki, and Ezard Ernst (2012) examined over 200 publications on the effects of aromatherapy on conditions such as depression, hypertension, anxiety, pain, and dementia. They concluded that "the evidence is not sufficiently convincing that aromatherapy is an effective therapy for any condition."

Chapter 1 pointed out that normal cognitive and social processes—such as the difficulties people have with methodological reasoning—may lead to pseudoscientific beliefs. One aspect of methodological reasoning that is relevant to this article is the need to consider how confounding variables—that is, variables other than aromatherapy that were present at the same time as the therapy—may explain changes in a person's health following a treatment. For example, if a person put a few drops of an aromatic oil into a warm bath in order to relieve stress, was it the aromatic oil or the warm bath that produced the decrease in stress? In this situation, the warm bath is confounded with the aromatherapy, and we cannot determine what caused the improvement. McCutcheon refers to this problem as "confused causation."

Reference

McCutcheon, L. (1996, May/June). What's that I smell? The claims of aromatherapy. *Skeptical Inquirer, 20,* 35–37.

ARTICLE 5.1

"WHAT'S THAT I SMELL? THE CLAIMS OF AROMATHERAPY"
LYNN McCUTCHEON

A small dose of aromatic oil may make for a pleasant experience, but the claims of aromatherapy go way beyond that.

Aromatherapy typically involves putting a few drops of some pleasant-smelling, plant-derived oil in your bath water, sniffing it from an inhaler, or massaging it directly into your skin. I sampled a number of these "essential oils," as they are called, and I was impressed with their unique aromas. So what's the problem with smelling something fragrant while you are bathing or while you are getting massaged? According to John Meisenheimer, who practices dermatology in Orlando, Florida, a tiny percentage of the population is allergic to some essential oils. But for the rest of us, the answer is, "nothing." A small dose of aromatic oil probably won't hurt you a bit, and if you enjoy the smell, that's fine!

The problem lies with the claims made by aromatherapy's most widely known practitioners—claims that are causally confused, ambiguous, dubious, and unsupported by scientific evidence. After reading several books and articles written by the enthusiastic supporters of aromatherapy, I believe that there are some recurrent themes that are worth a closer look.

One such theme is what I call "confused causation." Virtually all aromatherapists claim that if you relax for several minutes in warm bath water to which has been added a few drops of essential oil, you will get out of the tub feeling pleasant. I agree, but what causes the pleasantness? Is it the warmth, the water, the minutes spent resting, the few drops of oil, or some combination thereof? It would be easy to conduct an experiment in order to find out, but for some strange reason aromatherapists haven't seen fit to do this. Instead, they imply that the essential oil is the main cause. Says Meisenheimer: "The amount of essential oil from a few drops placed in your bath that might actually penetrate the stratum corneum [skin] is probably too small to have any meaningful, systemic, physiologic effect."

Other examples of confused causation permeate aromatherapists' writings. Hoffmann (1987, p. 94) claims that chamomile is good for insomnia *if* taken in a late bath. Is it the lateness or the chamomile that makes you sleepy? For stress, Lavabre (1990, p. 108) recommends relaxation, a better diet, nutritional supplements, more exercise, and a few drops of an oil blend. Heinerman informs us (1988, p. 197) that jasmine oil massaged into the abdomen and groin promotes sexual stimulation. I'll bet it does, with or without the jasmine. On page 301 he suggests that to make unsafe water safe, boil it and add rosemary, sage, or thyme before drinking. The heat probably kills most of

Lynn McCutcheon, "What's That I Smell? The Claims of Aromatherapy," *Skeptical Inquirer*, vol. 20, pp. 35-37. Copyright © 1996 by Center for Inquiry. Reprinted with permission.

the germs. Edwards (1994, p. 135) mentions that many patients in hospitals in England receive massages with essential oils. According to her, "the relaxing and uplifting effect of the oils helps boost the morale of the patients." Isn't it possible that the massage did as much to boost morale as the oils did?

One of the favorite tactics employed by aromatherapists is the use of ambiguous claims. Any good psychic can tell you that you *never* make a specific prediction. You always leave yourself enough room so that whatever the outcome, you can claim success. Judging from what I read, the aromatherapists have mastered this strategy. Here are some of my favorites, followed by my brief commentary.

According to Frawley (1992, p. 155), incense "cleanses the air of negative energies." What are negative energies? The reader is encouraged to get massaged with oil regularly (p. 155) because this "keeps the nerves in balance." How would we know an unbalanced nerve if we saw one? Hoffmann tells us (p. 95) that ylang ylang is "supposedly an aphrodisiac." Is it or or isn't it? Lavabre declares (p. 114) that benzoin resinoid will "drive our evil spirits." I'd love to see that. Presumably spruce oil is an even better essence because it is recommended (p. 64) "for any type of psychic work." Why limit yourself to evil spirits? Edwards (p. 134) quotes Visant Lad as saying that "life energy enters the body through breath taken through the nose." Is life energy the same thing as oxygen, and if so, why can't it enter through the mouth? About tea tree oil, Edwards opines (p. 135), "There is hope [it] may play a role in the successful treatment of AIDS." Is it hope or is it evidence? On the same page she tells readers that aromatherapy is good for "restoring harmony and balance between the mind and body." Such a phrase can mean almost anything you wish.

Not all of the claims are hopelessly ambiguous or unlikely to be true. I did a computer search of the psychological literature back to 1967, using the terms *essential oils, aromatherapy,* and the names of 23 common essences. I found that chamomile (Roberts and Williams 1992) can put people in a better mood, and lavender sometimes causes mistakes in arithmetic (Ludvigson and Rottman 1989). Furthermore, several of the odors used by aromatherapists are capable of producing physiological arousal as measured by electroencephalogram (EEG) recordings (Klemm et al. 1992); and emotional changes, as measured by self-report (Kikuchi et al. 1992; Nakano et al. 1992). Peppermint odor appears to be capable of causing very small EEG, electromyogram (EMG), and heart rare changes during sleep (Badia et al. 1990); and some odors can modify artificially induced sleep time in mice (Tsuchiya et al. 1991). There is evidence that specific odors can better enable one to recall information that was learned in the presence of that odor (Smith et al. 1992).

As a whole, these findings stretched to the limit would support only small craft, sailing cautiously near the shores of the aromatic sea. Unfortunately, some aromatherapists have been more than willing to sail boldly into uncharted waters. Consider these claims about specific essential oils, with my comments.

"A few drops of jasmine (Tisserand 1988, p. 87) cures postnatal depression." I didn't find any olfactory research that mentions postnatal depression. "Marjoram oil (Tisserand, p. 37) turns off sexual desire." The few studies I found that mentioned marjoram had nothing to do with sex. Price (1991, p. 93) tells us that juniper berry is "relaxing" and "stimulating" (both?), and she (p. 48) and Valner (1982, p. 87) recommend lavender for insomnia. The Klemm study showed that lavender was both arousing and unpleasant. Hoffmann (p. 94) claims that patchouli is good for anxiety. My computer search of the word *patchouli* turned up nothing. Valnet (p. 70) claims that ylang ylang is good for one's sex drive. *Ylang ylang* didn't turn up anything either.

Other claims of dubious validity are common to the writings of aromatherapists—broad claims that are related to the practice of aromatherapy in general. The following claims are my words, but they represent a synthesis of views expressed by the authors listed.

- *Smell is the most direct route to the brain.* (Avery 1992; Edwards 1994; Green 1992; Raphael 1994). The implication is that smell is superior to the other senses because olfactory information gets to the brain quickest, and since aromatherapy is concerned with smell, it is a superior method of treatment. Olfactory information gets to the brain very quickly, but so does auditory, tactile, and visual information. The differences would certainly be measured in milliseconds, and it would have no practical consequence. The olfactory sense is directly linked to the limbic system—a portion of the brain concerned with emotionality and memories. The aromatherapists make much of this—the smell of ginger evokes memories of grandma's cookies, etc. What they don't tell you is that the sight of grandma's photo or hearing her voice can do the same. All the senses are part of a massive network that links all parts of the brain. Smell enjoys no particular advantage when it comes to access to or speed of access to various parts of the brain.

- *Natural oils are better than synthetic ones.* (Avery 1992; Edwards 1994; Hillyer 1994; Lavabre 1999; Price 1991; Raphael 1994; Rose 1988). Most of these authors felt it unnecessary to explain such a statement, but Lavabre told readers that "natural" molecules work better because they have memory (p. 49). It is possible to make a synthetic preparation identical on a molecular level to the most important compound in an essential oil. John Renner, who has heard many of the bizarre claims made by aromatherapists, told me that if the molecules are the same, "I doubt seriously that your body could tell the difference." Given that essential oils contain several compounds, it seems possible that a natural oil might have more than one active agent. If that is so, then aromatherapists should be spearheading the research effort to determine which chemical compounds are inducing the changes they claim are taking place. Instead, most of them seem all too willing to assume that natural oils are better, and that there is no need to defend this assertion with any rationale or research evidence.

- *Essential oils can help your memory.* (Hoffmann 1987; Lavabre 1990; Price 1991; Valnet 1982). I found no evidence to support this, and none of these authors provided a hint about how they arrived at that conclusion. Psychologist Elizabeth

Loftus, a world-renowned human memory expert, told me in a personal communication that she knows "of no cogent scientific evidence that smells cure amnesia, or that they strengthen memory." There is such a phenomenon as context-dependent learning. It has been shown that it is easier to remember X when you can return to the environment or context in which you learned X. Presumably, the context provides cues that make it easier to recall X. It has further been shown that at least one essential oil can serve as a contextual cue (Smith et al. 1992). If this is the basis for the above-mentioned claim, it is highly misleading. The essence itself is not important, only the fact that it was a significant part of the context in which the original learning took place. In other words, if the essence wasn't present when you learned X, then it won't help you recall it later.

- *Scientists are doing a lot of research on essential oils.* (Avery 1992; Price 1991; Rose 1988; Valner 1982). Statements like this are usually followed by specific claims. The implication is that these claims are supported by scientific research. As we saw earlier, that isn't necessarily true. Whether or not scientists really *are* doing a lot of research on essential oils is debatable. By comparison with 50 years ago, there is probably more research on essential oils today. By comparison with hearing and vision, research on the consequences of smelling essential oils lags way behind. If there really is a lot of research on the effects of essential oils, why is it that these authors are so reluctant to cite it? Their books and articles rarely list or mention any scientific journal articles. Instead, if there are any references at all they are to books written by other aromatherapists.

All of this sounds as though I am strongly opposed to the use of essential oils. I'm not! If it pleases you to put some in your bath water or have a little rubbed on your back once in a while, by all means, go ahead. It is not the odor that arises from these fragrances that is troubling, it is the stench arising from the unwarranted claims made about them.

REFERENCES

Avery, A. 1992. *Aromatherapy and You.* Kailua, HI: Blue Heron Hill Press.

Badia, P., et al. 1990. Responsiveness to olfactory stimuli presented in sleep. *Physiology and Behavior* 48: 87–90.

Edwards, L. 1994. Aromatherapy and essential oils. *Healthy and Natural Journal.* October, pp. 134–137.

Frawley, D. 1992. Herbs and the mind. In *American Herbalism; Essays on Herbs and Herbalism,* ed. by M. Tierra. Freedom, Calif.: Crossing Press.

Green, M. 1992. Simpler scents: The combined use of herbs and essential oils. In *American Herbalism: Essays on Herbs and Herbalism,* ed. by M. Tierra. Freedom, Calif.: Crossing Press.

Heinerman, J. 1988. *Heinerman's Encyclopedia of Fruits, Vegetables, and Herbs,* West Nyack, N.Y.: Parker Publishing.

Hillyer, P. 1994. "Making $cents with Aromatherapy." *Whole Foods,* February, pp. 26–35.

Hoffmann, D. 1987. Aromatherapy. In *The Herbal Handbook.* Rochester, Vt.: Healing Arts Press.

Kikuchi, A., et al. 1992. Effects of odors on cardiac response patterns and subjective states in a reaction time task. *Psychological Folia* 51: 74–82.

Klemm, W. R. et al. 1992. Topographical EEG maps of human response to odors. *Chemical Senses* 17: 347–361.

Lavabre, M. 1990. *Aromatherapy Workbook.* Rochester, Vt.: Healing Arts Press.

Ludvigson, H., and T. Rottman. 1989. Effects of ambient odors of lavender and cloves on cognition, memory, affect and mood. *Chemical Sense* 14: 525-536.

Nakano, Y., et al. 1992. A study of fragrance impressions, evaluation and categorization. *Psychologica Folia* 51: 83-90.

Price, S. 1991. *Aromatherapy for Common Ailments.* New York: Simon and Schuster.

Raphael, A. 1994. "Ahh! Aromatherapy." *Delicious,* December pp. 47-48.

Roberts, A., and J. Williams, 1992. The effect of olfactory stimulation on fluency, vividness of imagery and associated mood: A preliminary study. *British Journal of Medical Psychology* 65: 197-199.

Rose, J. 1988. Healing scents from herbs: Aromatherapy. In *Herbal Handbook.* Escondido, Calif.: Bernard Jensen Enterprises.

Smith, D. G., et al. 1992. Verbal memory elicited by ambient odor. *Perceptual and Motor Skills* 74: 339-343.

Tisserand, M. 1988. *Aromatherapy for Women.* Rochester, Vt.: Healing Arts Press.

Tsuchiya, T., et al. 1991. Effects of olfactory stimulation on the sleep time induced by pentobarbital administration in mice. *Brain Research Bulletin* 26: 397-401.

Valnet, J. 1982. *The Practice of Aromatherapy.* London: C. W. Daniel.

REVIEW AND CONTEMPLATE

1. Explain and give two examples of the problem of "confused causation" with respect to claims made for the effects of aromatherapy.

2. Give three examples of how aromatherapists make ambiguous claims about aromatherapy, making it difficult to determine if the claims are accurate.

3. If there is some scientific evidence that odors can influence our mood and memory, why would aromatherapy be considered a pseudoscience?

4. Explain how odors might improve memory recall through context-dependent learning. How is this different from aromatherapists' claim that "essential oils can help your memory"?

5.2 "The Subtle Power of Hidden Messages"

SUBLIMINAL MESSAGES ARE those that are so faint or fast that people are unaware that they have been exposed to them. The public's fear over the potential power of subliminal messages to influence our behavior was prompted by a report by James Vicary in the late 1950s. Vicary claimed that he used subliminal messages to persuade people to buy more popcorn and Coke while they were watching a movie. The subliminal messages were the words "Eat popcorn" and "Drink Coke," which were flashed on the movie screen so fast that moviegoers could not detect the words. Today marketers sell subliminal messages for a variety of purposes, including self-improvement. You can purchase subliminal audio recordings designed to help you lose weight, improve your self-esteem, quit smoking or drinking, restore sexual urges, and improve your memory.

This selection by Wolfgang Stroebe examines research on the effects that subliminal messages have (and do not have) on our behavior and decisions. This article nicely illustrates the difference between scientific and pseudoscientific approaches to evaluating the effects of subliminal messages. A pseudoscientist might simply point to the testimonials of satisfied users of subliminal audio recordings; for example, people who use subliminal audio designed to improve their memory might report memory improvements after listening to the audio recordings. One problem with this evidence is that people's reports of memory improvement might be due more to their expectation that the recordings would work than to an actual effect of the subliminal messages. Stroebe also describes research that suggests that, under specific circumstances, subliminal messages can influence our decisions.

Reference

Stroebe, W. (2012). The subtle power of hidden messages. *Scientific American Mind, 23*(2), 46–51.

"THE SUBTLE POWER OF HIDDEN MESSAGES"
WOLFGANG STROEBE

Can subliminal advertisements influence our behavior?

New research says yes—but only under certain circumstances

The birth of subliminal advertising reads almost like a script from a television show. In this real-life story, the spotlight falls on James M. Vicary, an independent marketing researcher.

On September 12, 1957, Vicary called a press conference to announce the results of an unusual experiment. Over the course of six weeks during the preceding summer, he had arranged to have slogans—specifically, "Eat popcorn" and "Drink Coca-Cola"—flashed for three milliseconds, every five seconds, onto a movie screen in Fort Lee, N.J., while patrons watched *Picnic*. Vicary argued that these messages were too fast for filmgoers to read but salient enough for the audience to register their meaning subconsciously. As proof, he presented data indicating that the messages had increased soda sales at the theater by 18 percent and popcorn sales by 58 percent.

The public reacted with fury. Vicary's findings played directly into a popular fear at the time that Madison Avenue could manipulate consumers like mindless puppets. The idea that ads might be broadcast subliminally, below the threshold of conscious awareness, seemed akin to brainwashing. On October 5, 1957, some three weeks after Vicary's event, Norman Cousins, editor in chief of the *Saturday Review*, wrote an article called "Smudging the Subconscious," in which he lambasted ad campaigns designed to "break into the deepest and most private parts of the human mind and leave all sorts of scratch marks." The Central Intelligence Agency soon issued a report on the operational potential of subliminal perception. Vance Packard's book *The Hidden Persuaders*—which described Vicary's claims in detail—became an overnight best seller. As public pressure mounted in response, the U.K., Australia and the National Association of Broadcasters in America all banned subliminal advertising sight unseen.

There was a glitch, however. Researchers tried to replicate Vicary's findings during this time, but none succeeded. After five years Vicary confessed that his so-called experiment was "a gimmick." His admission garnered far less attention than his initial publicity stunt. Many in the U.S. and Europe continued to believe that subliminal advertising could shape consumer choice despite all the evidence to the contrary.

Recently, though, psychologists have begun to discover that subliminal messages can sometimes redirect our decisions, but not at all in the way Vicary had proposed. Subliminal

Wolfgang Stroebe, "The Subtle Power of Hidden Messages," *Scientific American Mind*, vol. 23, no. 2, pp. 46-51. Copyright © 2012 by Springer Nature America, Inc. Reprinted with permission.

messaging cannot override our intentions or commandeer our will. On the contrary, it seems that we are susceptible to these extremely brief suggestions only under special, somewhat limited circumstances. Because these subconscious hints streak through our memory almost as fleetingly as they flash on a screen, they hold no power unless they happen to relate to our immediate goals or natural proclivities.

BACKLASH AND GNIKSAMKCAB

In the decades after Vicary's experiment, marketers, politicians, film directors and even law-enforcement agencies tried to harness the powers of subliminal persuasion without measurable success. Their intimation tactics typically followed Vicary's lead, embedding millisecond flashes of words or images in other film clips. For example, in 1978 a Wichita, Kan., TV station received permission from the police to show a glimpse of the sentence "Now call the chief" during a report on the "BTK" serial killer, hoping he might then feel compelled to turn himself in. Unfortunately, the man they were after, Dennis Rader, eluded capture until 2005.

In 2000 subliminal messaging entered the U.S. presidential race. One Republican campaign spot spliced the word "rats" into a segment about Democratic candidate Al Gore. Although "rats" was part of a clearly visible line, "bureaucrats decide," the less than flattering four letters appeared on screen 30 milliseconds before the rest. Republican candidate George W. Bush claimed it was an accident, but television affiliates quickly pulled the commercial from the airwaves.

Other controversial campaigns have involved "backmasking," or backward masking—a technique in which audio engineers record spoken words backward onto a track. Proponents claimed that the reversed messages acted subliminally on listeners. In the 1980s religious groups in the U.S. feared that some rock bands used backmasking to convey satanic teachings. Two sets of parents sued British musician Ozzy Osbourne, claiming that backmasked phrases in his songs had prompted their children to commit suicide. The courts dismissed these cases—as they did similar suits brought against rock band Judas

FAST FACTS Conscious Consumers

1. For decades the public has feared subliminal advertising, viewing it as akin to brainwashing. Scientists, however, view it as largely a myth.
2. Recent experiments demonstrate that subliminal messages flashed onto a screen or computer monitor can influence our decisions only if we are open to persuasion because of a particular need, such as thirst.
3. Despite our fear of being manipulated, our surroundings exert an unconscious influence on our decisions every day. For example, the smell of grilling meats can make us feel hungry, and the music in a supermarket can steer us toward certain purchases.

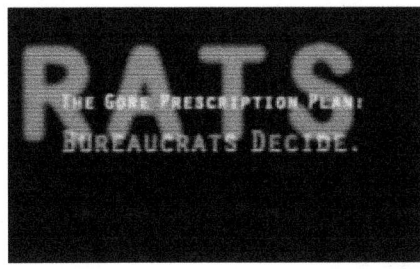 

GEORGE W. BUSH AND OZZY OSBOURNE: These men have both been accused of using hidden messages. Bush's 2000 presidential campaign ran ads against Al Gore that subliminally flashed the word "rats" (*left*). Parents unsuccessfully sued Osborne (*right*), claiming his music contained secret backmasked tracks that had driven their children to commit suicide.

Priest—because they found insufficient evidence that backmasking worked. Researchers repeatedly demonstrated that backmasking left no measurable traces in memory. Even so, the uproar led to public record burnings, and in 1983 California restricted the practice.

Also during the 1980s a flourishing trade arose around self-help cassette tapes that claimed to employ subliminally perceptible messages recorded in the correct direction. In 1991, though, Anthony G. Greenwald of the University of Washington and his colleagues proved that these recordings were also ineffective. Greenwald and his team gave 237 test subjects classical music cassettes that held subliminal tips to boost either self-confidence or memory. Unbeknownst to the study participants, who listened to the tapes daily for five weeks, half of the cassettes were deliberately mislabeled. The researchers found that the cassettes had no effect on self-confidence or memory. The participants, however, had a different experience: those who believed that their cassette would increase self-confidence perceived an improvement, as did listeners who expected supercharged memories.

For many scientists this experiment closed the books on subliminal messaging. In 1992 Anthony R. Pratkanis, a psychologist at the University of California, Santa Cruz, and one of the co-authors of the cassette study, wrote that belief in the efficacy of subliminal persuasion offered an example of what physicist Richard Feynman called a cargo-cult science, in reference to the phenomenon in which a tribal society encounters "cargo" from a technologically advanced culture and designs rituals around it. By Feynman's definition, given as part of a commencement speech at the California Institute of Technology in 1974, cargo-cult science appears to have all the trappings of real science—seeming objectivity and apparently careful experimentation—but is missing something fundamental: its practitioners lack skepticism. Throughout the 1990s subliminal messaging as a research field fell silent, relegated to the realm of reflexology, ESP and other dubious disciplines.

During the past decade, though, psychologists have taken a renewed interest in the topic, and their work has produced some intriguing results. In 2001 Ap Dijksterhuis of Radboud University Nijmegen in the Netherlands, then working with colleagues at the

University of Amsterdam, gave students a computerized attention test. Throughout the test he flashed either nonsense syllables or "cola" and "drink" on the screen. Afterward he asked the participants if they would like a cola or a mineral water. The subjects who watched the subliminal messages were more likely to ask for a drink. They did not, however, ask for cola more often. A year later Joel and Grant Cooper of Princeton University replicated the finding, planting subliminal suggestions—the word "thirsty" and images of cola cans—in an episode of The Simpsons. Again the people they subjected to the subliminal messages felt parched by comparison to those who watched unaltered shows.

DRINKING THE KOOL-AID

To understand why the subliminally cued participants in these studies felt thirstier but not necessarily more inclined to drink cola, consider what happens when you enter a convenience store in search of a drink. First you have to be able to retrieve from memory the name of a beverage. Chances are you will select whatever brand comes to mind fastest. If you drink Coca-Cola all the time, you are probably impervious to any subliminal suggestion to buy another brand. If, however, you sometimes drink Lipton iced tea, messaging that you experience below the threshold of consciousness might sway your choice, making that brand name at least temporarily more accessible in your memory.

We decided to test the theory that Coca-Cola as a brand name may be too deeply imprinted in most people's memories for subliminal stimuli to have any effect. Working with Jasper Claus at Utrecht University, John Karremans of Radboud and I conducted an initial study in 2006 in which we asked volunteers to perform a computerized attention task. We repeatedly bombarded half of our participants with 23-millisecond flashes of

WATCH THIS SPACE, BUY THIS BRAND: Recent studies suggest that subliminal messages can sometimes tip our decisions one way or another, but not at all in the way people have long feared. These fleeting messages have short-lived windows of influence.

the words "Lipton Ice," a brand of iced tea. Based on a questionnaire, we determined that Lipton Ice was well suited to our purposes: it is a good thirst quencher but not most people's first choice. The other half of our subjects saw 23-millisecond flashes of nonsense syllables. After the test, participants had to choose a beverage, either Lipton Ice or mineral water. As expected, the Lipton Ice group chose that brand far more often than the control group did. Again, as in the studies described above, only thirsty subjects reacted this way. Unless you are thirsty, it doesn't matter which drink brand is foremost in your mind.

In a second study, we used some pretense to give salt drops to half of our volunteers in the hopes of making them thirsty before we showed them the subliminal advertisement. In this scenario, more than 80 percent of the thirsty subjects—and about half of those who said they were not thirsty—chose Lipton Ice. Without subliminal messages, only 30 percent of the thirsty crew and 20 percent of our well-hydrated subjects took the iced tea. In 2011, working with our colleagues Thijs Verwijmeren and Daniël Wigboldus, Karremans and I refined these results and demonstrated that the subliminal priming worked only in thirsty test subjects who liked Lipton iced tea but did not drink it regularly. We could not influence people who said that Lipton iced tea was their favorite beverage. This finding might explain at least in part why earlier investigations, which typically involved Coca-Cola, failed to demonstrate a subliminal effect on brand choice. For decades Coke has been the favorite drink among university students, from whom researchers typically recruit their test subjects. Also, these studies did not take into account different levels of thirst.

Other researchers have observed a similar weakness to subliminal persuasion among tired, as opposed to thirsty, individuals. In 2009 Christina Bermeitinger of the University of Hildesheim in Germany, then working at Saarland University, with colleagues at the University of Western Australia, told the subjects that she and others planned to examine the effects of dextrose pills on concentration. They devised two fictitious brands of these pills and designed logos, each of which they presented subliminally to half of the participants while they played a computer game. During breaks the test subjects were offered dextrose pills labeled with the phony brand names. In the end, the more fatigued the participants said they were, the more they gravitated toward the brand they had seen flashed subliminally on the screen.

From these investigations it is clear that an individual's vulnerability to subliminal suggestion depends on a number of variables, including his or her physical needs and habits. A related effect, subliminal revulsion, also can be triggered under particular conditions. We showed this effect in a more recent study in which we subliminally projected the words "Lipton Ice" during two film clips: a funny sequence from the animated film *Madagascar* and a disturbing scene from a film about heroin addicts, *Trainspotting*. After the screening we offered participants Lipton Ice or mineral water. Compared with a control group, who were not subliminally primed, those who saw the brand embedded in

THIRSTY SUBCONSCIOUS: When test subjects viewed subliminal advertising for Lipton Ice, many more of them opted to drink this brand of tea instead of water. The effect was most pronounced among thirsty participants—their subconscious took notice of the subliminal hint.

Madagascar wanted more Lipton Ice. Those who watched *Trainspotting*, however, chose it less often. Once again, the subliminal messaging influenced only thirsty test subjects.

BRAINWASHING AT THE SUPERMARKET

The idea of subliminal advertising still terrifies many people. Research in the area remains somewhat taboo, and funding is scarce. *Programming the Nation*, a documentary film released in October 2011, sensationally asks, "Are we all brainwashed? Or have we lost our minds?" Such levels of fear simply are not justified. Certainly no one likes to feel manipulated, but the fact is that our surroundings color our choices all the time, without us consciously realizing it. The aroma of coffee escaping from a bakery can make us crave an espresso; the scent of grilled meat from a restaurant can set our stomach growling. Our research to date indicates that subliminal messages hold sway over our behavior in the same way as these environmental cues do. The thirsty test subject is more receptive to a subliminal hint about a drink just as the hungry shopper is more likely to overfill his or her cart at the supermarket.

To test the potency of everyday hidden persuaders, in 2005 Rob Holland and his colleagues at Radboud devised a clever experiment. The team asked 56 students to list five activities they hoped to undertake during the next few days. Half of the participants encountered the citrus smell of an all-purpose cleaner in the lab, whereas the other half worked in a scent-free room. The first group did not report noticing any odor. Even so, 36 percent of them wrote that they planned to clean their apartments. By comparison only 11 percent of the subjects who worked in the odor-free setting considered cleaning. Holland and his colleagues concluded that the citrus scent had increased the cognitive accessibility of the goal of cleaning. They did not find out how many of the would-be cleaners completed the task, however. Those good intentions may well have disappeared down the memory hole as soon as other, more urgent matters—such as studying for exams—came to the fore.

BRAINWASHING BACKGROUNDS:
Subliminal messages influence us in the same way environmental cues do: the smells from a cafe can make us feel hungry; a citrus scent can trigger thoughts about cleaning; even music can affect what we buy in a shop.

Indeed, such hints do not last long in our memory. Environmental triggers appear to be most potent in scenarios where we can act on them immediately, a fact that makes them useful in certain commercial settings. When department stores play Christmas music, it is meant to put us in a gift-giving mood and increase sales. In 1993 economists Charles Areni and David Kim of Texas Technical University revealed another way in which music can alter behavior. During several weeks at a wine store they played a variety of music, alternating between classical tracks, such as Antonio Vivaldi's "The Four Seasons," and popular tunes, including songs by Fleetwood Mac. They found that the musical selection had no bearing on the total number of bottles sold. Customers listening to classical selections, however, bought more expensive wine than did those listening to pop.

The spending habits of restaurant patrons appear to vary in response to musical cues as well. Adrian North, then at the University of Leicester in England, and his colleagues spent three weeks varying the music in a restaurant dining room from classical to pop to no music at all. When the background track was classical, guests spent an average of $45. By comparison they spent $40 when listening to pop songs and only $39 when there was no music at all.

In some cases, background music can even influence what types of products customers choose. In another experiment, North and his colleagues put a selection of four German or four French wines, equally priced, on display in a British supermarket. On some days the market played German brass band tracks, on others, French accordion music. When interviewed later, very few shoppers could say if they had heard any music. Those customers who heard French tunes, though, more frequently chose the French wines and vice versa.

We have every reason to believe that, just like the music in these examples, subliminal advertising could be used successfully in immediate, day-to-day situations. To have any genuine effect, however, subliminal slogans would have to be short, delivered near the time of a decision, and relate to a person's immediate intentions or habits. Given such constraints, it is unlikely that subliminal television ads could ever compel consumers days later to buy one brand or another on a weekly shopping trip.

Our work reveals that, in practice, subliminal messaging is far less potent or terrifying than it was first believed to be. It might even be put to good use. A handful of studies have shown that millisecond exposures to the words "angry" or "relax" can have definite, if short-lived, effects on a person's heart rate and blood pressure. Our subconscious registers many different kinds of suggestions, not just the ones advertisers may be aiming for.

Further Reading

- On the Psychology of Drinking: Being Thirsty and Perceptually Ready. Henk Aarts, Ap Dijksterhuis and Peter De Vries in *British Journal of Psychology,* Vol. 92, pages 631–642; 2001.

- Beyond Vicary's Fantasies: The Impact of Subliminal Priming and Brand Choice. Johan C. Karremans, Wolfgang Stroebe and Jasper Claus in *Journal of Experimental Social Psychology,* Vol. 42, No. 6, pages 792–798; November 2006.

- The Hidden Persuaders Break into the Tired Brain. Christina Bermeitinger, Ruben Goelz, Nadine Johr, Manfred Neumann, Ullrich K. H. Ecker and Robert Doerr in *Journal of Experimental Social Psychology,* Vol. 45, No. 2, pages 320–326; 2009.

- The Workings and Limits of Subliminal Advertising: The Role of Habits. Thijs Verwijmeren, Johan C. Karremans, Wolfgang Stroebe and Daniël H. J. Wigboldus in *Journal of Consumer Psychology,* Vol. 21, No. 2, pages 206–213; April 2011.

REVIEW AND CONTEMPLATE

1. Why, according to Stroebe (2012), is there reason to doubt the claim by James Vicary that subliminally flashing the words "Eat popcorn" and "Drink Coke" during a movie caused viewers to increase their consumption of popcorn and Coca-Cola?

2. Briefly describe the design and main results of the study published in 1991 by Anthony Greenwald and others. What did it suggest about the effects of subliminal audio recordings (i.e., can such recordings actually improve our memory or self-esteem)?

3. Stroebe (2012) described research that he conducted in which he found that people who were exposed to the visual subliminal message "Lipton Ice" were more likely to choose that product (instead of mineral water) compared to a control group that did not see the subliminal message. Why does Stroebe suggest that this approach would not work with a product like Coca-Cola? Also, what physical state do people have to be in for these subliminal messages to affect their choice of beverages?

4. Assume that the president of a large supermarket chain contacted you to ask your opinion about their plan to use subliminal messages to influence consumers' product choices in their stores. Specifically, they would like to include subliminal messages in the music they play while customers are shopping. Their goal is to get consumers to choose their "Private Selection" brand of peanut butter instead of Jif peanut butter by repeating the words "Private Selection peanut butter" over and over again in the background of the music at a volume so low that nobody will be consciously aware of hearing those words. Explain what you would tell the president about whether this approach would influence consumers' choices and, if so, which consumers are most likely to be influenced.

5.3 "Psychic Crime Detectives: A New Test for Measuring Their Successes and Failures"

IN MAY 2004, Charles Capel, a retired Miami University professor who had Alzheimer's disease, wandered away from his home in Oxford, Ohio. Despite extensive searches by police and volunteers, Capel was missing for months. In October, the police decided to hire self-proclaimed psychic detective Noreen Renier to assist in the search. Police sent Renier some of Capel's toothbrushes and shoes. From Virginia, Renier used visions she received from Capel's personal items to help her determine the location of Capel. According to Sgt. Jim Squance of the Oxford police, Renier said that Capel was approximately 8 miles from his house, and she mentioned seeing a stone, a wooded area, a creek, a fence, and a tower with an antenna on top of it. After the remains of Capel were found, news reports indicated that Renier's information was accurate and that she had helped the police find Capel's body. Sgt. Squance said, "When you see the results, you've got to be in awe."

Psychic crime detectives have been credited with helping police identify and locate criminals, find the bodies of murder victims, and fill in the missing details of a crime. Although television shows and news reporters sometimes make it appear as though psychics are amazingly accurate at such tasks, they typically do not test the psychics' abilities in a scientific manner.

We should not rely on after-the-fact reports of a psychic detective's apparent success to determine the psychic's accuracy. One problem with relying on these reports is that people have a tendency to make the psychic's statements fit the details of the crime after the fact, even if the psychic gave vague or inaccurate information. For example, near the location of Charles Capel's body was a subdivision named Stone Creek. This was interpreted as being consistent with Renier's statement about a "stone," but Renier did not say that Capel was near the Stone Creek subdivision. If you think about it, mentioning a "stone" is quite vague, and it could be considered consistent with a wide variety of scenarios. What if there had been a large stone near Capel's body, a stone in his shoe, or he had been hit with a stone; would we interpret these facts as being consistent with Renier's statement?

We also tend to remember information the psychic provided that was consistent with the facts and overlook information that was inconsistent. For example, Capel was found near a wooded area, but he was not 8 miles from his home; he was less than a mile away. How much of the information provided by Renier was inaccurate? It's difficult to answer this question without a full transcript of what Renier told the police.

Finally, we don't know whether Renier's statements were "accurate" simply by chance. Psychic detectives often say that bodies will be found near water or near wooded areas because killers typically hide bodies in such areas. Another interesting fact about the Capel case is that although the police credited Renier with helping them solve this case, the police did not find Capel's body. In fact, the police searched for 2 months after they received Renier's advice, and they still could not find Capel. His body was actually discovered by a hunter who saw the body while walking through the area.

If we cannot rely on anecdotal reports, such as the one involving Noreen Renier, to determine the accuracy of psychic detectives, how might we test these detectives in a more scientific manner? In this article, Wiseman et al. (1996) describe their efforts to test several psychic detectives' ability to determine the details of crimes after being given items related to those crimes. This classic study is a great example of the fact that scientific studies of psychic abilities do not support the claims of the "psychics."

Reference

Wiseman, R., West, D., & Stemman, R. (1996). Psychic crime detectives: A new test for measuring their successes and failures. *Skeptical Inquirer, 20,* 38–40, 58.

"PSYCHIC CRIME DETECTIVES: A NEW TEST FOR MEASURING THEIR SUCCESSES AND FAILURES"

RICHARD WISEMAN, DONALD WEST, AND ROY STEMMAN

A controlled test of 'psychic detectives,' using a novel method, found that they were no more accurate than college students. Yet the psychics all thought they had been successful.

Many psychics claim to be able to help the police solve serious crime. Recent surveys suggest that approximately 35 percent of urban United States police departments and 19 percent of rural departments (Sweat and Durm 1993) admit to having used a psychic at least once in their investigations. In addition, Lyons and Truzzi (1991) report the widespread use of psychic detectives in several other countries including Britain, Holland, Germany, and France.

Most of these psychics' claims are supported only by anecdotal evidence. This is unfortunate because it is often extremely difficult to rule out nonpsychic explanations. For example, Hoebens (1985) described how some psychics have made several (often conflicting) predictions relating to an unsolved crime. Once the crime was solved, the incorrect predictions were forgotten while the correct ones were exhibited as evidence of paranormal ability. Rowe (1993) cites examples of psychics making vague and ambiguous predictions that later were interpreted to fit the facts of the crime. Lyons and Truzzi (1991 noted that it is often difficult to obtain "baseline" information for many of these predictions. For example, a psychic may state that a murder weapon will be discovered "near, or in, a large body of water." Although this may later prove to be accurate, it is difficult to know how many criminals dump incriminating objects in areas that could be seen as "large bodies of water" (e.g., streams, lakes, rivers, the ocean, etc.) and therefore establish a statistical baseline for the prediction.

Some investigators have overcome these problems by carrying out controlled tests of psychic detection abilities. One of the earliest controlled studies was conducted by a Dutch police officer, Filippus Brink. Brink carried out a one-year study using four psychics. These psychics were shown various photographs and objects and asked to describe the crimes that had taken place. Some of the photographs and objects were connected with actual crimes; others were not. In a report to INTERPOL, Brink (1960) noted that the psychics had failed to provide any information that would have been of any use to an investigating officer. However, this report is brief and, as noted by Lyons and Truzzi (1991, p. 51): "Because Brink gives us few details of his method and analysis in this report, the strength, if not the value, of his conclusions cannot really be evaluated."

Richard Wiseman, Donald West, and Roy Stemman, "Psychic Crime Detectives: A New Test for Measuring Their Successes and Failures," *Skeptical Inquirer*, vol. 20, pp. 38-40, 58. Copyright © 1996 by Center for Inquiry. Reprinted with permission.

Studies have been carried out by Martin Reiser of the Los Angeles Police Department. An initial study by Reiser, Ludwig, Saxe, and Wagner (1979) involved twelve psychics. Each psychic was presented with several sealed envelopes containing physical evidence from four crimes (two solved, two unsolved). The psychics were asked to describe the crimes that had taken place. They were then allowed to open the envelopes and describe any additional impressions they received from the object. The study was double-blind, as neither the psychics nor the experimenters had any prior knowledge of the details of the crimes.

The psychics' statements were then coded into several categories (e.g., crime committed, victim, suspect, etc.) and compared with the information known about the crime. For each of the psychics' predictions that matched the actual information, they were awarded one point. The psychics' performances were less than impressive. For example, the experimenters knew that 21 key facts were true of the first crime. The psychics identified an average of only 4. Similarly, of the 33 known facts concerning the second crime, the psychics correctly identified an average of only 1.8. This data caused Reiser et al. to conclude: "The research data does not support the contention that psychics can provide significant additional information leading to the solution of major crime" (pp. 21–22).

Reiser and Klyver (1982) also carried out a follow-up study that used three groups of participants: psychic detectives, students, and police homicide detectives. Four crimes were used (two solved and two unsolved) and again physical evidence from each crime was presented to participants in sealed envelopes. Reiser and Klyver report that the data produced by the three groups was quite different in quantity and character. The psychic detectives produced descriptions that were, on average, six times the length of the student descriptions. In addition, the psychic detectives' statements sounded more confident and dramatic than those produced by either the students or the homicide detectives. Parts of the descriptions were separated into several categories (e.g., sex of criminal, age, height, etc.) and, if correct, assigned one point. A comparison between the three groups showed that although the psychics produced the greatest number of predictions, they were not any more accurate than either the students or the homicide detectives.

In August 1994 the authors of this article were contacted by a British television company involved in making a major documentary series on the paranormal (Arthur C. Clarke's "Mysterious Universe"). One of their programs was to be devoted to psychic detectives, and the producers were eager to film a well-controlled test of three British psychics. The company approached the authors and asked if we would design and carry out these tests. We agreed.

This was the first test of its type in Britain and one of only a handful carried out anywhere in the world. In addition, the methods used during previous studies have been the subject of some criticism (see Lyons and Truzzi 1991) so the authors thought it worthwhile to devise a new method for testing the claims of psychic detection.

This test compared the performance of two groups of participants: psychic detectives and a "control" group of college students. Two of the psychics were professional while the third (who will be referred to as "Psychic 1") was not, but had recently received a great deal of attention from the British media. The psychic's local police force (Herefordshire Police Force) described him as follows:

> When [psychic's name] comes to the police with his dreams, he is taken seriously and the information that he passes on to his established contact, Sgt. Richard Mac-Gregor, is acted upon immediately (*Psychic News*, November 26, 1994, p. 1)[1]

None of the students claimed to be psychic or had any special interest in criminology.

Each participant was shown three items that had been involved in one of three crimes: a bullet, a scarf, and a shoe. They were asked to handle each of the objects and speak aloud any ideas, images, or thoughts that might be related to these crimes. Participants were told that they were free to take as long as they wished and to say as little or as much as they thought necessary. During the test they were left alone in the room, but everything they said and did was filmed.

After they had finished commenting on all three objects, the participants were given three response sheets (one for each object), each containing 18 statements. Six of each of the 18 statements were true of each crime. The participants were then asked to mark the 6 statements that they believed were true about the crime in question.

Table 5.1 presents the individual scores for each of the six participants. None of the scores of any of the individuals was statistically significant or impressive.

TABLE 5.1: Individual/Group Means, Standard Deviations (in Brackets), Z-Scores, and P-Values.

	INDIVIDUAL SCORES (MIN = 0, MAX = 6)	GROUP SCORES (MIN = 0, MAX = 6)	Z-SCORE	P-VALUE (2 TAILED)
Psychic 1	2.3 (1.15)		.24	.8
Psychic 2	2.66 (0.57)	2.09 (0.68)	.73	.46
Psychic 3	1.33 (0.57)		.73	.46
Student 1	2(0.5)		0	1
Student 2	2(0.5)	2.33 (0.57)	0	1
Student 3	3(1.73)		1.21	.22

It could be argued that the above method of testing might *underestimate* participants' psychic ability. For example, a participant may have made several accurate comments describing the crime in question but, nevertheless, obtained a low score if this information was not included on the list of 18 statements. For this reason, a judge not involved in the test transcribed and separated all of the comments made by the participants as the participants handled the objects. The order of these statements was then randomized within each crime and presented to two additional judges. These judges were asked to read about each crime and rate the accuracy of each statement from 1 (very inaccurate) to 7 (very accurate). Table 5.2 contains the average of the two judges' ratings (inter-rater reliability = .77).

TABLE 5.2: Individual/Group Accuracy Means, Standard Deviations (in Brackets), and Number of Statements.

	ACCURACY RATING (MIN = 0, MAX = 7)	NUMBER OF STATEMENTS	GROUP SCORES (MIN = 0, MAX = 7)
Psychic 1	3.87 (2.57)	15	
Psychic 2	3.65 (1.83)	16	3.83 (0.17)
Psychic 3	4.00 (1.96)	8	
Student 1	6.37 (0.64)	8	
Student 2	4.14 (2.62)	7	5.63 (1.28)
Student 3	5.10 (2.13)	5	

Overall, the psychics made a total of 39 statements while the students made 20 statements. A paired *t*-test showed no significant differences for the accuracy ratings of students and psychics (t = 2.38, df = 4, p[2 tailed] = .074). This supports Reiser and Klyver's finding that even though psychics tend to make more predictions than students, they are no more accurate.

After their predictions had been recorded, the participants were told about the crimes associated with each of the target objects. This debriefing was filmed, and it is interesting to review the way in which the participants reacted to finding out the truth about each crime:

Crime 1. The Moat Farm murder, 1889–1903. In 1889 an army sergeant major named Samuel Herbert Dougal wished to have an affair with his maid but first needed to dispose of his wife. On May 16, 1889, he and his wife went out for a horse-and-trap ride into the town. During the trip Dougal shot his wife in the head and buried her in a ditch. The body remained buried for four years before the police eventually discovered it. The shoes worn by the corpse were identified by a cobbler as belonging to the dead woman, and Dougal was hung for the murder in 1903.

Crime 2. The murder of Constable Gutteride, 1927. In 1927 a police officer (Constable George William Gutteridge from the Essex Police Force) stopped a stolen car. The driver suddenly pulled out a gun and fired two shots—one into each of Constable Gutteridge's eyes. The car was later found abandoned in Brixton, London. A six-month-long investigation resulted in two men having been caught and hanged. An important part of the incriminating evidence was the bullet removed from the scene of the crime.

Crime 3. The killing of Margery Pattison, 1962. Margery Pattison, a 71-year-old widow, returned to her flat and disturbed her milkman who had entered through an unlocked door and had started to look for money. An argument ensued and the man grabbed the scarf around her neck, pulled it tight, and strangled her. The man was later caught and charged with murder.

All three psychics thought that they had been successful. On hearing that Crime 2 involved the killing of a police officer, Psychic 1 noted that one of his precognitive dreams involved Police Constable Keith Blakelock (who had been killed on duty in London a few years earlier). This participant noted that he thought at the time the dream was related to Blakelock's murder, but that he now believed it related to the killing of Constable Gutteridge. The same participant remarked that he felt he had given a successful description of Crime 1, as he had said it involved a woman having been raped and murdered and that "that is the fundamental theme of the crime." Psychic 1 failed to recall that he had also said the woman was murdered by a black man and that it happened on Tottenham Court Road. Both of these statements were incorrect. This lends support to the notion that some psychic detection may appear to work, in part, because inaccurate predictions may be forgotten about later, whereas successful ones are recalled and elaborated on.

Psychic 2 remarked that he believed that the experiment showed a "good conclusion all round" and that "my colleagues and I have put the jigsaw puzzle together." He emphasized that all three psychics believed that the scarf was involved in suffocation, had had trouble with Crime 2, but had predicted that the shoe-related crime involved some form of burial.

Psychic 3 also thought that there had been a consensus on the scarf and shoe. Remarking on the lack of information forthcoming on Crime 2, the psychic noted that "sometimes access to information is not appropriate at certain times." Despite this, he said that he was "relatively pleased with the outcome."

In short, this study provided no evidence to support the claims of psychic detection and, as such, the results are in accordance with other controlled studies. The study utilized a novel method of evaluating psychic detection. The way in which the participants responded to being told the true nature of the crimes gives some insight into some of the mechanisms that might cause individuals to believe erroneously that they are able to solve crimes by psychic means.

NOTES

This research was carried out with support from the Committee for the Scientific Investigation of Claims of the Paranormal.

The authors would like to thank Granite Television, London, Melvin Harris, and Sergeant Fred Feather for helping to set up our study described in this paper. Thanks also to Matthew Smith for helping to run the experiment, and Carol Hurst for carrying out the qualitative analysis of the data. Finally, our thanks to the psychics and students who kindly gave up their time to act as subjects. Correspondence regarding this article should be addressed to Richard Wiseman.

1. Richard Wiseman contacted Sgt. Richard MacGregor of the Herefordshire Police Force concerning this matter and received confirmation that the above statement was correct (personal communication, December 19, 1994).

REFERENCES

Brink, F. 1960. Parapsychology and criminal investigations. *International Criminal Police Reviews*, 134, 3–9.

Hoebens, P. H. 1985. Reflections on psychic sleuths. Edited by Marcello Truzzi in *A Skeptic's Handbook of Parapsychology*, ed. by P. Kurtz, part 6, pp. 631–643. Amherst, N.Y.: Prometheus Books.

Lyons, A. and M. Truzzi. 1991. *The Blue Sense*. New York: Warner Books.

Herts police admit to using psychic help. 1994. *Psychic News*, Nov. 26, 3259:1.

Reiser, M., L. Ludwig, S. Saxe, and C. Wagner. 1979. An evaluation of the use of psychics in the investigation of major crimes. *Journal of Police Science and Administration*, 7(1): 1825. (Reprinted in Nickel, J. [Ed.], *Psychic Sleuths*, Prometheus Books, Amherst, N.Y., 1994).

Reiser, M., and N. Klyver. 1982. A comparison of psychics, detectives, and students in the investigation of major crimes. In *Police Psychology: Collected Papers* by M. Reiser, Los Angeles, Calif.: Lehi.

Rowe, W. F. 1993. Psychic detectives: A critical examination. SKEPTICAL INQUIRER, 17(2): 159–165.

Sweat, J. A., and M. W. Durm. 1993. Psychics: Do police departments really use them? SKEPTICAL INQUIRER, 17(2): 148–158.

REVIEW AND CONTEMPLATE

1. Wiseman, West, and Stemman (1996) explained that most psychic detectives' claims are supported only by anecdotal evidence. Explain the problem with such evidence.

2. Briefly describe the design and results of the study conducted by Reiser and Klyver (1982).

3. Briefly describe the design and results of the study conducted by Wiseman, West, and Stemman (1996).

4. Explain how the psychics' comments—after they learned the true nature of the crimes—provide some insight into why individuals may believe incorrectly that they can solve crimes by psychic means.

Chapter 6

LEARNING AND MEMORY

6.1 "Do Visual, Auditory, and Kinesthetic Learners Need Visual, Auditory, and Kinesthetic Instruction?"

MY WIFE OFTEN tells me that she learns best by listening to an instructor's oral presentation, and she believes that I learn best by reading information. Would that make her an auditory learner and me a visual learner? The basic idea behind the notion of learning styles is that people have different styles or ways of learning and they learn best when information is provided to them in a manner that best suits their learning style. According to supporters of learning styles, visual learners learn best by seeing pictures, maps, illustrated textbooks, videos, or other visual media. Auditory learners, on the other hand, prefer to hear sound; thus, they may learn best by hearing a lecture or reading a book aloud.

To many people, the notion of learning styles sounds reasonable. In fact, if you search the Internet, you will find a variety of sites that help you assess your learning style and give advice on how to increase your ability to learn according to your style of learning. There are also companies that develop and sell learning-styles assessment tools for teachers to use in their classrooms. In this article, Daniel Willingham points out that although the notion of learning styles (or modality theory) has intuitive appeal, it doesn't fare well under scientific scrutiny. Willingham points out that teachers might believe in modality theory because they have been taught that it is true and because they notice and remember instances of student success that seem consistent with modality theory and overlook instances that are inconsistent with the theory (i.e., confirmation bias). This is a good example of the point made in Chapter 1: that people can develop beliefs in pseudoscientific phenomena due to common cognitive processes and biases.

Willingham's article provides a nice, brief overview of the research on learning styles. For readers who would like a more extensive review, an excellent article by Pashler, McDaniel, Rohrer, and Bjork was published in the journal *Psychological Science in the Public Interest* in 2008.

Reference

Willingham, D. T. (2005). Do visual, auditory, and kinesthetic learners need visual, auditory, and kinesthetic instruction? *American Educator, 29*(2), 31–35, 44.

"DO VISUAL, AUDITORY, AND KINESTHETIC LEARNERS NEED VISUAL, AUDITORY, AND KINESTHETIC INSTRUCTION?"

DANIEL WILLINGHAM

How does the mind work—and especially how does it learn? Teachers' instructional decisions are based on a mix of theories learned in teacher education, trial and error, craft knowledge, and gut instinct. Such gut knowledge often serves us well, but is there anything sturdier to rely on?

Cognitive science is an interdisciplinary field of researchers from psychology, neuroscience, linguistics, philosophy, computer science, and anthropology who seek to understand the mind. In this regular American Educator column, we consider findings from this field that are strong and clear enough to merit classroom application.

Question: What does cognitive science tell us about the existence of visual, auditory, and kinesthetic learners and the best way to teach them?

The idea that people may differ in their ability to learn new material depending on its modality—that is, whether the child hears it, sees it, or touches it—has been tested for over 100 years. And the idea that these differences might prove useful in the classroom has been around for at least 40 years.

What cognitive science has taught us is that *children do differ in their abilities with different modalities, but teaching the child in his best modality doesn't affect his educational achievement*. What does matter is whether the child is taught in the *content's* best modality. All students learn more when content drives the choice of modality. In this column, I will describe some of the research on matching modality strength to the modality of instruction. I will also address why the idea of tailoring instruction to a *student's* best modality is so enduring—despite substantial evidence that it is wrong.

* * *

Discussions of visual, auditory, and kinesthetic learners[1] are common in educational literature, teacher-preparation programs, and professional development workshops. The

---

1 The notion of kinesthetic learners is a big part of modality theory. However, this article will focus on the other two modalities because what's commonly considered a "kinesthetic learning experience" is almost always a misnomer. Kinesthetic information comes from the joints and muscles and tells the brain about the location of body parts. Kinesthetic learning

Daniel T. Willingham, "Do Visual, Auditory, and Kinesthetic Learners Need Visual, Auditory, and Kinesthetic Instruction?" *American Educator*, vol. 20, no. 2, pp. 31-35, 44. Copyright © 2005 by Daniel T. Willingham. Reprinted with permission.

theory that students learn more when content is presented in their best modality seems to make sense, seems to be supported by classroom experiences, and offers the hope of maximizing each child's learning by planning different lessons for each type of learner. For example, within one kindergarten class, the auditory learner could listen to stories about different holidays around the world, while the visual learner examined pictures of holiday celebrants, and the kinesthetic learner handled costumes and artifacts associated with the holidays. But is the theory correct? And, whether or not the theory is correct, might it not also be true that *all* of the kindergartners would learn the most about holidays by listening to stories, looking at pictures, *and* handling costumes?

Before we tackle the research on using modalities to enhance student learning, let's review a few things that cognitive scientists know about modalities.

1. Some memories are stored as visual and auditory representations—but most memories are stored in terms of meaning.

Cognitive psychologists have used formal laboratory tasks to investigate the role of modality in memory. An important finding from that research is that memory is usually stored independent of *any* modality. You typically store memories in terms of meaning—not in terms of whether you saw, heard, or physically interacted with the information. For example, your knowledge that a fire requires oxygen to burn is unlikely to be stored as a visual or an auditory memory. The initial experience by which you learned this fact may have been visual (watching a flame go out under a glass) or auditory (hearing an explanation), but the resulting representation of that knowledge in your mind is neither visual nor auditory.

How did cognitive scientists figure this out? An important clue that memories are stored by their meaning is the types of errors people make on memory tests. People who listen to a story will later confidently "recognize" sentences that never appeared in the story—so long as these new sentences are consistent with the story's meaning (Bransford and Franks, 1971). The same phenomenon is observed with purely visual stimuli. People rapidly lose the memory of the precise images that make up a picture story (e.g., whether a character faced left or right), but they retain the meaning or gist of the story (Gernsbacher, 1985).

These findings do not mean that you *can't* store auditory or visual information. You can, and you do. For example, if I ask you "Which is a darker green: a Christmas tree or a

---

is the process of making movements automatic: it's the type of learning you do as you slowly master typing, riding a bike, or mincing garlic. In the classroom, a "kinesthetic learning experience" is usually taken to mean any activity that involves movement, e.g., dissecting a worm or using blocks to explore fractions. But the learning that comes from these activities almost always goes along with changes in mental activity—the learning is not really part of the kinesthetic experience. For example, if I handle a Greek costume (rather than watch you handle it), I am the one who decides which part of it to explore, whether or not to try it on, and so on. True kinesthetic learning experiences, like practicing handwriting, do not make up much of the curriculum. To avoid continual qualifications about what is or is not a true kinesthetic learning experience, I will refer mainly to visual and auditory modalities. The conclusions drawn also apply to kinesthetic learning experiences.

frozen pea?" you'll likely report that you would answer this question by visually imagining the two objects side by side and evaluating which is a darker green. If I ask you whether Bill Clinton or George W. Bush has a deeper voice, you will likely report that you would answer by generating an auditory memory of each.

The mind is capable of storing memories in a number of different formats, and laboratory research indicates that a single experience usually leads to more than one type of representation. When subjects view a picture story, they *do* have a visual representation of what the pictures look like, in addition to the meaning-based representation. They usually don't remember the visual representation for long, however, largely because when they see the pictures, they are thinking about what they mean in order to understand the story. If, in contrast, they were asked to remember visual details of the pictures and to ignore the story they tell, they would have a better memory for the visual details and the meaning-based representation would be worse. (This principle is another example of a generalization made in a previous column: What's stored in memory is what you think about. To read that column, see www.aft.org/pubs-reports/american_educator/summer2003/cogsci.html.)

2. The different visual, auditory, and meaning-based representations in our minds cannot serve as substitutes for one another.

Our minds have these different types of representations for a reason: Different representations are more or less effective for storing different types of information. Visual representations, for example, are poor for storing meaning because they are often consistent with more than one interpretation: A static image of a car driving on a snowy hill could just as well depict a car struggling up the hill or slipping backwards down the hill. And some concepts do not lend themselves well to pictures: How would one depict "genius" or "democracy" in a picture? On the other hand, the particular shade of green of a frozen pea would be stored visually because the information is inherently visual.

Because these different memory representations store different types of information, you usually cannot use one representation to substitute for another. This point is illustrated in an experiment by Chad Dodson and Arthur Shimamura (2000). They asked subjects to listen to two word lists and to judge whether or not each word on the second list (new words) had appeared on the first list (studied words), as shown below. The interesting twist was that each word on both lists was spoken by either a man (depicted by boldface) or a woman (depicted by *italics*). If a word had appeared on both lists, it might be spoken in the same voice ("Window") or in different voices ("Doctor"). The question is whether changing the gender of the voice (and, therefore, the auditory experience) influenced memory for the studied words.

List **1**	List **2**
Shell	**Doctor**
Radio	*Fleet*
Doctor	*Midnight*
Table	*Thread*
Window	**Reason**
	Window

HOW HAS MODALITY THEORY BEEN TESTED?

The most comprehensive review of studies testing the effect of matching modality of instruction with students' modality preference was a meta-analysis conducted by Kenneth Kavale and Stephen Forness (1987). The study (see p. 34 of the main article) concluded such instruction produced no educational benefit. Here are three examples of the kinds of studies that were included in the meta-analysis.

In one carefully designed study, Thomas Vandever and Donald Neville (1974) examined the impact of modality on learning to read. To determine students' modality strengths and weaknesses, a teacher presented each student with an auditory, a visual, and a kinesthetic lesson on 12 novel words. In the auditory lesson, the sound of the word was emphasized; in the visual lesson, the shape and length or the word form was emphasized; and in the kinesthetic lesson, the words were traced and silently spoken. After each lesson the student's ability to read the words was tested. If a student had similar scores on the three tests, that student was determined to have no modality-based strength or weakness. But if the student scored much higher or lower on one test than on the other two, that student was categorized as having a strength or weakness in the modality. Of the 282 students tested, 72 showed a strength or weakness in a modality that was extreme enough to continue with the experiment.

The second phase of the study was designed to confirm whether or not these 72 students would benefit from ongoing instruction in their strongest modality. Subjects were assigned to further reading training with novel words using a variety of instructional methods that centered on each student's strong or weak modality. Sessions were 25 minutes, four days a week for six weeks. Students' ability to read the words was tested weekly. The data showed that the visual, auditory, and kinesthetic methods of instruction were equally effective, and that teaching to a student's modality strength or weakness made no difference.

Similar results were found in a study that tested the use of modalities to teach vocabulary (Ringler and Smith, 1973). One hundred twenty-eight students were classified according to their best modality and then taught new vocabulary words with instructional materials that were visual, auditory, kinesthetic, or combined (meaning all three modalities were used). The students were grouped for instruction such that each type of learner was represented in each type of instructional group. That way, the researchers could see if, for example, the visual learners did better in the visual instruction group than in the auditory instruction group. The results showed that the children did learn the new vocabulary—but the instructional modality made no difference at all.

A third study on the influence of modality preference on lesson comprehension also found similar results (Newcomer and Goodmnan, 1975). The researchers tested 167 fourth-graders on a battery of auditory and visual tests. In order to give modality theory the best chance of working, they selected 57 students who showed a relatively large difference on the auditory and visual tests. These students were then exposed to six brief lessons on new concepts. Each lesson was introduced with a theme (e.g., "The Solar System") and consisted of five related facts (e.g., the position of the planets, the function of the sun, etc.). Half of the lessons were presented via brief descriptions (auditorily) and half were presented pictorially, with printed captions (visually). Immediately after the lesson, students' comprehension and retention were tested. While 18 statements relating to the lesson were being read aloud by the experimenter, students silently read along and circled the ideas that had been presented in the lesson. The results showed that the "auditory" and "visual" learners showed no advantage when a lesson was presented in their preferred modality, compared to when it was not.

—D.W.

REFERENCES

Kavale, K. A. and Forness, S. R. (1987). Substance over style: Assessing the efficacy of modality testing and teaching. *Exceptional Children, 54(3)*, 228–239.

Newcomer, P. L. and Goodman, L. (1975). Effect of modality instruction on the learning of meaningful and nonmeaningful material by auditory and visual learners. *Journal of Special Education, 9,* 261–268.

Ringler, L. and Smith, I. (1973). Learning modality and word recognition of first-grade children. *Journal of Learning Disabilities,* 307–312.

Vandever, T. R. and Neville, D. D. (1974). Modality aptitude and word recognition. *Journal of Reading Behavior, 6,* 195–201.

Dodson and Shimamura found that whether the gender of the voice repeated or switched made no difference at all in remembering the word (75 percent versus 73 percent accuracy). That is, subjects were just as likely to remember "Doctor" as "Window." But when subjects judged that a word was on the first list, they also had to say whether a man or woman had said it. For this judgment, subjects were more accurate if the same gender voice spoke the word on the first and the second list (57 percent) than if the voice switched genders (39 percent). This experiment indicates that subjects do store auditory information, but it only helps them remember the part of the memory that is auditory—the sound of the voice—and not the word itself, which is stored in terms of its meaning.

3. Children probably do differ in how good their visual and auditory memories are, but in most situations, it makes little difference in the classroom.

Let's return to classroom education. We've said that some memories are stored visually, some auditorily, and some in terms of meaning. And it's likely that some students should have a relatively better visual memory or auditory memory. Shouldn't that mean that some students will more easily remember material that is presented in their stronger modality? It does, but what advantage would this superior memory provide for the student in a classroom? Teachers almost always want students to remember what things mean, not what they look like or sound like. For the vast majority of education, vision and audition are usually just vehicles that carry the important information teachers want students to learn. There are some limited types of materials for which an exact visual or auditory representation is helpful. The child with a good visual memory might have an edge over his peers in learning the location of capitals on a map of Europe, for example. That task is inherently visual. The child with a good auditory memory might learn the correct accent for a foreign language more quickly. (And the child with a good kinesthetic memory may have an edge in sports, handwriting, or painting.) But most of what we want children to learn is based on meaning, so their superior memory in a specific modality doesn't give them an advantage just because material is presented in their preferred modality. Whether information is presented auditorily or visually, the student must extract and store its meaning.

WHAT DOES THE RESEARCH SAY ABOUT TEACHING TO A CHILD'S STRONGEST MODALITY?

Because the vast majority of educational content is stored in terms of meaning and does not rely on visual, auditory, or kinesthetic memory, it is not surprising that researchers have found very little support for the idea that offering instruction in a child's best modality will have a positive effect on his learning. A few studies show a positive effect of accounting for students' best modality, but many studies show no effect (Kampwirth and Bates, 1980; Arter and Jenkins, 1979). The most comprehensive review was conducted by Kenneth Kavale and Steven Forness (1987); it is especially relevant for teachers because it includes many studies that tested the effectiveness of specific instructional approaches (as opposed to laboratory-based exercises). Kavale and Forness analyzed 39 studies using a technique called meta-analysis, which allows the combination of data from different studies. By combining many studies into a single statistical analysis, the researchers have greater power to detect a small effect, if one exists.

The initial results indicated that teaching in the child's best modality might have a small impact on learning, but closer inspection of the studies qualified that conclusion. The studies showing the largest effects had methodological problems. For example, a common error in studies of modality is a failure to ensure that the lesson plans and materials are equivalent in every way except modality (since that is the only way to be sure that any effect found is due to modality). Some studies have used materials specially-prepared for the visual and auditory conditions and then compared those to "regular teaching materials." It is possible that the specially prepared materials were more interesting or better organized than the "regular teaching" materials. This type of mistake calls the results into question because no one can tell if the results were caused by the change of modality or by the use of better materials. (The results may demonstrate that children learn more when teachers use better materials.) When Kavale and Forness limited the meta-analysis to studies with few or no such methodological problems, the modality effect disappeared.[2]

Kavale and Forness's meta-analysis provides substantial evidence that tailoring instruction to students' modality is not effective; across these many well-designed studies, such tailoring had no educational effect. But readers should bear in mind that it is impossible to prove a negative: We cannot be certain that modality theory is incorrect because it is always possible that we haven't looked for just the right sort of evidence. An inventive theorist could always create a new version of the theory with predictions that hadn't yet been tested. Nonetheless, the meta-analysis included a large number of studies that tested many different hypotheses (see box on p. 33 for examples).

Although it is technically true that the theory hasn't been (and will never be) disproved, we can say that the possible effects of matching instructional modality to a student's modality strength have been extensively studied and have yielded no positive evidence.

---

[2] This meta-analysis was not without controversy. Rita Dunn, who has proposed a theory consistent with modality effects (e.g., Dunn and Dunn, 1992; 1993; Dunn, Dunn and Perrin, 1994) wrote a rather acrimonious criticism of the Kavale and Forness study (Dunn, 1990), to which they replied (Kavale and Forness, 1990). Dunn later published her own meta-analysis (Dunn et al., 1995), which appeared to provide strong support for a large modality effect. Kavale and his colleagues (1998) noted, however, that only one of the studies reviewed had appeared in a peer-reviewed journal. All the others were unpublished doctoral dissertations, and 21 of these were from Dunn's home institution, St. John's University. This is a problem because of **confirmation bias**—a tendency in researchers to unconsciously slant the design of a study and its interpretation to favor the outcome they hope to observe (Wason, 1960; Mahoney and DeMonbreun, 1981). That's why having impartial, expert reviewers is vital to research. Almost none of the studies included in Dunn's meta-analysis underwent scrutiny by outside reviewers, which makes it hard to take seriously.

THE *CONTENT'S* BEST MODALITY IS KEY

The research presented in this article boils down to this: Modality of instruction is important, but it is equally important for all students—not more or less important depending on students' modality preference. There are several important implications for educators. First, teachers need not worry about differences between students in terms of modalities; there are not visual or auditory or kinesthetic learners. Indeed, applying this incorrect theory may actually shortchange some students. For example, a teacher introducing the concept of multiplication may show her students three boxes, each containing two marbles, but insist that the "auditory learners" in the class ignore this helpful visual aid, and instead listen to a verbal explanation. Imposing an ineffective explanation on a child because of a supposed modality fit is poor instruction. Second, modality does have an impact on learning, but this impact is the same for all students. Each modality is effective in carrying certain types of information: If it's important that children know what something looks like, sounds like, or feels like, they should experience the object in that modality. Third, as experienced teachers know, a change in modality can provide a welcome change of pace that brings students' attention back to a lesson. Students who have been primarily listening for 20 minutes will be glad to watch a short video. And students who have been watching a demonstration will benefit from solving a problem on their own. Teachers would do well to consider these uses of content-driven modality, and to disregard the idea that instruction needs to be tailored to a child's best modality. Fourth, as most teachers know, creating visual images is a good way to help you remember. (For example, to remember the parts of a perfect flower, you could imagine carefully peeling away the sepals, petals, pistil, and stamens until all that is left is the stem.) But this does not mean that having a good visual memory will improve memory for meaning. It turns out that the quality of the images people create doesn't seem to matter that much. People who report especially vivid images do not seem to be better at visual memory tasks than people who report poor quality images (Dickel and Slak, 1983; Ernest, 1983; Owens and Richardson, 1979). It is the process of creating the images that gives you the memory boost, and the quality of the final image is irrelevant. Moreover, creating visual images is a memory-boosting strategy that helps all people, not only those with a good visual memory.

—D.W.

REFERENCES

Dickel, M. J. and Slak, S. (1983). Imagery vividness and memory for verbal material. *Journal of Mental Imagery, 7,* 121–125.

Ernest, C. H. (1983). Imagery and verbal ability and recognition memory for pictures and words in males and females. *Educational Psychology, 3,* 227–244.

Owens, A. C. and Richardson, J. T. (1979). Mental imagery and pictorial memory. *British Journal of Psychology 70,* 497–505.

If there was an effect of any consequence, it is extremely likely that we would know it by now.

Teachers should focus on the content's best modality—not the student's

We have seen that the mind uses different representations to store different types of information and that these representations are poor substitutes for one another. That indicates that teachers should indeed think about the modality in which they present material, but their goal should be to find the content's best modality, not to search (in vain) for the students' best modality. If the teacher wants students to learn and remember what something looks like, then the presentation should be visual. For example, if students are to appreciate the appearance of a Mayan pyramid, it would be much more effective to view a picture than to hear a verbal description.

Many topics may call for information in more than one modality. In a unit on the Civil War, in addition to lectures and reading, it might be appropriate to include recordings of martial music used to inspire the troops, visual representations (maps) of battlefields, and perhaps a chance to handle the pack and equipment the troops carried so that students could appreciate their heft. Similarly, if students are to learn the form of an English sonnet, they should hear the stress forms of iambic pentameter, and then see a visual representation of it.

There are other ways in which modality of instruction can influence the effectiveness of a given lesson—but the influence applies to all children (see box, p. 34). Experiences in different modalities simply for the sake of including different modalities should not be the goal. Material should be presented auditorily or visually because the information that the teacher wants students to understand is best conveyed in that modality. There is no benefit to students in teachers' attempting to find auditory presentations of the Mayan pyramids for the students who have good auditory memory. Everyone should see the picture. The important idea from this column is that *modality matters in the same way for all students.*

IF MODALITY THEORY IS SO WRONG, WHY DOES IT FEEL SO RIGHT?

The belief in modality theory is very common among teachers. More than 25 years ago, Arter and Jenkins (1979) reported that more than 90 percent of special education teachers believed it. Today, the prevalence of books describing the theory and lesson plans suggesting ways to implement it suggest that it still enjoys widespread acceptance. Why is the theory so widely accepted if there is no research evidence to support it?

One factor is that it fits with a more general assumption that many teachers hold: There are genuinely important differences among students in how they learn. Modality gives us an easily understood way to think about the differences among children and it offers a hopeful message—a relatively easy adjustment to teaching practice may provide a boost to kids who are struggling. Further, everyone else believes it. Although false, the truth of modality theory has become "common knowledge."

I think that these factors may contribute to the belief, but I also think that most teachers wouldn't believe the theory if it did not seem consistent with their own experience. There are two ways that a teacher might see what looks like evidence for modality theory in the classroom. First, a teacher who believes the theory may interpret ambiguous situations as support for the theory. For example, a teacher might verbally explain to a student—several times—the idea of "borrowing" in subtraction without success. Then the teacher draws a diagram that more explicitly represents that the "3" in the tens place really represents "30." Suddenly, the concept clicks for the student. The teacher thinks "Aha. He's a visual learner. Once I drew the diagram, he understood." But the more likely explanation is that the diagram would have helped *any* student because it is a good way to represent a difficult concept. The teacher interprets the student's success in terms of modality theory because she has been told the theory is correct and because it seems to explain her experience. But cognitive scientists have long known that we all notice and remember examples that confirm our beliefs and, without meaning to, ignore and forget evidence that does not.

Modality theory may also seem correct because, as we have discussed, children probably do differ in their abilities with different types of memories. I remember my daughter commenting (out of the blue, as 4-year-olds will) that her preschool teacher said "white" in a way that made the "h" faintly, but distinctly, audible. I was impressed that she had noticed this difference, remembered it, and could reproduce it. So my daughter may have a good auditory memory, and that might help her in certain tasks, such as remembering regional accents, should she decide to be an actress. It does not mean that I want her teachers to ensure that she receives primarily auditory input in her coursework, because her superior auditory memory will not help her when she needs to remember meaning. But it is easy to see how one might (mistakenly) believe that complex material would be easier for her to master if presented auditorily. Further, as the box on p. 34 indicates, there are various ways in which modality does strengthen instruction (for all kids)—and it's easy to imagine that the effect has to do with a student's modal preference when in fact the effect is due to the content's best modality.

REFERENCES

Arter, J. A. and Jenkins, J. A. (1979). Differential diagnosis-prescriptive teaching: A critical appraisal. *Review of Educational Research, 49,* 517–555.

Bransford, J. D. and Franks, J. J. (1971). The abstraction of linguistic ideas. *Cognitive Psychology, 2,* 331–350.

Dodson, C. S. and Shimamura, A. P. (2000). Differential effects of cue dependency on item and source memory. *Journal of Experimental Psychology: Learning, Memory, & Cognition, 26,* 1023–1044.

Dunn, R. (1990). Bias over substance: A critical analysis of Kavale and Forness' report on modality-based instruction. *Exceptional Children, 56,* 352–356.

Dunn, R. and Dunn, K., (1992). *Teaching Elementary Students Through Their Individual Learning Styles*. Boston: Allyn and Bacon.

Dunn, R. and Dunn, K., (1993). *Teaching Secondary Students Through Their Individual Learning Styles*. Boston: Allyn and Bacon.

Dunn, R., Dunn, K., and Perrin, K.J. (1994). *Teaching Young Children Through Their Individual Learning Styles*. Boston: Allyn and Bacon.

Dunn, R., Griggs, S. A., Olson, J., Beasly, M. and Gorman, B. S. (1995). A meta-analytic validation of the Dunn and Dunn model of learning style preferences. *Journal of Educational Research, 88*, 353–362.

Gernsbacher, M. A. (1985). Surface information loss in comprehension. *Cognitive Psychology, 17*, 324–363.

Kampwirth, T. J. and Bates, M. (1980). Modality preference and teaching method. A review of the research. *Academic Therapy, 15*, 597–605.

Kavale, K. A. and Forness, S. R. (1990). Substance over style: A rejoinder to Dunn's animadversions. *Exceptional Children, 56(4)*, 357–361.

Kavale, K. A. and Forness, S. R. (1987). Substance over style: Assessing the efficacy of modality testing and teaching. *Exceptional Children, 54(3)*, 228–239.

Kavale, K. A., Hirshoren, A., Forness, S. R. (1998). Meta-analytic validation of the Dunn and Dunn Model of Learning-Style Preferences: A critique of what was Dunn. *Learning Disabilities Research & Practice, 13*, 75–80.

Mahoney, M. J. and DeMonbreun, B. G. (1981). Problem-solving bias in scientists. In R. D. Tweney, M. E. Doherty, and C. R. Mynatt (Eds.) *On Scientific Thinking* (pp. 139–144). New York: Columbia University Press.

Wason, P. C. (1960). On the failure to eliminate hypotheses in a conceptual task. *Quarterly Journal of Experimental Psychology, 12*, 129–140.

REVIEW AND CONTEMPLATE

1. What is the "learning styles" theory of educating children (i.e., what does it say about the best way to teach children)? Does scientific research support this theory?

2. What does research suggest about how we store memories? Do we store memories in terms of modality (i.e., whether we saw, heard, or physically interacted with information), or do we store them some other way?

3. Willingham (2005) states that "teachers should indeed think about modality in which they present material." What exactly does he mean by this? Should teachers teach according to each *student's* best modality (e.g., visual, auditory, or kinesthetic)?

4. According to Willingham (2005), why is learning-styles theory so widely accepted among educators if the research evidence does not support it? Describe two reasons.

6.2 "Past-Life Identities, UFO Abductions, and Satanic Ritual Abuse: The Social Construction of Memories"

IN HER BOOK entitled *Abducted,* Dr. Susan Clancy discussed how people come to believe they were abducted by aliens. She told the story of Will Andrews, a 42-year-old chiropractor. Dr. Clancy stated,

> For the past ten years he has had vivid memories of having been repeatedly taken away by "beings" and medically, psychologically, and sexually experimented on. During his abductions, he became close to his "alien guide"—a streamlined, sylph-like creature. Although they didn't communicate verbally, he feels they became "spiritually connected" and their connection resulted in a number of hybrid babies. He never sees his children, but he feels their presence; "I know they're out there, and they know who I am."

Although some believe that anecdotal reports of alien abductions are evidence that aliens have actually visited our planet and abducted people, you read in Chapter 1 that scientists do not rely on anecdotal evidence or testimonials for evidence. One problem with anecdotal reports of alien abductions is that although the people who give such reports may truly believe the abduction occurred, it is possible that they are remembering events that never actually took place.

Spanos, Burgess, and Burgess discuss fascinating stories of people who believe they (a) lived a past life, (b) have many different personalities living within them, (c) were abducted by aliens, or (d) participated in ritualized satanic abuse involving the rape and murder of children. Although these beliefs and memories are very real to many people who experience them, the authors present evidence that suggests that socially influenced false memories underlie these amazing beliefs.

Reference

Spanos, N. P., Burgess, C. A, and Burgess, M. F. (1994). Past-life identities, UFO abductions, and satanic ritual abuse. *The International Journal of Clinical and Experimental Hypnosis, 42,* 433–446.

"PAST-LIFE IDENTITIES, UFO ABDUCTIONS, AND SATANIC RITUAL ABUSE: THE SOCIAL RECONSTRUCTION OF MEMORIES"

NICHOLAS SPANOS, CHERYL BURGESS AND MELISSA FAITH BURGESS

It is now generally acknowledged that recall involves reconstructive processes and is strongly influenced by current beliefs and expectations (Bower, 1990; Loftus, 1979). As pointed out by Bartlett (1932) many years ago, people typically organize their recall of past events in a way that makes sense of their present situation and is congruent with their current expectations. What they recall frequently involves a mixture of correctly remembered and misremembered information that is often impossible to disentangle. Often there is little or no correlation between the accuracy of recall and the confidence that people place in their recall. It is not unusual for people to be convinced about the accuracy of a remembrance that turns out to be false (Loftus, 1979; Wells, Ferguson, & Lindsay, 1981). Contrary to popular belief, hypnotic procedures do not reliably enhance the accuracy of recall and, at least under some circumstances, may lead subjects to become even more overconfident than usual in their inaccurate recall (Smith, 1983; Spanos, Quigley, Gwynn, Glatt, & Perlin, 1991). Leading questions and other suggestive interview procedures, whether or not they are administered in a hypnotic context, can produce a very substantial deterioration in recall accuracy even when subjects remain highly confident in their inaccurate remembrances (Spanos, Gwynn, Comer, Baltruweit, & deGroh, 1989).

To a large extent, these ideas about memory have been developed and refined in the context of studying eyewitness testimony. The implications of these ideas have been particularly influential at shaping the critical attitudes taken by many psychologists toward the reliability of eyewitness testimony, and toward the usefulness of hypnotic and other procedures that are touted as "refreshing" such testimony (Loftus, 1979; Orne, 1979; Smith, 1983; Wagstaff, 1989). In the typical eyewitness situation, however, the memory distortions under consideration involve inaccuracies in detail (e.g., identifying the wrong suspect of real crime) rather than fabrications of entire complex scenarios (e.g., detailed descriptions of an entire gun battle that never occurred). Little systematic research is available that examines the applications of reconstructive and expectancy-guided views of memory to situations in which people "remember" entire scenarios that never happened. This article describes research of this kind conducted in our laboratory and examines the implications of our findings for three phenomena that appear to involve the wholesale "remembering" of fictitious events; past-life identities (Warnbach, 1979), UFO alien contact and abduction reports (Jacobs, 1992), and reports of satanic ritual

Nicholas P. Spanos, Cheryl A. Burgess and Melissa Faith Burgess, "Past-Life Identities, UFO Abductions, and Satanic Ritual Abuse," *The International Journal of Clinical and Experimental Hypnosis*, vol. 42, pp. 433-446. Copyright © 1994 by Taylor & Francis Group. Reprinted with permission.

child abuse from patients diagnosed with multiple personality disorder (Fraser, 1990; Young, Sachs, Braun, & Watkins, 1991).

EXPERIMENTAL CREATION OF PAST-LIFE PERSONALITIES

Several studies have examined factors that influence the formation of false memories by employing the phenomenon of past-life hypnotic regression. Some believers in reincarnation contend that people can be hypnotically regressed back to a time before their birth when they led previous lives (e.g., Wambach, 1979). The available evidence does not support this hypothesis and suggests instead that "memories" of having lived a past life are fantasy constructions (Baker, 1992; Spanos, Menary, Gabora, DuBreuil, & Dewhirst, 1991; Wilson, 1982). These fantasy constructions are important, however, because they can shed light on the processes by which people come to treat their fantasies as real, and because past-life identities are similar in many respects to the secondary or alter identities of multiple personality disorder patients. Like multiple personality disorder patients, subjects who report past lives behave as if they are inhabited by secondary selves. These selves display moods and personality characteristics that are different from the person's primary self, have a different name than the primary self, and report memories of which the primary self was previously unaware. Just as multiple personality disorder patients come to believe that their alter identities are real personalities rather than self-generated fantasies, many of the subjects who remember past lives continue to believe in the reality of their past lives after termination of the hypnotic session.

Kampman (1976) found that 41% of highly hypnotizable subjects reported a past-life identity and called themselves by different names when given hypnotic suggestions to regress back before their birth. Contrary to the notion that multiple identity experiences are a sign of mental illness, Kampman's (1976) past-life responders scored higher on measures of psychological health than did subjects who failed to report a past life.

In a series of experiments, Spanos, Menary, et al. (1991) also obtained past-life identity reports following hypnotic regression suggestions. Frequently the past-life identities were quite elaborate. They had their own names and frequently described their lives in great detail. Subjects who reported past-life experiences scored higher on measures of hypnotizablity and fantasy proneness, but no higher on measures of psychopathology than those who did not exhibit a past life.

The social nature of past-life identities was demonstrated by showing that the characteristics that subjects attributed to these identities were influenced by expectations transmitted by the experimenter (Spanos, Menary, et al, 1991; Experiment 2). Subjects provided with prehypnotic information about the characteristics of their identities (e.g., information about the identities' expected race and sex) were much more likely than those who did not receive such information to incorporate these characteristics into their descriptions of their past-life selves.

A different study (Spanos, Menary, et al., 1991, Experiment 3) tested the hypothesis that experimenter expectations influence the extent to which past-life identities describe themselves as having been abused during childhood. Before past-life regression, subjects were informed that their past-life identities would be questioned about their childhoods to obtain information about child-rearing practices in earlier historical times. Those in one condition were further told that children in past times had frequently been abused. Those in the other condition were given no information about abuse. The past-life identities of subjects given abuse information reported significantly higher levels of abuse during childhood than did the past-life identities of control subjects. In summary, these studies indicate that both the personal attributes and memory reports elicited from subjects during past-life identity enactments are influenced by the beliefs and expectations conveyed by the experimenter/hypnotist. When constructing their past lives, subjects shape the attributes and biographies attributed to these identities to correspond to their understandings of what significant others believe these characteristics to be.

After termination of the hypnotic regression procedure, some past-life reporters believed that their past-life experiences were memories of actual, reincarnated personalities, whereas others believed that their past-life identities were imaginary creations. Hypnotizability did not predict the extent to which subjects assigned credibility to their past-life identities. Instead, the degree of credibility assigned to these experiences correlated significantly with the degree to which subjects believed in reincarnation before the experiment, and the extent to which they expected to experience a real past life.

In a final study Spanos, Menary, et al. (1991; Experiment 4) manipulated prehypnotic information that concerned the reality of past-life experiences. Subjects in one condition were informed that past-life experiences were interesting fantasies rather than evidence of real past-life memories. Those in another condition were provided with background information which suggested that reincarnation was a scientifically credible notion, and that past-life identities were real people who had lived earlier lives. Subjects in the two conditions were equally likely to construct past-life experiences, but those assigned to the imaginary creation condition assigned significantly less credibility to these identities than did those told that reincarnation was scientifically credible.

Taken together these findings indicate that experiences of having lived a past life are social creations that can be elicited easily from many normal people, and that are determined by the understandings that subjects develop about such experiences from the information to which they are exposed. Past-life identities can be quite complex and detailed, and subjects draw from a wide array of sources outside of the immediate situation (e.g., television shows, historical novels, aspects of their own past, wish-fulfilling daydreams) to flesh out their newly constructed identity and to provide it with the history and characteristics that are called for by their understanding of the current task demands. The most important factor in influencing the extent to which past-life experiences are defined as real memories appears to be the extent to which subjects hold a belief system that is congruent with this interpretation (i.e., a belief in reincarnation). Information from an authoritative source which legitimates or delegitimates reincarnation beliefs also influences the extent to which subjects define their experiences as real memories rather than imaginings.

All of these past-life experiments either tested only highly hypnotizable subjects or found that the reporting of past lives was correlated significantly with hypnotizablity. Hypnotizablity refers to the extent to which subjects respond to hypnotic suggestions, and it correlates significantly with such dimensions as fantasy proneness and an openness to unusual experiences (see deGroh, 1989, for a review). One interpretation suggests that hypnotizablity or its imaginal correlates may constitute cognitive abilities which predispose individuals to construct secondary identities when such experiences are called for by contextual demands, and when these subjects are motivated to respond to those demands.

However, an alternative hypothesis suggests that hypnotizablity is correlated with the development of past-life identities because the suggestions that called for these experiences were administered in a hypnotic context and therefore were likely to call up the same attitudes and expectations as the hypnotizablity test situation. Whether circumstances can be created that will elicit multiple identity enactments from low hypnotizables remains to be determined.

ENCOUNTERS WITH UFO ALIENS

Reports of seeing unidentified flying objects (UFOs) and belief that such objects are extraterrestrial spacecraft have increased dramatically since World War II. Nevertheless, the available scientific evidence fails to support the hypothesis that these reports reflect the sighting of alien spacecraft (Sheaffer, 1986). Initially, UFO reports focused on the purported sightings of the crafts themselves. However, by the mid-1960s purportedly true accounts of people who claimed to have been abducted by UFO aliens began to appear (e.g., Fuller, 1966). Some of these accounts gained a great deal of notoriety. In addition, uncritical and sensationalistic documentary-type television shows and movies that featured alien contact became popular (Sheaffer, 1986). At the same time, reports of contact and abduction by aliens mushroomed, and such reports appear to be increasing in frequency (Klass, 1989).

Recently, Spanos, Cross, Dickson, and DuBreuil (1993) interviewed subjects who claimed UFO experiences. One group of these subjects simply reported distant lights or shapes in the night sky that appeared to move in erratic patterns and that they interpreted as UFOs. However, a second group of 20 subjects reported more elaborate experiences that included close contact with alien spaceships and/or alien beings, and occasionally, abduction by the aliens. Subjects in both UFO groups failed to differ in hypnotizablity or fantasy proneness from comparison subjects, and either failed to differ, or scored higher, than comparison subjects on indexes of mental health and IQ. However, subjects in both UFO groups believed more strongly in the reality of UFOs than did comparison subjects, and those with elaborate UFO experiences also held other esoteric beliefs (e.g., reincarnation) more strongly than comparison subjects.

Subjects who reported elaborate UFO experiences were much more likely to report their experience was sleep related than were those who reported more mundane (i.e., lights in the sky) experiences. Many of the elaborate experiences were clearly night dreams or hypnagogic imagery. In addition, almost a quarter of those in the elaborate UFO group reported frightening experiences that included full body paralysis and, frequently, vivid multisensorial hallucinations. For example, one subject reported:

> I was lying in bed facing the wall, and suddenly my heart started to race. I could feel the presence of three entities standing beside me. I was unable to move my body but could move my eyes. One of the entities, a male, was laughing at me, not verbally but with his mind. *(Spanos et al., 1993, p. 627)*

Experiences of this kind are most probably explicable as sleep paralysis; a phenomenon that is usually estimated as occurring in approximately 15% to 25% of the population, and that is commonly associated with feelings of suffocation, the sense of a presence, and hallucinations (Bell et al., 1984; Hufford, 1982). These findings suggest that at least some of the characteristics common to many elaborate UFO reports (e.g., being paralyzed by the aliens) may be grounded in the physiological changes that underlie sleep paralysis experiences.

Not all elaborate UFO experiences were sleep related. Moreover, the elaborateness of UFO experiences was positively correlated with questionnaire variables that assessed propensities toward experiencing unusual body sensations, and fantasy proneness. Hypnotizablity, however, failed to correlate significantly with elaborateness.

Taken together, the findings of Spanos et al. (1993) indicate that elaborate UFO experiences that are later described as memories are particularly likely to occur in people who believe in alien visitation, and who also interpret unusual sensory and imaginal experiences in terms of the alien hypothesis.

People who believe that they might have been abducted by aliens but cannot remember, or who dream of aliens or experience gaps in memory that they are unable to explain, sometimes undergo hypnotic (or non-hypnotic) interviews aimed at uncovering, "hidden memories" of their alien abduction (Jacobs, 1992; Klass, 1989). Frequently, the interviews include two phases. In the first phase background information is obtained and clients are asked about unusual or inexplicable experiences that have occurred during their life. These include "missing time" experiences, unusual or bizarre dreams, and experiences that suggest hypnagogic imagery or sleep paralysis (e.g., having seen a ghost, strange lights, or a monster). Such experiences are defined as distorted memories of alien abduction that call for further probing (Jacobs & Hopkins, 1992). Moreover, making such experiences salient enhances the likelihood that some of their characteristics (e.g., paralysis, feelings of suffocation) will be incorporated into any abduction memories that are recalled in Phase 2. Phase 2 typically involves hypnotic or nonhypnotic guided imagery employed to facilitate recall. This may involve leading questions (Baker, 1992), or the subject may be pressed repeatedly for more details (Jacobs, 1992). In addition, subjects may be informed that some material is so deeply hidden that several such interviews are required, Subjects who have difficulty "remembering" some or all of their abduction are defined as "blocking" and are provided with strategies for facilitating recall. These include asking subjects to imagine a curtain and then to peek behind it to view their abduction, or to imagine a movie screen on which they see their abduction replayed (Jacobs & Hopkins, 1992).

Given that subjects in past-life experiments frequently reported elaborate past-life identities on the basis of much less prodding, it is not surprising that such interviewing procedures lead clients to generate imaginative scenarios in which they are abducted by aliens. It is also not surprising that clients typically interpret their abduction fantasies as memories rather than as fantasies. After all, they usually sought help because they believed that they might have been abducted. In other words, they already possessed a set of background beliefs and current expectations that facilitated the interpretation of such fantasies as memories. In addition, their abduction fantasies are legitimated as memories by the interviewers who treat them as such and who do not provide alternative explanations. Finally, it is worth noting that people who believe that they have been abducted frequently join support groups that include other abductees (Jacobs, 1992). The sharing of abduction experiences in such groups can only serve to enhance their uniformity and further legitimate them as real memories.

RITUAL SATANIC ABUSE AND MULTIPLE PERSONALITY DISORDER

The large majority of patients who eventually receive a multiple personality disorder diagnosis do not display symptoms of multiplicity and are unaware that they have alter identities before they enter treatment with the therapist who "discovers" their multiplicity (Kluft, 1985). Moreover, this "discovery" frequently involves the use of highly leading hypnotic interviews in which patients are explicitly informed that they have alter personalities and attempts are made to communicate directly with these alters, learn their names, their functions, and so on (Bliss, 1986; Spanos, Weekes, & Bertrand, 1985; Wilbur, 1984).

Most studies find that multiple personality disorder patients report extremely high rates of childhood sexual and/or physical abuse (e.g., Ross, Miller, Bjornson, Reagor, & Fraser, 1991). Contrary to the majority opinion in the multiple personality disorder literature, however, these data do not demonstrate that child abuse causes multiplicity. At least three noncausal factors appear to influence the high rates of reported child abuse obtained from multiple personality disorder patients: (a) high base rates of reported child abuse in the clinical samples from which patients who will be diagnosed with multiple personality disorder are drawn, (b) use of a child abuse history to justify implementing leading "diagnostic" interviews that generate displays of multiplicity, and (c) confabulation of abuse in patients who generate such "memories" only after exposure to leading interviews that call for and legitimate such reports (Spanos, in press).

The strong connection between child abuse and multiple personality disorder is of recent origin. Early cases (i.e., pre-1920) were much less likely than modern ones to be associated with reports of child abuse (Bowman, 1990; Kenny, 1986), and the abuse that was reported in these early cases lacked the lurid ritualistic satanic elements that are becoming increasingly prominent in the abuse memories proffered by modern multiple personality disorder patients.

Although controversy remains concerning its actual rate of occurrence (Wakefield & Underwager, 1992), there is general agreement that the sexual abuse of children in our society is a good deal more common than was once believed (Finkelhor, 1987). Frequently, people who were sexually abused as children retain their memories of these experiences (Femina, Yeager, & Lewis, 1990). In some cases, however, adults in psychotherapy report for the first time remembering early child abuse. According to many multiple personality disorder therapists (e.g., Bliss, 1986), these reports reflect memories of actual abuse that was repressed at the time of its occurrence and recovered later during the therapeutic process. However, an alternative hypothesis suggests that these reports may frequently reflect confabulations induced by the unwitting suggestions of therapists (Loftus, 1993; Spanos, in press). Unfortunately, in such cases it is usually difficult or impossible to either corroborate or disconfirm the validity of these memory reports (Wakefield & Underwager, 1992). Reported memories of ritual satanic child abuse are an exception. These reports are of theoretical importance for memory researchers because the available data indicate that they are almost always believed-in fantasy constructions rather than memories of actual events (Jenkins & Maier-Katkin, 1991; Mulhern, 1991b; Spanos, in press).

By 1980 the idea of a relationship between child abuse and multiple personality disorder was well established. In that year a book titled *Michelle Remembers* (Smith & Pazdec, 1980) reported on ritual satanic tortures that a woman had purportedly experienced during childhood and then forgotten until they were recovered during therapy. Michelle's story became a part of the propaganda used by the Evangelical Christian movement that became increasingly prominent in American social and political life during the 1980s. This movement reinvigorated the mythology of satanism—the idea that there exists a powerful but secret international satanic conspiracy that carries out heinous crimes. These crimes supposedly include the kidnapping, torture, and sexual abuse of countless children as well as mass murder, forced pregnancies, and cannibalism (Bromley, 1991; Hicks, 1991; Lyons, 1989).

Large numbers of therapists who identified themselves as active Christians joined the multiple personality disorder movement in the 1980s (Mulhern, 1993), and soon accounts like those of Michelle began to be reported by the alters of multiple personality disorder patients during therapy (Frazer, 1990; Young et al., 1991). By the mid-1980s, 25%

of multiple personality disorder patients in therapy had recovered memories of ritual satanic abuse, and by 1992 the percentage of patients recovering such memories was as high as 80% in some treatment facilities (Mulhern, 1993).

If they were real, the ritual satanic crimes "remembered" by multiple personality disorder patients would require a monumental criminal conspiracy that has been in existence for at least 50 years and that has been responsible for the murder of thousands of people (Hicks, 1991). The FBI and other law enforcement agencies throughout North America have investigated many satanic abuse allegations made by multiple personality disorder patients but have been unable to substantiate the existence of the requisite criminal conspiracy (Lanning, 1992). These repeated failures to find evidence of satanic ritual abuse strongly indicate that the vast majority of these allegations are false, and that the "memories" on which they are based are fantasies rather than remembrances of actual events (Hicks, 1991).

Bottoms, Shaver, and Goodman (1991) surveyed psychotherapists across the United States about the frequency with which they had seen patients who reported ritual abuse memories. Seventy percent of the therapists who responded indicated no contact with such patients. A small minority, however, reported having seen large numbers of patients who reported ritual abuse. This pattern of findings suggests that therapists who regularly obtain such reports play an active role in shaping the ritual abuse "memories" of their patients.

Frequently, satanic abuse memories are elicited during hypnotic interviews that explicitly suggest such abuse. In such cases it is common for the therapist to explicitly describe satanic rituals and possibly to show the patient pictures of satanic symbols or photographs of possible cult leaders. The therapist then addresses the patient's alters and asks if any of them recognize the material or remember similar experiences (Mulberry, 1991a).

Multiple personality disorder patients are often chronically unhappy people with well-developed imaginations, who become strongly attached to and dependent on their therapists. Consequently, they are motivated to use the information from such interviews to construct an autobiography that will make sense of their lives and their symptoms, and that will win approval and validation from their therapist (Spanos, in press). In this context it is worth recalling the ease with which highly hypnotizable college students were induced to report past life personalities who "remembered" that they had been abused as children, when the expectation of such abuse had been conveyed to them before their hypnotic regression (Spanos, Menary, et al., 1991).

Recently, Ofshe (1992) described the case of a fundamentalist Christian man named Paul Ingram who, after highly leading interrogations confessed to having participated in the satanic ritual abuse of his own children. The case provides a "real life" example of the ease with which false memories can be generated in people who hold a belief system that is congruent with the false information. Ingram was initially accused of incest by one of his daughters after she had attended a church-sponsored retreat intended to reveal sexual abuse. Ingram initially denied the charges, but after being convinced that his children would not lie, he agreed that Satan may have hidden from him his own crimes. Many of the events to which Ingram eventually confessed were suggested to him by the police officers and psychologist who interrogated him, and he was supported in his confessions by his minister. Along with repeatedly raping his children, Ingram confessed to belonging to a satanic cult and participating in the murder of 25 babies. Although Ingram had no history of mental illness before his arrest, he was diagnosed as suffering from multiple personality disorder by at least one psychologist. Ofshe (1992) demonstrated Ingram's willingness to accept suggested fantasies as real memories by concocting a set of ritual abuse events that had not been alleged against Ingram. When Ofshe questioned Ingram about these false events using guided imagery and other interrogative procedures employed by the police, Ingram readily confessed to them. Later Ingram insisted that the false events had really happened and had not been suggested to him during the interrogation.

Some patients report memory fragments or dreams with satanic content and only after are exposed to hypnotic interviews aimed at confirming such abuse. However, since many multiple personality disorder patients are enmeshed in a social network where they hear about satanic abuse from other patients, therapists, and shared newsletters, and where they or their fellow patients attend workshops devoted to such abuse, "spontaneous" dreams and memories do not provide serious evidence of actual ritual abuse (Mulhern, 1991b).

CONCLUSION

The findings reviewed above are consistent with the view that recall is reconstructive and guided by current motivations and expectations. In addition, these findings indicate that social factors can lead people to generate complex fantasy scenarios and to define such experiences as actual memories of real events. In many cases some elements in these fantasies are memories. For instance, past-life reporters frequently incorporate information from their own past, or events and plots recalled from books and movies into their past-life identities, and UFO reporters sometimes experience abduction dreams or complex sleep paralysis episodes. The memory of these experiences can then form the core of their abduction fantasies and help to legitimate these fantasies as memories. Some multiple personality disorder patients may use memories of actual abuse around which they add elaborate satanic elements. Despite the inclusion of real memory elements, however, past-life, UFO and satanic ritual abuse "memories" are primarily fantasy constructions. Typically they are organized around expectations derived from external sources, embedded in a belief system that is congruent with their classification as memories, and legitimated as memories by significant others. In short, whether experiences are counted as memories of actual happenings or as fantasies may, under some circumstances, have less to do with characteristics intrinsic to these experiences than to the internal context (i.e., supportive belief structures) in which they are embedded and the external context (i.e., social legitimation) in which they are validated (Johnson, 1988).

Manuscript submitted March 23, 1993; final revision received January 27, 1994.

1. The writing of this article was supported by a grant to the first author from the Soscial Sciences and Humanities Research Council of Canada.
2. Requests for reprints should be addressed to Cheryl A. Burgess, Department of Psychology, 8550 Loeb Building, 1125 Colonel By Drive, Carleton University, Ottawa, Ontario K1S 3B6, Canada.

The International Journal of Clinical and Experimental Hypnosis, Vol. XLII. No. 4, October 1994, 433-446 (c) 1994 The International Journal of Clinical and Experimental Hypnosis.

REFERENCES

Baker, R.A. (1992), *Hidden memories,* Buffalo, NY, Prometheus.

Bartlett, E.C. (1032), *Remembering,* Cambridge, Cambridge University Press.

Bell, C.C., Shakoor, B., Thompson, B., Dew, D., Hughley, E., Mays, R., and Shorter-Gooden, K. (1984). Prevalence of isolated sleep paralysis in Black subjects. *Journal of the National Medical Association, 76,* 501-508.

Bliss, E.I. (1986) *Multiple personality, allied disorders and hypnosis,* New York, Oxford.

Bottoms, B. L., Shaver, P.R., & Goodman, G.S. (1991, August). *Profile of ritual and religion related abuse allegations reported to clinical psychologists in the United States.* Paper presented at the 99th annual convention of the American Psychological Association, San Francisco.

Bower, G. (1990). Awareness, the unconscious and repression: An experimental psychologist's perspective. In J.L. Singer (Ed.), *Repression and dissociation: Implications for personality, theory, psychopathology, and health* (pp. 209-222). Chicago, University of Chicago Press.

Bowman, E.S. (1990). Adolescent multiple personality disorder in the nineteenth and early twentieth centuries, *Dissociation, 3,* 179-187.

Bromley, D.G. (1991). Satanism: The new cult scare. In J.T. Richardson, J. Best, & D.G. Bromley (Eds.), *The satanism scare* (pp. 49-72). New York: Aldine deGruyter.

DeGroh, M. (1989). Correlates of hypnotic susceptibility. In N.P. Spanos & J.F. Chaves (Eds.), *Hypnosis the cognitive behavioral perspective.* Buffalo, NY, Prometheus.

Femina, D.D., Yeager, C.A., & Lewis, D.O. (1990). Child abuse: Adolescent records vs. adult recall. *Child Abuse and Neglect, 14,* 227-231.

Finkelhor, D. (1987). The sexual abuse of children: Current research reviewed. *Psychiatric Annals, 17,* 233-241.

Fraser, G.A. (1990). Satanic ritual abuse: A cause of multiple personality disorder. *Journal of Child and Youth Care*, pp. 55-66.

Fuller, J.G. (1966). *The interrupted journey,* New York: Dell.

Hicks, R.D. (1991). *In pursuit of Satan,* Buffalo, NY: Prometheus.

Hufford, D. (1992). *The terror that comes in the night.* Philadelphia University of Pennsylvania Press.

Jacobs, D.M. (1992), *Secret life: Firsthand accounts of UFO abductions.* New York: Simon & Schuster.

Jacobs, D.M., & Hopkins, B. (1992). *Suggested techniques for hypnosis and therapy of abductees.* Unpublished manuscript, Department of History, Temple University, Philadelphia, PA.

Jenkins, P., & Maier-Katkin, D. (1991). Occult survivors: The making of a myth. In J.T. Richardson, K. Best, & D.G. Bromley (Eds.), *The satanism scare* (pp. 49-72). New York: Aldine deGryter.

Johnson, M.K. (1988). Discriminating the origin of information. In T.F. Oltmanns & B.A. Maher (eds.), *Delusional beliefs* (pp. 34-65). New York: Wiley.

Kampman, R. (1976). Hypnotically induced multiple personality: An experimental study. *International Journal of Clinical and Experimental Hypnosis, 24,* 215-217.

Kenny, M.G. (1981), Multiple personality and spirit possession. *Psychiatry, 44,* 337-356.

Kenny, M.G. (1986). *The passion of Ansel Bourne: Multiple personality and American culture.* Washington, DC: Smithsonian Institution Press.

Klass, P.J. (1989). *UFO abductions: A dangerous game.* Buffalo, NY: Prometheus.

Kluft, R.P. (1985). The natural history of multiple personality disorder. In R.P. Kluft (Ed.), *Childhood antecedents of multiple personality* (pp. 197-238). Washington, DC: American Psychiatric Press.

Lanning, K.V. (1992). A law enforcement perspective on allegations of ritual abuse. In D.K. Sakheim & S.E. Devine (eds.), *Out of darkness: Exploring satanism and ritual abuse* (pp. 109-146). New York: Lexington.

Loftus, E.F. (1979). *Eyewitness testimony.* Cambridge, MA: Harvard University Press.

Loftus, E.F. (1993). The reality of repressed memories. *American Psychologist 48,* 518-537.

Lyons, A. (1989). *Satan wants you: The cult of devil worship in America.* New York: Mysterious Press.

Merskey, H. (1992). The manufacture of personalities: The production of multiple personality disorder. *British Journal of Psychiatry, 160,* 327-340.

Mulhern, S. (1991a). Letter to the editor. *Child Abuse and Neglect, 14,* 609-611.

Mulhern, S. (1991b). Satanism and psychotherapy: A rumor in search of an inquisition. In J.T. Richardson, J. Best, & D.G. Bromley (eds.), *The satanism scare* (pp. 145-172) New York: Aldine de Gruyter.

Mulhern, S. (1993). *Le trouble de la personnalite multiple a la recherche du trauma perdu* [The trouble of multiple personality in the research of lost trauma]. Unpublished manuscript, Laboratorie des Rumeurs des Mythes du Futur et des Sectes, U.F.R. Anthropologie, Ethnologie, Science des Relgions, Universite de Paris, France.

Ofshe, R.J. (1992). Inadvertent hypnosis during interrogation: False confession due to dissociative state; mis-identified multiple personality and the satanic cult hypothesis. *International Journal of Clinical and Experimental Hypnosis, 40,* 125–156.

Orne, M.T. (1979). The use and misuse of hypnosis in court. *International Journal of Clinical and Experimental Hypnosis, 27,* 311–341.

Ross, C.A., Miller, S.D., Bjornson, L., Reagor, P., & Fraser, G.A. (1991). Abuse histories in 102 cases of multiple personality disorder. *Canadian Journal of Psychiatry, 36,* 97–101.

Sheaffer, R. (1986). *The UFO verdict.* Buffalo, NY: Prometheus.

Smith, M. & Pazder, L. (1980). *Michelle remembers.* New York: Pocket Books.

Smith, M.C. (1983). Hypnotic memory enhancement of witnesses: Does it work? *Psychological Bulletin, 94,* 387–407.

Spanos, N.P. (1989). Hypnosis, demonic possession and multiple personality: Strategic enactments and disavowals of responsibility for actions. In C.A. Ward (ed.), *Altered states of consciousness and mental health: Theoretical and methodological issues* (pp. 96–124). Newbury Park, CA: Sage.

Spanos, N.P. (in press). Multiple identity enactments and multiple personality disorder: A sociocognitive perspective. *Psychological Bulletin.*

Spanos, N.P., Cross, P., Dickson, K., & DuBreuil, S.C. (1993). Close encounters: An examination of UFO experiences. *Journal of Abnormal Psychology, 102,* 624–632.

Spanos, N.P., Gwynn, M.I., Comer, S.L., Baltruweit, W.J., & deGroh, M. (1989). Are hypnotically induced pseudomemories resistant to cross-examination? *Law and Human Behavior, 13,* 271–289.

Spanos, N.P., Menary, E., Gabora, N.J., DuBreuil, S.C., & Dewhirst, B. (1991). Secondary identity enactments during hypnotic past-life regression: A sociocognitive perspective. *Journal of Personality and Social Psychology, 61,* 308–320.

Spanos, N.P., Quigley, C.A., Gwynn, M.I., Glatt, R.L., & Perlini, A.H. (1991). Hypnotic interrogation, pretrial preparation, and witness testimony during direct and cross-examination. *Law and Human Behavior, 15,* 639–653.

Wagstaff, G.F. (1989). Forensic aspects of hypnosis. In N.P. Spanos &J.F. Chaves (Eds.), *Hypnosis: The cognitive-behavioral perspective* (pp. 340–357). Buffalo, NY: Prometheus.

Wakefield, H., & Underwager, R. (1992). Recovered memories of alleged sexual abuse: Lawsuits against parents. *Behavioral Sciences and the Law, 10,* 483–507.

Wambach, H. (1979). *Life before life.* New York: Bantam.

Wells, G.L., Ferguson, T.J., & Lindsay, R.C.L. (1981). The tractability of eyewitness confidence and its implications for triers of fact. *Journal of Applied Psychology, 66,* 688–696.

Wilbur, C.B. (1984). Treatment of multiple personality. *Psychiatric Annals, 14,* 27–31.

Wilson, I. (1982). *Reincarnation? The claims investigated.* Harmondsworth, Middlesex, England: Penguin.

Young, W.C., Sachs, R.G., Braun, G.G., & Watkins, R.T. (1991). Patients reporting ritual abuse in childhood: A clinical syndrome. Report of 37 cases. *Child Abuse and Neglect, 15,* 181–189.

REVIEW AND CONTEMPLATE

1. Describe the research findings that suggest memories of past-life identities are fantasy constructions rather than real memories. How might people come to mistakenly believe they have led a past life?

2. Explain two different ways that people might come to believe they were visited or abducted by aliens. (HINT: One way is sleep related, the other is not).

3. What evidence suggests that multiple personality disorder (also known as Dissociative Identity Disorder) is socially constructed (i.e., people learn to exhibit the disorder rather than develop it spontaneously or as a result of abuse)?

4. What evidence suggests that memories of satanic ritual abuse are false memories (cite at least two types of evidence)?

6.3 "Memory Recovery Techniques in Psychotherapy: Problems and Pitfalls"

AFTER EXPERIENCING SEVERE postpartum depression, Patricia Burgess sought inpatient psychiatric care in a large Chicago hospital in 1986. Patricia's therapists helped her uncover previously hidden memories of her role as the High Priestess of a satanic cult. She recalled participating in satanic rituals, being abused by numerous men, abusing her own children, murdering adults and babies, and engaging in cannibalism. After her condition worsened, she was transferred to another psychiatric unit, where she began to doubt the reality of her new memories. Patricia eventually realized that none of the events her therapists helped her "remember" actually happened. She was not the High Priestess of a satanic cult, nor had she abused or murdered anyone. Her therapists had used a mixture of psychiatric drugs, hypnotism, and highly suggestive questioning to bring out these false memories. Patricia eventually won a $10.6 million lawsuit against the hospital and the psychiatrists.

Patricia's story is a rather extreme example of the destructive power of various pseudoscientific techniques for unearthing supposedly repressed memories. Sigmund Freud believed that some of our thoughts, wishes, and memories—especially those that may cause us psychological distress—get pushed back into our unconscious minds so that we are no longer consciously aware of them. He called this phenomenon "repression." Although reliable scientific evidence for repressed memories is lacking, a substantial number of mental health professionals believe they exist and use a variety of memory recovery techniques to help patients remember traumatic memories. Lynn, Loftus, Lilienfeld, and Lock describe these memory-recovery techniques and discuss scientific evidence that suggests they may result in the creation rather than the recovery of traumatic memories.

Reference

Lynn, S. J., Loftus, E. F., Lilienfeld, S. O., & Lock, T. (2003, July/August). Memory recovery techniques in psychotherapy: Problems and pitfalls. *Skeptical Inquirer, 27,* 40–46.

"MEMORY RECOVERY TECHNIQUES IN PSYCHOTHERAPY: PROBLEMS AND PITFALLS"

STEVEN JAY LYNN, ELIZABETH LOFTUS, SCOTT LILIENFELD, AND TIMOTHY LOCK

Memory recovery techniques that are widely used in psychotherapy including hypnosis, age regression, guided imagery, dream interpretation, bibliotherapy, and symptom interpretation can distort or create—rather than reveal—allegedly repressed traumatic memories.

In 1997, Nadean Cool won a $2.4 million malpractice settlement against her therapist in which she alleged that he used a variety of suggestive memory recovery procedures to persuade her that she had suffered horrific abuse and harbored more than 130 personalities including demons, angels, children, and a duck. Prior to therapy, Nadean recounted problems typical of many women including a history of bulimia, substance abuse, and mild depression. During her five-year treatment, Nadean's therapist allegedly maintained that she could not improve unless she uncovered repressed traumatic memories. To do so, Nadean participated in repeated hypnotic age regression and guided imagery sessions, and was subjected to an exorcism and fifteen-hour marathon therapy sessions. Nadean recalled frightening images of participating in a satanic cult, eating babies, being raped, having sex with animals, and being forced to watch the murder of her eight-year-old friend after these interventions, and her psychological health deteriorated apace. Eventually Nadean came to doubt that the recovered memories were "real," terminated treatment with her therapist, and recouped much of the ground she had lost.

Although Nadean Cool's therapy strayed far beyond conventional practice, her therapist is in the company of many professionals who perform so-called "memory work" to help clients retrieve memories of ostensibly repressed abuse. Poole, Lindsay, Mcmon, and Bull (1995) reported that 25 percent of licensed doctoral level psychologists surveyed in the United States and Great Britain indicated that they: (a) use two or more techniques such as hypnosis and guided imagery to facilitate recall of repressed memories; (b) consider memory recovery an important part of treatment; and (c) can identify patients with repressed or otherwise unavailable memories as early as the first session (see Polousny and Follecte 1996 for similar findings). In addition, over three-quarters of the U.S. doctoral-level psychotherapists reported using at least one memory recovery technique to "help clients remember childhood sexual abuse." In this article we consider

Steven Jay Lynn, Timothy Lock, Elizabeth F. Loftus, and Scott O. Lilienfeld, "Memory Recovery Techniques in Psychotherapy: Problems and Pitfalls," *Skeptical Inquirer*, vol. 27, pp. 40-46. Copyright © 2003 by Center for Inquiry. Reprinted with permission.

a number of widely used memory recovery procedures, and whether they can distort or create, rather than reveal, traumatic memories.

CLINICAL TECHNIQUES

Guided Imagery

One important class of techniques relies on guided imagery, in which patients imagine scenarios described by the therapist. So long as imagery techniques focus on current problems, as in visualizing pleasant scenes to develop relaxation skills, there is probably little cause for concern about false memory creation. However, the use of imagery to uncover allegedly repressed memories is controversial and warrants concern because people frequently confuse real and imagined memories, particularly when memories are initially hazy or unavailable. Roland (1993), for example, proposed using visualization to jog "blocked" memories of sexual abuse, and a "reconstruction" technique for recovering repressed memories of abuse. According to Poole et al. (1995), 32 percent of U.S. therapists report using "imagery related to the abuse."

Suggesting False Memories

Memory errors are not random. What is recalled depends on current beliefs, inferences, guesses, expectancies, and suggestions. People can clearly be led by suggestions to integrate a fabricated event into their personal histories. In Loftus's research (Loftus, Coan, and Pickrell 1996; Loftus and Pickrell 1995), twenty-four participants were asked by an older sibling to remember real and fictitious events (e.g., getting lost in a shopping mall). The older sibling initially provided a few details about the false event, such as where the event allegedly occurred, after which the subjects were interviewed one to two weeks apart. A quarter of the subjects claimed to remember the false event; some provided surprisingly detailed accounts of the event that they came to believe had actually occurred. Similar studies with college students have shown that approximately 20–25 percent report experiencing such fictitious events as: (a) an overnight hospitalization for a high fever and a possible ear infection, accidentally spilling a bowl of punch on the parents of the bride at a wedding reception, and evacuating a grocery store when the overhead sprinkler systems erroneously activated (Hyman et al. 1995); and (b) a serious animal attack, serious indoor accident, serious outdoor accident, a serious medical procedure, and being injured by another child (Porter, Yuille, and Lehman 1998).

Hypnosis

Many therapists endorse popular yet mistaken beliefs about hypnosis. Yapko's (1994) survey revealed that 47 percent of a sample composed of professionals had greater faith in the accuracy of hypnotic than non-hypnotic memories, 54 percent believed to some degree that hypnosis is effective for recovering memories as far back as birth, and 28 percent believed that hypnosis is an effective means of recovering past life memories.

If hypnosis were able to accurately retrieve forgotten memories, confidence in its use for recovering memories would be warranted. But this is not the case. The following conclusions are based on major reviews of the literature[1]:

1. Hypnosis increases the sheer volume of recall, resulting in both more incorrect and correct information. When the number of responses is statistically controlled, hypnotic recall is no more accurate than nonhypnotic recall.
2. Hypnosis produces more recall errors and higher levels of memories for false information.
3. False memories are associated with subjects' levels of hypnotic suggestibility. However, even relatively non-suggestible participants report false memories.
4. Hypnotized persons sometimes exhibit less accurate recall in response to misleading questions compared with nonhypnotized participants.
5. In general, hypnotized individuals are more confident about their recall accuracy than are nonhypnotized individuals, and an association between hypnotizability and confidence has been well documented.
6. Even when participants are warned about possible memory problems associated with hypnosis, they continue to report false memories during and after hypnosis, although some studies indicate that warnings decrease pseudomemories.
7. Contrary to the claim that hypnosis facilitates the recall of emotional or traumatic memories, hypnosis does not improve recall of emotionally arousing events (e.g., films of shop accidents, depictions of fatal stabbings, a mock assassination, an actual murder videotaped serendipitously), and arousal level is not associated with hypnotic recall.
8. Hypnosis does not necessarily produce more false memories or unwarranted confidence in memories than highly suggestive nonhypnotic procedures. However, simply asking participants to focus on the task at hand and to do their best to recall specific events yields accurate recall comparable to hypnosis, but with fewer or comparable recall errors.

Our dour assessment of hypnosis for recovering memories has been echoed by professional societies, including divisions and task forces of the American Psychological Association and the Canadian Psychiatric Association. The American Medical Association (1994) has asserted that hypnosis be used only for investigative purposes in forensic contexts. However, even when hypnosis is used solely for investigative purposes, there are attendant risks. Early in an investigation, the information obtained through hypnosis could lead investigators to pursue erroneous leads and even to interpret subsequent leads as consistent with initial and perhaps mistaken hypnotically generated evidence.

Searching for Early Memories

According to Adler (1931), "The first memory will show the individual's fundamental view of life … . I would never investigate a personality without asking for the first memory (p. 75)." More recently, Olson (1979) articulated a belief shared by many therapists (Papanek 1979) that "[Early memories] when correctly interpreted often reveal very quickly the basic core of one's personality … and suggest … bedrock themes with which the therapist must currently deal in treating the client" (p. xvii).

Most adults' earliest reported memories date back to between 36 and 60 months of age. Virtually all contemporary memory researchers agree that accurate memory reports of events that occur before 24 months of age are extremely rare (see Malinoski, Lynn, and Sivec 1998), due to developmental changes that influence how children process, retrieve, and share information. Adults' memory reports from 24 months of age or earlier are likely to represent confabulations, condensations, and constructions of early events, as well as current concerns and stories heard about early events (Spanos 1996). Although certain early memories might well have special significance,[2] such memories are highly malleable. Malinoski, Lynn, and Green (1999) examined early memories in a study in which interviewers probed for increasingly early memories until participants twice denied any earlier memories. Participants then received "memory recovery techniques" similar to those advocated by some therapists (e.g., Farmer 1989, Meiselman 1990). Interviewers asked participants to see themselves "in their mind's eye" as a toddler or infant, and "get in touch" with memories of long ago. Participants were informed that most young adults can retrieve memories of very early events—including their second birthday—if they "let themselves go" and try hard to visualize and concentrate. Interviewers then asked for subjects' memories of their second birthdays and reinforced increasingly early memory reports.

The average age of the initial reported memory was 3.7 years: Only 11 percent of individuals reported memories at or before age 24 months, and 3 percent reported a memory from age 12 months or younger. However, after receiving the visualization instructions, 59 percent of the participants reported a memory of their second birthday. After interviewers pressed for even earlier memories, the earliest memory reported was 1.6 years, on average. Fully 78.2 percent of the sample reported at least one memory that occurred at or earlier than 2 years, outside the boundary of infantile amnesia. More than half (56 percent) of the participants reported a memory between birth and 18 months of life; a third (33 percent) reported a memory that occurred at age 12 months or earlier, and 18 percent reported memories dated from six months or earlier. Remarkably, 4 percent of the sample reported memories from the first week of life!

Age-regression

Age-regression involves "regressing" a person back through time to an earlier life period. Subjects are typically asked to mentally re-create events that occurred at successively earlier periods in life, or to focus on a particular event at a specific age, with suggestions to fully relive the event. A televised documentary (*Frontline* 1995) showed a group therapy session in which a woman was age-regressed through childhood, to the womb, and eventually to being trapped in her mother's Fallopian tube. The woman provided a convincing demonstration of the emotional and physical discomfort that one would experience if one were indeed stuck in such an uncomfortable position. Although the woman may have believed in the veracity of her experience, research indicates that her regression experiences were not memory-based. Instead, age-regressed subjects behave according to situational cues and their knowledge, beliefs, and assumptions about age-relevant behaviors. According to Nash (1987), age-regressed adults do not show the expected patterns on many indices of development, including brain activity (EEGs) and visual illusions. No matter how compelling, "age-regressed experiences" do not represent literal reinstatements of childhood experiences, behaviors, and feelings.

Hypnotic Age-regression

Although hypnosis is often used to facilitate the experience of age-regression, it can distort memories of early life events. Nash, Drake, Wiley, Khalsa, and Lynn (1986) attempted to corroborate the memories of subjects who had participated in an earlier age-regression experiment. This experiment involved age-regressing hypnotized and role-playing (control) subjects to age three to a scene in which they were in the soothing presence of their mothers. During the experiment, subjects reported the identity of their transitional objects (e.g., blankets, teddy bears). Third-party verification (parent report) of the accuracy of recall was obtained for fourteen hypnotized subjects and ten control subjects. Hypnotic subjects were less able than were control subjects to identify the transitional objects actually used. Hypnotic subjects' hypnotic recollections matched their parent's reports only 21 percent of the time, whereas control subjects' reports were corroborated by their parents 70 percent of the time.

Sivec and Lynn (1997) age-regressed participants to the age of five and suggested that they played with a Cabbage Patch Doll (if a girl) or a He-Man toy (if a boy). These toys were not released until two or three years after the target time of the age-regression suggestion. Half of the subjects received hypnotic age-regression instructions and half received suggestions to age-regress that were not administered in a hypnotic context. While none of the nonhypnotized persons was influenced by the suggestion, 20 percent of the hypnotized subjects rated the memory as real and were confident that the event occurred at the age to which they were regressed.

Past Life Regression

The search for traumatic memories can extend to well before birth (see Mills and Lynn 2000). "Past life regression therapy" is based on the premise that traumas that occurred in previous lives contribute to current psychological and physical symptoms. For example, psychiatrist Brian Weiss (1988) published a widely publicized series of cases focusing on patients who were hypnotized and age-regressed to "go back to" the origin of a present-day problem. When patients were regressed, they reported events that Weiss interpreted as having their source in previous lives.

Vivid and realistic experiences during age-regression can seem very convincing to both patient and therapist. However, Spanos, Menary, Gabora, DuBreuil, and Dewhirst (1991) determined that the information participants provided about specific time periods during their hypnotic age-regression was almost "invariably incorrect" (p. 137). For example, one participant who was regressed to ancient times claimed to be Julius Caesar, emperor of Rome, in 50 B.C., even though the designations of B.C. and A.D. were not adopted until centuries later, and even though Julius Caesar died decades prior to the first Roman emperor. Spanos et al. (1991) informed some participants that past life identities were likely to be of a different gender, culture, and race from that of the present personality, whereas other participants received no prehypnotic information about past life identities. Participants' past life experiences were elaborate, conformed to induced expectancies about past life identities (e.g., gender, race), and varied in terms of the pre-hypnotic information participants received about the frequency of child abuse during past historical periods. In summary, hypnotically-induced past life experiences are fantasies constructed from available cultural narratives about past lives and known or surmised facts regarding specific historical periods, as well as cues present in the hypnotic situation (Spanos 1996).

Symptom Interpretation

Therapists often inform suspected abuse victims that their symptoms suggest a history of abuse (Blume 1990, Fredrickson 1992). Examples of symptom interpretation can be found in many popular psychology and self-help sources (e.g., Bass and Davis 1992). Some popular self-help books on the topic of incest include lists of symptoms (e.g., "Do you use work or achievements to compensate for inadequate feelings in other parts of your life?") that are presented as possible or probable correlates of childhood incest. Blume's "Incest Survivors' Aftereffects Checklist" consists of thirty-four such correlates. The scale instructions read: "Do you find many characteristics of yourself on this list? If so, you could be a survivor of incest." Blume also indicates that "clusters" of these items predict childhood sexual abuse, and that "the more items endorsed by an individual the more likely that there is a history of incest." Many of the characteristics on such checklists are vague and applicable to many non-abused individuals. Much of the seeming "accuracy" of such checklists could stem from "P.T. Barnum effects"—the tendency to believe that highly general statements true of many individuals in the population apply specifically to oneself (Emery 2002).

Although there may be numerous psychological correlates of sexual abuse (but see Rind, Tromovitch, and Bauserman 1998, for a competing view), no known constellation of specific symptoms, let alone diagnosis, is indicative of a history of abuse. Some genuine victims of childhood incest experience many symptoms, others only some, and still others none. Moreover, nonvictims experience many of the same symptoms often associated with sexual abuse (Tavris 1993). Nevertheless, Poole et al. (1995) found that more than one-third of the U.S. practitioners surveyed reported that they used symptom interpretation to recover suspected memories of abuse.

Bogus Personality Interpretation

For ethical reasons, researchers have not directly tested the hypothesis that false memories of childhood abuse can be elicited by informing individuals that their personality characteristics are suggestive of such a history. However, studies have shown that personality interpretation can create highly implausible or false memories. Spanos and his colleagues (Spanos, Burgess, Burgess, Samuels, and Blois 1999) informed participants that their personality indicated that they had a certain experience during the first week of life. After participants completed a questionnaire, they were told that a computer-generated personality profile based on their responses indicated they were "High Perceptual Cognitive Monitors," and that people with this profile had experienced special visual stimulation by a mobile within the first week of life. Participants were falsely told that the study was designed to recover memories to confirm the personality test scores. The participants were age-regressed to the crib; half of the participants were hypnotized and half received non-hypnotic age-regression instructions. In the non-hypnotic group, 95 percent of the participants reported infant memories and 56 percent reported the target mobile. However, all of these participants indicated that the memories were fantasy constructions or they were unsure if the memories were real. In the hypnotic group, 79 percent of the participants reported infant memories, and 46 percent reported the target mobile. Forty-nine percent of these participants believed the memories were real, and only 16 percent classified the memories as fantasies.

DuBreuil, Garry, and Loftus (1998) used the bogus personality interpretation paradigm and non-hypnotic age-regression to implant memories of the second day of life (crib group) or the first day of kindergarten (kindergarten group). College students were administered a test that purportedly measured personality and were told that, based on their scores, they were likely to have participated in a nationwide program designed to enhance the development of personality and cognitive abilities by means of red and green moving mobiles. The crib group was told that this enrichment occurred in the hospital immediately after birth, and the kindergarten group was told that the mobiles were placed in kindergarten classrooms. Participants were given the false information that memory functions "like a videotape recorder" and that age-regression can access otherwise inaccessible memories. Participants were age-regressed (non-hypnotically) to the appropriate time period and given suggestions to visualize themselves at the target age. Twenty-five percent of the kindergarten group and 55 percent of the crib group reported the target memory. All kindergarten participants believed that their memories corresponded to real events. In the crib group, 33 percent believed in the reality of their memories, 50 percent were unsure, and 17 percent of participants did not believe in the reality of their memories.

Dream Interpretation

Viewed by Freud as the "royal road to the unconscious," dreams have been used to provide a window on past experiences, including repressed traumatic events. For example, van der Kolk, Britz, Burr, Sherry, and Hartmann (1984) claimed that dreams can represent "exact replicas" of traumatic experiences (p. 188), a view not unlike that propounded by Fredrickson (1992), who argued that dreams are a vehicle by which "Buried memories of abuse intrude into ... consciousness" (p. 44).

The popularity of dream interpretation has waned in recent years. However, survey research indicates that at least a third of U.S. psychotherapists (37–44 percent) still use this technique (see also Brenneis 1997, Polusny and Follette 1996). These statistics are noteworthy given that no data exist to support the idea that dreams can be interpreted as indicative of a history of child abuse (Lindsay and Read 1994). When dreams are interpreted in this manner by an authority figure such as a therapist, rather than as reflecting the residues of the day's events or as the day's concerns seeping into dreams, it can constitute a strong suggestion to the patient that abuse actually occurred.

Mazzoni and her colleagues simulated the effects of dream interpretation of stressful yet non-abuse-related life events. Mazzoni, Lombardo, Malvagia, and Loftus (1997) had participants report on their childhood experiences on two occasions, three to four weeks apart. Between sessions, some subjects were exposed to a brief (half hour) therapy simulation in which an expert clinician analyzed a dream report that they had brought to the session. No matter what participants dreamed, they received the suggestion that their dream was indicative of having experienced certain events (e.g., being lost in a public place or abandoned by parents) before the age of three. Although subjects had indicated that they had not experienced these events before age three, many individuals revised their accounts of their past. Relative to controls who had not received the personalized suggestion, "therapy" participants were far more likely to develop false beliefs that before age three they had been lost in a public place, had felt lonely and lost in an unfamiliar place, and had been abandoned by their parents.

Mazzoni, Loftus, Seitz, and Lynn (1999) extended this paradigm to a memory of having been bullied as a child; dream interpretation increased participants' confidence that the event (being bullied or getting lost) had occurred, compared with control participants who were given a brief lecture about dreams. Six of the twenty-two participants in the dream interpretation condition recalled the bullying event and four of the five participants in the dream interpretation condition recalled getting lost. In conclusion, it is possible to implant childhood memories using personality and dream interpretation.

Bibliotherapy

Many therapists who treat patients with suspected abuse histories prescribe "survivor books" or self-help books written specifically for survivors of childhood abuse to provide "confirmation" that the individual's symptoms are due to past abuse and to provide a means of gaining access to memories. The books typically provide imaginative exercises and stories of other survivors' struggles, as well as potential support for actual abuse survivors. However, the fact that the writers interpret current symptoms as indicative of an abuse history and include suggestive stories of abuse survivors may increase the risk that readers will develop false memories of abuse. Some of the most influential popular books of this genre include Bass and Davis' (1988) *Courage to Heal,* Fredrickson's (1992) *Repressed Memories,* and Blume's (1990) *Secret Survivors: Uncovering Incest and Aftereffects in Women.*

Mazzoni, Loftus, and Kirsch (2001) provided a dramatic illustration of how reading material and psychological symptom interpretation can increase the plausibility of an initially implausible memory of witnessing a demonic possession. The study was conducted in Italy, where demonic possession is viewed as a more plausible occurrence than in America. However, in an initial testing session, all of the participants indicated that demonic possession was not only implausible, but that it was very unlikely that they had personally witnessed an occurrence of possession as children. A month after the first session, participants in one group read three short articles indicating that demonic possession is more common than is generally believed and that many children have witnessed such an event. Participants were compared with individuals who read three short articles about choking and with individuals who received no manipulation. Participants exposed to one of the manipulations returned the following week and, based on their responses to a fear questionnaire they completed, were informed (regardless of their actual responses) that their fear profile indicated that they had probably either witnessed a possession or had almost choked during early childhood.

When the original questionnaire was completed in a final session, 18 percent of the students indicated that they had probably witnessed possession. No changes in memories were evident in the control condition. In summary, events that were not experienced during childhood and initially thought to be highly implausible can, with sufficient credibility-enhancing information, come to be viewed as having occurred in real life.

HYPOTHESIZED PATH OF FALSE MEMORY CREATION

Imaginative narratives of sexual abuse that never occurred and past life reports arise when patients come to believe that the narrative provides a plausible explanation for current life difficulties. The narrative can achieve a high degree of plausibility due to many factors:

> (1) the prevalent belief that abuse and psychopathology are associated; (2) the therapist's support or suggestion of this interpretation; (3) the failure to

consider alternative explanations for everyday problems; (4) the search for confirmatory data; (5) the use of suggestive memory recovery techniques that increase the plausibility of abuse and yield remembrances consistent with the assumption that abuse occurred; (6) increasing commitment to the narrative on the part of the client and therapist, escalating dependence on the therapist, and anxiety reduction associated with ambiguity reduction; (7) the encouragement of a "conversion" or "coming out" experience by the therapist or supportive community (e.g., therapy group), which solidifies the role of "abuse victim," and which is accompanied by reinforcing feelings of empowerment; and (8) the narrative's provision of continuity to the past and the future, as well as a sense of comfort and identity.

People are not equally vulnerable to the potentially suggestive influences of memory recovery procedures. At the very least it is necessary to believe that at least some memories remain intact indefinitely so that they can be retrieved, and that memory recovery techniques can retrieve these stored memories, In addition, fantasy prone, imaginative, compliant, as well as highly hypnotically suggestible people appear to be especially vulnerable to suggestive influences and to the development of false memories.

The evidence provides little support for the use of memory recovery techniques in psychotherapy. Contrary to the idea that people repress memories in the face of trauma, traumatic events are highly memorable (Shobe and Kihlstrom 1997). Even if a small percentage of accurate memories can be recovered in psychotherapy, there is no evidence for a causal connection between non-remembered abuse and psychopathology. In addition, the mere experience of painful emotions, when not tied to attempts to bolster positive coping and mastery, can be harmful (Littrell 1998). Indeed, there is no empirically supported psychotherapy that relies on the recovery of traumatic memories to achieve a positive therapeutic outcome. Adshead (1997) argued that if memory work with trauma patients is not effective, then "it would therefore be just as unethical to use memory work for patients who could not use it or benefit by it, as it would be to prescribe the wrong medication, or employ a useless surgical technique" (p. 437).

Before concluding, let us be clear about what the findings reviewed do not mean as well as what they do mean. First, all memory recovery techniques are not necessarily problematic. For example, the "cognitive interview" (Fisher and Geiselman 1992), which incorporates a variety of techniques derived from experimental research on memory (e.g., providing subjects with retrieval cues, searching for additional memorial details), holds promise as a method of enhancing memory in eyewitness contexts. Second, we do not wish to imply that all uses of hypnosis in psychotherapy are problematic. Controlled research evidence suggests that hypnosis may be useful in treating pain, medical conditions, and habit disorders (e.g., smoking cessation), and as an adjunct to cognitive-behavioral therapy (e.g., anxiety, obesity). Nevertheless, the extent to which hypnosis provides benefits above and beyond relaxation in such cases remains unclear (Lynn, Kirsch, Barabasz, Cardena, and Patterson 2001). The questionable scientific status of hypnosis as a memory recovery technique has no bearing on the therapeutic efficacy of hypnosis, which must ultimately be investigated and judged on its own merits. Finally, we do not wish to claim that all memories recovered after years or decades of forgetting are necessarily false. We remain open to the possibility that certain recovered childhood memories are veridical, although further research is needed to document their existence and possible prevalence. These important and unresolved issues notwithstanding, the conclusion that certain suggestive therapeutic practices can foster false memories in some clients appears indisputable.

NOTES

1. The following reviews were used as sources: Erdelyi 1994; Lynn, Lock, Myers, and Payne 1997; Lynn, Neuschatz, Fite, and Rhue 2001; Nash 1987; Spanos 1996; Steblay & Bothwell 1994; Witehouse, Dinges, E. C. Orne, and M.T. Orne 1988.
2. Some therapists do not assume that early memories reports are necessarily accurate but posit that such memories nevertheless provide a window into clients' personalities; the claim of these therapists is not of concern to us here.

REFERENCES

Adler, A. 1927. *Understanding Human Nature*. New York: Greenberg.

Adshead, G. 1997. Seekers after truth: Ethical issues raised by the discussion of "false" and "recovered" memories. In J.D. Read and D.S. Lindsay (Eds.), *Recollections of Trauma: Scientific Evidence and Clinical Practice*. New York: Plenum Press.

American Medical Association. 1994. Council on Scientific Affairs. *Memories of Childhood Abuse*. CSA Report 5-A-94.

American Psychological Association. 1995. *Psychotherapy guidelines for working with clients who may have an abuse or trauma history*. Division 17 Committee on Women, Division 42 Trauma and Gender Issues Committee.

Bass, E., and L. Davis. 1988. *The Courage to Heal*. New York: Harper & Row.

Blume, E.S. 1990. *Secret Survivors: Uncovering Incest and Its Aftereffects in Women*. New York: John Wiley and Sons.

Canadian Psychiatric Association. 1996, March 25. Position statement: Adult recovered memories of childhood sexual abuse. *Canadian Journal of Psychiatry* 41: 305–306.

DuBreuil, S.C., M. Garry, and E.F. Loftus. 1998. Tales from the crib: Age-regression and the creation of unlikely memories. In S.J. Lynn and K.M. McConkey (Eds.), *Truth in Memory*. Washington, D.C.: American Psychological Association.

Emery, C.L. 2002. The validity of childhood sexual abuse victim checklists in popular psychology literature: A Barnum effect. Unpublished honors thesis, Emory University, Atlanta.

Erdelyr, M. 1994. Hypnotic hypermnesia: The empty set of hypermnesia. *International Journal of Clinical and Experimental Hypnosis* 42: 379–390.

Fisher, R.P., and R.E. Griselman. 1992. *Memory Enhancement Techniques for Investigative Interviewing*. Springfield, Illinois: Charles C. Thomas.

Frederickson, R. 1992. *Repressed Memories*. New York: Fireside/Parkside. *Frontline*. 1995. Divided memories. Producer, Ofra Bikel.

Hyman, J.E. Jr., T.H. Husband, and F.J. Billings. 1995. False memories of childhood experiences. *Applied Cognitive Psychology* 9: 181–197.

Lindsay, D. S., and D. Read. 1994. Psychotherapy and memories of childhood sexual abuse: A cognitive perspective. *Applied Cognitive Psychology* 8: 281–338.

Littrell, J. 1998. Is the experience of painful emotion therapeutic? *Clinical Psychology Review* 18: 71–102.

Loftus, E.F. 1993. The reality of repressed memories. *American Psychologist* 48: 518–537.

Loftus, E.F., and G. Mazzoni. 1998. Using imagination and personalized suggestion to change behavior. *Behavior Therapy* 29: 691–708.

Loftus, E.F., and J.E. Pickrell. 1995. The formation of false memories. *Psychiatric Annals* 25: 720–725.

Lynn, S.J., I. Kirsch, A. Barabasz, E. Cardena, and D. Patterson. 2000. Hypnosis as an empirically supported adjunctive technique: The state of the evidence. *International Journal of Clinical and Experimental Hypnosis* 48: 343–361

Lynn, S.J., T.G. Lock, B. Myers, and D.G. Payne. 1997. Recalling the unrecallable: Should hypnosis be used to recover memories in psychotherapy? *Current Directions in Psychological Science* 6: 79–83.

Lynn, S.J., B. Myers, and P. Malinoski. 1997. Hypnosis, pseudomemories, and clinical guidelines: A sociocognitive perspective. In D. Read and S. Lindsay (Eds.), *Recollections of Trauma: Scientific Research and Clinical Practice*. New York: Plenum Press.

Lynn, S.J., J. Neuschatz, R. Fire, and J.W. Rhue. 2001. Hypnosis and memory: Implications for the courtroom and psychotherapy. In M. Eisen, and G. Goodman (Eds.), *Memory, Suggestion, and the Forensic Interview*. New York: Guilford.

Malinoski, P., and S.J. Lynn. 1999. The plasticity of very early memory reports: Social pressure, hypnotizability, compliance, and interrogative suggestibility. *International Journal of Clinical and Experimental Hypnosis* 47: 320–345.

Malinoski, P., S.J. Lynn, and H. Sivec. 1998. The assessment, validity, and determinants of early memory reports: A critical review. In S.J. Lynn and K. McConkey (Eds.), *Truth in Memory*. New York: Guilford.

Mazzoni, G.A., E.F. Loftus, and I. Kirsch. 2001. Changing beliefs about implausible autobiographical memories. *Journal of Experimental Psychology: Applied* 7: 51–59.

Mazzoni, G.A., E.F. Loftus, A. Seitz, and S.J. Lynn. 1999. Creating a new childhood: Changing beliefs and memories through dream interpretation. *Applied Cognitive Psychology* 13: 125–144.

Mazzoni, G.A., P. Lombardo, S. Malvagia, and E.F. Loftus. 1997. Dream Interpretation and False Beliefs. Unpublished manuscript, University of Florence and University of Washington.

Meiselman, K. 1990. *Resolving the Trauma of Incest: Reintegration Therapy with Survivors*. San Francisco: Jossey-Bass.

Mills, A., and S.J. Lynn. 2000. Past-life experiences. In E. Cardena, S.J. Lynn, and S. Krippner (Eds.), *The Varieties of Anomalous Experience*. New York: Guilford.

Nash, M.R. 1987. What, if anything, is regressed about hypnotic age regression? A review of the empirical literature. *Psychological Bulletin* 102: 42–52.

Nash, M.J., M. Drake, R. Wiley, S. Khalsa, and S.J. Lynn. 1986. The accuracy of recall of hypnotically age regressed subjects. *Journal of Abnormal Psychology* 95: 298–300.

Olson, H.A. 1979. The hypnotic retrieval of early recollections. In H.A. Olson (Ed.), *Early Recollections: Their Use in Diagnosis and Psychotherapy*. Springfield, Illinois: Charles C. Thomas.

Papanek, H. 1979. The use of early recollections in psychotherapy. In H.A. Olson (Ed.), *Early Recollections: Their Use in Diagnosis and Psychotherapy*. Springfield Illinois: Charles C. Thomas.

Polusny, M.A., and V.M. Follene. 1996. Remembering childhood sexual abuse: A national survey of psychologists' clinical practices, beliefs, and personal experiences. *Professional Psychology: Research and Practice* 27: 41–52.

Poole, D.A., D.S. Lindsay, A. Memon, and R. Bull. 1995. Psychotherapists' opinions, practices, and experiences with recovery of memories of incestuous abuse. *Journal of Consulting and Clinical Psychology* 68: 426–437.

Porter, S., J.C. Yuille, and D.R. Lehman. 1999. The nature of real, implanted, and fabricated childhood emotional events: Implications for the recovered memory debate. *Law and Human Behavior* 23: 517–537.

Roland, C.B. 1993. Exploring childhood memories with adult survivors of sexual abuse: Concrete reconstruction and visualization techniques. *Journal of Mental Health Counseling* 15: 363–372.

Shobe, K.K., and J.F. Kihlstrom. 1997. Is traumatic memory special? *Current Directions in Psychological Science* 6: 70–74.

Sivec, H.J., S.J. Lynn, and P.T. Malinoski. 1997. Hypnosis in the cabbage patch: Age regression with verifiable events. Unpublished manuscript, State University of New York at Binghamton.

Spanos, N.P. 1996. *Multiple Identities and False Memories: A Sociocognitive Perspective*. Washington, D.C.: American Psychological Association.

Spanos, N.P., C.A. Burgess, M.F. Burgess, C. Samuels, and W.O. Blois. 1999. Creating false memories of infancy with hypnotic and nonhypnotic procedures. *Applied Cognitive Psychology* 13: 201–218.

Spanos, N.P., E. Menary, M.J. Gabota, S.C. DuBreuil, and B. Dewhirst. 1991. Secondary identity enactments during hypnotic past-life regression: A sociocognitive perspective. *Journal of Personality and Social Psychology* 61: 308–320.

Steblay, N.M., and R.K. Bothwell. 1994. Evidence for hypnotically refreshed testimony: The view from the laboratory. *Law and Human Behavior* 18: 635–651.

Tavris, C. 1993. Beware the incest survivor machine. *New York Times Book Review*, January 3, pp. 1, 16–17.

Van der Kolk, B.A. 1994. The body keeps the score: Memory and the evolving psychobiology of posttraumatic stress. *Harvard Review of Psychiatry* 1: 253–265.

Weiss, B.L. 1988. *Many Lives, Many Masters*. New York: Simon & Schuster.

Yapko, M.D. 1994. Suggestibility and repressed memories of abuse: A survey of psychotherapists' beliefs. *American Journal of Clinical Hypnosis* 36: 163–171.

REVIEW AND CONTEMPLATE

1. Briefly describe the clinical techniques of guided imagery and hypnosis, and explain why they are problematic with respect to memory recovery.

2. Describe one study that suggests hypnotic age-regression can distort people's memories.

3. Explain the problem with using a person's dreams to determine if the person has a history of child abuse.

4. Describe five of the eight factors that lead patients to perceive a high degree of plausibility in imaginative narratives of sexual abuse that never occurred.

Chapter 7

COGNITION

7.1 "Nostradamus's Clever 'Clairvoyance': The Power of Ambiguous Specificity"

PERHAPS YOU'VE HEARD of Michel Nostradamus. He's the famous 16th-century French astrologer who apparently predicted, hundreds of years in advance, such events as the assassination of President John F. Kennedy, the atrocities committed by Adolph Hitler, and the September 11, 2001 terrorist attacks in the United States. Some believe that Nostradamus predicted Hurricane Katrina, a Category 5 hurricane that hit New Orleans in 2005, causing billions of dollars in damage and more than a thousand deaths. Could the "shaking of land and sea" in the city of "Orleans" mentioned in the quote below from Nostradamus refer to Hurricane Katrina?

> The cities of Tours, Orleans, Blois, Angers, Reims and Nantes
> are troubled by sudden change.
> Tents will be pitched by (people) of foreign tongues;
> rivers, darts at Rennes, shaking of land and sea.

Did Nostradamus have amazing psychic abilities, or do people's interpretations of his prophecies tell us more about the psychology of living individuals than about the psychic abilities of a man who died hundreds of years ago? Yafeh and Heath discuss how some of the common cognitive strategies we use may lead us to perceive Nostradamus as an amazing prophet, even when his prophecies are scrambled in a random fashion. Thus, this article is an excellent example of the point made in Chapter 1: that normal cognitive processes can lead to paranormal beliefs. One cognitive tendency that is particularly relevant to this article is called "confirmation bias," or our tendency to search for information that confirms (rather than disconfirms) our hypotheses or beliefs.

Reference

Yafeh, M., & Heath, C. (2003, September/October). Nostradamus's clever 'clairvoyance': The power of ambiguous specificity. *Skeptical Inquirer, 27,* 36–40.

"NOSTRADAMUS'S CLEVER 'CLAIRVOYANCE': THE POWER OF AMBIGUOUS SPECIFICITY"

MAZIAR YAFEH AND CHIP HEATH

How did a French astrologer, dead for over 400 years, become a premier commentator on world events in 2001? The authors' research shows that Nostradamus's dark prophecies are ambiguous enough to "work" for events selected at random and even when they are scrambled.

Amidst the chaos and confusion after the September 11 terrorist attacks, anxious people flocked to the Internet for any information that would shed light on the horrific event and its implications. In the weeks after the attack, Google, the most widely used World Wide Web search engine, predictably reported sharp increases in searches for "Osama Bin Laden" and "Al Qaeda."

Yet Google also reported that in the two weeks following the attacks, searches for a sixteenth-century astrologer surpassed those for Bin Laden and his organization (Grossman 2001). In fact, "Nostradamus" became one of Google's top searches, surpassing even the perennial favorite topic of "sex"! (See Figure 7.1 for converging results from the "Buzz Index" on Yahoo, another popular search engine.) How did a French astrologer, dead for over 400 years, become a premier commentator on world events in 2001?

Michel Nostradamus was a sixteenth-century French physicist and astrologer who gained fame in the Renaissance for *Centuries,* his ten-volume collection of 942 four-line poetic prophecies, which he published in 1555. These prophecies have been eagerly studied for centuries.

In the tumult after tragic events, people over the last 400 years may have turned to Nostradamus to understand their world, just as modern citizens did right after the September 11 attacks. If so, then Nostradamus doesn't really have to predict events before they occur, he just has to look as though he predicted them *after* they have already occurred. That in itself is a pretty clever accomplishment: How could Nostradamus do it?

After spending a year researching his work and running controlled experiments, we suggest a combination of two factors: ambiguously specific prophecies that focus on dark, foreboding events.

AMBIGUOUSLY SPECIFIC PROPHECIES

Anyone who has visited a card reader or psychic knows that the lifeblood of the fortune-telling trade is vagueness (such as "You will face an important decision soon"). In

Maziar Yafeh and Chip Heath, "Nostradamus's Clever 'Clairvoyance': The Power of Ambiguous Specificity," *Skeptical Inquirer*, vol. 27, pp. 27, 36-40. Copyright © 2003 by Center for Inquiry. Reprinted with permission.

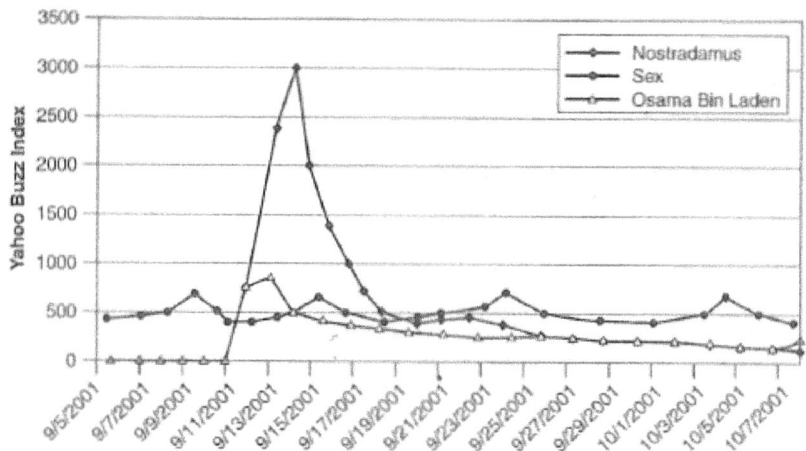

FIGURE 7.1: Popular searches on Yahoo in the days after September 11, 2001. (Note that "Nostradamus" beats out "Osama Bin Laden" and even perennial favorite "sex.")

part, Nostradamus's prophecies seem to match this vagueness test. He used a famously cryptic, poetic style, interspersing his original French with selected Hebrew, Latin, and Spanish words and phrases, to create an aura of vagueness around each prophecy. Hence, each prophecy is difficult to attribute to an exact event.

But is vagueness enough? Clearly, it is not vagueness that drew Internet searchers to the following Nostradamus prophecy in the days after September 11:

> At forty-five degrees the sky will burn,
> Fire to approach the great new city,
> In an instant a great scattered flame will leap up,
> When one will want to demand proof of the Normans.

On the contrary, it is the prophecy's unnerving similarities to the attacks; it seems written specifically for our time.

Or was it? The art of Nostradamus, our research shows, is that what appears to be specific is in fact generalizable. Nostradamus's gift is that he writes poetry that is apparently specific (at least when someone examines it with a specific historical event in mind), but that is in fact ambiguous—which we use in the dictionary sense of "allowing for multiple meanings." Indeed, it may be ambiguous enough that it could apply to many different tragic events.

But how could we test the hypothesis that this ambiguity contributes to Nostradamus's ability to appear prophetic? One way might be to choose two different events and see whether a particular prophecy could be equally well applied to each. If the same prophecy seems equally prophetic for two very different events, this indicates that Nostradamus is appealing at least in part because of his ambiguity.

With this test in mind, we chose two events for comparison: the September 11 attack on World Trade Center and the London Blitz (the fifty-seven consecutive nights during World War II in which Germany bombarded London). We selected these two events because they both took place in a specific city and are characterized in pictures, videos, and people's minds by explosions and vivid images of fire.

We concentrated on the words *city* and *fire* because these were key words in the Nostradamus prophecy we mentioned previously that circulated widely on the Internet after the World Trade Center attacks. We found eleven prophecies that contained these key words, and randomly picked ten to use in our experiment. We presented these ten prophecies to two groups of participants; one group was asked to say whether each prophecy indicated that Nostradamus might have predicted the events of September 11, the other whether each prophecy predicted the London Blitz.

Our participants were eighty Stanford University undergraduates, who are typically quite skeptical of notions of prophecy, so any results we find might underestimate the actual success of the prophecies with a less skeptical audience. For each of the ten prophecies, we asked our participants whether the prophecy predicted either September 11 or the Blitz, and gave them three choices: yes, no, and maybe. The "yes" option was almost never used, and the "no" option was used frequently. However, across the ten prophecies, the "maybe" option was chosen a surprising amount. Participants who were asked to think about the September 11 attacks on average thought that 3.2 of the prophecies may have predicted the attacks, and participants asked to think about the Blitz thought that 2.8 may have predicted those attacks. This overall difference was not statistically significant, so our participants in effect said that Nostradamus's prophecies were equally foresightful about (and relevant to) September 11 and the Blitz.

This level of "maybe" responses could suggest that Nostradamus was a pretty good prophet—about a third of his prophecies seemed at least somewhat prophetic about events that occurred 400 years after his death. However this interpretation is disputed by one key fact: participants in both groups were impressed by the *same* prophecies, regardless of whether they considered September 11 or the Blitz. For example, 68 percent of participants thought that the following prophecy might have predicted the September 11 attacks:

> Earthshaking fire from the centre of the earth,
> Will cause tremors around the new city,
> Two great rocks will war for a long time,
> Then arethusa will redden a new river.

Here, the "earthshaking fire" causing "tremors around the new city" might have seemed very applicable; the "new city" seems a good code word for "New York," and the "two great rocks" a good analogy for the twin towers.

However, 61 percent of our participants thought this same prophecy might also refer to the events of the Blitz; the "earthshaking fire" causing "tremors" seemed applicable to the Blitz as well. The word "new" seems to have been ignored since London is not one of Europe's newest cities, but in the case of the Blitz the "two great rocks" warring may have been seen as emblematic of the two strongest European armies—Germany and England—facing off across the English Channel. This "successful" prophecy is thus ambiguous enough that it seems almost equally applicable to two very different events, yet it contains enough specific detail that it looks as though Nostradamus is on to something.

Our results here are consistent with research in psychology on individual decision making. Research on "confirmation bias" and related topics has shown that individuals don't naturally consider alternative hypotheses for a particular pattern of data (see Klayman 1995; Nisbett and Ross 1980). Our participants, though smart and skeptical, fell into this same well-documented trap. Implicitly they were asking "Did Nostradamus predict the event I'm considering?" As they searched for evidence that confirmed or disconfirmed whether he did so, they probably weren't paying attention to the ambiguity of his prose, and they almost certainly weren't asking themselves whether the same prophecy could have predicted *other* events. Yet by neglecting competing hypotheses, our participants left themselves open to be fooled by the ambiguous predictions. Those participants thinking about the Blitz and its connection to the "two great rocks" probably did not consider that the same "evidence" would look equally prescient if they had been considering the New York City attacks instead.

In contrast to the ambiguity of the "successful" prophecies, the least successful prophecies contained imagery that was less ambiguous and offered concrete evidence that could be historically verified. Only 12 percent of our participants thought the following prophecy might fit September 11 and 17 percent thought it fit the Blitz:

> The great city will be thoroughly desolated,
> Of the inhabitants not a single one will remain there,
> Wall, sex, temple and virgin violated,
> Through sword, fire, plague, cannon people will die.

This prophecy is partially applicable to both events because it evokes a "great city" where some people die by fire. However, it is less convincing than the first because it is more specific: New York and London were not "thoroughly" destroyed and neither event prominently featured sex, temples, virgins, or swords.

Across the ten different prophecies, we found a high correlation between the prophecies that supposedly predicted the two events—events that were separated by half a century, different geographies, and different political contexts. True, both events involved "fire" and a "city," but so did most other wars in the last 2,000 years. These results suggest that Nostradamus's true genius was his ability to write descriptions of crises that are sufficiently ambiguous that they could describe almost any crisis.

But how far could we push the ambiguity hypothesis? Nostradamus's prophecies frequently predict "war"—indeed, war is featured in a conspicuous 104 of his 942 prophecies. Are his prophecies ambiguous enough that any of those 104 prophecies could be applied to *any* war? We asked a group of Stanford undergrads to list all the wars they could think of, and we took the top thirteen mentions. Because our students were at an American university, there was an American bias to the wars they remembered, but that did not affect the test we wanted to run. We randomly selected thirteen from 104 war prophecies and assigned them at random to the thirteen different wars; then we asked seventy-four students to indicate whether the prophecy might have predicted the war.

Because we're assigning prophecies to wars at random, we might expect the overall success to be quite low: historical accounts of various wars could not be interchanged at random. If the prophecies had any (unambiguous) content, they shouldn't be interchangeable either.

However, the prophecies were ambiguous enough that on average 29 percent of our participants said any prophecy selected at random "may have" predicted a war selected at random. When the same prophecy can apply equally well to the French Revolution, World War II, and the war on terrorism, this makes Nostradamus a relatively imprecise prophet but a very clever wartime poet—able to capture the overall atmosphere of war in a seemingly specific way, yet speaking ambiguously enough that this prophecies are for the most part not limited in time or location.

To take the poet-versus-prophet test a step further, we thought about how to preserve the poetry while destroying any potential prophecy. Nostradamus's poetry is ambiguous enough that we thought it could be largely preserved even if we scrambled the lines from different prophecies. If Nostradamus had any prophetic ability, this scrambling procedure should destroy any coherent aspects of his prophecies—certainly reducing historical accounts or news stories to gibberish.

We randomly scrambled the lines of our thirteen prophecies, and matched one scrambled prophecy with each of the thirteen wars. Then we asked a second group of seventy-two participants to assess whether the prophecy predicted the war.

With the *original* prophecies, 29 percent had said maybe. With our *scrambled* prophecies, 34 percent said maybe. Thus, if anything, our scrambled prophecies impressed people as *more prophetic* than Nostradamus's originals. (The difference wasn't statistically significant.)

DARK PROPHECIES

While ambiguity is probably the most important feature of Nostradamus's prophecies, another notable feature is their dark, foreboding quality. People are more likely to discuss and try to explain negative events than positive ones. When we're upset or surprised in a negative way, we look for explanations; when we're satisfied or things are proceeding according to our expectations, we don't (Wong and Weiner 1981; for more general discussion, Weiner 1985; Taylor 1995). By writing many prophecies involving negative

Can You Find the Original Nostradamus Prophecies?

Three of the prophecies in this table are from Nostradamus. The other three are versions we created by scrambling the lines of his original prophecies. Can you tell which is which?

1. Arms will be heard clashing in the sky. That very same year the divine one's enemies. They will want unjustly to discuss the holy laws. Through lightning and war the complacent one put to death.
2. The two nephews brought up in diverse places,
   He assembles the pardoned before the gods,
   They will come to be elevated very high in making war,
   Far away where their prince and rector will die.
3. The great younger son will make an end of the war,
   Will have carried off the prize from one greater than he,
   He holds a flowering branch in this beak,
   Without armor he will be surprised suddenly.
4. Two royal brothers will wage war so fiercely,
   That between them the war will be so mortal,
   That both will occupy the strong places,
   Then great quarrel will fill realm and life.
5. The two nephews brought up in diverse places,
   Naval battle, land, fathers fallen,
   They will come to be elevated very high in making war,
   To avenge the injury, enemies succumbed.
6. Through long war all the army exhausted,
   To great a faith will betray the monarch instead of gold or silver
   they will come to coin leather,
   To avenge the injury enemies succumbed.

(#1,4,5 are original and 2,3,6 are our scrambled versions)
Prophecies taken from www.ebooks3.com/ebooks/nostradamus_centuries.html

The top thirteen wars recalled by our participants. We used these to test whether any of Nostradamus's "war" prophecies could be randomly assigned to any randomly selected war.

American Revolution	Gulf War
World War	Korean War
War on Terrorism	Spanish Civil War
American Civil War	French-Indian War
Vietnam War	War of 1812
World War 1	Thirty Years War
French Revolution	

events, Nostradamus maximized the chances that someone confronted with a crisis might look for—and find—something in his prophecies that would remind them of their own current crisis.

To test how much Nostradamus focused on the negative, we randomly sampled 100 of his prophecies and asked a group of students to assess whether they concerned positive or negative events. More than three times as many prophecies discussed negative events as positive ones. We also asked a group of students to list words associated with events of good fortune and misfortune. The top examples of good fortune were *birth* and *discovery,* while *war* and *death* topped the misfortune list. Searching through all of Nostradamus's prophecies, we found that while less than five of them dealt with either *birth* or *discovery,* 104 mentioned *war* and ninety-four mentioned *death.* We're not sure that this focus on the negative makes Nostradamus a good prophet—after all, prophecies of great discoveries and the births of great people might come in handy. On the other hand, when people search for explanations after a tragic event, Nostradamus allows himself many opportunities to provide them with an "answer."

Nostradamus, a clever poet, offers pronouncements of ambiguous doom— so ambiguous, in fact, that his war prophecies can apply to *any* war, and appear equally prophetic even when scrambled.

Our results show that there is about a 30 percent chance that any randomly selected war prophecy will remind some readers of any randomly selected war. But Nostradamus was sufficiently prolific that his readers don't have to stop with just one prophecy. Imagine someone who was sufficiently intrigued to read all 942 prophecies; wouldn't at least one of the 104 prophecies about "war" seemingly provide an even better match than one selected at random? By writing many prophecies, Nostradamus could take advantage of people's natural tendency to search longer and harder for explanations at times of crisis.

We offer a recipe for a modern prophet: Write a lot of prophecies, focusing on the negative. Take care to keep your prophecies as dark and ambiguous as possible—lots

How Effectively Does the Following Prophecy Predict WWII?

For a long time a gray bird will be seen in the sky,
They will be thoroughly devastated by sea and by land
Those (actions) started in France will end there
Captured, dead, bound, pillaged without law of war
58% of our participants thought that Nostradamus may have predicted WWII with this prophecy but it's actually one of our scrambled versions.

of doom and gloom, very few unambiguous specifics. And someday you too might be invoked as a commentator on world events.

Now if someone could only figure out how to collect royalties from beyond the grave....

REFERENCES

Grossman, L. 2001. In search of ... *Time,* October 29, 2001, p. 92.

Klayman, J. 1995. Varieties of confirmation bias. *The Psychology of Learning and Motivation,* 32: 385–418.

Nisbett, R., and L. Ross. 1980. *Human Inference: Strategies and Shortcomings of Social Judgment.* Englewood Cliffs, New Jersey: Prentice-Hall.

Taylor, S.E. 1991. Asymmetrical effects of positive and negative events: The mobilization/minimization hypothesis. *Psychological Bulletin* 110: 67–85.

Weiner, B. 1985. "Spontaneous" causal thinking. *Psychological Bulletin* 97: 74–84.

Wong, P.T., and B. Weiner. 1981. When people ask "Why" questions and the heuristics of attributional search. *Journal of Personality and Social Psychology* 40: 650–663. Who is Michel Nostradamus, and for what is he famous?

REVIEW AND CONTEMPLATE

1. Briefly describe the evidence that suggests the predictions of Nostradamus appear accurate because they are ambiguous enough to apply to many different tragic events.

2. Define "confirmation bias" and describe how it explains people's tendency to see ambiguous predictions as related to specific events.

3. What "recipe" does the article offer for those who want to be a "modern prophet"?

4. Collect the daily horoscope for your astrological sign and three other astrological signs. How are the statements used in horoscopes similar to those used by Nostradamus?

7.2 "Like Goes With Like: The Role of Representativeness in Erroneous and Pseudoscientific Beliefs"

ONE EARLY THEORY of medicine, popularized in the 1600s, was the Doctrine of Signatures. This doctrine stated that natural substances such as plants have well-marked signs that indicate the maladies for which they may be used as treatments. For example, the spotted leaves of the lungwort plant resemble a diseased lung and could therefore be used to treat lung ailments. Goldenrod (which has yellow flowers) could be used to treat jaundice (a condition in which the skin appears yellow); bloodroot (the root of which contains a red liquid) could be used to treat blood disorders; toothwort (which has a white root) was thought to be useful for treating toothaches; and the maidenhair fern (which has fine hairs on its roots) could be used to treat baldness.

This early medical thinking relies on a common cognitive shortcut—called the "representativeness heuristic"—that people use to simplify everyday decisions and judgments. As mentioned in Chapter 1, heuristics are normal cognitive strategies that can sometimes lead to paranormal and pseudoscientific beliefs. The representativeness heuristic is one of several such heuristics. One way we use this heuristic is to estimate the likelihood that a substance can be used to treat a disease based on how similar the substance is to the symptoms of the disease. Thus, goldenrod might have been used to treat jaundice because its yellow flowers resembled the yellow skin of those who had jaundice.

Although early medical beliefs guided by the Doctrine of Signatures may seem obviously faulty to you, similar reasoning is behind a number of more recent practices and beliefs. Gilovich and Savitsky discuss how the representativeness heuristic may underlie faulty medical beliefs, pseudoscientific beliefs, and the popularity of psychoanalytic theory and projective tests.

Reference

Gilovich, T., & Savitsky, K. (1996, March/April). Like goes with like: The role of representativeness in erroneous and pseudoscientific beliefs. *Skeptical Inquirer, 20,* 34–40.

"LIKE GOES WITH LIKE: THE ROLE OF REPRESENTATIVENESS IN ERRONEOUS AND PSEUDOSCIENTIFIC BELIEFS"

THOMAS GILOVICH AND KENNETH SAVITSKY

The misguided premise that effects should resemble their causes underlies a host of erroneous beliefs, from folk wisdom about health and the human body to elaborate pseudoscientific belief systems.

It was in 1983, at an infectious-disease conference in Brussels, that Barry Marshall, an internal-medicine resident from Perth, Australia, first staked his startling claim. He argued that the peptic ulcer, a painful crater in the lining of the stomach or duodenum, was not caused by a stressful lifestyle as everyone had thought. Instead, the malady that afflicts millions of adults in the United States alone was caused by a simple bacterium, and thus could be cured using antibiotics (Hunter 1993; Monmaney 1993; Peterson 1991; Wandycz 1993).

Although subsequent investigations have substantiated Marshall's claim (e.g., Hentschel et al. 1993), his colleagues initially were highly skeptical. Martin Blaser, director of the Division of Infectious Diseases at the Vanderbilt University School of Medicine, described Marshall's thesis as "the most preposterous thing I'd ever heard" (Monmaney 1993).

What made the idea so preposterous? Why were the experts so resistant to Marshall's suggestion? There were undoubtedly many reasons. For one, the claim contradicted what most physicians, psychiatrists, and psychologists knew (or thought they knew): Ulcers were caused by stress. As one author noted, "No physical ailment has ever been more closely tied to psychological turbulence" (Monmaney 1993, p. 64). In addition, science is necessarily and appropriately a rather conservative enterprise. Although insight, creativity, and even leaps of faith are vital to the endeavor, sound empirical evidence is the true coin of the realm. Much of the medical establishment's hesitation doubtless stemmed from the same healthy skepticism that readers of the SKEPTICAL INQUIRER have learned to treasure. After all, Marshall's results at the time were suggestive at best—no cause-effect relationship had yet been established.

But there may have been a third reason for the reluctance to embrace Marshall's contention, a reason we explore in this article. The belief that ulcers derive from stress is particularly seductive—for physicians and laypersons alike—because it flows from a general tendency of human judgment, a tendency to employ what psychologists Amos Tversky and Daniel Kahneman have called the "representativeness heuristic" (Kahneman

Thomas Gilovich and K. Savitsky, "Like Goes with Like: The Role of Representativeness in Erroneous and Pseudoscientific Beliefs," *Skeptical Inquirer*, vol. 20, pp. 34-40. Copyright © 1996 by Thomas Gilovich. Reprinted with permission.

and Tversky 1972, 1973; Tversky and Kahneman 1974, 1982). Indeed, we believe that judgment by representativeness plays a role in a host of erroneous beliefs, from beliefs about health and the human body to handwriting analysis and astrology (Gilovich 1991). We consider a sample of these beliefs in this article.

THE REPRESENTATIVENESS HEURISTIC

Representativeness is but one of a number of heuristics that people use to render complex problems manageable. Heuristics are often described as judgmental shortcuts that generally get us where we need to go—and quickly—but at the cost of occasionally sending us off course. Kahneman and Tversky liken them to perceptual cues, which generally enable us to perceive the world accurately, but occasionally give rise to misperception and illusion. Consider their example of using clarity as a cue for distance. The clarity of an object is one cue people use to decide how far away it is. The cue typically works well because the farther away something is, the less distinct it appears. On a particularly clear day, however, objects can appear closer than they are, and on hazy days they can appear farther away. In some circumstances, then, this normally accurate cue can lead to error.

Representativeness works much the same way. The representativeness heuristic involves a reflexive tendency to assess the similarity of objects and events along salient dimensions and to organize them on the basis of one overarching rule: "Like goes with like." Among other things, the representativeness heuristic reflects the belief that a member of a given category ought to resemble the category prototype, and that an effect ought to resemble the cause that produced it. Thus, the representativeness heuristic is often used to assess whether a given instance belongs to a particular category, such as whether an individual is likely to be an accountant or a comedian. It is also used in assigning causes to effects, as when deciding whether a meal of spicy food caused a case of heartburn or determining whether an assassination was the product of a conspiracy.[1]

Note that judgment by representativeness often works well. Instances often resemble their category prototypes and causes frequently resemble their effects. Members of various occupational groups, for example, frequently do resemble the group prototype. Likewise, "big" effects (such as the development of the atomic bomb) are often brought about by "big" causes (such as the Manhattan Project).

Still, the representativeness heuristic is only that—a heuristic or shortcut. As with all shortcuts, the representativeness heuristic should be used with caution. Although it can help us to make some judgments with accuracy and ease, it can also lead us astray. Not all members fit the category prototype. Some comedians are shy or taciturn, and some accountants are wild and crazy. And although causes are frequently representative of their effects, this relationship does not always hold: Tiny viruses give rise to devastating epidemics like malaria or AIDS; and splitting the nucleus of an atom releases an awesome amount of energy. In some cases, then, representativeness yields inaccuracy and error.

Or even superstition. A nice example is provided by craps shooters, who roll the dice gently to coax a low number, and more vigorously to encourage a high one (Hanslin 1967). A small effect (low number) requires a small cause (gentle roll), and a big effect (high number) requires a big cause (vigorous roll).

How might the belief in a stress-ulcer link derive from the conviction that like goes with like? Because the burning feeling of an ulcerated stomach is not unlike the gut-wrenching, stomach-churning feeling of extreme stress (albeit more severe), the link seems natural: Stress is a representative cause of an ulcer.[2] But as Marshall suggested (and subsequent research has borne out), the link may be overblown. Stress alone does not appear to cause ulcers (Glavin and Szabo 1992; Soll 1990).

REPRESENTATIVENESS AND THE CONJUNCTION FALLACY

One of the most compelling demonstrations of how the representativeness heuristic can interfere with sound judgment comes from a much-discussed experiment in which participants were asked to consider the following description (Tversky and Kahneman 1982, 1983):

> Linda is 31 years old, single, outspoken, and very bright. She majored in philosophy. As a student, she was deeply concerned with issues of discrimination and social justice, and also participated in anti-nuclear demonstrations.
>
> Now, based on the above description, rank the following statements about Linda, from most to least likely:
>
> a. Linda is an insurance salesperson.
> b. Linda is a bank teller.
> c. Linda is a bank teller and is active in the feminist movement.

If you are like most people, you probably thought it was more likely that "Linda is a bank teller and is active in the feminist movement" than that "Linda is a bank teller." It is easy to see why: A feminist bank teller is much more representative of the description of Linda than is "just" a bank teller. It reflects the political activism, social-consciousness, and left-of-center politics implied in the description.

It may make sense, but it cannot be. The category "bank teller" subsumes the category "is a bank teller and is active in the feminist movement." The latter therefore cannot be more likely than the former. Anyone who is a bank teller and is active in the feminist movement is automatically also a bank teller. Indeed, even if one thinks it is impossible for someone with Linda's description to be solely a bank teller (that is, one who is not a feminist), being a bank teller is still *as* likely as being both. This error is referred to as the "conjunction fallacy" because the probability of two events co-occurring (i.e., their conjunction) can never exceed the individual probability of either of the constituents (Tversky and Kahneman 1982, 1983; Dawes and Mulford 1993).

Such is the logic of the situation. The psychology we bring to bear on it is something else. If we start with an unrepresentative outcome (being a bank teller) and then add a representative element (being active in the feminist movement), we create a description that is at once more psychologically compelling but objectively less likely. The rules of representativeness do not follow the laws of probability. A detailed description can seem compelling precisely because of the very details that, objectively speaking, actually make it less likely. Thus, someone may be less concerned about dying during a trip to the Middle East than about dying in a terrorist attack while there, even though the probability of death due to a *particular* cause is obviously lower than the probability of death due to the set of all possible causes. Likewise, the probability of global economic collapse can seem remote until one sketches a detailed scenario in which such a collapse follows, say, the destruction of the oil fields in the Persian Gulf. Once again, the additional details make the outcome less likely at the same time that they make it more psychologically compelling.

REPRESENTATIVENESS AND CAUSAL JUDGMENTS

Most of the empirical research on the representativeness heuristic is similar to the work on the conjunction fallacy in that the judgments people make are compared to a normative standard—in this case, to the laws of probability. The deleterious effect of judgment by representativeness is thereby established by the failure to meet such a standard. Previous work conducted in this fashion has shown, for example, that judgment by representativeness leads people to commit the "gambler's fallacy," to overestimate the reliability of small samples of data, and to be insufficiently "regressive" in making predictions under conditions of uncertainty.

The ulcer example with which we began this article does not have this property of being obviously at variance with a clear-cut normative standard. The same is true of nearly all examples of the impact of representativeness on causal judgments: It can be difficult to establish with certainty that a judgmental error has been made. Partly for this reason, there has been less empirical research on representativeness and causal judgments than on other areas, such as representativeness and the conjunction fallacy. This is not because representativeness is thought to have little impact on causal judgments, but because without a clear-cut normative standard it is simply more difficult to conduct research in this domain. The research that has been conducted, furthermore, is more suggestive than definitive. Nonetheless, the suggestive evidence is rather striking, and it points to the possibility that representativeness may exert at least as much influence over causal judgments as it does over other, more exhaustively researched types of judgments. To see how much, we discuss some examples of representativeness-thinking in medicine, in pseudoscientific systems, and in psychoanalysis.

REPRESENTATIVENESS AND MEDICAL BELIEFS

One area in which the impact of representativeness on causal judgments is particularly striking is the domain of health and medicine. Historically, people have often assumed that the symptoms of a disease should resemble either its cause or its cure (or both). In ancient Chinese medicine, for example, people with vision problems were fed ground bat in the mistaken belief that bats had particularly keen vision and that some of this ability might be transferred to the recipient (Deutsch 1977). Evans-Pritchard (1937) noted many examples of the influence of representativeness among the African Azande (although he discussed them in the context of magical-thinking, not representativeness). For instance, the Azande used the ground skull of the red bush monkey to cure epilepsy. Why? The cure should resemble the disease, so the herky-jerky movements of the monkey make the essence of monkey appear to be a promising candidate to settle the violent movements of an epileptic seizure. As Evans-Pritchard (quoted in Nisbett and Ross 1980, p. 116) put it:

> Generally the logic of therapeutic treatment consists in the selection of the most prominent external symptoms, the naming of the disease after some object in nature it resembles, and the utilization of the object as the principal ingredient in the drug administered to cure the disease. The circle may even be completed by belief that the external symptoms not only yield to treatment by the object which resembles them but are caused by it as well.

Western medical practice has likewise been guided by the representativeness heuristic. For instance, early Western medicine was strongly influenced by what was known as the "doctrine of signatures," or the belief that "every natural substance which possesses any medicinal virtue indicates by an obvious and well-marked external character the disease for which it is a remedy, or the object for which it should be employed" (quoted in Nisbett and Ross 1980, p. 116). Thus, physicians prescribed the lungs of the fox (known for its endurance) for asthmatics, and the yellow spice turmeric for jaundice. Again, disease and cure are linked because they resemble one another.

Or consider the popularity of homeopathy, which derives from the eighteenth-century work of the German physician Samuel Hahnemann (Barrett 1987). One of the bedrock principles of homeopathy is Hahnemann's "law of similars," according to which the key to discovering what substance will cure a particular disorder lies in noting the effect that various substances have on healthy people. If a substance causes a particular reaction in an unafflicted person, then it is seen as a likely cure for a disease characterized by those same symptoms. As before, the external symptoms of a disease are used to identify a cure for the disease—a cure that manifests the same external characteristics.

Of course, there are instances in which substances that cause particular symptoms *are* used effectively as part of a therapeutic regimen to cure, alleviate, or prevent those very symptoms. Vaccines deliver small quantities of disease-causing viruses to help individuals develop immunities. Likewise, allergy sufferers sometimes receive periodic doses of the exact substance to which they are allergic so that they will develop a tolerance over time. The problem with the dubious medical practices described above is the *general* assumption that the symptoms of a disease should resemble its cause, its cure, or both. Limiting the scope of possible cures to those that are representative of the disease can seriously impede scientific discovery. Such a narrow focus, for example, would have inhibited the discovery of the two most significant developments of modern medicine: sanitation and antibiotics.

Representativeness-thinking continues to abound in modern "alternative" medicine, a pursuit that appears to be gaining in perceived legitimacy (Cowley, King, Hager, and Rosenberg 1995). An investigation by Congress into health fraud and quackery noted several examples of what appear to be interventions inspired by the superficial appeal of representativeness (U.S. Congress, House Subcommittee on Health and Long-Term Care 1984). In one set of suggested treatments, patients are encouraged to eat raw organ concentrates corresponding to the dysfunctional body part: e.g., brain concentrates for mental disorders, heart concentrates for cardiac conditions, and raw stomach lining for ulcers. Similarly, the fingerprints of representativeness are all over the practice of "rebirthing," a New Age therapeutic technique in which individuals attempt to reenact their own births in an effort to correct personality defects caused by having been born in an "unnatural" fashion (Ward 1994). One person who was born breech (i.e., feet first) underwent the rebirthing procedure to cure his sense that his life was always going in the wrong direction and that he could never seem to get things "the right way round." Another, born Caesarean, sought the treatment because of a lifelong difficulty with seeing things to completion, and always relying on others to finish tasks for her. As one author quipped, "God knows what damage forceps might inflict... a lifelong neurosis that you're being dragged where you don't want to go?" (Ward 1994, p. 90).

A more rigorous examination of the kind of erroneous beliefs about health and the human body that can arise from the appeal of representativeness has dealt with the adage, "You are what you eat." Just how far do people take this idea? In certain respects, the saying is undeniably true: Bodies are composed to a large extent of the molecules that were once ingested as food. Quite literally, we are what we have eaten. Indeed, there are times when we take on the character of what we ingest: People gain weight by eating fatty foods, and a person's skin can acquire an orange tint from the carotene found in carrots and tomatoes. But the notion that we develop the characteristics of the food we eat sometimes goes beyond such examples to almost magical extremes. The Hua of Papua New Guinea, for example, believe that individuals will grow quickly if they eat rapidly growing food (Meigs 1984, cited by Nemeroff and Rozin 1989).

But what about a more "scientifically minded" population? Psychologists Carol Nemeroff and Paul Rozin (1989) asked college students to consider a hypothetical culture known as the "Chandorans," who hunt wild boar and marine turtles. Some of the students learned that the Chandorans hunt turtles for their shells, and wild boar for their meat. The others heard the opposite: The tribe hunts turtles for their meat, and boar for their tusks.

After reading one of the two descriptions of the Chandorans, the students were asked to rate the tribe members on numerous characteristics. Their responses reflected a belief that the characteristics of the food that was eaten would "rub off' onto the tribe members. Boar-eaters were thought to be more aggressive and irritable than their counterparts—and more likely to have beards! The turtle-eaters were thought to live longer and be better swimmers.

However educated a person may be (the participants in Nemeroff and Rozin's experiment were University of Pennsylvania undergraduates), it can be difficult to get beyond the assumption that like goes with like. In this case, it leads to the belief that individuals tend to acquire the attributes of the food they ingest. Simple representativeness.

REPRESENTATIVENESS AND PSEUDOSCIENTIFIC BELIEFS

A core tenet of the field of astrology is that an individual's personality is influenced by the astrological sign under which he or she was born (Huntley 1990). A glance at the personality types associated with the various astrological signs reveals an uncanny concordance between the supposed personality of someone with a particular sign and the characteristics associated with the sign's namesake (Huntley 1990; Howe 1970; Zusne and Jones 1982). Those born under the sign of the goat (Capricorn) are said to be tenacious, hardworking, and stubborn; whereas those born under the lion (Leo) are proud, forceful leaders. Likewise, those born under the sign of Cancer (the crab) share with their namesake a tendency to appear hard on the outside; while inside their "shells" they are soft and vulnerable. One treatment of astrology goes so far as to suggest that, like the crab, those born under the sign of Cancer tend to be "deeply attached to their homes" (Read et al. 1978).

What is the origin of these associations? They are not empirically derived, as they have been shown time and time again to lack validity (e.g., Carlson 1985; Dean 1987; for reviews see Abell 1981: Schick and Vaughn 1995: Zusne and Jones 1982). Instead, they are conceptually driven by simple, representativeness-based assessments of the personalities that *should* be associated with various astrological signs. After all, who is more likely to be retiring and modest than a Virgo (the virgin)? Who better to be well balanced, harmonious, and fair than a Libra (the scales)? By taking advantage of people's reflexive associations, the system gains plausibility among those disinclined to dig deeper.

And it doesn't stop there. Consider another elaborate "scientific" system designed to assess the "secrets" of an individual's personality—graphology, or handwriting analysis. Corporations pay graphologists sizable fees to help screen job applicants by developing personality profiles of those who apply for jobs (Neter and Ben-Shakhar 1989). Graphologists are also called upon to provide "expert" testimony in trial proceedings, and to help the Secret Service determine if any real danger is posed by threatening letters to government officials (Scanlon and Mauro 1992). How much stock can we put in the work of handwriting analysts?

Unlike astrology, graphology is not worthless. It has been, and continues to be, the subject of careful empirical investigation (Nevo 1986), and it has been shown that people's handwriting can reveal certain things about them. Particularly shaky writing can be a clue that an individual suffers from some neurological disorder that causes hand tremors; whether a person is male or female is often apparent from his or her writing. In general, however, what handwriting analysis can determine most reliably tends to be things that can be more reliably ascertained through other means. As for the "secrets" of an individual's personality, graphology has yet to show that it is any better than astrology.

This has not done much to diminish the popularity of handwriting analysis, however. One reason for this is that graphologists, like astrologers, gain some surface plausibility or "face validity" for their claims by exploiting the tendency for people to employ the representativeness heuristic. Many of their claims have a superficial "sensible" quality, rarely violating the principle that like goes with like. Consider, for instance, the "zonal theory" of graphology, which divides a person's handwriting into the upper, middle, and lower regions. A person's "intellectual," "practical," and "instinctual" qualities supposedly correspond to the different regions (Basil 1989). Can you guess which is which? Could our "lower" instincts be reflected anywhere other than the lower region, or our "higher" intellect anywhere other than the top?

The list of such representativeness-based "connections" goes on and on. Handwriting slants to the left? The person must be holding something back, repressing his or her true emotions. Slants to the right? The person gets carried away by his or her feelings. A signature placed far below a paragraph suggests that the individual wishes to distance himself or herself from what was written (Scanlon and Mauro 1992). Handwriting that stays close to the left margin belongs to individuals attached to the past, whereas writing that hugs the right margin comes from those oriented toward the future.

What is ironic is that the very mechanism that many graphologists rely upon to argue for the persuasive value of their endeavor—that the character of the handwriting resembles the character of the person—is what ultimately betrays them: They call it "common sense"; we call it judgment by representativeness.

REPRESENTATIVENESS AND PSYCHOANALYSIS

Two prominent social psychologists, Richard Nisbett and Lee Ross, have argued that "the enormous popularity of Freudian theory probably lies in the fact that, unlike all its competitors among contemporary views, it encourages the layperson to do what comes naturally in causal explanation, that is, to use the representativeness heuristic" (Nisbett and Ross 1980, p. 244). Although this claim would be difficult to put to empirical test, there can be little doubt that much of the interpretation of symbols that lies at the core of psychoanalytic theory is driven by representativeness. Consider the interpretation of dreams, in which the images a client reports from his or her dreams are considered indicative of underlying motives. An infinite number of potential relationships exist between dream content and underlying psychodynamics, and it is interesting that virtually all of the "meaningful" ones identified by psychodynamically oriented clinicians are ones in which there is an obvious fit or resemblance between the reported image and inner dynamics. A man who dreams of a snake or a cigar is thought to be troubled by his penis or his sexuality. People who dream of policemen are thought to be concerned about their fathers or authority figures. Knowledge of the representativeness heuristic compels one to wonder whether such connections reflect something important about the psyche of the client, or whether they exist primarily in the mind of the therapist.

One area of psychodynamic theorizing in which the validity of such superficially plausible relationships has been tested and found wanting is the use of projective tests. The most widely known projective test is the Rorschach, in which clients report what they "see" in ambiguous blotches of ink on cards. As in all projective tests, the idea is that in responding to such an unstructured stimulus, a person must "project," and thus reveal, some of his or her inner dynamics. Countless studies, however, have failed to produce evidence that the test is valid—that is, that the assessments made about people on the basis of the test correspond to the psychopathological conditions from which they suffer (Burros 1978).[3]

The research findings notwithstanding, clinicians frequently report the Rorschach to be extremely helpful in clinical practice. Might representativeness contribute to this paradox of strongly held beliefs coexisting with the absence of any real relationship? You be the judge. A person who interprets the whole Rorschach card, and not its specific details, is considered by clinicians to suffer from a need to form a "big picture," and a tendency toward grandiosity, even paranoia. In contrast, a person who refers only to small details of the ink blots is considered to have an obsessive personality—someone who attends to detail at the expense of the more important holistic aspects (Dawes 1994). Once again, systematic research has failed to find evidence for these relationships, but the sense of representativeness gives them some superficial plausibility.

CONCLUSION

We have described numerous erroneous beliefs that appear to derive from the overuse of the representativeness heuristic. Many of them arise in domains in which the reach for solutions to important problems exceeds our grasp—such as the attempt to uncover (via astrology or handwriting analysis) simple cues to the complexities of human motivation and personality. In such domains in which no simple solutions exist, and yet the need or desire for such solutions remains strong, people often let down their guard. Dubious cause-effect links are then uncritically accepted because they satisfy the principle of like goes with like.

Representativeness can also have the opposite effect, inhibiting belief in valid claims that violate the expectation of resemblance. People initially scoffed at Walter Reed's suggestion that malaria was carried by the mosquito. From a representativeness standpoint, it is easy to see why: The cause (a tiny mosquito) is not at all representative of the result (a devastating disease). Reed's claim violated the notion that big effects should have big causes, and thus was difficult to accept (Nisbett and Ross 1980). Although skepticism is a vital component of critical thought, it should not be based on an excessive adherence to the principle that like goes with like.

Indeed, it is often those discoveries that violate the expected resemblance between cause and effect that are ultimately hailed a significant breakthroughs, as with the discovery of *Helicobacter pylori*, as the ulcer-causing bacterium is now named. As one author put it, "The discovery of *Helicobacter* is no crummy little shift. It's a mindblower—tangible, reproducible, unexpected, and, yes, revolutionary. Just the fact that a bug causes peptic ulcers, long considered the cardinal example of a psychosomatic illness, is a spear in the breast of New Age medicine" (Monmaney 1993, p. 68). Given these stakes, one might be advised to avoid an overreliance on the shortcut of representativeness, and instead to devote the extra effort needed to make accurate judgments and decisions. (But not too much effort—you wouldn't want to give yourself an ulcer.)

NOTES

We thank Dennis Regan for his helpful comments on an earlier draft of this article.

1. The reason that the heuristic has been dubbed "representativeness" rather than, say, "resemblance" or "similarity" is that it also applies in circumstances in which the assessment of "fit" is not based on similarity. For example, when assessing whether a series of coin flips was produced by tossing a fair coin, people's judgments are influenced in part by whether the sequence is representative of one produced by a fair coin. A sequence of five heads and five tails is a representative outcome, but a sequence of nine heads and one tail is not. Note, however, that a fifty-fifty split does not make the sequence "similar" to a fair coin, but is does make it representative of one.
2. Some theories of the link between stress and ulcers are even more tinged with representativeness. Since the symptoms of an ulcer manifest themselves in the stomach, the cause "should" involve something that is highly characteristic of the stomach as well, such as hunger and nourishment. Thus, one theoriest asserts, "The critical factor in the development of ulcers is the frustration associated with the wish to receive love—when this wish is rejected, it is converted into a wish to be fed," leading ultimately "to an ulcer." Echoing such ideas, James Masterson writes in his book *The Search for the Real Self* that ulcers affect those who are "hungering for emotional supplies that were lost in childhood or that were never sufficient to nourish the real self' (both quoted in Monmaney 1993).
3. Actually, a nonprojective use of the Rorschach, called the Exner System, has been shown to have some validity (Exner 1986). The system is based on the fact that some of the inkblots *do* look like various objects, and a person's responses are scored for

the number and proportion that fail to reflect this correspondence. Unlike the usual Rorschach procedure, which is subjectively scored, the Exner system is a standardized test.

REFERENCES

Abell, G. O. 1981. Astrology. In *Science and the Paranormal: Probing the Existence of the Supernatural,* ed. by G. O. Abell and B. Singer. New York: Charles Scribner's Sons.

Barrett, S. 1987. Homeopathy: Is it medicine? SKEPTICAL INQUIRER 12(1) (Fall): 56–62.

Basil, R. 1989. Graphology and personality: Let the buyer beware. SKEPTICAL INQUIRER 13 (3) (Spring): 241–243.

Burros, O. K. 1978. *Mental Measurement Yearbook.* 8th ed. Highland Park, N.J.: Gryphon Press.

Carlson, S. 1985. A double-blind test of astrology. *Nature* 318: 419–425.

Cowley, G., P. King, M. Hager, and D. Rosenberg. 1995. Going mainstream. *Newsweek* June 26: 56–57.

Dawes, R. M. 1994. *House of Cards: Psychology and Psychotherapy Built on Myth.* New York: Free Press.

Dawes, R. M., and M. Mulford. 1993. Diagnoses of alien kidnappings that result from conjunction effects in memory. SKEPTICAL INQUIRER 18(1) (Fall): 50–51.

Dcan, G. 1987. Does astrology need to be true? Part 2: The answer is no. SKEPTICAL INQUIRER 11(3) (Spring): 257–273.

Deutsch, R. M. 1977. *The New Nuts among the Berriex: How Nutrition Nonsense Captured America.* Palo Alto, Calif.: Ball Publishing.

Evans-Pritchard, E. E. 1937. *Witsberuft, Oracles and Magic among the Axands.* Oxford: Clarendon.

Exnet, J. E. 1986. *The Rorschach: A comprehensive System.* 2d ed. New York: John Wiley.

Gilovich, T. 1991. *How We Know What Isn't So: The Fallibility of Human Reason in Everyday Life.* New York: The Free Press.

Glavin, G. B., and S. Szabo. 1992. Experimental gastric muscatel injury: Laboratory models reveal mechanisms of pathogenesis and new therapeutic strategies. *FASEB Journal* 6:825–831.

Hanslin, J. M. 1967. Craps and magic. *American Journal of Sociology* 73:316–330.

Hentschel, E., G. Brandstattet, B, Dragosics, A. M. Hirschel, H. Nemec, K. Schurze, M. Taufer, and H. Wurzet. 1993. Effect of ranitidine and amoxicillin plus metronidazole on the eradication of Helicobacter pylori and the recurrence of duodenal ulcer. *New England Journal of Medicine* 328: 308–312.

Howe, E. 1970. Astrology. In *Man, Myth, and Magic: An Illustrated Encyclopedia of the Supernatural,* ed. by R. Cavendish. New York: Marshall Cavendish.

Hunter, B. T. 1993. Good news for gastric sufferers. *Consumer's Research* 76 (October): 8–9.

Huntley, J. 1990. *The Elements of Astrology.* Shaftesbury, Dorset, Great Britain: Element Books.

Kahneman, D., and A. Tversky. 1972. Subjective probability: A judgment of representativeness. *Cognitive Psychology* 3: 430–454.

Kahneman, D., and A. Tversky. 1973. On the psychology of prediction. *Psychological Review* 80: 237–251.

Meigs, A. S. 1984. *Food, Sex, and Pollution: A New Guinea Religion.* New Brunswick, N.J.: Rutgers University Press.

Monmaney, T. 1993. Marshall's hunch. *The New Yorker* 69 (September 20): 64–72.

Nemeroff, C., and P. Rozin. 1989. 'You are what you eat': Applying the demand-free "impressions" technique to an unacknowledged belief. *Erhos* 17: 50–69.

Neter, E., and G. Ben-Shakhar. 1989. The predictive validity of graphological inferences: A meta-analytic approach. *Personality and Individual Differences* (10) 737–745.

Nevo, B. 1986. ed. *Scientific Aspects of Graphology: A Handbook.* Springfield, Ill.: Charles C. Thomas.

Nisbett, R., and L. Ross. 1980. *Human Inference: Strategies and Shortcomings of Social Judgment.* Englewood Cliffs, N.J.: Prentice-Hall.

Peterson, W. L. 1991. Helicobacter pylori and peptic ulcer disease. *New England Journal of Medicine* 324: 1043–1048.

Read, A. W. et al. eds. 1978. *Funk and Wagnall's New Comprehensive International Dictionary of the English Language.* New York: Publishers Guild Press.

Scanlon, M., and J. Mauro. 1992. The lowdown on handwriting analysis: Is it for real? *Psychology Today* (November/December): 46–53; 80.

Schick, T., and L. Vaughn. 1995. *How to Think about Weird Things: Critical Thinking for a New Age.* Mountain View, Calif.: Mayfield Publishing Company.

Soll, A. H. 1990. Pathogenesis of peptic ulcer and implications for therapy. *New England Journal of Medicine* 322: 909–916.

Tversky, A., and D. Kahneman. 1974. Judgment under uncertainty: Heuristics and biases. *Science* 185: 1124–1131.

Tversky, A., and D. Kahneman. 1982. Judgments of and by representativeness. In *Judgment under Uncertainty: Heuristics and Biases,* ed. by D. Kahneman, P. Slovic, and A. Tversky. Cambridge: Cambridge University Press.

Tversky, A., and D. Kahneman. 1983. Extensional versus intuitive reasoning: The conjunction fallacy in probability judgment. *Psychological Review* 90: 293–315.

U.S. Congress. 1984. *Quackery. A $10 Billion Scandal: A Report by the Chairman of the (House) Subcommittee on Health and Long-Term Care.* Washington, D.C.: United States Government Printing Office.

Wandyez, K. 1993. The H. Pylori factor. *Forbes* 152 (August 2): 128.

Ward, R. 1994. Maternity ward. *Mirabella* (February): 89–90.

Zusne, L. and W. H. Jones 1982. *Anomalistic Psychology.* Hillsdale, N.J.: Lawrence Erlbaum Associates.

REVIEW AND CONTEMPLATE

1. What is the representativeness heuristic?

2. Give two examples of how the representativeness heuristic can lead to mistaken medical beliefs.

3. Give two examples of how the representativeness heuristic can lead to pseudoscientific beliefs.

4. Explain how the representativeness heuristic plays a role in clinicians' beliefs about the validity of the Rorschach Inkblot Test.

7.3 "Some Systematic Biases of Everyday Judgment"

WHILE WRITING THIS introduction, I came across the website for a man named Brian who claims to have predictive dreams, 84% of which he says have come true. He claims to have predicted (a) Hurricane Katrina's landfall and the resulting flooding of New Orleans, (b) a school shooting in Tennessee, (c) a fireman waking up after 10 years in a coma, and many more events. Every day, he updates his website with a number of scanned images of his "dream drawings" from the previous night. The drawings often consist of words and figures hastily scrawled on a piece of paper, and Brian typically interprets the drawing in a brief sentence placed below the image. Visitors to the website are invited to use a web search engine to search for news stories or events that appear to match Brian's prediction. For example, one year on February 6, Brian posted a drawing that said "ship sinks." Later that same month, a visitor posted a story about 50 people who were missing after a ferry sank in a river in Bangladesh on February 27; thus, Brian's prediction was apparently confirmed.

Is Brian really psychic, or might believers in his psychic abilities be misled by normal cognitive tendencies that make Brian's predictive dreams seem more accurate than they actually are? In this article, Gilovich discusses several cognitive tendencies that may lead people to develop inaccurate, pseudoscientific, or paranormal beliefs. One of these tendencies—which Gilovich calls the "compared to what?" problem—is people's failure to consider a relevant baseline of comparison or control group. For example, with respect to Brian's "ship sinks" prediction, how frequent are events that involve a ship or boat sinking? Predicting a frequent event is not exactly an impressive feat. For example, I could predict that an automobile accident will occur in the near future on a major highway, but it's not a very impressive prediction because such accidents happen regularly. When I typed Brian's "ship sinks" prediction into a web search engine, I found a number of stories consistent with Brian's prediction, including a freighter that sank in China, a cargo ship that sank off the coast of Egypt, and an Egyptian passenger ship that sank in the Red Sea. All of these events happened within a 6-week period, so which one is the event he predicted?

Of course, there are additional reasons why people might overestimate the accuracy of Brian's dreams, one of which is his use of "ambiguous specificity," a topic discussed in the first article in this chapter. Other reasons are discussed in this article by Gilovich.

Reference

Gilovich, T. (1997, March/April). Some systematic biases of everyday judgment. *Skeptical Inquirer, 21*, 31–35.

ARTICLE 7.3

"SOME SYSTEMATIC BIASES OF EVERYDAY JUDGMENT"
THOMAS GILOVICH

Skeptics have long thought that everyday judgment and reasoning are biased in predictable ways. Psychological research on the subject conducted during the past quarter century largely confirms these suspicions.

Two types of explanations are typically offered for the dubious beliefs that are dissected in SKEPTICAL INQUIRER. On one hand, there are motivational causes: Some beliefs are comforting, and so people embrace that comfort and convince themselves that a questionable proposition is true. Many types of religious beliefs, for example, are often explained this way. On the other hand, there are cognitive causes: faulty processes of reasoning and judgment that lead people to misevaluate the evidence of their everyday experience. The skeptical community is convinced that everyday judgment and reasoning leave much to be desired.

Why are skeptics so unimpressed with the reasoning abilities and habits of the average person? Until recently, this pessimism was based on simple observation, often by those with a particularly keen eye for the foibles of human nature. Thus, skeptics often cite such thinkers as Francis Bacon, who stated:

> ... all superstition is much the same whether it be that of astrology, dreams, omens, retributive judgment, or the like ... [in that] the deluded believers observe events which are fulfilled, but neglect or pass over their failure, though it be much more common. (Bacon 1899/1620)

John Stuart Mill and Bertrand Russell are two other classic scholars who, along with Bacon, are often quoted for their trenchant observations on the shortcomings of human judgment. It is also common to see similar quotes of more recent vintage—in SKEPTICAL INQUIRER and elsewhere—from the likes of Richard Feynman, Stephen Jay Gould, and Carl Sagan.

During the past twenty-five years, a great deal of psychological research has dealt specifically with the quality of everyday reasoning, and so it is now possible to go beyond simple observation and arrive at a truly rigorous assessment of the shortcomings of everyday judgment. In so doing, we can determine whether or not these scholars we all admire are correct. Do people misevaluate evidence in the very ways and for the very reasons that Bacon, Russell, and others have claimed? Let us look at the research record and see.

Thomas Gilovich, "Some Systematic Biases of Everyday Judgment ," *Skeptical Inquirer*, vol. 21, pp. 31-35. Copyright © 1997 by Thomas Gilovich. Reprinted with permission.

THE "COMPARED TO WHAT?" PROBLEM

Some of the common claims about the fallibility of human reasoning stand up well to empirical scrutiny. For example, it is commonly argued that people have difficulty with what might be called the "compared to what" problem. That is, people are often overly impressed with an absolute statistic without recognizing that its true import can only be assessed by comparison to some relevant baseline.

For instance, a 1986 article in *Discover* magazine (cited in Dawes 1988) urges readers who fly in airplanes to "know where the exits are and rehearse in your mind exactly how to get to them." Why? The article approvingly notes that someone who interviewed almost two hundred survivors of fatal airline accidents found that "... more than 90% had their escape routes mentally mapped out beforehand." Good for them, but note that whoever did the study cannot interview anyone who perished in an airplane crash. Air travel being as scary as it is to so many people, perhaps 90 percent or more of those who died in airline crashes rehearsed their escape routes as well. Ninety percent sounds impressive because it is so close to 100 percent. But without a more pertinent comparison, it really does not mean much.

Similarly, people are often impressed that, say, 30 percent of all infertile couples who adopt a child subsequently conceive. That is great news for that 30 percent to be sure, but what percentage of those who do not adopt likewise conceive? People likewise draw broad conclusions from a cancer patient who goes into remission after steadfastly practicing mental imagery. Again, excellent news for that individual, but might the cancer have gone into remission even if the person had not practiced mental imagery?

This problem of failing to invoke a relevant baseline of comparison is particularly common when the class of data that requires inspection is inherently difficult to collect. Consider, for example, the commonly expressed opinion, "I can always tell that someone is wearing a hairpiece." Are such claims to be believed, or is it just that one can tell that someone is wearing a hairpiece ... when it is obvious that he is wearing a hairpiece? After all, how can one tell whether some have gone undetected? The goal of a good hairpiece is to fool the public, and so the example is one of those cases in which the confirmations speak loudly while the disconfirmations remain silent.

A similar asymmetry should give pause to those who have extreme confidence in their "gaydar," or their ability to detect whether someone is gay. Here, too, the confirmations announce themselves. When a person for whatever reason "seems gay" and it is later determined that he is, it is a salient triumph for one's skill at detection. But people who elude one's gaydar rarely go out of their way to announce, "By the way, I fooled you: I'm gay."

At any rate, the notion that people have difficulty invoking relevant comparisons has received support from psychological research. Studies of everyday reasoning have shown that the logic and necessity of control groups, for example, is often lost on a large segment of even the educated population (Boring 1954; Einhorn and Hogarth 1978; Nisbett and Ross 1980).

THE "SEEK AND YE SHALL FIND" PROBLEM

Another common claim that stands up well to empirical research is the idea that people do not assess hypotheses even-handedly. Rather, they tend to seek out confirmatory evidence for what they suspect to be true, a tendency that has the effect of "seek and ye shall find." A biased search for confirmatory information frequently turns up more apparent support for a hypothesis than is justified.

This phenomenon has been demonstrated in numerous experiments explicitly designed to assess people's hypothesis-testing strategies (Skov and Sherman 1986; Snyder and Swann 1978). But it is so pervasive that it can also be seen in studies designed with an entirely different agenda in mind. One of my personal favorites is a study in which participants were given the following information (Shafir 1993):

> Imagine that you serve on the jury of an only-child sole-custody case following a relatively messy divorce. The facts of the case are complicated by ambiguous, economic, social, and emotional considerations, and you decide to base your decision entirely on the following few observations. To which parent would you award sole custody of the child?
>
> Parent A: average income
> average health
> average working hours
> reasonable rapport with the child
> relatively stable social life
>
> Parent B: above-average income
> minor health problems
> lots of work-related travel
> very close relationship with the child
> extremely active social life

Faced with this version of the problem, the majority of respondents chose to award custody to Parent B, the "mixed bag" parent who offers several advantages (above-average income), but also some disadvantages (health problems), in comparison to Parent A. In another version of the problem, however, a different group is asked to which parent they would *deny* custody of the child. Here, too, a majority selects Parent B. Parent B, then, is paradoxically deemed both more and less worthy of caring for the child.

The result is paradoxical, that is, unless one takes into account people's tendencies to seek out confirming information. Asked which parent should be *awarded* the child, people look primarily for positive qualities that warrant being awarded the child—looking less vigilantly for negative characteristics that would lead one to favor the other parent. When asked which parent should be *denied* custody, on the other hand, people look primarily for negative qualities that would disqualify a parent. A decision to award or deny, of course, should be based on a comparison of the positive *and* negative characteristics of the two parents, but the way the question is framed channels respondents down a narrower path in which they focus on information that would confirm the type of verdict they are asked to render.

The same logic often rears its head when people test certain suppositions or hypotheses. Rumors of some dark conspiracy, for example, can lead people to search disproportionately for evidence that supports the plot and neglect evidence that contradicts it.

THE SELECTIVE MEMORY PROBLEM

A third commonly sounded complaint about everyday human thought is that people are more inclined to remember information that fits their expectations than information at variance with their expectations. Charles Darwin, for example, said that he took great care to record any observation that was inconsistent with his theories because "I had found by experience that such facts and thoughts were far more apt to escape from the memory than favourable ones" (cited in Clark 1984).

This particular criticism of the average person's cognitive faculties is in need of revision. Memory research has shown that often people have the easiest time recalling information that is *inconsistent* with their expectations or preferences (Bargh and Thein 1985; Srull and Wyer 1989). A little reflection indicates that this is particularly true of those "near misses" in life that become indelibly etched in the brain. The novelist Nicholson Baker (1991) provides a perfect illustration:

> [I] told her my terrible story of coming in second in the spelling bee in second grade by spelling *keep* "c-e-e-p" after successfully tossing off *microphone,* and how for two or three years afterward I was pained every time a yellow garbage truck drove by on Highland Avenue and I saw the capitals printed on it, "Help Keep Our City Clean," with that impossible irrational K that had made me lose so humiliatingly....

Baker's account, of course, is only an anecdote, possibly an apocryphal one at that. But it is one that, as mentioned above, receives support from more systematic studies. In one study, for example, individuals who had bet on professional football games were later asked to recall as much as they could about the various bets they had made (Gilovich 1983). They recalled significantly more information about their losses—outcomes they most likely did not expect to have happen and certainly did not *prefer* to have happen (see Figure 7.2).

Thus, the simple idea that people remember best that which they expect or prefer needs modification. Still, there is something appealing and seemingly true about the idea, and it should not be discarded prematurely. When considering people's belief in the accuracy of psychic forecasts, for example, it certainly seems to be fed by selective memory for successful predictions.

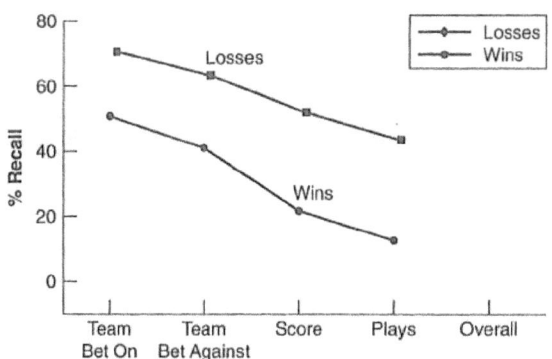

FIGURE 7.2: Gamblers' recall of information about bets won and lost. (From Gilovich 1983.)

How then can we reconcile this idea with the finding that often *inconsistent* information is better recalled? Perhaps the solution lies in considering when an event is *eventful*. With respect to their capacity to grab attention, some events are one-sided and others two-sided. Two-sided events are those that stand out and psychologically register as events regardless of how they turn out. If you bet on a sporting event or an election result, for example, either outcome—a win or a loss—has emotional significance and is therefore likely to emerge from the stream of everyday experience and register as an event. For these events, it is doubtful that confirmatory information is typically better remembered than disconfirmatory information.

In contrast, suppose you believe that "the telephone always rings when I'm in the shower." The potentially relevant events here are one-sided. If the phone happens to ring while showering, it will certainly register as an event, as you experience great stress in deciding whether to answer it, and you run dripping wet to the phone only to discover that it is someone from AT&T asking if you are satisfied with your long-distance carrier. When the phone does *not* ring when you are in the shower, on the other hand, it is a non-event. Nothing happened. Thus, with respect to the belief that the phone always rings while you are in the shower, the events are inherently one-sided: Only the confirmations stand out.

Perhaps it is these one-sided events to which Bacon's and Darwin's comments best apply. For one-sided events, as I discuss below, it is often the outcomes consistent with expectations that stand out and are more likely to be remembered. For two-sided events, on the other hand, the two types of outcomes are likely to be equally memorable; or, on occasion, events inconsistent with expectations may be more memorable.

But what determines whether an event is one- or two-sided? There are doubtless several factors. Let's consider two of them in the context of psychic predictions. First, events relevant to psychic predictions are inherently one-sided in the sense that such predictions are disconfirmed not by any specific event, but by their accumulated failure to be confirmed. Thus, the relevant comparison here is between confirmations and non-confirmations, or between events and non-events. It is no surprise, surely, that events are typically more memorable than non-events.

In one test of this idea, a group of college students read a diary purportedly written by another student, who described herself as having an interest in the prophetic nature of dreams (Madey 1993). To test whether there was any validity to dream prophecy, she decided to record each night's dreams and keep a record of significant events in her life, and later determine if there was any connection between the two. Half of the dreams (e.g., "I saw lots of people being happy") were later followed by events that could be seen as fulfilling ("My professor cancelled our final, which produced cheers throughout the class"). The other half went unfulfilled.

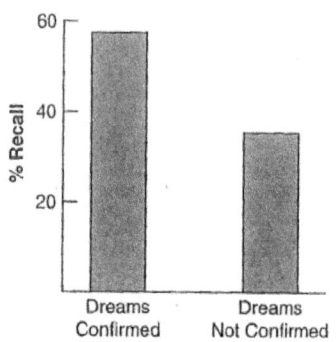

FIGURE 7.3: Participants' recall of dream prophecies that were either confirmed or unconfirmed. (Adapted from Madey 1993.)

After reading the entire diary and completing a brief "filler" task, the participants were asked to recall as many of the dreams as they could. As Figure 7.3 shows, they recalled many more of the prophecies that were fulfilled than those that were not. This result is hardly a surprise, of course, because the fulfillment of a prophecy reminds one of the original prediction, whereas a failure to fulfill it is often a non-event. The relevant outcomes are therefore inherently one-sided, and the confirmations are more easily recalled. The end result is that the broader belief in question—in this case, dream prophecy—receives spurious support.

The events relevant to psychic predictions are one-sided in another way as well. Psychic predictions are notoriously vague about when the prophesied events are supposed to occur. "A serious misfortune will befall a powerful leader" is a more common prophecy than "The President will be assassinated on March 15th." Such predictions are *temporally unfocused,* in that there is no specific moment to which interested parties are to direct their attention. For such predictions, confirmatory events are once again more likely to stand out because confirmations are more likely to prompt a recollection of the original prophecy. The events relevant to temporally unfocused expectations, then, tend to be one-sided, with the confirmations typically more salient and memorable than disconfirmations.

Temporally focused expectations, on the other hand, are those for which the timing of the decisive outcome is known in advance. If one expects a particular team to win the Super Bowl, for example, one knows precisely when that expectation will be confirmed or refuted—at the end of the game. As a result, the events relevant to temporally focused expectations tend to be two-sided because one's attention is focused on the decisive moment, and both outcomes are likely to be noticed and remembered.

In one study that examined the memory implications of temporally focused and unfocused expectations, participants were asked to read the diary of a student who, as part of an ESP experiment, was required to try to prophesy an otherwise unpredictable event every week for several weeks (Madey and Gilovich 1993). The diary included the student's weekly prophecy as well as various passages describing events from that week. There were two groups of participants in the experiment. In the *temporally unfocused* condition, the prophecies made no mention of when the prophesied event was likely to occur ("I have a feeling that I will get into an argument with my Psychology research group"). In the *temporally focused* condition, the prediction identified a precise day on which the event was to occur ("I have a feeling that I will get into an argument with my Psychology research group on Friday"). For each group, half of the prophecies were confirmed (e.g., "Our professor assigned us to research groups, and we immediately disagreed over our topic") and half were disconfirmed (e.g., "Our professor assigned us to research groups, and we immediately came to a unanimous decision on our topic"). Whether confirmed or disconfirmed, the relevant event was described in the diary entry for the day prophesied in the temporally focused condition. After reading the diary and completing a short distracter task, the participants were asked to recall as many prophecies and relevant events as they could.

Knowing when the prophesied events were likely to occur helped the respondents' memories, but only for those prophecies that were disconfirmed (see Figure 7.4). Confirmatory events were readily recalled whether temporally focused or not. Disconfirmations, on the other hand, were rarely recalled unless they disconfirmed a temporally

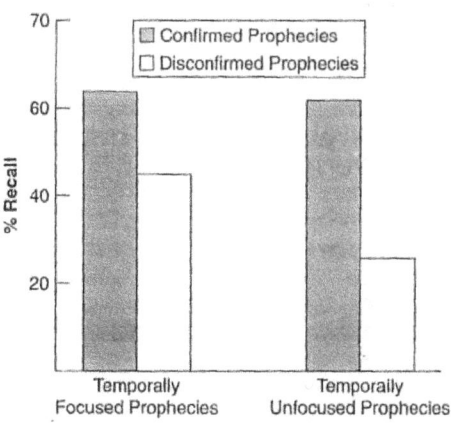

FIGURE 7.4: Participants' recall of prophecies that were confirmed or disconfirmed, as a function of whether or not the prophecies specified when the critical events were to occur. (Adapted from Madey and Gilovich 1993.)

focused prediction. When one considers that most psychic predictions are temporally unfocused, the result, once again, is that the evidence for psychic predictions can appear more substantial than it is.

CONCLUSION

There is, of course, much more psychological research on the quality of everyday judgment than that reviewed here (see, for example, Baron 1988; Dawes 1988; Gilovich 1991; Nisbett and Ross 1980; Kahneman, Slovic, and Tversky 1982). But even this brief review is sufficient to make it clear that some of the reputed biases of everyday judgment turn out to be real, verifiable shortcomings. Systematic research by and large supports the suspicions of much of the skeptical community that everyday judgment is not to be trusted completely. At one level, this should not come as a surprise: It is precisely because everyday judgment cannot be trusted that the inferential safeguards known as the scientific method were developed. It is unfortunate that those safeguards are not more widely taught or more generally appreciated.

REFERENCES

Bacon, F. 1899. *Advancement of Learning and the Novum Organum* (rev. ed.). New York: Colonial Press. (Original work published 1620).

Baker, N. 1991. *Room Temperature*. New York: Vintage.

Bargh, J. A., and R. D. Thein. 1985. Individual construct accessibility, person memory, and the recall-judgment link: The case of information overload. *Journal of Personality and Social Psychology* 49: 1129–1146.

Baron, J. 1988. *Thinking and Deciding*. New York: Cambridge University Press.

Boting, E. G. 1954. The nature and history of experimental control. *American Journal of Psychology* 67: 573–589.

Clark, R. W. 1984. *The Survival of Charles Darwin: A Biography of a Man and an Idea*. New York: Random House.

Dawes, R. M. 1988. *Rational Choice in an Uncertain World*. San Diego, Calif.: Harcourt Brace Jovanovich.

Einhorn, H. J., and R. M. Hogarth. 1978. Confidence in judgment: Persistence in the illusion of validity. *Psychological Review* 85: 395–416.

Gilovich, T. 1983. Biased evaluation and persistence in gambling. *Journal of Personality and Social Psychology* 44: 1110–1126.

———. 1991. *How We Know What Isn't So: The Fallibility of Human Reason in Everyday Life*. New York: Free Press.

Kahneman, D., P. Slovic, and A. Tversky. 1982. *Judgment under Uncertainty: Heuristics and Biases*. Cambridge: Cambridge University Press.

Madey, S. E. 1993. Memory for expectancy-consistent and expectancy-inconsistent information: An investigation of one-sided and two-sided events. Unpublished doctoral dissertation, Cornell University.

Madey, S. F., and T. Gilovich. 1993. Effect of temporal focus on the recall of expectancy-consistent and expectancy-inconsistent information. *Journal of Personality and Social Psychology* 65: 458–468.

Nisbett, R. E., and L. Ross. 1980. *Human Inference: Strategies and Shortcomings of Social Judgment.* Englewood Cliffs, N.J.: Prentice-Hall.

Shafir, E. 1993. Choosing versus rejecting: Why some options are both better and worse than others. *Memory and Cognition* 21: 546–556.

Skov, R. B., and S. J. Sherman. 1986. Information-gathering processes: Diagnosticity, hypothesis-confirmatory strategies, and perceived hypothesis confirmation. *Journal of Experimental Social Psychology* 22: 93–121.

Snyder, M., and W. B. Swann. 1978. Hypothesis-testing processes in social interaction. *Journal of Personality and Social Psychology* 36: 1202–1212.

Stull, T. K., and R. S. Wyer. 1989. Person memory and judgment. *Psychological Review* 96: 58–83.

REVIEW AND CONTEMPLATE

1. Describe and give an example of the "compared to what?" problem.
2. Describe and give an example of the "seek and ye shall find" problem.
3. Describe and give an example of the "selective memory" problem.
4. Explain two reasons why we are more likely to remember information that *confirms* psychic predictions.
5. In the introduction to this article, I described how Brian's predictive dreams were related to the "compared to what?" problem. Explain how Brian's dreams are related to the "seek and ye shall find" problem and the "selective memory" problem.

Chapter 8

PERSONALITY AND PSYCHOLOGICAL TESTING

8.1 "Criminal Profiling: Granfalloons and Gobbledygook"

IN 2002, THE FBI released their criminal profile of a serial killer who had murdered several women in the Baton Rouge area. The profile indicated that the killer was a White man between the ages of 25 and 35. Unfortunately, this profile caused the police to overlook an African American man, Derrick Todd Lee, who had been arrested for stalking and assaulting multiple women in the years prior to 2002. During the year after the FBI profile was released, Derrick is believed to have murdered at least two other women. The authorities began collecting DNA evidence from other victims in the area; this evidence was linked to Derrick, who was convicted in 2004.

Was the failure of the FBI to accurately profile Derrick Todd Lee an unusual fluke? Can the FBI or other criminal profilers accurately determine the demographic and personality characteristics of criminals based on the behaviors of those criminals at a crime scene? In this article, Snook, Gendreau, Bennell, and Taylor explain that criminal profiling is a popular practice for police investigations and is portrayed as an accurate technique in television crime dramas. However, they also explain why the practice of criminal profiling is not supported by scientific evidence. In addition, Snook et al. touch on a theme presented in Chapter 1: beliefs in pseudoscientific practices might arise from normal cognitive and social processes. For example, they describe how people's belief in profiling might stem from confirmation bias, overconfidence, or overreliance on anecdotal evidence or fictional accounts of successful profiling in television shows.

Reference

Snook, B., Gendreau, P., Bennell, C., & Taylor, P. J. (2008). Criminal profiling: Granfalloons and gobbledygook. *Skeptic, 14*(2), 42–47.

"CRIMINAL PROFILING: GRANFALLOONS AND GOBBLEDYGOOK"

BRENT SNOOK, PAUL GENDREAU, CRAIG BENNELL, AND PAUL TAYLOR

Reading the claims of criminal profilers and watching popular television programs like *Criminal Minds* can leave one with the impression that Criminal Profiling (CP)—the task of inferring demographic and personality details of an offender from his or her crime scene actions—is a well-practiced and reliable investigative technique. Over the past three decades, CP has gained tremendous popularity as a media topic, an academic area of study, and a tool for police investigations worldwide.

However, as we demonstrate in this article, the acceptance of CP by many police officers, profilers, and the public is at odds with the absence of scientific evidence to confirm its reliability or validity. We think this confusion has arisen for two related reasons. The first is that people have developed a biased picture of CP because they typically hear only about its glowing successes. The second, related, reason relates to what we know about cognition and the manner by which people process information, which typically serves to support the credibility of CP.

THE 5 W'S OF CRIMINAL PROFILING

1. *What is profiling?* When CP was originally popularized by the FBI, a profile consisted primarily of a list of very basic characteristics (e.g., age, previous convictions) that were likely to be possessed by the unknown offender of the crime(s) under consideration.[1] Profiles were generally used to narrow a list of potential suspects, focus investigations, and construct interview strategies.[2] In more recent years, the potential forms that a profile can take and the ways in which it can be used within a criminal investigation have expanded to include suggestions regarding resource prioritization, case management, strategies for dealing with the media, and so on.[3] (To view a profile, see http://www.brgov.com/TaskForce/pdf/profile.pdf.) Notwithstanding these developments, the core focus of CP remains the derivation of inferences about an unknown offender's characteristics. Yet, a 2001 study regarding the content of criminal profiles found that only 25% of statements in profiles were inferences about offender characteristics. Of that 25%, 82% of the inferences were unsubstantiated, 55% were unverifiable, 24% were ambiguous, and 6% contained opposing alternatives.[4]

The specific process that profilers use to make their inferences appears to be shaped by their training. Profilers who emphasize a clinical/psychological perspective draw on their psychological training, knowledge and experience with criminal behavior, and possibly their intuition, as they make their inferences. At its worse, this type of CP appears to differ little from what "psychic detectives" allegedly do when helping law enforcement

Brent Snook, Paul Gendreau, Craig Bennell, and Paul J.Taylor, "Criminal Profiling: Granfalloons and Gobbledygook," *Skeptic Magazine*, vol. 14, no. 2, pp. 42-47. Copyright © 2008 by Skeptic Magazine. Reprinted with permission.

agencies catch criminals or find missing persons[5] In fact, you can probably take any article or book written on psychic detectives and replace the term "psychic detective" with "criminal profiler" and the argument would continue to make perfect sense. By contrast, statistically oriented profilers claim to base their inferences on the statistical analysis of data, which comes from offenders who have previously committed crimes that are similar to those being investigated.

2. *Who are profilers?* Surprisingly, there is no consensus about who is qualified to be a profiler. Some have maintained that a profiler is anyone who labels themselves a profiler and has engaged in the practice of constructing a profile for a criminal investigation,[6] whereas others have argued that only individuals who have considerable investigative experience should be profilers.[7] Although some attempts have been made to regulate and accredit profilers (e.g., The International Criminal Investigative Analysis Fellowship), there is no recognized regulatory body that provides a professional CP designation. Thus, those presenting themselves as profiles may vary widely in their level of experience and education.

3. *When is profiling used?* The use of profilers has typically been limited to certain low-volume crimes such as sexual assaults committed by strangers and homicides that appear to lack a motive. Profiles are seen to be most useful in these types of cases because offenders are more likely to exhibit psychopathology such as psychopathy, schizoid thinking, and sadism.[8] This is assumed to increase the degree to which offenders behave consistently across their crimes and other aspects of their lives.[9] It is also the case that a profiler may be consulted at various stages of the investigation.[10]

4. *Where is profiling used?* It appears that the majority of CP occurs in the United States through the FBI, with the most recent estimates indicating that CP is being applied in approximately 1000 cases per year.[11] CP is also being used heavily in the United Kingdom, with 242 instances of CP advice being reported between 1981 and 1994.[12]

Although exact estimates of CP prevalence in other countries are not directly available, its use has been documented in Sweden, Finland, New Zealand, South Africa, Germany, Canada, Ireland, Malaysia, Russia, Zimbabwe, and The Netherlands.

5. *Why is profiling used?* The most obvious reason why police officers use CP is that they believe it "works". Indeed, survey results indicate that some officers believe profiles are operationally useful, often because they reinforce their own opinions, further their understanding of the offender, and/or focus the investigation.[13] Of course, it is also possible that some officers may use CP simply because they believe they have "nothing to lose" by consulting a profiler, and/or they are forced to do so in order to satisfy judicial requirements to exploit *all* available investigative options to solve the crime.

POLICE OFFICERS' OPINIONS OF CRIMINAL PROFILING

The few surveys that have assessed police officers' opinions about CP suggest they generally find CP useful for their investigations. An early survey found that solving cases was attributed to CP advice in 46% of the 192 instances where FBI profiling was requested.[14] Similarly, a 1993 study found that 5 out of 6 surveyed police officers in The Netherlands reported some degree of usefulness for advice given by an FBI trained profiler.[15] Likewise, a 1995 study found that 83% of a sample of 184 police officers in the United Kingdom claimed that CP was operationally useful and 92% reported that they would seek CP advice again.[16] Consistent with these results, a 2001 study showed that a significant portion of police officers in the United States believe that CP has value.[17] Finally, a 2007 survey of Canadian police officers found that 66% of the officers believed that it contributed to their investigation. Moreover, most officers reported that the profiler made accurate predictions.[18]

PUTTING CP TO THE TEST

Despite the fact that police officers hold these views, a review of the CP literature reveals that: (a) the majority of CP approaches are based on an outdated theory of personality that lacks strong empirical support, and (b) professional profilers have a dismal performance record when the accuracy of their profiles have been examined.

Is CP based on an empirically supported theory? In a similar way to a theory of personality (the classic trait theory) that was popular in personality psychology up until the late 1960s,[19] the overwhelming majority of CP approaches assume that criminal behavior is determined by underlying dispositions (i.e., traits) within offenders that make them behave in a particular way.[20] The assumptions that emerge from this theory are fundamental to CP. For example, the trait theory leads to an assumption that offenders will exhibit similar behaviors across their offenses because traits, rather than situational factors, are the determinants of their behavior. Perhaps more important for the practice of CP, the theory also suggests that offenders will display similar behaviors in their crimes and in other aspects of their lives (e.g., in their interpersonal relationships).

The sole reliance on trait-based models of profiling is fundamentally flawed. Criminal profilers do not seem to recognize that a consensus began to emerge in the psychological literature some 40 years ago that it was a mistake to rely on traits as the primary explanation for behavior.[21] Situational factors contribute as much to the prediction of behavior as personality dispositions. This is equally true when predicting criminal behavior.

The importance of situational factors is apparent when one considers research in the profiling domain. For example, offenders rarely display high levels of behavioral consistency across the crimes they commit.[22] A similar picture emerges when evaluating the degree to which offenders exhibit consistency across their crimes and other aspects of their lives. At best, small pockets of consistency have been identified, whereby a specific crime scene behavior is found to relate to a specific background characteristic. For example, a 1997 study found that rapists who forced entry into premises were four times more likely to have prior convictions for property offenses than those who did not engage in that behavior.[23] In general, profilers seem to ignore this empirical research.

Profilers also appear to be oblivious to research in closely related fields. For example, despite a massive effort to identify predictors of consistency in offender samples within community and prison settings, research has failed to turn up anything of value to criminal profilers. While it is possible to make reasonably accurate predictions of criminal behavior with respect to recidivism,[24] these inferences are based on the analysis of behaviors beyond those exhibited at an offender's crime scene. Indeed, the well-established predictors of criminal behavior (e.g., antisocial attitudes, cognition) are not the sorts of variables typically focused on by profilers (e.g., crime scene behaviors), which raises unanswered questions about why profilers might expect that behaviorally-based profiling approaches will be effective.

Can professional profilers make accurate inferences? Within the CP domain, negligible quantitative differences have been found between the predictive ability of "professional profilers" and "non-profilers". The accuracy of profiler inferences has been tested by comparing the performance of so-called professional profilers with that of non-profiler groups in mock profiling scenarios.[25] In a typical experiment, profilers and non-profiler groups are asked to review details of a solved crime and make inferences about the likely offender (via a multiple choice questionnaire). Inferences are typically divided into four categories: cognitive processes (e.g., whether or not offender exhibits remorse), physical attributes (e.g., presence of facial hair), offense behaviors (e.g., whether the offender removed items from the crime scene), and social history/habits (e.g., alcohol consumption). The results from these four categories are also combined to form an overall profile performance measure. The accuracy of these inferences is then checked against the actual perpetrator's physical characteristics, thoughts, and behaviors.

Two 2007 meta-analyses of these studies were revealing.[26] The first analysis compared the predictive accuracy of a group of self-labeled profilers and experienced investigators against non-profilers (e.g., college students and psychologists). The profilers/investigators were found to be more accurate than non-police personnel on an overall measure of profile accuracy ($r = .24$) and on the physical attribute category ($r = .10$). On the other hand, the predictive accuracy of the profilers/investigators was marginally worse or no better than the non-profilers when it came to inferences of cognitive processes ($r = -.06$), offense behaviors ($r = .00$), and social history/habits ($r = -.09$).

In the second analysis, the experienced investigators were included in the non-profiler group. In this analysis, the results favored the profilers across all five predictor categories, but the differences were not large enough to be statistically significant. The best result came when the overall profile was considered ($r = .32$). However, even if this most optimistic of results could be replicated, it warrants consideration that many variables included in this analysis of profilers' expertise are well known in the criminological literature (e.g., the likelihood that a serial offender will be of a particular age, have particular convictions, suffer substance abuse problems, etc.). This means, and we hasten to emphasize this point, that any police professional with a good knowledge of the criminological literature should be able to achieve this level of success simply by relying on base rate information. In other words, success in CP does not appear to be based on specialized knowledge of the peculiarities and idiosyncrasies found at a given crime scene.

WHY DO PEOPLE BELIEVE THAT CRIMINAL PROFILING WORKS?

Given the state of affairs with CP research, one can only wonder why police officers and the public would have faith in such a dubious technique. Below are eight potential reasons. The first four relate to how information about CP is presented to people. The second four relate to how people might process that information.

1. *The power of anecdotes.* CP accounts in books, magazines, law enforcement bulletins, and peer-reviewed journal articles often rely entirely on a "case in point", "case study", "actual case," or "success story" to illustrate how profiling is useful in catching a criminal. For instance, a 2007 study found that 60% of the CP literature relied on anecdotes as a source of evidence.[27] But anecdotes are inadequate for effectively validating CP for at least three reasons. First, in attempting to convince others that profiling works, a profiler can surely find at least one anecdote in which a profile appears to have helped investigators. Second, anecdotal evidence from any source may exaggerate the actual usefulness of a profile in various ways. Third, profiling anecdotes are prone to be distorted in some way to make them more entertaining and informative.

2. *Repetition of the message that "profiling works."* Repeating the message that "CP is an effective investigative tool" or "police officers seek profilers' input" can contribute to the CP illusion because people tend to believe messages they hear repeatedly. The 2007 study noted above found that the message "profiling works" is clearly stated in 52% of the 130 profiling articles reviewed, whereas only 3% of articles unequivocally stated that profiling does not work. As previously argued, that positive message is unsupported by the research on the predictive ability of profilers.[28]

3. *Counting the hits and discounting the misses.* Profilers create the impression that their inferences are highly accurate by over-emphasizing their correct inferences.[29] When all the necessary and pertinent information is not explicitly reported, readers may form beliefs based solely upon the information that is presented to them. Findings from psychological research suggest that the exclusive presentation of correct inferences can lead people to overestimate the accuracy and potential utility of profiles. It is therefore not surprising that reading articles about profiling might lead people to conclude that it is a viable tool.

4. *Profilers are not "experts."* Experts are people who have professional competence in a specialized area. People have a tendency to accept information that is reported to them by supposed experts. However, problems can arise when people wholeheartedly believe in the power of an expert's "specialized knowledge" when that knowledge has little foundation. In practice, profilers present themselves as experts by implying that they possess accumulated wisdom, investigative and behavioral science experience, and training and/or knowledge of abnormal behavior that provide them with the necessary skills to collect and analyze crime scene information and peek inside the criminal mind. In addition, research has shown that police officers tend to believe that profiles written by supposed experts are more accurate than those written by other consultants, even when identical information appeared in both profiles.[30] The problem with this state of affairs is that there is little evidence supporting the proposition that profilers' possess specialized skills that warrant labeling them as experts.[31]

5. *Humans are pattern-seekers.* Humans attempt to find order and meaning in the uncertain world and then form beliefs that can guide future behaviors.[32] In attempting to find useful patterns, however, people sometimes find patterns that are meaningless. When information is presented in such a way as to make us believe that CP works, it is no wonder that this is the conclusion that is reached. The information, however, may be biased in several ways. Profilers may wish to inflate their own usefulness (self-serving bias) and may actually be more confident in their abilities than is warranted (over-confidence); people might believe that a profiler's advice solved an investigation because they are unaware of, or do not consider, the rest of the police work that was involved in the case (attribution error); profilers, police officers, and the public are prone to make errors whenever they partake in after-the-fact reasoning; and, perhaps most important, there may be a tendency to seek evidence that supports an existing belief that CP works and ignore or filter out evidence that contradicts such a belief (confirmation bias).

6. *Vague profiles fit any case.* The inferences in some profiles are so ambiguous, vague, and/or general that the profile (like horoscopes) can appear to describe any suspect.[33] This is problematic for both practice and research. For example, in a case with multiple suspects, profiles that contain many ambiguous inferences may not assist in the elimination of the innocent. It is also possible that interpreting ambiguous statements

(and subsequently using that interpretation to guide investigative decision-making) may contribute to the arrest of an innocent suspect and thus the release of, or the cessation of a search for, the actual criminal. In this latter regard, readers should be reminded of the frequent reporting in the media of wrongful convictions. Regarding research, it is difficult to retrospectively determine and report the actual accuracy of profiles if they can be interpreted to fit many individuals. Moreover, ambiguous inferences are not falsifiable, thus the profiler can never be shown to be wrong.

7. *Imitation.* People tend to believe things or do things a certain way because they were believed or done that way by others in the past.[34] In fact, a large amount of what we know is naturally acquired from other people's behavior and instructions. Thus, those who observe other people using CP are likely to both use it and believe it works, even if the initial user does not hold this belief. Police officers may believe CP is a good investigative technique because they observe other police officers using it. Police officers spend time with other officers, communicating various skills and proper policing behaviors through both formal and informal teachings. Through police culture, profiling advocates (e.g., those officers trained to use CP) can directly and/or indirectly instruct other officers that CP is effective. In any case, it is unlikely that any of the other officers would have access to all of the information needed to properly determine whether CP works.

8. *Mistaking fiction for fact.* Because people are generally intrigued by the criminal mind, profiling activities tend to generate a lot of public fascination. The increasing number of books, films, and television programs that deal with profiling, as well as the recent growth in college and university courses that address profiling issues, supports this observation. Exposure to primarily fictional accounts of CP unfortunately means people may base their beliefs upon those accounts; especially since people are not very adept at remembering the source of information that they acquire during routine daily activities.[35]

CONCLUSION

There is a growing belief that profilers can accurately and consistently predict a criminal's characteristics based on crime scene evidence. This belief is evident from the fact that CP is becoming increasingly prevalent as an investigative technique and that positive opinions of CP are being communicated in the published literature. Such a belief is premature because the technique has yet to be theoretically or empirically supported. Belief in this unscientific policing practice appears to be due to the erroneous information that police officers (and the public) receive about CP and the way that this information is processed. Since profiling has the potential to mislead criminal investigators, it is a practice that must be approached with the utmost caution.

REFERENCES

1. Hicks, S. J., & Sales, B. D. 2006. *Criminal Profiling: Developing an Effective Science and Practice.* Washington, DC: The American Psychological Association.
2. Douglas, J. E., Ressler, R. K., Burgess, A. W., & Hartman. C. R. 1986. "Criminal Profiling from Crime Scene Analysis." *Behavioral Sciences and the Law, 4,* 401–421.
3. Ainsworth, P. B. 2001. *Offender Profiling and Crime Analysis.* Cullompton, Devon: Willan.
4. Alison, L. J., Smith, M. D., Eastman. O., & Rainbow, L. 2003. "Toulmin's Philosophy of Argument and its Relevance to Offender Profiling." *Psychology, Crime, and Law, 9,* 173–183.
5. Lyons, A. & Truzzi, M. 1991. *The Blue Sense: Psychic Detectives and Crime.* The Mysterious Press: New York.
6. Kocsis, R. N. 2004. "Psychological Profiling of Serial Arson Skills: An Assessment of Skills and Accuracy." *Criminal Justice and Behavior, 31,* 341–361; Kocsis, R. N., & Hayes, A. F. 2004. "Believing is Seeing? Investigating the Perceived Accuracy of Criminal Psychological Profiles." *International Journal of Offender Therapy and Comparative Criminology. 48,* 149–160.
7. Hazelwood. R. R., Ressler, R. K., Depue, R. L., & Douglas, J. E. 1995. "Criminal Investigative Analysis: An Overview." In A. W. Burgess & R. R. Hazelwood (Eds.), *Practical Aspects of Rape Investigation: A Multidisciplinary Approach.* Boca Raton, FL: CRC Press.
8. Geberth, V. 1995. "Criminal Personality Profiling." *Law and Order, 43,* 46–49.
9. Pinizzotto, A. J., & Finkel, N. J. 1990. "Criminal Personality Profiling: An Outcome and Process Study." *Law and Human Behavior, 14,* 215–233.
10. Copson, G. 1995. *Coals to Newcastle? Part 1: A Study of Offender Profiling.* London: Home Office, Police Research Group: Snook, B., Haines, A., Taylor, P. J., & Bennell, C. 2007. "Criminal Profiling Belief and Use: A Survey of Canadian Police Officer Opinion." *Canadian Journal of Police and Security Services, 5,* 169–179.
11. Witkin, G.1996. "How the FBI Paints Portraits of the Nations Most Wanted." *U.S. News and World Report, 120,* April 22, 32.
12. Copson, op cit.
13. Copson, op cit.; Snook, et al. op cit.
14. Pinizzotto, A. J. 1984. "Forensic Psychology: Criminal Personality Profiling." *Journal of Police Science and Administration, 12,* 32–40.
15. Jackson, J. L, van Koppen, P. J., & Herbrink, J. C. M. 1993. *Does the Service Meet the Needs? An Evaluation of Consumer Satisfaction with Specific Profile Analysis and Investigative Advice Offered by the Scientific Research Advisory Unit of the National Criminal Intelligence Division (CRI)—The Netherlands.* Leiden: NISCALE: Netherlands Institute for the Study of Criminality and Law Enforcement.

16. Copson. op cit.
17. Trager, J., & Brewster, J. 2001. "The Effectiveness of Psychological Profiles." *Journal of Police and Criminal Psychology, 16,* 20–28.
18. Snook, et al. op cit. B., Eastwood. J., Gendreau, P., Goggin, C., & Cullen, R. M. 2007. "Taking Stock of Criminal Profiling: A Narrative Review and Meta-analysis." *Criminal Justice and Behavior, 34,* 437–453.
19. Mischel, W. 1968. *Personality and Assessment.* New York: Wiley.
20. Homant, R. J., & Kennedy, D. B. 1998. "Psychological Aspects of Crime Scene Profiling." *Criminal Justice and Behavior, 25,* 319–343.
21. Mischel, op cit.
22. Bateman. A. L, & Salfati, C. G. 2007. "An Examination of Behavioral Consistency Using Individual Behaviors or Groups of Behaviors in Serial Homicide." *Behavioral Sciences and the Law, 25,* 527–544.
23. Davies, A., Wittebrood, K., & Jackson, J. L. 1997. "Predicting the Criminal Antecedents of a Stranger Rapist from his Offence Behaviour." *Science and Justice, 37,* 161–170.
24. Gendreau, P., Little, T., & Goggin, C. 1996. "A Meta-analysis of the Predictors of Adult Offender Recidivism: What Works!" *Criminology, 31,* 401–433.
25. Kocsis, R. N., Hayes, A. F., & Irwin, H. J. 2002. "Investigative Experience and Accuracy in Psychological Profiling of a Violent Crime." *Journal of Interpersonal Violence. 17,* 811–823.
26. Snook, et al., op cit.
27. Ibid.
28. Ibid.
29. Douglas, op cit.
30. Kocsis and Hayes, 2004, op cit.
31. Snook, Eastwood, et al., op cit.
32. Shermer, M. 2002. *Why People Believe Weird Things: Pseudoscience, Duperstition, and Other Confusions of Our Time.* New York: Henry Holt and Company.
33. Alison, L. J., Smith, M., & Morgan, K. 2003. "Interpreting the Accuracy of Offender Profiles." *Psychology, Crime, and Law, 9,* 185–195.
34. Dawkins, R. 2003. *A Devil's Chaplain: Reflections on Home, Lies. Science, and Love.* New York: Houghton Mifflin Company.
35. Johnson. M. K. 1997. "Source Monitoring and Memory Distortion." *Philosophical Transactions of the Royal Society of London B, 352,* 1733–1745.

REVIEW AND CONTEMPLATE

1. What is criminal profiling? What consensus exists about who qualifies as a professional criminal profiler?

2. Snook et al. (2008) explain that criminal profiling is based on the trait theory of personality. What assumptions does this theory lead to about the behaviors of criminals across their offenses? Why do Snook et al. say that this trait-based model is "fundamentally flawed"?

3. Snook et al. (2008) describe research in which professional profilers and nonprofilers are compared in a mock profiling scenario. On which aspects of the profiles do profilers appear to do slightly better than nonprofilers? According to Snook et al., why might criminal profilers be slightly better than nonprofilers on some aspects of the profiles; are they better at using "specialized knowledge of the peculiarities and idiosyncrasies found at a crime scene"?

4. Why do people believe that criminal profiling works, after research has shown that profilers are not very accurate? Describe at least three reasons.

8.2 "What's wrong with this picture?"

DURING THE 1960S, psychologists Loren and Jean Chapman noticed a disturbing problem with clinicians' beliefs about a psychodiagnostic test called the Draw-a-Person Test (DAP). In the DAP, a client draws pictures of people, and the clinician examines these drawings to infer information about the person's personality or psychological problems. There was fairly consistent agreement among the clinicians who used the DAP that people with certain psychological symptoms drew pictures with particular characteristics. For example, the clinicians believed that people who were paranoid or suspicious of other people drew pictures with atypical eyes and that men who were worried about their manliness drew broad-shouldered, muscular figures. The problem was that even though experienced clinicians believed in the existence of these correlations between drawing characteristics and the psychological symptoms of the test takers, research studies showed their beliefs were erroneous. In other words, paranoid or suspicious people did not draw atypical eyes more often than those who were not paranoid or suspicious. The clinicians had developed illusory correlations—that is, they perceived relationships that did not exist. Apparently, the clinicians saw these illusory correlations because they expected to see them, even though the data they observed showed no such correlations. This is a good example of a point raised in Chapter 1: Difficulties we have with statistical reasoning can lead to pseudoscientific beliefs. In this case, difficulties with statistical reasoning led to the belief that the DAP accurately measured personality and psychological problems.

Projective tests, which include the DAP and other tests, are used by psychologists to assess personality, identify mental disorders, and estimate a person's violent or criminal tendencies. These tests involve ambiguous stimuli, such as an inkblots or drawings, that test takers are asked to interpret. People's responses to these ambiguous stimuli supposedly reflect their hidden or unconscious motives, thoughts, and conflicts. Lilienfeld, Wood, and Garb discuss the scientific evidence concerning the reliability and validity of a variety of projective techniques, including the Rorschach Inkblot Test, Thematic Apperception Test, and Draw-a-Person Test.

Reference

Lilienfeld, S. O., Wood, J. M., & Garb, H. N. (2001). What's wrong with this picture? *Scientific American, 284*(5), 81–87.

"WHAT'S WRONG WITH THIS PICTURE?"
SCOTT LILIENFELD, JAMES WOOD, AND HOWARD GARB

What if you were asked to describe images you saw in an inkblot or to invent a story for an ambiguous illustration—say, of a middle-aged man looking away from a woman who was grabbing his arm? To comply, you would draw on your own emotions, experiences, memories and imagination. You would, in short, project yourself into the images. Once you did that, many practicing psychologists would assert, trained evaluators could mine your musings to reach conclusions about your personality traits, unconscious needs and overall mental health.

But how correct would they be? The answer is important because psychologists frequently apply such "projective" instruments (presenting people with ambiguous images, words or objects) as components of mental assessments, and because the outcomes can profoundly affect the lives of the respondents. The tools often serve, for instance, as aids in diagnosing mental illness, in predicting whether convicts are likely to become violent after being paroled, in evaluating the mental stability of parents engaged in custody battles, and in discerning whether children have been sexually molested.

We recently reviewed a large body of research into how well projective methods work, concentrating on three of the most extensively used and best-studied instruments. Overall our findings are unsettling.

BUTTERFLIES OR BISON?

The Famous Rorschach inkblot test—which asks people to describe what they see in a series of 10 inkblots—is by far the most popular of the projective methods, given to hundreds of thousands, or perhaps millions, of people every year. The research discussed below refers to the modern, rehabilitated version, not to the original construction, introduced in the 1920s by Swiss psychiatrist Hermann Rorschach.

The initial tool came under server attack in the 1950s and 1960s, in part because it lacked standardized procedures and a set of norms (averaged results from the general population). Standardization is important because seemingly trivial differences in the way an instrument is administered can affect a person's responses to it. Norms provide a reference point for determining when someone's responses fall outside an acceptable range.

In the 1970s John E. Exner, Jr., then at Long Island University, ostensibly corrected those problems in the early Rorschach test by introducing what he called the Comprehensive

Scott O. Lilienfeld, "What's Wrong with This Picture?," *Scientific American*, vol. 284, no. 5, pp. 81-87. Copyright © 2001 by Springer Nature America, Inc. Reprinted with permission.

System. This set of instructions established detailed rules for delivering the inkblot exam and for interpreting the responses, and it provided norms for children and adults.

In spite of the Comprehensive System's current popularity, it generally falls short on two crucial criteria that were also problematic for the original Rorschach: scoring reliability and validity. A tool possessing scoring reliability yields similar results regardless of who grades and tabulates the responses. A valid technique measures what it aims to measure: its results are consistent with those produced by other trustworthy instruments or are able to predict behavior, or both.

To understand the Rorschach's scoring reliability defects, it helps to know something about how reactions to the inkblots are interpreted. First, a psychologist rates the collected reactions on more than 100 characteristics, or variables. The evaluator, for instance, records whether the person looked at whole blots or just parts, notes whether the detected images were unusual or typical of most test takers, and indicates which aspects of the inky swirls (such as form or color) most determined what the respondent reported seeing.

Then he or she compiles the findings into a psychological profile of the individual. As part of that interpretive process, psychologists might conclude that focusing on minor details (such as stray splotches) in the blots, instead of on whole, images, signals obsessiveness in a patient and that seeing things in the white spaces within the larger blots, instead of in the inked areas, reveals a negative, contrary streak.

For the scoring of any variable to be considered highly reliable, two different assessors should be very likely to produce similar ratings when examining any given person's responses. Recent investigations demonstrate, however, that strong agreement is achieved for only about half the characteristics examined by those who score Rorschach responses; evaluators might well come up with quite different ratings for the remaining variables.

Equally troubling, analyses of the Rorschach's validity indicate that it is poorly equipped to identify most psychiatric conditions—with the notable exceptions of schizophrenia and other disturbances marked by disordered thoughts, such as bipolar disorder (manic-depression). Despite claims by some Rorschach proponents, the method does not consistently detect depression, anxiety disorders or psychopathic personality (a condition characterized by dishonesty, callousness and lack of guilt).

Moreover, although psychologists frequently administer the Rorschach to assess propensities toward violence, impulsiveness and criminal behavior, most research suggests it is not valid for these purposes either. Similarly, no compelling evidence supports its use for detecting sexual abuse in children.

Other problems have surfaced as well. Some evidence suggests that the Rorschach norms meant to distinguish mental health from mental illness are unrepresentative of the U.S. population and mistakenly make many adults and children seem maladjusted. For instance, in a 1999 study of 123 adult volunteers at a California blood bank, one in six had scores supposedly indicative of schizophrenia.

RORSCHACH TEST: WASTED INK?

"It looks like two dinosours with huge heads and tiny bodies. They're moving away from each other but looking back. The black blob in the middle reminds me of a spaceship."

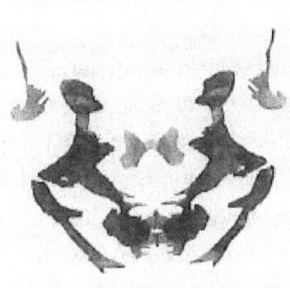

Once deemed an "x-ray of the mind," the Rorschach inkblot test remains the most famous—and infamous—projective psychological technique. An examiner hands 10 symmetrical inkblots one at a time in a set order to a viewer, who says what each blot resembles. Five blots contain color; five are black and gray. Respondents can rotate the images. The one on the right is an inverted version of an Andy Warhol rendering; the actual Rorschach blots cannot be published.

Responses to the inkblots purportedly reveal aspects of a person's personality and mental health. Advocates believe, for instance, that references to moving animals—such as the dinosaurs mentioned above—often indicate impulsiveness, whereas allusions to a blot's "blackness"—as in the spaceship—often indicate depression.

Swiss psychiatrist Hermann Rorschach probably got the idea of showing inkblots from a European parlor game. The test debuted in 1921 and reached high status by 1945. But a critical backlash began taking shape in the 1950s, as researchers found that psychologists often interpreted the same responses differently and that particular responses did not correlate well with specific mental illnesses or personality traits.

Today the Comprehensive System, meant to remedy those weaknesses, is widely used to score and interpret Rorschach responses. But it has been criticized on similar grounds. Moreover, several recent findings indicate that the Comprehensive System incorrectly labels many normal respondents as pathological.

The inkblot results may be even more misleading for minorities. Several investigations have shown that scores for African-Americans, Native Americans, Native Alaskans, Hispanics, and Central and South Americans differ markedly from the norms. Together the collected research raises serious doubts about the use of the Rorschach inkblots in the psychotherapy office and in the courtroom.

DOUBTS ABOUT TAT

Another projective tool—the Thematic Apperception Test (TAT)—may be as problematic as the Rorschach. This method asks respondents to formulate a story based on ambiguous scenes in drawings on cards. Among the 31 cards available to psychologists are ones depicting a boy contemplating a violin, a distraught woman clutching an open door, and the man and woman who were mentioned at the start of this article. One card, the epitome of ambiguity, is totally blank.

The TAT has been called "a clinician's delight and a statistician's nightmare," in part because its administration is usually not standardized: different clinicians present different numbers and selections of cards to respondents. Also, most clinicians interpret people's stories intuitively instead of following a well-tested scoring procedure. Indeed, a recent survey of nearly 100 North American psychologists practicing in juvenile and family courts discovered that only 3 percent relied on a standardized TAT scoring system. Unfortunately, some evidence suggests that clinicians who interpret the TAT in an intuitive way are likely to over-diagnose psychological disturbance.

Many standardized scoring systems are available for the TAT, but some of the more popular ones display weak "test-retest" reliability: they tend to yield inconsistent scores from one picture-viewing session to the next. Their validity is frequently questionable as well; studies that find positive results are often contradicted by other investigations. For example, several scoring systems have proved unable to differentiate normal individuals from those who are psychotic or depressed.

A few standardized scoring systems for the TAT do appear to do a good job of discerning certain aspects of personality—notably the need to achieve and a person's perceptions of others (a property called "object relations"). But many times individuals who display a high need to achieve do not score well on measures of actual achievement, so the ability of that variable to predict a person's behavior may be limited. These scoring systems currently lack norms and so are not yet ready for application outside of research settings, but they merit further investigation.

FAULTS IN THE FIGURES

In contrast to the Rorschach and the TAT, which elicit reactions to existing images, a third projective approach asks the people being evaluated to draw the pictures. A number of these instruments, such as the frequently applied Draw-a-Person Test, have examinees depict a human being; others have them draw houses or trees as well. Clinicians commonly interpret the sketches by relating specific "signs"—such as features of the body or clothing—to facets of personality or to particular psychological disorders. They might associate large eyes with paranoia, long ties with sexual aggression, missing facial features with depression, and so on.

As is true of the other methods, the research on drawing instruments gives reason for serious concern. In some studies, raters agree well on scoring, yet in others the

THEMATIC APPERCEPTION TEST: PICTURE IMPERFECT

The Thematic Apperception Test [TAT], created by Harvard University psychiatrist Henry A. Murray and his student Christiana Morgan in the 1930s, is among the most commonly used projective measures. Examiners present individuals with a subset [typically five to 12] of 31 cards displaying pictures of ambiguous situations, mostly featuring people. Respondents then construct a story about each picture, describing the events that are occurring, what led up to them, what the characters are thinking and feeling, and what will happen later. Many variations of the TAT are in use, such as the Children's Apperception Test, featuring animals interacting in ambiguous situations, and the Blacky Test, featuring the adventures of a black dog and its family.

Psychologists have several ways of interpreting responses to the TAT. One promising approach—developed by Boston University psychologist Drew Westen—relies on a specific scoring system to assess people's perceptions of others ["object relations"]. According to that approach, if someone wove a story about an older woman plotting against a younger person in response to the image visible in the photograph above, the story would imply that the respondent tends to see malevolence in others—but only if similar themes turned up in stories told about other cards.

Surveys show, however, that most practitioners do not use systematic scoring systems to interpret TAT stories, relying instead on their intuitions. Unfortunately, research indicates that such "impressionistic" interpretations of the TAT are of doubtful validity and may make the TAT a projective exercise for both examiner and examinee.

Reprinted by permission of the publishers from Henry A. Murray, Thematic Apperception Test, plate 12F, Cambridge, Mass.: Harvard University Press, Copyright (c) 1943 by the President and Fellows of Harvard College, (c) 1971 by Henry A. Murray.

agreement is poor. What is worse, no strong evidence supports the validity of the sign approach to interpretation; in other words, clinicians apparently have no grounds for linking specific signs to particular personality traits or psychiatric diagnoses. Nor is there consistent evidence that signs purportedly linked to child sexual abuse (such as tongues or genitalia) actually reveal a history of molestation. The only positive result found repeatedly is that, as a group, people who draw human figures poorly have somewhat elevated rates of psychological disorders. On the other hand, studies show that clinicians are likely to attribute mental illness to many normal individuals who lack artistic ability.

Certain proponents argue that sign approaches can be valid in the hands of seasoned experts. Yet one group of researchers reported that experts who administered the Draw-a-Person Test were less accurate than graduate students at distinguishing psychological normality from abnormality.

A few global scoring systems, which are not based on signs, might be useful. Instead of assuming a one-to-one correspondence between a feature of a drawing and a personality trait, psychologists who apply such methods combine many aspects of the pictures to come up with a general impression of a person's adjustment. In a study of 52 children, a global scoring approach helped to distinguish normal individuals from those with mood or anxiety disorders. In another report, global interpretation correctly differentiated 54 normal children and adolescents from those who were aggressive or extremely disobedient. The global approach may work better than the sign approach because the act of aggregating information can cancel out "noise" from variables that provide misleading or incomplete information.

Our literature review, then, indicates that, as usually administered, the Rorschach, TAT and human figure drawings are useful only in very limited circumstances. The same is true for many other projective techniques, some of which are described in the box on the following page.

We have also found that even when the methods assess what they claim to measure, they tend to lack what psychologists call "incremental validity": they rarely add much to information that can be obtained in other, more practical ways, such as by conducting interviews or administering objective personality tests. (Objective tests seek answers to relatively clear-cut questions, such as, "I frequently have thoughts of hurting myself—true or false?") This shortcoming of projective tools makes the costs in money and time hard to justify.

WHAT TO DO?

Some mental health professionals disagree with our conclusions. They argue that projective tools have a long history of constructive use and, when administered and interpreted properly, can cut through the veneer of respondents' self-reports to provide a picture of the deepest recesses of the mind. Critics have also asserted that we have emphasized negative findings to the exclusion of positive ones.

OTHER PROJECTIVE TOOLS: WHAT'S THE SCORE?

Psychologists have dozens of projective methods to choose from beyond the Rorschach Test, the TAT and figure drawings. As the sampling below indicates, some stand up well to the scrutiny of research, but many do not.

Hand Test
Subjects say what hands pictured in various positions might be doing. This method is used to assess aggression, anxiety and other personality traits, but it has not been well studied.

Handwriting Analysis (Graphology)
Interpreters rely on specific "signs" in a person's handwriting to assess personality characteristics. Though useless, the method is still used to screen prospective employees.

Lüscher Color Test
People rank colored cards in order of preference to reveal personality traits. Most studies find the technique to lack merit.

Play with Anatomically Correct Dolls
Research finds that sexually abused children often play with the dolls' genitalia, however, that behavior is not diagnostic, because many nonabused children do the same thing.

Rosenzweig Picture Frustration Study
After one cartoon character makes a provocative remark to another, a viewer decides how the second character should respond. This instrument, featured in the movie A *Clockwork Orange*, successfully predicts aggression in children.

Sentence Completion Test
Test takers finish a sentence, such as, "If only I could..." Most versions are poorly studied, but one developed by Jane Loevinger of Washington University is valid for measuring aspects of ego development, such as morality and empathy.

Szondi Test
From photographs of patients with various psychiatric disorders, viewers select the ones they like most and least, this technique assumes that the selections reveal something about the choosers' needs, but research has discredited it.

HUMAN FIGURE DRAWINGS: MISLEADING SIGNS

Psychologists have many projective drawing instruments at their disposal, but the Draw-a-Person Test is among the most popular—especially for assessing children and—adolescents. A clinician asks the child to draw someone of the same sex and then someone of the opposite sex in any way that he or she wishes. [A variation involves asking the child to draw a person, house and tree.] Those who employ the test believe that the drawings reveal meaningful information about the child's personality or mental health.

In a sketch of a man, for example, small feet would supposedly indicate insecurity or instability—a small head, inadequacy. Large hands or teeth would be considered signs of aggression; short arms, a sign of shyness. And feminine features—such as long eyelashes or darkly colored lips—would allegedly suggest sex-role confusion.

Yet research consistently shows that such "signs" bear virtually no relation to personality or mental illness. Scientists have denounced these sign interpretations as "phrenology for the 20th century," recalling the 19th-century pseudoscience of inferring people's personalities from the pattern of bumps on their skulls.

Still, the sign approach remains widely used. Some psychologists even claim they can identify sexual abuse from certain key signs. For instance, in the child's drawing at the right, alleged signs of abuse include a person older than the child, a partially unclothed body, a hand near the genitals, a hand hidden in a pocket, a large nose and a mustache. In reality, the connection between these signs and sexual abuse remains dubious, at best.

Yet we remain confident in our conclusions. In fact, as negative as our overall findings are, they may paint an overly rosy picture of projective techniques because of the so-called file drawer effect. As is well known, scientific journals are more likely to publish reports demonstrating that some procedure works than reports finding failure. Consequently, researchers often quietly file away their negative data, which may never again see the light of day.

We find it troubling that psychologists commonly administer projective instruments in situations for which their value has not been well established by multiple studies; too many people can suffer if erroneous diagnostic judgments influence therapy plans, custody rulings or criminal court decisions. Based on our findings, we strongly urge psychologists to curtail their use of most projective techniques and, when they do select such instruments, to limit themselves to scoring and interpreting the small number of variables that have been proved trustworthy.

Our results also offer a broader lesson for practicing clinicians, psychology students and the public at large: even seasoned professionals can be fooled by their intuitions and their faith in tools that lack strong evidence of effectiveness. When a substantial body of research demonstrates that old intuitions are wrong, it is time to adopt new ways of thinking.

HOW OFTEN THE TOOLS ARE USED: POPULARITY POLL

In 1995 a survey asked 412 randomly selected clinical psychologists in the American Psychological Association how often they used various projective and non-projective assessment tools, including those listed below. Projective instruments present people with ambiguous pictures, words or things; the other measures are less open-ended. The number of clinicians who use projective methods might have declined slightly since 1995, but these techniques remain widely used.

PROJECTIVE TECHNIQUES	USE ALWAYS OR FREQUENTLY	USE AT LEAST OCCASIONALLY
Rorschach	43%	82%
Human Figure Drawings	39%	80%
Thematic Apperception Test [TAT]	34%	82%
Sentence Completion Tests	34%	84%
CAT [Children's versions of the TAT]	6%	42%

NONPROJECTIVE TECHNIQUES*	USE ALWAYS OR FREQUENTLY	USE AT LEAST OCCASIONALLY
Weshler Adult Intelligence Scale [WAIS]	59%	93%
Minnesota Multiphasic Personality Inventory-2 [MMPI-2]	58%	85%
Weschler Intelligence Scale for Children [WISC]	42%	69%
Beck Depression Inventory	21%	71%

* These listed are the most community used nonprojective tests for assessing adult IQ (WAIS) personality (MMPI-2), childhood IQ (WISC) and depression [Beck Depression inventory].
SOURCE: "Contemporary Practice of Psychological Assessment by Clinical Psychologists" by C.E. Watkins et al. In *Professional Psychology Research and Practice*, Vol. 26: No. 1, pages 54-60, 1995.

REVIEW AND CONTEMPLATE

1. Define "scoring reliability" and "validity."

2. Briefly describe the Rorschach Inkblot Test. What does research indicate about the validity of this test?

3. Briefly describe the Thematic Apperception Test (TAT). What does research indicate about the validity of this test with respect to diagnosing mental disorders and personality?

4. What does it mean to say that projective tests such as the Rorschach and TAT lack incremental validity?

5. Describe one reason why professional clinicians might believe in the validity of projective tests despite research evidence suggesting that these tests are not valid (HINT: The reason is related to statistical reasoning).

8.3 "Portrait of a Lie"

IN FEBRUARY 2003, United States Secretary of State Colin Powell addressed the United Nations Security Council about whether Iraq had complied with a UN resolution that required Iraq to destroy its alleged weapons of mass destruction. Mr. Powell presented evidence suggesting that Iraq still possessed weapons of mass destruction and had failed to comply with the resolution, setting the stage for the U. S. to invade Iraq in March 2003. Part of the evidence presented by Mr. Powell was information from an Iraqi defector who told U. S. intelligence officials that Iraq had mobile biological weapons factories. Because the informant had passed a polygraph test, his information appeared reliable. But should a polygraph test be trusted as an accurate lie detector in matters of such importance? Unfortunately, intelligence officials later acknowledged that the informant may have fabricated or exaggerated the information about the mobile weapons factories. No such mobile factories were ever found in Iraq.

Polygraph testing involves measuring people's physiological responses to questions designed to determine if they are guilty of deceit or some misdeed. You've probably heard of many examples of the use of polygraph testing in professional settings, such as by police to determine if a suspect is guilty of a crime or by the CIA to determine if their employees are involved in espionage. Polygraph use is also prevalent in the popular media. On several talk shows, it's been used to determine whether men have had sexual affairs. On one reality television show, it was used when a man's children wanted to determine which of several women would be a suitable marriage partner for him. On another reality show, it was used when the parents of an attractive young woman wanted to learn which of several young men would be a suitable dating partner for their daughter.

A crucial question underlying all uses of the polygraph is whether it can accurately detect when people are lying. In this article, Matthias Gamer explains problems with the validity of the polygraph test and discusses other, more scientifically supported techniques for detecting deception.

Reference

Gamer, M. (2009). Portrait of a lie. *Scientific American Mind, 20*(1), 50–55.

"PORTRAIT OF A LIE"

MATTHIAS GAMER

A young man steals across the hallway, slips through a door and scans the room. He opens a drawer, snatches a wristwatch inside and puts it in his pocket. Then he hurries out the door.

Sixty more people perform the same drill, half of them filching a watch and the others, a ring. Psychiatrist F. Andrew Kozel, now at the University of Texas Southwestern Medical Center at Dallas, and his colleagues promised to give a bonus payment to anyone who could conceal the deed from the scientists, who planned to look into their brains for signs of a cover-up.

Kozel and his co-workers scanned the volunteers' brains using functional magnetic resonance imaging, which provides a measure of neural activity in different brain areas. During the scans, the subjects answered questions about the theft such as "Did you steal a watch?" or "Did you steal a ring?" The researchers also asked neutral yes/no queries as well as questions about minor wrongful acts. Each participant could truthfully deny stealing one of the objects but had to lie about the other to conceal the deed. (The volunteers were supposed to answer the unrelated questions truthfully.)

Kozel and his team initially identified typical neural activity patterns for true and false statements. Then, in the first use of fMRI to detect deception in individuals, the researchers used the patterns they identified to correctly determine whether each of the subjects had taken a watch or a ring 90 percent of the time.

The use of fMRI represents the cutting edge of lie-detection technology. As far as we know, no region of the brain specializes in lies. But investigators have found that lying activates brain regions involved in suppressing information and in resolving conflicts—such as that between the impulse to describe reality and the wish to contradict it. The use of fMRI combined with a clever questioning strategy could lead to a better method for detecting lies or, more precisely, for getting at the truth despite a person's attempts to hide it.

Improved ability to detect falsehoods would be of significant use in solving crimes, for example, and perhaps also in ferreting out military spies. Unraveling the neurocircuitry of deception, moreover, might help doctors better understand, diagnose and treat patients with disorders in which compulsive lying is a prominent component, including antisocial personality disorder and substance dependence.

Matthias Gamer, "Portrait of a Lie," *Scientific American Mind*, vol. 20, no. 1, pp. 51-55. Copyright © 2009 by Springer Nature America, Inc. Reprinted with permission.

QUESTIONING THE TRUTH

Virtually everybody lies. Indeed, the ability to fabricate, at least to some extent, is important for normal social interactions and the maintenance of a healthy state of mind [see "Natural-Born Liars," by David Livingstone Smith; SCIENTIFIC AMERICAN Mind, Vol. 16, No. 2; June 2005]. Nevertheless, law-enforcement officials and employers, among others, often want to know whether someone is lying—either to cover up a crime or to simply make himself or herself look better.

Laypeople and psychologists alike have thus looked for behavioral clues such as slight hesitations or mistakes in speech, awkward gestures or lack of eye contact. These signs do not reliably indicate untruthfulness, however. We cannot distinguish a fabrication from the facts by observation alone. We are correct only 45 to 60 percent of the time, a rate barely better than chance.

Similarly, researchers have not found any specific verbal, behavioral or physiological cue that uniquely indicates lying. In contrast to Pinocchio, whose nose grows whenever he lies, the "tells" that betray dishonest intent in humans are more nonspecific. In the early 20th century psychologist William Moulton Marston invented the first polygraph, popularly known as a lie detector, to pick up some of these nonspecific signals. The polygraph measures physiological activity from a subject that may help an examiner glean the truth from his or her reactions to questions and statements. The instrument records such physical signs as heart rate dips, blood pressure boosts, slowed breathing and increased sweating on separate tracks in a graphical printout [see box on opposite page].

The polygraph picks up emotional and peripheral nervous system arousal that is not specific to lying. Thus, blips on a polygraph can reflect fear or agitation resulting from just being hooked up to a machine and having to answer probing questions. To minimize that problem, researchers have designed questioning strategies that compare physical reactions to questions or answer choices that are connected to a crime with those of

FAST FACTS: DETECTING DECEPTION

1. There is no telltale sign that reliably shows someone is a liar, although investigators have long used physical indications of arousal such as sweating and changes in heart rate.
2. More recently, researchers have probed the brain for a neural signature of a fib. They found that lying activates brain regions involved in suppressing information and in resolving conflicts—such as that between the impulse to describe reality and the wish to contradict it.
3. The use of brain imaging combined with physiological measures, along with a clever questioning strategy, could lead to an improved method for detecting lies.

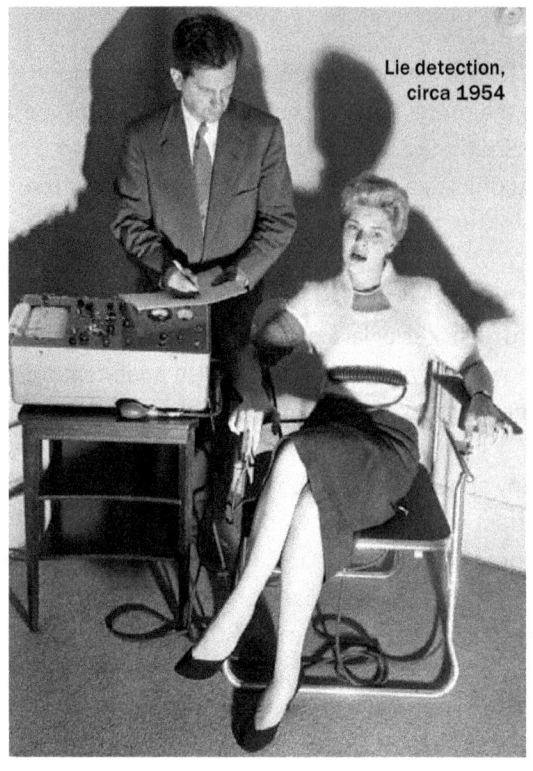

Lie detection, circa 1954

questions or choices that have nothing to do with the deed.

In the Control Question Test, for example, a practitioner compares the physiological responses to crime-linked inquiries such as the direct "Did you do it?" with the responses to incriminatory control questions about past acts such as minor traffic violations or lying to parents. In a pretest interview, an examiner leads subjects to believe that the control questions are important indicators of dishonesty so that they will trigger large physiological responses when subjects lie about them in an attempt to appear respectable. In theory, a perpetrator should still react more strongly to crime-related queries than to the control questions. In contrast, innocent individuals should respond less vigorously to the crime questions, which they can deny with a clear conscience. Thus, the results of a polygraph test are supposed to point to guilt or innocence—and, indirectly, to deception by perpetrators trying to hide their ties to a misdeed.

GUILTY KNOWLEDGE

Such tactics are imperfect, however. When combined with a Control Question Test, a polygraph may detect a reaction pattern in an innocent person that is very similar to that of the perpetrator if the blameless individual merely thinks he or she is being accused of a crime. Some researchers say that this combination wrongly implicates the innocent in up to 30 percent of cases. Conversely, if a person can remain calm, he or she could beat the test and successfully hide falsehoods.

Another questioning strategy, developed by the late psychologist David T. Lykken of the University of Minnesota, reduces such misplaced anxiety by not prodding a suspect directly about guilt. Instead of asking, "Did you steal the watch?" Lykken's Guilty Knowledge Test probes a person for inside information about the crime. It compares physiological responses to different multiple-choice answers, one of which contains information only the investigators and criminal would know. For the misdeed described above, one such inquiry might read, "Where did the thief find a watch? Did he find it (a) on the table, (b) in the jewelry box, (c) in the drawer or (d) in a shopping bag?"

BODY LANGUAGE

Can your body betray a lie? The so-called Guilty Knowledge Test is based on the idea that people react physiologically to information they recognize but are trying to conceal—such as that connected to a crime. When someone recognizes a crime-related detail, for example, he or she typically breaks out in a sweat and shows a brief heart rate drop, a reaction that might relate to enhanced attention. A polygraph (aka lie detector) tracks such responses. Tubes placed around the chest and stomach record respiratory rate (through chest and abdominal movement); two small metal plates on the fingers measure skin conductivity, which indicates the amount of sweat on the fingertips; and an electrocardiogram picks up the heart rate.

In the case shown here, the examiner compared a suspect's physiological responses when she heard a multiple-choice answer that was related to a crime (R) to her bodily reactions to four plausible control answers (C_1-C_4). Physiological aberrations that occur in connection with the crime facts may indicate involvement in an illegal activity. The reaction profile suggests that the person being interrogated has knowledge of the crime: when a crime detail is mentioned, her breathing slows (*blue arrow*); she sweats more, indicated by increased skin conductivity (*green arrow*); and her heart rate momentarily drops (*red arrow*).

—M.G.

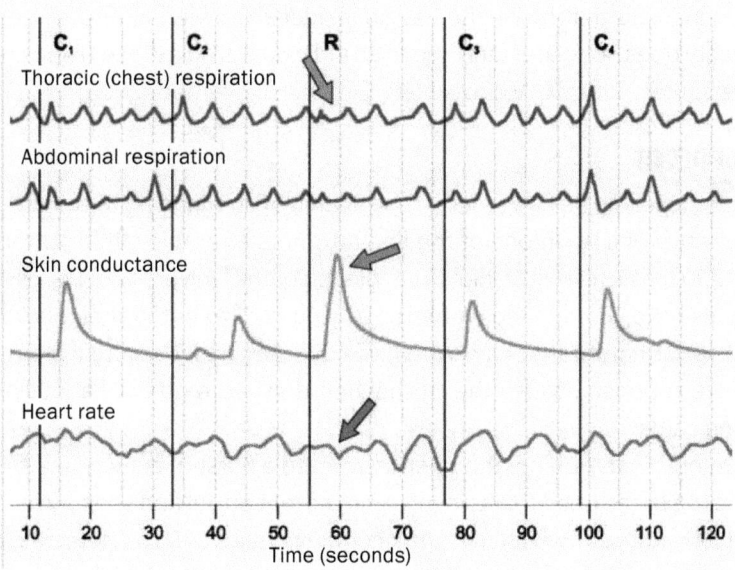

If the person being interrogated responds systematically differently to the correct answer ("in the drawer"), he has an insider's knowledge of the crime, indicating guilt. In contrast, an innocent person should not react differently to the theft-related answers. The Guilty Knowledge Test relies on recognition, which is hard to suppress, rather than on fear or comprehension of culpability. It accurately detects concealed recognition of crime details 80 to 90 percent of the time. What is more, it incriminates the innocent in only 0 to 10 percent of cases, far fewer than the Control Question Test does.

As a practical matter, the Guilty Knowledge Test requires that investigators have several pieces of insider information so that conclusions are based on more than just one or two deviant responses. Furthermore, interrogators must make certain that the general public is not privy to facts about the circumstances of the crime; otherwise innocent suspects might distinguish these facts from the neutral alternatives and react as a perpetrator would.

But in addition to trying to improve such interrogation procedures, many scientists are looking for a more precise physiological measure of deception. In particular, psychologists have been trying to outline the signature of a lie in the brain. Deception is, after all, a cognitive event, so it ought to leave a trace in the neural machinery that underlies the ability to deceive.

Early efforts to perform brain "fingerprinting" involved attaching electrodes to a subject's head and recording his or her brain waves on an electroencephalogram. A characteristic brain wave called the P300 shows up when a person recognizes something familiar, which could indicate that he or she has an insider's knowledge of a crime, although such familiarity does not necessarily mean an individual is guilty [see "Exposing Lies," by Thomas Metzinger; Scientific American Mind, October/November 2006].

PATTERNS OF DECEIT

More recently, researchers have used sophisticated brain scanning to search for a neural portrait indicative of a lie. In one of the first attempts to employ fMRI for this purpose, reported in 2002, psychiatrist Daniel D. Langleben of the University of Pennsylvania and his colleagues gave 18 men and women a playing card to put in their pocket and told them to lie about having that card when asked if they had it during a brain scan. The subjects were supposed to tell the truth when they were queried about possessing other playing cards.

When a subject was fibbing, the scientists noted a burst of activity in a strip of brain tissue at the top of the head that is involved in motor control and sensory feedback and in the anterior cingulate, which performs cognitive tasks such as detecting discrepancies that could result in errors [see "Minding Mistakes," by Markus Ullsperger; Scientific American Mind, August/September 2008]. Langleben's team suggests that this neural pattern reflects the mental conflict that arises in the telling of a lie and the increased demand for motor control when suppressing the truth. Such inhibition of the truth, the

TELLING THE TRUTH

Finding the facts of a criminal case does not necessarily require fancy machinery. A method called Criteria-Based Content Analysis relies on evaluating the retelling of an incident for a set of defined narrative features that hint at whether it is a true account. The method is based on research indicating that a story of a real recollection differs from a fabrication in specific ways, according to a 2005 analysis by psychologist Aldert Vrij of the University of Portsmouth in England.

This idea suggests that descriptions of actual experiences have the following properties:

- They are coherent and consistent but generally not in chronological order.
- They contain a lot of detail and include unusual and superfluous elements.
- They depict personal interactions and reiterate speech and conversation.
- They describe feelings and thoughts—the narrator's and in many cases those the storyteller ascribes to the perpetrator.
- They contain spontaneous corrections, the admission of memory gaps and doubts about the believability of the story.

These criteria may be used in cases of suspected sexual abuse in children to assess the believability of the events as described by the underage victims. Some studies suggest, however, that testimony gained in this manner is somewhat less valid than that derived from polygraph tests. Indeed, the error rate of the method in experimental settings is as high as 30 percent. —M.G.

authors state, may be a basic component of intentional deception. Because no brain regions were *less* active during deceit, the researchers contend that truth is the baseline cognitive state.

Other studies have similarly associated dishonesty with activation in the anterior cingulate. In their 2005 study, described earlier, Kozel and his colleagues showed that they could use an activation pattern in the brain that included this area to determine whether individuals had "stolen" a watch or a ring. The scientists theorize that the anterior cingulate monitors the incorrect and deceptive response to a question and then spurs other frontal brain regions to produce a falsehood. The ability to recognize a mark of deception in the brain further suggests that brain imaging might work as a lie detector in the courtroom and in other applications.

In a study published in 2007 my colleagues at the University of Mainz in Germany and I found additional support for the role of frontal brain regions in concealing knowledge. We asked 14 men to choose one of three envelopes containing money and a playing card and to keep them secret. While the men were in an MRI scanner, we gave them a Guilty Knowledge Test that included images of the contents of the envelope and of various other objects. In addition, we recorded skin conductivity to determine whether activity in the brain regions involved in concealing information is linked to the response of sweat glands to questions about crime details.

As expected, skin conductivity increased more when subjects saw the information they were trying to conceal than when they looked at the other options. The same held true for activity in certain regions of the frontal lobe, which plays a key role in memory and attention [*see illustration below*]. Apparently, our volunteers recognized the secret information and mobilized additional brain resources to conceal their knowledge of it.

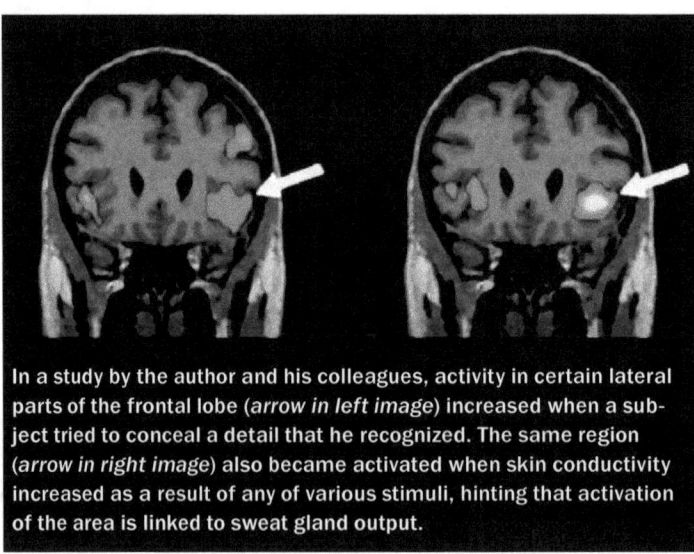

In a study by the author and his colleagues, activity in certain lateral parts of the frontal lobe (*arrow in left image*) increased when a subject tried to conceal a detail that he recognized. The same region (*arrow in right image*) also became activated when skin conductivity increased as a result of any of various stimuli, hinting that activation of the area is linked to sweat gland output.

In fact, we found that activity in inferior frontal regions and in the right anterior insula, which interprets bodily states as emotions, directly paralleled sweat gland productivity, lending credence to both brain and skin responses as indicators of fibbing.

IMAGING ON TRIAL

Still, many questions remain about the use of brain imaging to detect lies in real-world settings such as law enforcement. For one, experimental tests of the technology typically involve normal adults whose brains may be substantially different from those of individuals who have frequent problems with the law. Studies of people with antisocial personality disorders, for example, indicate that such patients may have damaged frontal lobes. Because of these discrepancies, a sociopath, psychopath or someone who is simply a good liar might well be able to suppress any suspicious neural responses to the "insider" choices and thus avoid detection. [For more on the use of brain scans in the courtroom, see "Brain Scans Go Legal," by Scott T. Grafton et al.; Scientific American Mind, December 2006/January 2007.]

And of course, the consequences of being caught in a lie in experimental settings are typically low: the subjects are usually asked to lie, after all. The brain activity recorded in such studies therefore is not necessarily the same as that which occurs in real-world scenarios in which people deceive to avoid severe social, emotional or monetary repercussions.

Functional MRIs of brain activity are far more expensive than polygraph exams, too, and we do not yet know whether they are really more sensitive and accurate than these traditional tests are. We can be fairly certain that neither polygraphs nor fMRI can identify responses that are exclusive to lying or identify the guilty with 100 percent confidence. Nevertheless, researchers may eventually identify a combination of brain images and signals from the body that comes much closer than do current methods to providing an accurate depiction of deception.

REVIEW AND CONTEMPLATE

1. How accurate are laypeople or psychologists when they use behavioral clues (e.g., hesitations in speech, awkward gestures, lack of eye contact) to determine whether someone is lying?

2. Explain how the Control Question Test is conducted with a polygraph to determine if someone is lying. What pattern of responses supposedly indicates deception? Is the CQT an accurate lie detector?

3. Explain how a Guilty Knowledge Test (GKT) is conducted and what pattern of responses suggests deception. What percentage of the time does the GKT accurately detect concealed recognition of crime details (i.e., deception)? Can the GKT be used in cases where all of the important details of a crime that are known to police have been shared with the public?

4. Gamer (2008) described a study conducted by Andrew Kozel in which they used functional magnetic resonance imaging (fMRI) to detect deception among subjects who had been asked to take a watch or a ring. What percentage of the time were they able to determine which item the subjects had taken? Gamer (2008) explained that "many questions remain about the use of brain imaging to detect lies in real-world settings"; describe two issues that make it unclear whether fMRI would be useful in real-world settings.

8.4 "Voice Stress Analysis: Only 15% of Lies About Drug Use Detected in Field Test"

THE NATIONAL INSTITUTE of Truth Verification (NITV) sells a popular Computerized Voice Stress Analyzer (CVSA) used by a wide variety of law enforcement, federal government, and other agencies. The CVSA is touted by the NITV as "a technological achievement in detecting deception born from a desire to achieve the most accurate results in truth verification for law enforcement, government, military, and private sector applications." On their website, they have a section entitled "Real Cases Solved" that provides many anecdotes about how the CVSA was used to solve a variety of criminal cases. For example, in one case, Detective Phil Kleman reports that he was asked by the Fostoria, Ohio police department to "test an individual who was suspected of murder." The story continues as follows:

> The suspect had just taken a polygraph examination from an Ohio Bureau of Criminal Investigations polygraph examiner who reported the results of the polygraph examination to be inconclusive bordering on truthful. The subject denied any involvement in or knowledge of the murder and agreed to take the CVSA, just as he had agreed to take the polygraph. The CVSA showed very clearly that the subject had committed the murder and when confronted with his deceptive charts, gave a full confession. The Fostoria P.D. has now purchased their own CVSA and trained several detectives as examiners.

As discussed in Chapter 1, pseudoscientists often rely on testimonial or anecdotal evidence to support their claims rather than relying on well-controlled scientific research. In addition, pseudoscientists tend to focus only on information that is consistent with their claims, ignoring information that contradicts their claims. Thus, the fact that the NITV's website reflects both of these characteristics of pseudoscience might be red flags that suggest that the CVSA is pseudoscience.

In this selection, Kelly Damphousse reports the results of scientific research on voice stress analysis. This article by Damphousse and other recent research, such as that published by Hollien and Harnsberger (2013) in *Investigative Sciences Journal,* leads to the conclusion that the CVSA does not live up to the claims made by its manufacturer.

Reference

Damphousse, K. R. (2008, March). Voice stress analysis: Only 15% of lies about drug use detected in field test. *National Institute of Justice Journal,* 259, 8–12.

"VOICE STRESS ANALYSIS: ONLY 15 % OF LIES ABOUT DRUG USE DETECTED IN FIELD TEST"

KELLY DAMPHOUSSE

Law enforcement agencies across the country have invested millions of dollars in voice stress analysis (VSA) software programs.[1] One crucial question, however, remains unanswered:

Does VSA actually work?

According to a recent study funded by the National Institute of Justice (NIJ), two of the most popular VSA programs in use by police departments across the country are no better than flipping a coin when it comes to detecting deception regarding recent drug use. The study's findings also noted, however, that the mere presence of a VSA program during an interrogation may deter a respondent from giving a false answer.

VSA manufacturers tout the technology as a way for law enforcers to accurately, cheaply, and efficiently determine whether a person is lying by analyzing changes in their voice patterns. Indeed, according to one manufacturer, more than 1,400 law enforcement agencies in the United States use its product.[2] But few studies have been conducted on the effectiveness of VSA software in general, and until now, none of these tested VSA in the field—that is, in a real-world environment such as a jail. Therefore, to help determine whether VSA is a reliable technology, NIJ funded a field evaluation of two programs: Computer Voice Stress Analyzer® (CVSA®)[3] and Layered Voice Analysis™ (LVA).

Researchers with the Oklahoma Department of Mental Health and Substance Abuse Services (including this author) used these VSA programs while questioning more than 300 arrestees about their recent drug use. The results of the VSA output—which ostensibly indicated whether the arrestees were lying or telling the truth—were then compared to their urine drug test results. The findings of our study revealed:

- **Deceptive respondents.** Fifteen percent who said they had not used drugs—but who, according to their urine tests, had—were *correctly* identified by the VSA programs as being deceptive.

- **Nondeceptive respondents.** Eight and a half percent who were telling the truth—that is, their urine tests were consistent with their statements that they had or had not used drugs—were *incorrectly* classified by the VSA programs as being deceptive.

K. R. Damphousse, "Voice Stress Analysis: Only 15% of Lies about Drug Use Detected in Field Test," *National Institute of Justice Journal*, vol 259, pp. 8-12, 2008.

Using these percentages to determine the overall accuracy rates of the two VSA programs, we found that their ability to accurately detect deception about recent drug use was about 50 percent.

Based solely on these statistics, it seems reasonable to conclude that these VSA programs were not able to detect deception about drug use, at least to a degree that law enforcement professionals would require—particularly when weighed against the financial investment. We did find, however, that arrestees who were questioned using the VSA instruments were less likely to lie about illicit drug use compared to arrestees whose responses were recorded by the interviewer with pen and paper.

So perhaps the answer to the question "Does VSA work?" is ... it depends on the definition of "work."

WHAT IS VSA?

VSA software programs are designed to measure changes in voice patterns caused by the stress, or the physical effort, of trying to hide deceptive responses.[4] VSA programs interpret changes in vocal patterns and indicate on a graph whether the subject is being "deceptive" or "truthful."

Most VSA developers and manufacturers do not claim that their devices detect lies; rather, they claim that VSA detects micro-tremors, which are caused by the stress of trying to conceal or deceive.

VSA proponents often compare the technology to polygraph testing, which attempts to measure changes in respiration, heart rate, and galvanic skin response.

Even advocates of polygraph testing, however, acknowledge its limitations, including that it is inadmissible as evidence in a court of law; requires a large investment of resources; and takes several hours to perform, with the subject connected to a machine. Furthermore, a polygraph cannot test audio or video recordings, or statements made either over a telephone or in a remote setting (that is, away from a formal interrogation room), such as at an airport ticket counter. Such limitations of the polygraph—along with technological advances—prompted the development of VSA software.

OUT OF THE LAB, INTO THE FIELD

Although some research studies have shown that several features of speech pattern differ under stress,[5,6] it is unclear whether VSA can detect *deception-related* stress. In those studies that found that this stress *may* be detectable, the deception was relatively minor and no "jeopardy" was involved—that is, the subjects had nothing to lose by lying (or by telling the truth, for that matter). This led some researchers to suggest that if there is no jeopardy, there is no stress—and that if there is no stress, the VSA technology may not have been tested appropriately.[7]

EDITOR'S NOTE
POLYGRAPH AND VOICE STRESS ANALYSIS: TRYING TO FIND THE RIGHT TOOL

The validity of the polygraph as a lie-detection device has been under fire for years. In 2003, the National Academy of Sciences issued a report identifying major deficiencies in polygraph technology.[9] The report and other analyses led to the research and development of potential alternatives to the polygraph; one technology that emerged is voice stress analysis (VSA).

The National Institute of Justice funded a study to evaluate two of the most popular VSA software programs in a real-world (that is, nonlaboratory) setting in which jeopardy—the threat of penalty—was present.

The study found that the average accuracy rate of these programs in detecting deception regarding drug use was approximately 50 percent—about as accurate as flipping a coin. But the research also found that subjects may be deterred from lying if they think their responses can be "proven" false.

It remains to be seen, however, if any deterrence factor dissipates as word spreads about the accuracy rate of VSA software programs. Prospective users of VSA should weigh all these factors, including that there may be an investigative, even if there is no evidentiary, use for this technology.

The NIJ-funded study was designed to address these criticisms by testing VSA in a setting where police interviews commonly occur (a jail) and asking arrestees about relevant criminal behavior (drug use) that they would likely hide.[8]

Our research team interviewed a random sample of 319 recent arrestees in the Oklahoma County jail. The interviews were conducted in a relatively private room adjacent to the booking facility with male arrestees who had been in the detention facility for less than 24 hours. During separate testing periods, data were collected using CVSA® and LVA.

The arrestees were asked to respond to questions about marijuana use during the previous 30 days, and cocaine, heroin, methamphetamine, and PCP use within the previous 72 hours. The questions and test formats were approved by officials from CVSA® and LVA. The VSA data were independently interpreted by the research team and by certified examiners from both companies.

Following each interview, the arrestee provided a urine sample that was later tested for the presence of the five drugs. The results of the urinalysis were compared to the responses about recent drug use to determine whether the arrestee was being truthful or deceptive. This determination was then compared to the VSA output results to see whether the VSA gave the same result of truthfulness or deceptiveness.

CAN VSA ACCURATELY DETECT DECEPTION?

Our findings suggest that these VSA software programs were no better in determining deception about recent drug use among arrestees than flipping a coin. To arrive at this conclusion, we first calculated two percentage rates[10]:

- **Sensitivity rate.** The percentage of deceptive arrestees correctly identified by the VSA devices as deceptive.

- **Specificity rate.** The percentage of non-deceptive arrestees correctly classified by the VSA as nondeceptive.

Both VSA programs had a low sensitivity rate, identifying an average of 15 percent of the responses by arrestees who lied (based on the urine test) about recent drug use for all five drugs. LVA correctly identified 21 percent of the deceptive responses as deceptive; CVSA® identified 8 percent.

The specificity rates—the percentage of nondeceptive respondents who, based on their urine tests, were correctly classified as nondeceptive—were much higher, with an average of 91.5-percent accuracy for the five drugs. Again, LVA performed better, correctly identifying 95 percent of the nondeceptive respondents; CVSA® correctly identified 90 percent of the nondeceptive respondents.

We then used a plotting algorithm, comparing the sensitivity and specificity rates, to calculate each VSA program's overall "accuracy rate" in detecting deception about drug use.[11] We found that the average accuracy rate for all five drugs was approximately 50 percent.

DOES VSA DETER PEOPLE FROM LYING?

Although the two VSA programs we tested had about a 50-percent accuracy rate in determining deception about recent drug use, might their very presence during an interrogation compel a person to be more truthful?

This phenomenon—that people will answer more honestly if they believe that their responses can be tested for accuracy—is called the "bogus pipeline" effect.[12] Previous research has established that it is often present in studies that examine substance use.[13]

To determine whether a bogus pipeline effect existed in our study, we compared the percentage of deceptive answers to data from the Oklahoma City Arrestee Drug Abuse Monitoring (ADAM) study (1998–2004), which was conducted by the same VSA researchers in the same jail using the same protocols. The only differences—apart from the different groups of arrestees—were that the ADAM survey was longer (a 20-minute survey compared with the VSA study's 5-minute survey) and did not involve the use of VSA technology.

In both studies, arrestees were told that they would be asked to submit a urine sample after answering questions about their recent drug use. In the VSA study, arrestees were told that a computer program was being used that would detect deceptive answers.

Arrestees in the VSA study were much less deceptive than ADAM arrestees, based on responses and results of the urine test (that is, not considering the VSA data). Only 14 percent of the VSA study arrestees were deceptive about recent drug use compared to 40 percent of the ADAM arrestees. This suggests that the arrestees in the VSA study who thought their interviewers were using a form of "lie detection" (i.e., the VSA technology) were much less likely to be deceptive when reporting recent drug use. (See sidebar on p. 250, "Editor's Note, Polygraph and Voice Stress Analysis: Trying to Find the Right Tool.")

THE BOTTOM LINE: TO USE OR NOT USE VSA

It is important to look at both "hard" and "hidden" costs when deciding whether to purchase or maintain a VSA program. The monetary costs are substantial: it can cost up to $20,000 to purchase LVA. The average cost of CVSA® training and equipment is $11,500. Calculating the current investment nationwide—more than 1,400 police departments currently use CVSA®, according to the manufacturer—the total cost is more than $16 million not including the manpower expense to use it.

The hidden costs are, of course, more difficult to quantify. As VSA programs come under greater scrutiny—due, in part, to reports of false confessions during investigations that used VSA—the overall value of the technology continues to be questioned.[14]

Therefore, it is not a simple task to answer the question: Does VSA work? As our findings revealed, the two VSA programs that we tested had approximately a 50-percent accuracy rate in detecting deception about drug use in a field (i.e., jail) environment; however, the mere presence of a VSA program during an interrogation may deter a respondent from answering falsely. Clearly, law enforcement administrators and policy-makers should weigh all the factors when deciding to purchase or use VSA technology.

NCJ 221502

The products, manufacturers, and organizations discussed in this document are presented for informational purposes only and do not constitute product approval or endorsement by the U.S. Department of Justice.

NOTES

1. The National Institute for Truth Verification (manufacturer of CVSA®) states that more than 1,400 law enforcement agencies use its product. See www.nitv1.com/Agenciesusing.htm.
2. Ibid.

3. CVSA® was introduced into the market in 1988 by the National Institute for Truth Verification and has undergone a number of changes and system upgrades over the years. The version used in this field test was the CVSA® introduced in 1997.
4. Hopkins, C.S., R.J. Ratley, D.S. Benincasa, and J. Grieco, "Evaluation of Voice Stress Analysis Technology," *Proceedings of the 38th Annual Hawaii International Conference on System Sciences,* 2005.
5. In the few studies in which the theory behind VSA has been tested, there has generally been solid support. Cestaro, V.L., "A Comparison Between Decision Accuracy Rates Obtained Using the Polygraph Instrument and the Computer Voice Stress Analyzer (CVSA) in the Absence of Jeopardy," *Polygraph* 25 (2) (1996): 117–127; and Fuller, B.F., "Reliability and Validity of an Interval Measure of Vocal Stress," *Psychological Medicine* 14 (1) (1984): 159–166.
6. Researchers at the Air Force Research Laboratory concluded that two VSA devices (Lantern™ and the Psychological Stress Evaluator—a precursor of CVSA®) could measure these differences in speech patterns. Hansen, J., and G. Zhou, *Methods for Voice Stress Analysis and Classification: Final Technical Report,* Rome, NY: U.S. Air Force Research Laboratory, 1999; and Haddad, D., S. Walter, R. Ratley, and M. Smith, *Investigation and Evaluation of Voice Stress Analysis Technology,* final report submitted to the National Institute of Justice, 2002 (NCJ 193832), available at www.ncjrs.gov/pdffiles1/nij/193832.pdf.
7. Barland, G., "The Use of Voice Changes in the Detection of Deception," *Polygraph* 31 (2) (2002): 145–153. This study suggests simulated stress in a laboratory setting may not be sufficient to allow VSA to detect deception. This leads to the argument, by some VSA proponents, that mock deception in a staged (lab) scenario fails to create the necessary degree of jeopardy (and therefore stress) to stimulate a measurable response indicating deception. In an experiment in which the subject is not worried about getting "caught" because there are no real consequences or is pretending to lie, it is, they argue, more difficult for the software to detect deception, as the necessary stress levels are not present.
8. Previous arrestee studies suggest that respondents are commonly deceptive about recent drug use. Fendrich, M., and Y. Xu, "Validity of Drug Use Reports from Juvenile Arrestees," *International Journal of the Addictions* 29 (8) (1994): 971–985; Hser, Y.I., "Self-Reported Drug Use: Results of Selected Empirical Investigations of Validity," *NIDA Research Monograph* 167 (1997): 320–343; Lu, N.T., B.J. Taylor, and K.G. Riley, "The Validity of Adult Arrestee Self-Reports of Crack Cocaine," *American Journal of Drug and Alcohol Abuse* 27 (3) (2000): 399–407; Mieczkowski, T., D. Barzelay, B. Gropper, and E. Wish, "Concordance of Three Measures of Cocaine Use in an Arrestee Population: Hair, Urine, and Self-Report," *Journal of Psychoactive Drugs* 23 (3) (1991): 241–249; and Harrison, L., "The Validity of Self-Reported Data on Drug Use," *Journal of Drug Issues* 25 (1) (1995): 91–111.

9. Committee to Review the Scientific Evidence on the Polygraph, National Research Council, *The Polygraph and Lie Detection,* Washington, DC: National Academies Press, 2003.
10. Ibid.
11. Sensitivity and specificity should be examined jointly, because an overly sensitive but not specific instrument—that is, one that indicates all responses as deceptive—is not very useful. The standard way to compare these two scores simultaneously is by examining them on a receiver operating characteristic chart. Programs with high sensitivity and specificity scores will efficiently predict who is being deceptive and who is not. If either the sensitivity or the specificity score is low, the usefulness of the programs for predicting deception is diminished.
12. Jones, E.E., and H. Sigall, "The Bogus Pipeline: A New Paradigm for Measuring Affect and Attitude," *Psychological Bulletin* 76 (5) (1971): 349–364.
13. Aguinis, H., C.A. Pierce, and B.M. Quigley, "Conditions Under Which a Bogus Pipeline Procedure Enhances the Validity of Self-Reported Cigarette Smoking: A Meta-Analytic Review," *Journal of Applied Social Psychology* 23 (5) (1993): 352–373; Botvin, E.M., G.J. Botvin, N.L. Renick, A.D. Filazzola, and J.P. Allegrante, "Adolescents' Self-Reports of Tobacco, Alcohol, and Marijuana Use: Examining the Comparability of Video Tape, Cartoon and Verbal Bogus-Pipeline Procedures," *Psychological Reports* 55 (1984): 379–386; and Sprangers, M., and J. Hoogstraten, "Response-Style Effects, Response-Shift Bias and a Bogus-Pipeline," *Psychological Reports* 61 (1987): 579–585.
14. Hansen, M., "Untrue Confessions," *ABA Journal,* July 1999, 50–53; Wagner, D., "Arguments Rage Over Voice-Stress Lie Detector," *Arizona Republic,* October 10, 2005; and "Innocent Until Proved Guilty?" *ABC News,* March 30, 2006, available at www.abcnews.go.com/Primetime/story?id=1786421&page=1.

REVIEW AND CONTEMPLATE

1. What is voice stress analysis, and what physiological changes supposedly indicate lying?

2. Briefly describe the design and results of the study conducted by Damphousse (2008) on individuals about their recent drug use. Can voice stress analysis accurately detect deception (what was its overall accuracy rate and the accuracy rates with subjects who were lying and with those who were truthful)?

3. What evidence from the study by Damphousse (2008) suggests that voice stress analysis programs might deter people from lying?

4. Which characteristics of pseudoscience mentioned in Chapter 1 seem most relevant to how the NITV promotes the CVSA on its website?

Chapter 9

PSYCHOLOGICAL DISORDERS AND THERAPIES

9.1 "Dissociative Identity Disorder: A Contemporary Scientific Perspective"

THE 1973 BOOK and 1976 movie *Sybil* was based on the true story of a woman who was diagnosed with multiple personality disorder (currently known as Dissociative Identity Disorder). Her psychiatrist—Dr. Cornelia Wilbur—believed that Sybil developed the disorder as a way to cope with the severe abuse she received as a child from her cruel mother. Sybil's 16 personalities included a self-assured blond woman, a male carpenter, a baby, and a carefree, fun-loving teenage girl. It's a fascinating story, but now it appears that Sybil never actually had multiple personalities that were caused by severe trauma.

In the late 1990s, after reviewing tape recordings of conversations between Dr. Wilbur and the author of a book about Sybil, psychologist Robert Rieber concluded that Sybil's personalities may have been created during therapy as a result of suggestions given by Dr. Wilbur. Similarly, Dr. Herbert Spiegel, who served as Sybil's psychiatrist when Dr. Wilbur was out of town, suspected that Sybil's multiple personalities came about as a result of Dr. Wilbur's therapeutic technique of assigning people's names to various emotional states Sybil exhibited and encouraging her to be those people while describing her past experiences.

In 2011, Debbie Nathan published a book entitled *Sybil Exposed*, in which she explained that Sybil (whose real name was Shirley Mason) had written a letter to Dr. Wilbur stating, "I do not really have any multiple personalities. ... I am all of them. I have been lying in my pretense of them." But Dr. Wilbur rejected the confession, thinking that Sybil was just trying to get out of any further therapy for her multiple personalities.

In the 1970s, there were fewer than 200 cases of people diagnosed with multiple personality disorder. By the 1990s, clinicians specializing in the treatment of the disorder estimated there were tens of thousands of cases, most of which were in North America. Psychologists believe that the book and film about Sybil contributed to the massive increase in diagnosed cases of DID by influencing the beliefs of psychotherapists and the public about the causes and features of DID. Psychologists now question whether Dissociative Identity Disorder more likely reflects a socially constructed condition than a psychological disorder brought about by childhood trauma. In the following excerpt from a chapter written by Lilienfeld and Lynn, they discuss the controversy surrounding this disorder and the problems with the theory that trauma causes DID (a theory that many psychologists consider pseudoscientific).

Reference

Lilienfeld, S. O., & Lynn, S. J. (2015). Dissociative identity disorder: A contemporary scientific perspective. In Lilienfeld, S. O., Lynn, S. J., & Lohr, J. M. (Eds.), *Science and pseudoscience in clinical psychology* (2nd ed.). New York: Guilford Press.

ARTICLE 9.1

"DISSOCIATIVE IDENTITY DISORDER: A CONTEMPORARY SCIENTIFIC PERSPECTIVE"

SCOTT LILIENFELD AND STEVEN JAY LYNN

Dissociative identity disorder (DID), known formerly as multiple personality disorder (MPD), has long been among the most controversial of all psychiatric diagnoses (see McCann, Lynn, Lilienfeld, Shindler, & Hammond, Chapter 4, this volume, for a review of other controversial psychiatric diagnoses and their legal status). The controversies surrounding DID have centered primarily on its descriptive psychopathology, diagnosis, etiology, and treatment (see also Elzinga, van Dyck, & Spinhoven, 1998; Giesbrecht, Lynn, Lilienfeld, & Merkelbach, 2008; Lynn, Lilienfeld, Merckelbach, Giesbrecht, McNally, et al., 2014). Although these controversies have a lengthy history, they have become especially divisive and even acrimonious over the past two decades. To a large extent, these debates center on fundamental questions regarding the nature, boundaries, and etiology of the diagnosis itself.

Some prominent researchers (e.g., Ross, 1997) believe that DID is one of the most commonly overlooked diagnoses in psychiatry and clinical psychology. According to these investigators, DID's prevalence and impact on psychiatric disability have been greatly underestimated (see also Dell, 2001; Dell & O'Neil, 2010). Yet surveys of clinicians indicate that many professionals are deeply skeptical of the DID diagnosis and of many prevailing theories of its etiology (Cormier & Thelen, 1998; Dell, 2001; Pope, Oliva, Hudson, Bodkin, & Gruber, 1999). These critics typically contend that DID is overdiagnosed, inadvertently created by careless mental health professionals, or both (McHugh, 2008). Some even argue that DID is a fad that enjoyed a brief stint of popularity that is now waning. For example, Pope, Barry, Bodkin, and Hudson (2005) found that the number of publications on DID peaked in the mid-1990s and declined precipitously by 2003 (see also Paris, 2012). Because many of the points of contention surrounding DID's scientific status bear potentially important implications for the causes and treatment of other psychological conditions, they may serve as a valuable object lesson for mental health professionals.

In this chapter, we provide an overview of the major controversies regarding the scientific status of DID and, to a lesser extent, dissociative disorders in general. In addition, we attempt to outline areas of potential common ground among individuals who hold markedly differing viewpoints regarding DID and also to delineate fruitful areas for further investigation.

Selections from Scott O. Lilienfeld and Steven Jay Lynn, "Dissociative Identity Disorder: A Contemporary Scientific Perspective," *Science and Pseudoscience in Clinical Psychology*, pp. 113-114, 121-134, 143-152. Copyright © 2015 by Guilford Press. Reprinted with permission.

THE ETIOLOGY OF DID: TWO COMPETING MODELS

DID's "Existence": A Pseudocontroversy

The principal controversy regarding the scientific status of DID has often been framed in terms of whether this condition "exists" (e.g., Arrigo & Pezdek, 1998; Dunn, Paolo, Ryan, & van Fleet, 1994; Mai, 1995; see also Hacking, 1995). Nevertheless, as we and our colleagues have argued elsewhere (Lilienfeld et al., 1999), the question of DID's "existence" is a pseudocontroversy. There is little dispute that DID "exists," in that a number of individuals exhibit multiple identity enactments (i.e., apparent alters) in conjunction with reported autobiographical memory gaps in childhood or adolescence. This point was aptly put by McHugh (1993): "Students often ask me whether multiple personality disorder (MPD) really exists. I usually reply that the symptoms attributed to it are as genuine as hysterical paralysis and seizures" (p. 4). Somatoform conditions, like DID, are unquestionably genuine, although their origins remain largely obscure.

The central question at stake therefore is not DID's existence but rather its etiology. As we will learn shortly, some researchers contend that DID is a spontaneously occurring consequence of childhood trauma, whereas others contend that it emerges primarily in response to suggestive therapist cueing, media influences, and broader sociocultural expectations. But even these skeptical researchers believe that DID is "genuine" in the sense that its signs and symptoms are typically not faked or intentionally produced.

There is general agreement, however, that at least some individuals have successfully pretended to have DID (Farrell, 2011; Merten & Merckelbach, 2013). For example, Kenneth Bianchi, one of the Hillside Strangler murderers, is widely believed to have faked DID to escape criminal responsibility (Orne, Dinges, & Orne, 1984). Nevertheless, outside of criminal settings, cases of malingered DID are believed to be quite rare, and both proponents and skeptics of the DID diagnosis agree that the substantial majority of individuals with this condition are not intentionally producing their symptoms (see Boon & Drajer, 1993, for a discussion of the problem of intentionally produced DID).

The Central Controversy: Two Competing Etiological Models

In general, two major competing views regarding the etiology of DID have emerged (see Gleaves, 1996; Lynn, Lilienfeld, Merckelbach, Giesbrecht, McNally, et al., 2014): the posttraumatic model (PTM) and the sociocognitive model (SCM). Although these two models are not mutually exclusive, they differ substantially in emphasis concerning the causes of DID. To oversimplify these views slightly, the PTD model posits that core DID features, particularly alters, are *discovered* by therapists, whereas the SCM model posits that these features are *created* by therapists. Because we believe that the bulk of the research evidence supports the SCM, we devote much of the remainder of the chapter to a discussion of this model. At the same time, we believe that certain aspects of the PTM have yet to be convincingly falsified, and therefore this model requires additional investigation. Moreover, we believe that a meaningful rapprochement between at least certain aspects of these two models may ultimately prove possible.

The Posttraumatic Model

Proponents of the PTM (e.g., Dell, 2006; Gleaves, 1996; Gleaves, May, & Cardena, 2001; Ross, 1997) posit that DID is a posttraumatic condition that arises primarily from a history of severe physical and/or sexual abuse in childhood. They typically argue that individuals who undergo horrific trauma in early life often dissociate or compartmentalize their personalities into discrete alters as a means of coping with the intense emotional pain of this trauma (Dalenberg et al., 2012). According to Ross (1997), "MPD is a little girl imagining that the abuse is happening to someone else" (p. 59). In support of this assertion, proponents of the PTM cite data suggesting that a large proportion—perhaps 90% or more—of individuals with DID report a history of severe child abuse (Gleaves, 1996). Another, more indirect, source of evidence for the PTM derives from structural brain imaging data demonstrating that the hippocampi of DID appear to be smaller than those of healthy comparison participants (Vermetten, Schmahl, Lindner, Loewenstein, & Bremner, 2006). This finding is broadly consistent with evidence from animal studies that severe stress, including that induced by abuse, may produce hippocampal damage (Bremner, 1999). Nevertheless, it is unknown whether this smaller hippocampal size preceded or followed the onset of DID in participants.

The essence of the PTM has been well articulated by philosopher Daniel Dennett (1991):

> The evidence is now voluminous that there are not a handful or a hundred but thousands of cases of MPD diagnosed today, and it almost invariably owes its existence to prolonged early childhood abuse, usually sexual, and of sickening severity .... These children have often been kept in such extraordinarily terrifying and confusing circumstances that I am more amazed that they survive psychologically at all than I am that they manage to preserve themselves by a desperate redrawing of their boundaries. What they do, when confronted with overwhelming conflict and pain, is this: They "leave." They create a boundary that the horror doesn't happen to them; it either happens to no one, or to some other self. (p. 150)

Proponents of the PTM attribute the dramatic increase in the reported prevalence of DID over the past few decades to the heightened awareness and recognition of this condition by psychotherapists. Specifically, they maintain that clinicians have increasingly become attuned to the presence of possible DID in their clients and as a consequence inquire more actively about potential symptoms of this condition (Gleaves, 1996). They also point out that a number of conditions, such as posttraumatic stress disorder (PTSD) and obsessive-compulsive disorder, were apparently underdiagnosed in previous decades (e.g., Zohar, 1998) and that a relatively abrupt massive increase (as occurred with

DID at least through the mid-1990s) in the reported prevalence of a condition does not necessarily call into question its validity. In many cases, the proponents of the PTM advocate the use of hypnosis, sodium amytal, or sodium pentothal (see Lynn, Krackow, Loftus, Locke, & Lilienfeld, Chapter 8, this volume), guided imagery, and other suggestive therapeutic techniques to call forth alters that have otherwise been inaccessible, as well as to recover apparently repressed memories of child abuse.

The Sociocognitive Model

In contrast to advocates of the PTM, proponents of the SCM (Spanos, 1994, 1996; see also Aldridge-Morris, 1989; Lilienfeld et al., 1999; Lynn et al., 2012a; Lynn et al., 2012b; Lynn & Pintar, 1997; McHugh, 1993, 2008; Merskey, 1992; Sarbin, 1995) contend that DID is largely a socially constructed condition that results from inadvertent therapist cueing (e.g., suggestive questioning regarding the existence of possible alters), media influences (e.g., film and television portrayals of DID), and broader sociocultural expectations regarding the presumed clinical features of DID. For example, proponents of the SCM believe that the release of the book and film *Sybil* in the 1970s played a substantial role in shaping conceptions of DID in the minds of both of the general public and psychotherapists, and in inadvertently encouraging individuals to adopt the core features of this condition (Paris, 2012). According to Spanos (1996), Sybil "became a model of the MPD survivor that greatly influenced the expectations of therapists and patients alike" (p. 267). Interestingly, as noted earlier, reported cases of child abuse in patients with DID became widespread only following the release of *Sybil*.

Spanos (1994) and other proponents of the SCM (McHugh, 2008) contend that individuals with DID are engaged in a form of unconscious "role playing" that is similar in some ways to the intense sense of imaginative involvement that some actors report when playing a part. Because individuals who engage in role playing essentially "lose themselves" in the enacted part, this phenomenon should not be confused with simulation or conscious deception. Some authors have erroneously assumed that the SCM posits that individuals with DID are intentionally producing these features. But the SCM is careful to distinguish role playing from simulation (Lilienfeld et al. 1999; in contrast, see Gleaves, 1996).

According to the SCM, the dramatic "epidemic" in cases of DID observed in recent decades stems largely from iatrogenic (therapist-induced) influences and the increased media attention accorded to DID. Specifically, according to the SCM, as DID has become more familiar to both psychotherapists and the general public, an autocatalytic feedback loop (Hacking, 1995; see Shermer, 1997, for examples) has been set in motion. In this feedback loop, therapeutic and societal expectations regarding the features of DID have given rise to greater numbers of cases of DID, in turn influencing therapeutic and societal expectations regarding the features of DID, in turn giving rise to a greater number of cases of DID, and so on. It is critical to emphasize that the SCM does not contend that DID is *entirely* iatrogenic because media influences and broader sociocultural expectations often play an important role in the genesis of DID. The notion that the SCM posits that DID is entirely iatrogenic represents another frequent misconception concerning this model. For example, Gleaves et al. (2001) referred to the SCM as the "iatrogenic" theory of DID (see Brown, Frischholz, & Scheflin, 1999; and Gleaves, 1996, for other examples).

Another important brick in the edifice of the SCM is the assumption that DID is merely one variant of a much broader constellation of conditions characterized by multiple identity enactments, including cases of purported demonic possession, channeling, mass hysteria, transvestism, and glossolalia that traverse cultural and historical boundaries (Spanos, 1996). From this perspective, DID is not a unique condition but is instead a superficially different manifestation of the same diathesis that gives rise to many other conditions marked by dramatically different behaviors over time, cultures, and situations. Although the protean manifestations of these role enactments are shaped by cultural and historical expectations, their underlying commonalities are suggestive of a shared etiology (Lilienfeld et al., 1999; see also Flacking, 1995).

Some proponents of the SCM (e.g., Spanos, 1994, 1996) have placed more emphasis on social-role expectations and iatrogenic influences than on individual difference variables. Nevertheless, the SCM is entirely compatible with the possibility that individual differences in certain personality traits, such as proneness to fantasy (Giesbrecht et ah, 2008; Lynn, Rhue, & Green, 1988) or absorption (Tellegen & Atkinson, 1974), render certain individuals especially susceptible to suggestive therapeutic, media, and cultural influences (Lynn et ah, 2012). In addition, this model is consistent with findings indicating that a substantial proportion of patients with DID meet criteria for borderline personality disorder (BPD) and other psychiatric conditions marked by unstable and unpredictable behavior, such as bipolar disorder (Ganaway, 1995; Lilienfeld et ah, 1999; Lynn et ah, 2011). For example, clients with BPD—who typically exhibit severe disturbances of identity, dramatic mood swings, sudden changes in feelings toward other people, and impulsive and seemingly inexplicable behaviors (e.g., self-mutilation)—may often be seeking an explanation for these puzzling symptoms, as may their therapists. Therapists who repeatedly ask such questions as "Is it possible that there is another part of you with whom I haven't yet spoken?" may gradually begin to elicit previously "latent alters" that ostensibly account for their clients' otherwise enigmatic behaviors.

Many of the key features of the SCM were nicely summed up by Frances and First (1998), who ironically were two of the principal architects (chairperson and editor, respectively) of DSM-IV, which had endorsed the traditional view of DID as a condition marked by multiple indwelling identities:

> Dissociative Identity Disorder ... is a fascinating condition. Perhaps too much so. The idea that people can have distinct, autonomous, and rapidly alternating personalities has captured the attention of the general

public, of some therapists, and of hordes of patients. As a result, especially in the United States, there has been a marked increase in the diagnosis of Dissociative Identity Disorder. Much of the excitement followed the appearance of books and movies (like *Sybil* and *The Three Faces of Eve*) and the exploitation of the diagnosis by enthusiastic TV talk show guests ... . Many therapists feel that the popularity of Dissociative Identity Disorder represents a kind of social contagion. It is not so much that there are lots of personalities as that there are lots of people and lots of therapists who are very suggestible and willing to climb onto the bandwagon of this new fad diagnosis. As the idea of multiple personality pervades our popular culture, suggestible people coping with a chaotic current life and a severely traumatic past express discomfort and avoid responsibility by uncovering "hidden personalities" and giving each of them a voice. This is especially likely when there is a zealous therapist who finds multiple personality a fascinating topic of discussion and exploration, (pp. 286–287)

Advocates of the SCM have invoked a wide variety of pieces of research evidence in support of this theoretical position (see Lilienfeld et al., 1999; McHugh, 2008; Piper & Merskey, 2004; Spanos, 1994, 1996). In the following section, we present the major sources of evidence consistent with the SCM and examine common criticisms of the SCM by proponents of the PTM.

EVIDENCE FOR THE SOCIOCOGNITIVE MODEL OF DID

Recommended Treatment Practices for DID

One important source of evidence in favor of the SCM is the mode of treatment practices employed by some advocates of the PTM. Claims by a number of proponents of the PTM to the contrary (Brand et al., 2012; Brown et al., 1999; Gleaves, 1996), many standard therapeutic practices for DID—especially those performed by certain PTM advocates—are geared toward encouraging the appearance of alters and treating them as though they were distinct identities.

Indeed, inspection of the mainstream DID treatment literature reveals that therapists are often encouraged to reify the existence of multiple identities by mapping the system of alters and to establish direct contact with alters if they are not otherwise forthcoming (Piper, 1997). These reifying techniques are especially common in the early stages of psychotherapy, although the later stages often focus on achieving integration among alters (Ross, 1997).

For example, Kluft (1993) argued that "when information suggestive of MPD is available, but an alter has not emerged spontaneously, asking to meet an alter directly is an increasingly accepted intervention" (p. 29). Kluft further acknowledged that his most frequent hypnotic instruction to patients with DID is "Everybody listen" (see Ganaway, 1995). Braun (1980) wrote that "after inducing hypnosis, the therapist asks the patient 'if there is another thought process, part of the mind, part, person or force that exists in the body'" (p. 213). Bliss (1980) noted that in the treatment of DID "alter egos are summoned, and usually asked to speak freely … . When they appear, the subject is asked to listen. [The subject] is then introduced to some of the personalities" (p. 1393). Putnam (1989) suggested using a technique known as the "bulletin board," which allows patients with DID to have a "place where personalities can 'post' messages to each other … . I suggest that the patient buy a small notebook in which personalities may write messages to each other" (p. 154). Ross (1997) and other therapists (e.g., Putnam, 1989) have recommended giving names to each alter in order to "'crystallize' it and make it more distinct" (p. 311). Ross (1997) also advocated the use of "inner board meetings" as "a good way to map the system, resolve issues, and recover memories" (p. 350). He described this technique as follows:

> The patient relaxes with a brief hypnotic induction, and the host personality walks into the boardroom. The patient is instructed that there will be one chair for every personality in the system … . Often there are empty chairs because some alters are not ready to enter therapy. The empty chairs provide useful information, and those present can be asked what they know about the missing people, (p. 351)

In addition, one increasingly popular therapeutic method, internal family systems therapy, is premised on the notion that the mind houses separate subpersonalities (e.g., protectors, firefighters, exiles) that must be accessed and integrated for healing to occur (Goulding & Schwartz, 2002; see also Pignotti & Thyer, Chapter 7, this volume).

These and other treatment recommendations derived from the mainstream DID literature (see Piper, 1997, pp. 61–68, for additional examples) strongly suggest that many therapists are explicitly encouraged to reify the existence of alters by acknowledging and validating their independent existence. Even the slightly more cautious guidelines issued recently by the International Society for the Study of Trauma and Dissociation (ISSTD) inform therapists that "in times of repeated acting out by the patient, and/or at times of therapeutic impasse, it can be essential to directly elicit or make contact with alternate identities previously known or not, that are related to these difficulties" (ISSTD, 2011, p. 140). From a behavioral or social learning perspective, the process of attending to and reifying alters may adventitiously reinforce patients' displays of multiplicity.

Another treatment practice that may inadvertently facilitate the emergence of alters is hypnosis. Clinicians who treat patients with DID frequently use hypnosis in an effort to discover or call forth presumed latent alters (Spanos, 1994, 1996). The evidence regarding the use of hypnosis in such patients provides mixed support for the SCM. On the one hand, the results of several studies reveal few or no differences in the diagnostic features (e.g., alters, number of DID criteria) of patients with DID who have and have not been hypnotized (e.g., Putnam, Guroff, Silberman, Barban, & Post, 1986; Ross & Norton, 1989; see Gleaves, 1996, for a review). In addition, several studies indicate that many or most patients with DID have never been hypnotized (Gleaves, 1996), a finding that strongly suggests that hypnosis is not necessary for the emergence of DID.

In contrast, the finding that hypnotized and nonhypnotized patients with DID do not differ significantly in many characteristics (e.g., number of DID criteria) is difficult to interpret in light of ceiling effects (Lilienfeld et al., 1999; Powell & Gee, 1999). Specifically, given that almost all of the patients in these studies met the criteria for DID according to various diagnostic criterion sets (e.g., DSM-III), the differences in the number of DID criteria between hypnotized and nonhypnotized patients are not surprising.

In addition, in a reanalysis of the dataset of Ross and Norton (1989), Powell and Gee (1999) found that hypnotized patients exhibited greater variance in the number of alters at the time of diagnosis and in later treatment. Although the meaning of this finding is not entirely clear, it may reflect bimodal attitudes toward iatrogenesis among practitioners who use hypnosis, with some (who believe that hypnosis is potentially iatrogenic) using hypnosis never or rarely and others (who believe that hypnosis is not iatrogenic) using hypnosis frequently. Powell and Gee (1999) also found that clinicians who used hypnosis reported a significantly higher number of patients with DID in their caseloads than did practitioners who did not use hypnosis. Although this finding is open to several interpretations (e.g., DID specialists may be more likely to use hypnosis than are other clinicians), it is consistent with iatrogenesis.

Moreover, the SCM does not posit that hypnosis is necessary for the creation of DID alters. Hypnotic procedures do not possess any inherent or unique features that are necessary to facilitate responsivity to suggestion (Spanos & Chaves, 1989). Other methods, such as suggestive and leading questions, may be equally likely to induce clients' adoption of multiple identities (Barber, 1979; Spanos, 1996).

None of this implies, of course, that all or even most treatment for DID is ineffective or harmful. Naturalistic data indicate that DID often remits following treatment (Brand, Classen, McNary, & Zaveri, 2009), raising the possibility that certain DID interventions are effective. Nevertheless, studies do not permit an evaluation of the extent to which symptom reduction in dissociative patients in naturalistic studies is due to regression to the mean, the passage of time, placebo effects, or other artifacts. Other methodological limitations in treatment studies of DID include variability in treatments offered to patients (e.g., Choe & Kluft, 1995), lack of controls for nonspecific effects (e.g., Ellason & Ross, 1997), dropout rates as high as 68% (Gantt & Tinnin, 2007), and the failure to document clinically meaningful changes following treatment. Because there are no randomized controlled trials of DID treatment, it is unknown which, if any, extant treatments are effective for DID.

The Clinical Features of Patients with DID Before and After Psychotherapy

There is compelling evidence that a large proportion—perhaps even a substantial majority—of patients with DID exhibit very few or no unambiguous signs of this condition (e.g., alters) prior to psychotherapy. For example, Kluft (1991) estimated that only 20% of patients with DID exhibit unambiguous signs of this condition and that the remaining 80% exhibit only transient "windows of diagnosability," that is, short-lived periods during which the core features of DID are observable. Virtually all authors in this literature agree that a large proportion, and perhaps a majority, of patients with DID exhibit few or no clear-cut signs of this condition prior to psychotherapy (Kluft, 1984; Putnam, Guroff, Silberman, Barban, & Post, 1986; Ross, 1997). Moreover, individuals with DID typically are in treatment for an average of 6 to 7 years before being diagnosed with this condition (Gleaves, 1996). Such evidence raises the possibility that these patients often develop unambiguous features of DID only after receiving psychotherapy.

Moreover, although systematic data are lacking, the DID literature shows general agreement that many or most patients with DID are unaware of the existence of their alters prior to psychotherapy. For example, Putnam (1989) estimated that 80% of patients with DID possess no knowledge of their alters before entering treatment, and Dell and Eisenhower (1990) reported that all 11 of their adolescent patients with DID had no awareness of their alters at the time of diagnosis. Similarly, Lewis, Yeager, Swica, Pincus, and Lewis (1997) reported that none of the 12 murderers with DID in their sample reported any awareness of their alters.

Some authors have also reported that the number of DID alters tends to increase over the course of treatment (Kluft, 1984; Ross et al., 1989). In addition, although the number of alters per DID case at the time of initial diagnosis has remained roughly constant over time (Ross et al., 1989), the number of alters per DID case in treatment has increased over time (North et al., 1993).

These findings are consistent with the SCM, as they suggest that many psychotherapeutic practices for DID may inadvertently encourage the emergence of new alters. Moreover, as we noted elsewhere (Lilienfeld et al., 1999, p. 512), one would be hard-pressed to find another DSM-5 disorder whose principal psychopathological feature (i.e., alters) is typically unobservable prior to standard treatment and becomes substantially more florid following this treatment.

At the same time, some proponents of the PTM argue that these findings are potentially consistent with this model. Specifically, they maintain that alters were merely "latent" at the time of initial diagnosis and became observable only after prompting and elicitation by therapists (e.g., Gleaves, 1996). Without independent evidence of these alters, however, this position raises serious concerns regarding the falsifiability of the PTM. That is, if the number of alters either decreased or remained constant over the course of therapy, proponents of the PTM could maintain that psychotherapy for DID either ameliorated the symptoms of the condition or successfully held potential deterioration at bay. In contrast, the finding that the number of alters tends to increase over the course of therapy has been interpreted by proponents of the PTM as indicating that psychotherapy successfully uncovered alters that were merely latent (Gleaves, 1996). Because a theoretical model that is consistent with any potential set of observations is difficult or impossible to falsify and is therefore of questionable scientifically utility (Popper, 1959), proponents of the PTM will need to make explicit what types of evidence could falsify this model.

Some critics of the SCM (e.g., Brown et al., 1999; Gleaves, 1996) have also attempted to argue that suggestive therapeutic practices can produce additional alters in patients who already meet the criteria for DID, but that these practices cannot create DID *de novo*. This assertion hinges on the assumption that iatrogenic influences can lead patients with one alter to develop additional alters, but cannot lead patients with no alters to develop one or more alters. The theoretical basis underlying this assumption has not been clearly articulated by critics of the SCM (Lilienfeld et al., 1999). Moreover, this assertion appears extremely difficult, if not impossible, to falsify given that many critics of the SCM maintain that DID alters can be "latent" (e.g., Kluft, 1992). That is, if a patient with no alters developed alters following suggestive therapeutic practices, critics of the SCM could readily maintain that this patient merely had latent alters and in fact suffered from DID all along (Piper, 1997). In addition, even some of the most vociferous proponents of the PTM acknowledge that DID can indeed be iatrogenically created in certain cases. Ross (1977), for example, estimated that approximately 17% of DID cases are predominantly iatrogenic (see also Coons, 1994). Thus, the more important question appears to be not whether DID can be created largely by iatrogenic factors, but rather what is the relative importance of iatrogenesis compared with other potential causal variables, including media influences, sociocultural factors, and individual differences in personality and psychopathology.

The Distribution of Cases of DID across Clinicians

The distribution of cases of DID across therapists is strikingly nonrandom, demonstrating that a relatively small number of clinicians account for a large number of cases of DID. For example, a 1992 survey study in Switzerland revealed that 66% of DID diagnoses were made by 0.09% (!) of all clinicians. Moreover, 90% of respondents reported that they had never seen a single patient with DID, whereas three psychiatrists reported that they had seen over 20 patients with DID (Modestin, 1992). Ross et al. (1989) reported that members of the International Society for the Study of Multiple Personality and Dissociation (now called the ISSTD) were between 10 and 11 times more likely than members of the Canadian Psychiatric Association to report having seen a case of DID. In addition, Mai (1995) found evidence for substantial variability in the number of DID diagnoses across Canadian psychiatrists and reported that the lion's share of DID diagnoses derived from a relatively small number of psychotherapists. Boysen (2011) reported that four American research teams accounted for two-thirds of all reported published cases of childhood DID (N = 255). In a later review, Boysen and VanBergen (2013) found that, between 2000 and 2010, an equally remarkable two-thirds of all new cases of adult DID derived from five investigative teams.

Interestingly, these findings dovetail with those of Qin, Goodman, Bottoms, and Shaver (1998), who stated that reports of satanic ritual abuse similarly derive from a small number of psychotherapists. Reports of satanic ritual abuse are closely associated with diagnoses of DID (Mulhern, 1995).

Findings on the nonrandom distribution of DID cases are compatible with several explanations. For example, such findings could be explained by positing that patients with actual or possible DID are selectively referred to DID experts. Alternatively, perhaps certain therapists are especially adept at either detecting or eliciting the actual features of DID. Nevertheless, these findings are also consistent with the SCM and with Spanos's (1994, 1996) contention that only a handful of clinicians are diagnosing DID, producing DID symptoms in their patients, or both.

At this point, the data do not permit any adjudication among these possibilities, which are not mutually exclusive. Nevertheless, these findings provide one useful test of the SCM, because if DID diagnoses were not made disproportionately by a subset of clinicians—namely, those who are ardent proponents of the DID diagnosis—the SCM would be called into question. Longitudinal investigations examining whether patients tend to exhibit the core features of DID, especially alters, prior to or following referrals to DID specialists, would help to determine whether these findings are attributable primarily to iatrogenesis, as posited by the SCM, or to either differential referral patterns or the use of more sensitive diagnostic practices, as posted by the PTM.

Role-Playing Studies

Another source of evidence in support of the SCM derives from laboratory studies of role playing. These investigations are designed to test the hypothesis, derived from the SCM, that cues, prompts, and suggestions from a psychotherapist can trigger participants without DID to display the overt features of this condition.

In one of these studies, Spanos, Weekes, and Bertrand (1985) provided participants with suggestions for DID (e.g., "I think perhaps there might be another part of [you] that I haven't talked to") in the context of a simulated psychiatric interview. They found that many role-playing participants, but not control participants (who were not provided with these suggestions), spontaneously adopted a different name, referred to their host personality in the third person (e.g., "He"), and exhibited striking differences between the host and alter "personalities" on psychological measures (e.g., sentence completion tests and semantic differential questionnaires). In addition, most role-playing participants, but not control participants, spontaneously reported amnesia for their alters following hypnosis. It is crucial to note that participants were not explicitly told or asked to display any of these characteristics, which are similar to those exhibited by patients with DID. These findings were essentially replicated with a similar methodology by Spanos, Weekes, Menary, and Bertrand (1996; but see Frischolz, Lipman, Braun, & Sachs, 1992). Stafford and Lynn (1998) similarly found that, given adequate situational inducements, normal participants can readily role-play a variety of life history experiences often reported among patients with DID, including reports of physical, sexual, and satanic ritual abuse.

Role-playing studies have been commonly misinterpreted by critics of the SCM. For example, Gleaves (1996) argued that "to conclude that these studies prove that DID is simply a form of role-playing is unwarranted" (p. 47). Similarly, Brown et al. (1999) contended that role-playing studies do not demonstrate that DID "can be created in the laboratory" (p. 580) and that "these role enactments are not identical with alter behavior in MPD patients, nor are they proof that a major psychiatric condition, MPD, has been created" (p. 581). But role-playing studies were not designed to reproduce the full range or subjective experience of DID symptoms, nor to create DID itself, but rather to demonstrate the ease with which subtle cues and prompts can trigger normal participants to display some of the key features of this condition. The findings of these studies (e.g., Spanos et al., 1985) provide support for the SCM because they demonstrate that (1) the behaviors and reported experiences are familiar to many members of the general population and (2) individuals without DID can be readily induced to exhibit some of the key features of DID following prompts and cues, even though these specific features were not explicitly suggested to them. Were this not the case, the SCM would not be able to account for a number of the core features of DID. Role-playing studies therefore provide corroboration for one important and potentially falsifiable precondition of the SCM, although they do not provide dispositive evidence for this model (Lilienfeld et al., 1999).

Cross-Cultural Studies

As noted earlier, the SCM posits that the overt expression of multiple identity enactments is shaped substantially by cultural and historical factors. Consistent with this presupposition is the fact that until fairly recently, DID was largely unknown outside of North America (see also Hochman & Pope, 1997, for data suggesting considerably greater acceptance of DID in North American countries compared with non-North American English-speaking countries). Indeed, between 2000 and 2010, only 18% of all reported DID cases emanated from non-Western countries (Boysen & VanBergen, 2013). For example, during the 20th century, there were only 35 reported cases of DID in Japan (Sekine, 2000; see also Takahashi, 1990). In addition, until fairly recently, DID was quite rare in England, Russia, and India (Spanos, 1996). Interestingly, the cross-cultural expression of DID appears to be different in India than in North America. In the relatively rare cases of DID reported in India, the transition between alters is almost always preceded by sleep, a phenomenon not observed in North American cases of DID. Media portrayals of DID in India similarly include periods of sleep prior to the transitions between alters (North et al., 1993).

Cleaves (1996), noting that DID has recently been diagnosed in Holland (see also Sno & Schalken, 1999) and several other European countries, used this finding to argue against the SCM. Nevertheless, this finding is difficult to interpret and does not necessarily call the SCM into question. In Holland, for example, the writings of several well-known researchers (e.g., van der Hart, 1993; van der Kolk, van der Hart, & Marmar, 1996) have resulted in substantially increased media and professional attention to DID. Recent data also point to the possibility of a relatively recent increased prevalence of DID in other countries, including Turkey, Australia, Germany, and China (Martinez-Taboas, Dorahy, Sar, Middleton, & Kruger, 2013), with Turkey accounting for 79% of all non-Western cases between 2000 and 2010 (Boysen & VanBergen, 2013). Again, however, it is unclear whether such increases reflect increases in the genuine prevalence of DID in these countries or enhanced detection or creation of DID features.

Moreover, "culturally, influenced" is not equivalent to "culture bound." In other words, the fact that a condition initially limited to only a few countries subsequently spreads to other countries does not necessarily indicate that this condition is independent of cultural influence. To the contrary, the fact that the features of DID are becoming better known in certain countries would lead one to expect DID to be diagnosed with increasing frequency in these countries. The spread of DID to countries in which the characteristics of this condition are becoming more familiar constitutes one important and potentially falsifiable prediction of the SCM.

DID in Childhood

If the PTM is correct, then cases of DID should sometimes be observed in childhood, prior to extensive treatment and media exposure to the expected signs and symptoms of the condition. In a review of the literature, Boysen (2011) found at best mixed support for this possibility. As he noted, childhood DID "appears to be an extremely rare phenomenon" (p. 329). Moreover, he found that reported cases of DID in childhood have almost never been observed outside of treatment. At the same time, he reported a total of 255 cases of childhood DID in the world literature, but, as noted earlier, two-thirds of these cases originated from a very small number of research groups. Although these findings are not conclusive, they raise questions concerning the potential existence of childhood DID, a phenomenon that would be predicted by the PTM.

Summary

A variety of pieces of evidence, including commonly prescribed treatment practices of DID proponents, the clinical features of patients with DID before and after psychotherapy, the distribution of cases of DID across psychotherapists, data from role-playing studies, recent cross-cultural epidemiological data, and the extremely low prevalence of childhood DID outside of treatment, provide support for several important predictions of the SCM. In addition, these data call into question a "strong" form of the PTM (e.g., Bremner,

2010; Gleaves, 1996)—viz., a version of the PTM that essentially excludes sociocultural influence as an explanation of DID's etiology and accords virtually exclusive causal import to early trauma. These data may, however, be consistent with a "weak" form of the PTM that accords a predisposing role to early trauma but also grants a substantial causal role to sociocultural influences, including iatrogenesis (e.g., Dalenberg et al., 2012). To provide more compelling support for the PTM, proponents of this model will need to make more explicit predictions that could in principle permit this model to be falsified.

REFERENCES

Aldridge-Morris, R. (1989). *Multiple personality: An exercise in deception*. Hillsdale, NJ: Erlbaum.

Arrigo, J. M., & Pezdek, K. (1998). Textbook models of multiple personality: Source, bias, and social consequences. In S. J. Lynn (Ed.), *Truth in memory* (pp. 372–393). New York: Guilford Press.

Barber, T. X. (1979). Suggested ("hypnotic") behavior: The trance paradigm versus an alternative paradigm. In E. Fromm & R. E. Shor (Eds.), *Hypnosis: Developments in research and new perspectives* (2nd ed., pp. 217–271). New York: Aldine.

Bliss, E. L. (1980). Multiple personalities: A report of 14 cases with implications for schizophrenia and hysteria. *Archives of General Psychiatry, 37,* 1388–1397.

Boon, S., & Draijer, N. (1993). Multiple personality disorder in the Netherlands: A clinical investigation of 71 cases. *American Journal of Psychiatry, 150,* 489–494.

Boysen, G. A. (2011). The scientific status of childhood dissociative identity disorder: A review of published research. *Psychotherapy and Psychosomatics, 80,* 329–334.

Boysen, G. A., & VanBergen, A. (2013). A review of published research on adult dissociative identity disorder: 2000–2010. *Journal of Nervous and Mental Disease, 201,* 5–11.

Brand, B. L., Classen, C. C., McNary, S. W., & Zaveri, P. (2009). A review of dissociative disorders treatment studies. *The Journal of Nervous and Mental Disease, 197,* 646–654.

Brand, B. L., McNary, S. W., Myrick, A. C., Classen, C. C., Lanius, R., Loewenstein, R. J., et al. (2012). A longitudinal naturalistic study of patients with dissociative disorders treated by community clinicians. *Psychological Trauma: Theory, Research, and Practice, 5,* 301–308.

Braun, B. G. (1980). Hypnosis for multiple personalities. In H. J. Wain (Ed.), *Clinical hypnosis in medicine* (pp. 209–217). Chicago: Year Book Medical.

Bremner, J. D. (1999). Does stress damage the brain? *Biological Psychiatry, 45,* 797–805.

Bremner, J. D. (2010). Cognitive processes in dissociation: Comment on Giesbrecht et al. (2008). *Psychological Bulletin, 136,* 1–11.

Brown, D., Frischoltz, E. J., & Scheflin, A. W. (1999). Iatrogenic dissociative identity disorder: An evaluation of the scientific evidence. *Journal of Psychiatry and Law, 27,* 549–637.

Choe, B. M., & Kluft, R. P. (1995). The use of the DES in studying treatment outcome with dissociative identity disorder: A pilot study. *Dissociation: Progress in the Dissociative Disorders, 8,* 160–164.

Coons, P. M. (1994). Confirmation of childhood abuse in child and adolescent cases of multiple personality disorder and dissociative identity disorder not otherwise specified. *Journal of Nervous and Mental Disease, 182,* 461–464.

Cormier, J. F., & Thelen, M. H. (1998). Professional skepticism of multiple personality disorder. *Professional Psychology: Research and Practice, 29,* 163–167.

Dalenberg, C. J., Brand, B. L., Gleaves, D. H., Dorahy, M. J., Loewenstein, R. J., Cardeña, E., et al. (2012). Evaluation of the evidence for the trauma and fantasy models of dissociation. *Psychological Bulletin, 138,* 550–588.

Dell, P. F. (2001). Why the diagnostic criteria for dissociative identity disorder should be changed. *Journal of Trauma and Dissociation, 2,* 7–37.

Dell, P. F. (2006). A new model of dissociative identity disorder. *Psychiatric Clinics of North America, 29,* 1–26.

Dell, P. F., & Eisenhower, J. W. (1990). Adolescent multiple personality disorder: A preliminary study of eleven cases. *Journal of the American Academy of Child and Adolescent Psychiatry, 29,* 359–366.

Dell, P. F., & O'Neil, J. A. (Eds.). (2010). *Dissociation and the dissociative disorders: DSM-V and beyond.* New York: Routledge.

Dennett, D. (1991). *Consciousness explained.* Boston: Little, Brown.

Dunn, G. E., Paolo, A. M., Ryan, J. J., & van Fleet, J. N. (1994). Belief in the existence of multiple personality disorder among psychologists and psychiatrists. *Journal of Clinical Psychology, 50,* 454–457.

Ellason, J. W., & Ross, C. A. (1997). Two-year follow-up of inpatients with dissociative identity disorder. *American Journal of Psychiatry, 154,* 832–839.

Elzinga, B. M., van Dyck, R., & Spinhoven, P. (1998). Three controversies about dissociative identity disorder. *Clinical Psychology and Psychotherapy, 5,* 13–23.

Farrell, H. M. (2011). Dissociative identity disorder: Medicolegal challenges. *Journal of the American Academy of Psychiatry and the Law Online, 39,* 402–406.

Frances, A., & First, M. B. (1998). *Your mental health: A layman's guide to the psychiatrist's Bible.* New York: Scribner.

Frischholz, E. J., Lipman, L. S., Braun, B. G., & Sachs, R. (1992). Suggested posthypnotic amnesia in psychiatric patients and normals. *American Journal of Clinical Hypnosis, 35,* 29–39.

Ganaway, G. K. (1995). Hypnosis, childhood trauma, and dissociative identity disorder: Toward an integrative theory. *International Journal of Clinical and Experimental Hypnosis, 43*, 127-144.

Gantt, L., & Tinnin, L. W. (2007). Intensive trauma therapy of PTSD and dissociation: An outcome study. *Arts in Psychotherapy, 34*, 69-80.

Giesbrecht, T., Lynn, S. J., Lilienfeld, S. O., & Merckelbach, H. (2008). Cognitive processes in dissociation: An analysis of core theoretical assumptions. *Psychological Bulletin, 134*, 617-647.

Gleaves, D. H. (1996). The sociocognitive model of dissociative identity disorder: A reexamination of the evidence. *Psychological Bulletin, 120*, 42-59.

Gleaves, D. H., May, M. C., & Cardena, E. (2001). An examination of the diagnostic validity of dissociative identity disorder. *Clinical Psychology Review, 21*, 577-608.

Goulding, R. A., & Schwartz, R. C. (2002). *The mosaic mind: Empowering the tormented selves of child abuse survivors*. Oak Park, IL: Trailheads.

Hacking, I. (1995). *Rewriting the soul: Multiple personality and the science of memory*. Princeton, NJ: Princeton University Press.

Hochman, J., & Pope, H. G. (1997). Debating dissociative diagnoses. *American Journal of Psychiatry, 153*, 887-888.

International Society for the Study of Trauma and Dissociation (ISSTD). (2011). Guidelines for treating dissociative identity disorder in adults, third revision. *Journal of Trauma and Dissociation, 12*, 115-187.

Kluft, R. P. (1984). Treatment of multiple personality disorder: A study of 33 cases. *Psychiatric Clinics of North America, 7*, 20-29.

Kluft, R. P. (1991). Multiple personality disorder. In A. Tasman & S. M. Goldfinger (Eds.), *American Psychiatric Press review of psychiatry* (Vol. 10, pp. 161-188). Washington, DC: American Psychiatric Association Press.

Kluft, R. P. (1993). Multiple personality disorders. In D. Spiegel (Ed.), *Dissociative disorders: A clinical review* (pp. 17-44). Lutherville, MD: Sidran Press.

Lewis, D. O., Yeager, C. A., Swica, Y., Pincus, J. H., & Lewis, M. (1997). Objective documentation of child abuse and dissociation in 12 murderers with dissociative identity disorder. *American Journal of Psychiatry, 143*, 1703-1710.

Lilienfeld, S. O., Lynn, S. J., Kirsch, L, Chaves, J. F., Sarbin, T. R., Ganaway, G. K., et al. (1999). Dissociative identity disorder and the sociocognitive model: Recalling the lessons of the past. *Psychological Bulletin, 125*, 507-523.

Lynn, S. J., Berg, J., Lilienfeld, S. O., Merckelbach, H., Giesbrecht, T., Accardi, M., et al. (2012a). Dissociative disorders. In M. Hersen & D. C. Beidel (Eds.), *Adult psychopathology and diagnosis* (pp. 497-538). New York: Wiley.

Lynn, S. J., Lilienfeld, S. O., Merckelbach, H., Giesbrecht, T., & van der Kloet, D. (2012b). Dissociation and dissociative disorders: Challenging conventional wisdom. *Current Directions in Psychological Science, 21*, 48-53.

Lynn, S. J., Lilienfeld, S. O., Merckelbach, H., Giesbrecht, T., McNally, R. J., Loftus, E. F., et al. (2014). The trauma model of dissociation: Inconvenient truths and stubborn fictions. *Comment on Dalenberg et al. (2012), 140,* 896-910.

Lynn, S. J., & Pintar, J. (1997). A social narrative model of dissociative identity disorder. *Australian Journal of Clinical and Experimental Hypnosis, 25,* 1-7.

Lynn, S. J., Rhue, J. W., & Green, J. P. (1988). Multiple personality and fantasy proneness: Is there an association or dissociation. *British Journal of Experimental and Clinical Hypnosis, 5,* 138-142.

Mai, F. M. (1995). Psychiatrists' attitudes to multiple personality disorder: A questionnaire study. *Canadian Journal of Psychiatry, 40,* 154-157.

Martínez-Taboas, A., Dorahy, M., Sar, V., Middleton, W., & Krüger, C. (2013). Growing not dwindling: International research on the worldwide phenomenon of dissociative disorders. *Journal of Nervous and Mental Disease, 201,* 353-354.

McHugh, P. R. (1993). Multiple personality disorder. *Harvard Mental Health Newsletter, 10*(3), 4-6.

McHugh, P. R. (2008). *Try to remember: Psychiatry's clash over meaning, memory, and mind.* New York: Dana Press.

Merskey, H. (1992). The manufacture of personalities: The production of multiple personality disorder. *British Journal of Psychiatry, 160,* 327-340.

Merten, T., & Merckelbach, H. (2013). Symptom validity testing in somatoform and dissociative disorders: A critical review. *Psychological Injury and Law, 6,* 1-16.

Modestin, J. (1992). Multiple personality disorder in Switzerland. *American Journal of Psychiatry, 149*(1), 88-92.

Mulhern, S. (1995). Les aleas de la therapie des reminscences: Le trouble de la personalite. In M. Gabel, S. Lebovic, & P. Mazet (Eds.), *Le traumatisme de l'inceste.* Paris: Presses Universitaires de France.

North, C. S., Ryall, J.-E. M., Ricci, D. A., & Wetzel, R. D. (1993). *Multiple personalities, multiple disorders.* New York: Oxford University Press.

Orne, M. T., Dinges, D. F., & Orne, E. C. (1984). On the differential diagnosis of multiple personality in the forensic context. *International Journal of Clinical and Experimental Hypnosis, 32,* 118-169.

Paris, J. (2012). The rise and fall of dissociative identity disorder. *Journal of Nervous and Mental Disease, 200,* 1076-1079.

Piper, A. (1997). *Hoax and reality: The bizarre world of multiple personality disorder.* Northvale, NJ: Aronson.

Piper, A., & Merskey, H. (2004). The persistence of folly: A critical examination of dissociative identity disorder: Part I. The excesses of an improbable concept. *Canadian Journal of Psychiatry, 49,* 592-600.

Pope, H. G., Jr., Barry, S., Bodkin, A., & Hudson, J. I. (2005). Tracking scientific interest in the dissociative disorders: A study of scientific publication output 1984-2003. *Psychotherapy and Psychosomatics, 75*(1), 19-24.

Pope, H. G., Oliva, P. S., Hudson, J. I., Bodkin, J. A., & Gruber, A. J. (1999). Attitudes toward DSM-IV dissociative disorders diagnoses among board-certified American psychiatrists. *American Journal of Psychiatry, 156,* 321–323.

Popper, K. R. (1959). *The logic of scientific discovery.* London: Hutchinson.

Powell, R. A., & Gee, T. L. (1999). The effects of hypnosis on dissociative identity disorder: A reexamination of the evidence. *Canadian Journal of Psychiatry, 44,* 914–916.

Putnam, F. W. (1989). *Diagnosis and treatment of multiple personality disorder.* New York: Guilford Press.

Putnam, F. W., Guroff, J. J., Silberman, E. K., Barban, L., & Post, R. M. (1986). The clinical phenomenology of multiple personality disorder: Review of 100 recent cases. *Journal of Clinical Psychiatry, 47,* 285–293.

Qin, J. J., Goodman, G. S., Bottoms, B. L., & Shaver, P. R. (1998). Repressed memory: An inquiry into allegations of ritual abuse. In S. J. Lynn (Ed.), *Truth in memory.* New York: Guilford Press.

Ross, C. A. (1997). *Dissociative identity disorder: Diagnosis, clinical features, and treatment of multiple personality.* New York: Wiley.

Ross, C. A., & Norton, G. R. (1989). Effects of hypnosis on the features of multiple personality disorder. *Dissociation, 3,* 99–106.

Ross, C. A., Norton, G. R., & Wozney, K. (1989). Multiple personality disorder: An analysis of 236 cases. *Canadian Journal of Psychiatry, 34,* 413–418.

Sarbin, T. R. (1995). On the belief that one body may be host to two or more personalities. *International Journal of Clinical and Experimental Hypnosis, 43,* 163–183.

Sekine, Y. U. Y. (2000). Dissociative identity disorder (DID) in Japan: A forensic case report and the recent increase in reports of DID. *International Journal of Psychiatry in Clinical Practice, 4,* 155–160.

Shermer, M. (1997). *Why people believe weird things: Pseudoscience, superstition, and other confusions of our time.* New York: Freeman.

Sno, H. N., & Schalken, H. F. (1999). Dissociative identity disorder: Diagnosis and treatment in the Netherlands. *European Psychiatry, 5,* 270–277.

Spanos, N. P. (1994). Multiple identity enactments and multiple personality disorder: A sociocognitive perspective. *Psychological Bulletin, 116,* 143–165.

Spanos, N. P. (1996). *Multiple identities and false memories: A sociocognitive perspective.* Washington, DC: American Psychological Association.

Spanos, N. P. & Chaves, J. F. (1989). *Hypnosis: The cognitive-behavioral perspective.* Buffalo, NY: Prometheus.

Spanos, N. P., Weekes, J. R., & Bertrand, L. D. (1985). Multiple personality: A social psychological perspective. *Journal of Abnormal Psychology, 94,* 362–376.

Spanos, N. P., Weekes, J. R., Menary, E., & Bertrand, L. D. (1986). Hypnotic interview and age regression procedures in the elicitation of multiple personality symptoms. *Psychiatry, 49,* 298–311.

Stafford, J., & Lynn, S. J. (1998). *Cultural scripts, childhood abuse, and multiple identities: A study of role-played enactments*. Manuscript submitted for publication.

Takahashi, Y. (1990). Is multiple personality disorder really rare in Japan?: Dissociation. *Progress in the Dissociative Disorder, 3*, 57–59.

Tellegen, A., & Atkinson, G. (1974). Openness to absorbing and self-altering experiences ("absorption"), a trait related to hypnotic susceptibility. *Journal of Abnormal Psychology, 83*, 268–277.

van der Hart, O. (1993). Multiple personality disorder in Europe: Impressions. *Dissociation, 6*, 102–118.

van der Kolk, B. A., van der Hart, O., & Marmar, C. R. (1996). Dissociation and information processing in posttraumatic stress disorder. In B. A. van der Kolk, A. C. McFarlane, & L. Weisaeth (Eds.), *Traumatic stress: The effects of overwhelming stress on mind, body, and society.* New York: Guilford Press.

Vermetten, E., Schmahl, C., Lindner, S., Loewenstein, R. J., & Bremner, J. D. (2006). Hippocampal and amygdalar volumes in dissociative identity disorder. *American Journal of Psychiatry, 163*, 630–636.

Zohar, J. (1998). Post-traumatic stress disorder: The hidden epidemic of modern times. *CNS Spectrums, 3*(7, Suppl. 2), 4–51.

REVIEW AND CONTEMPLATE

1. Explain Lilienfeld and Lynn's (2015) position on whether DID "exists." What do they say about whether most individuals with DID are faking or intentionally producing their symptoms?

2. Briefly describe the two competing etiological models of DID (i.e., the posttraumatic model and the sociocognitive model). What does each model say about the causes of DID?

3. Describe two sources of evidence for the PTM model that you found most convincing. Describe three of the six sources of evidence for the SCM model mentioned in the reading that you found most convincing. Which of the two models of DID seems to be most accurate, given all of the evidence discussed by Lilienfeld and Lynn (2015)?

4. The famous book written about Sybil suggests that her multiple personalities developed as a result of severe child abuse (consistent with the PTM model of DID). Explain why this case study of Sybil is not convincing evidence for the PTM model of DID (i.e., why is there reason to doubt that Sybil's supposed multiple personalities existed and were caused by child abuse?).

9.2 "Can We Really Tap Our Problems Away? A Critical Analysis of Thought Field Therapy"

IN AUGUST OF 1998, Dr. Jenny Edwards, a practitioner of thought field therapy, was in Nairobi, Kenya conducting a training program for human service workers when the U. S. Embassy was bombed. She went to a nearby hospital to help the bombing victims, and she encountered a woman whose shoes had been blown off in the bombing. The woman was just staring into space. After talking with the woman, Dr. Edwards discovered that she was traumatized, had an extreme level of pain, and could not stop thinking that a bomb might go off any minute in the hospital. Dr. Edwards quickly performed thought field therapy—which involves tapping various parts of the body in specific sequences—on the woman and found that her pain, trauma, and intrusive thoughts disappeared. Dr. Edwards then moved on to another woman who "was just staring into space; her arm was bandaged, and her hand was limp … she was a '10' on both trauma and pain." After performing thought field therapy, the woman's trauma and pain disappeared, and "she was moving her hand all around, color was restored to her face, and she was smiling and laughing."

Today, the website for Dr. Roger Callahan's thought field therapy explains that it "provides a code to nature's healing system. When applied to problems, TFT solves the fundamental causes, balancing the body's energy system and eliminates most negative emotions … within minutes." It is used primarily for weight loss, stress relief, and treating anxiety and trauma. In this article, Gaudiano and Herbert discuss why thought field therapy should be considered a pseudoscientific practice.

Reference

Gaudiano, B. A., & Herbert, J. D. (2000, July/August). Can we really tap our problems away? A critical analysis of thought field therapy. *Skeptical Inquirer, 24,* 29–33, 36.

ARTICLE 9.2

"CAN WE REALLY TAP OUR PROBLEMS AWAY? A CRITICAL ANALYSIS OF THOUGHT FIELD THERAPY"

BRANDON GAUDIANO AND JAMES HERBERT

> Thought Field Therapy is marketed as an extraordinarily fast and effective body-tapping treatment for a number of psychological problems. However, it lacks even basic empirical support and exhibits many of the trappings of a pseudoscience.
>
> —Brandon A. Gaudiano and James D. Herbert

It is nothing new to find enterprising entrepreneurs seeking to profit from their novel inventions, which are often claimed to produce miraculous results for their users. The field of mental health is no exception. In fact, there has recently been a surge of putatively revolutionary treatments for various psychological problems that claim to be far superior to standard treatments in both effectiveness and efficiency. Known as "power" or "energy" therapies (Gist, Woodall, and Magenheimer 1999; Herbert et al. in press; Swenson 1999), these treatments are gaining widespread acceptance among mental health practitioners, despite their frankly bizarre theories and techniques, extraordinary claims, and absence of scientific support. One of the most popular of these power therapies, known as Eye Movement Desensitization and Reprocessing (EMDR), involves a therapist waving his or her fingers in front of the patient's eyes while the client imagines various disturbing scenes that are thought to be related to the patient's problems. In fact, EMDR, a "power therapy" that alludes to neural networks instead of energy fields for its theoretical basis, has been described as a prototypical case of pseudoscience within mental health (Herbert et al. in press; Lohr, Montgomery, Lilienfeld, and Tolin 1999; Lilienfeld 1996).

There is another treatment approach on the rise that threatens to overtake EMDR as the premiere power therapy for the twenty-first century: Thought Field Therapy (TFT; Callahan 1985). Roger Callahan, TFT's inventor, claims that he can train therapists to be over 97% effective using his "revolutionary" procedures in treating a variety of common psychological problems including anxiety and depression. Since the history of psychotherapy is replete with treatments that failed to live up to their initial hype, it seems prudent to take a closer look at TFT.

ORIGINS AND METHODS

Callahan (1997) states that he accidentally discovered TFT while treating a client named Mary, who had a severe fear of water. Inspired by an acupuncture class he was taking at the time, Callahan instructed Mary to firmly tap the area under her eye with her

Brandon A. Gaudiano and James D. Herbert, "Can We Really Tap Our Problems Away? A Critical Analysis of Thought Field Therapy," *Skeptical Inquirer*, vol. 24, pp. 29-33, 36. Copyright © 2000 by Center for Inquiry. Reprinted with permission.

fingers, leading to a miraculous and immediate resolution of Mary's phobia. Callahan subsequently developed the comprehensive set of techniques and theory that is now known as TFT. The therapy is based on the idea that invisible energy fields called "thought fields" exist within the body (Callahan and Callahan 1997). Environmental traumas and inherited predispositions are theorized to cause blockages, or what Callahan terms "perturbations," in the flow of energy in these thought fields. Callahan theorizes that the commonly observed neurochemical, behavioral, and cognitive indicators of disorders such as depression are the result of these perturbations. In other words, the root cause of all psychological problems are blockages in energy fields.

In order to correct these perturbations, clients are directed by the TFT therapist to tap on the body's "energy meridians" in specific sequences, called "algorithms," which vary based on the particular problem being treated (Callahan and Callahan 1997). For example, the client may be instructed to tap at the corner of the eyebrow five times and then continue tapping on other parts of the body in a specific sequence as instructed by the therapist. In addition, the clients are told to roll their eyes, count, and hum a few bars of a song at various points during the treatment. Callahan states that when the thought field is "attuned," that is, when the person is thinking about the distressing event or image, perturbations are able to be located and corrected. The tapping is theorized to add energy to the system, which then re-balances the overall energy flow, thereby eliminating the distress at the source.

THEORETICAL UNDERPINNINGS

The theory behind TFT is a hodgepodge of concepts derived from a variety of sources. Foremost among these is the ancient Chinese philosophy of *chi*, which is thought to be the "life force" that flows throughout the body. Beyerstein and Sampson (1996) argue that *chi* is more accurately conceptualized as a philosophy, not a science, and its existence is not empirically supported. In addition, they note that while acupuncture, a procedure used to correct the flow of *chi*, has been shown to provide some minor analgesic effects, its utility has not been demonstrated for treating illnesses or diseases. TFT also borrows techniques from a procedure known as Applied Kinesiology that is used to test muscles for "weaknesses" caused by certain food or chemical pathogens (Sampson and Beyerstein 1996). Applied Kinesiology is a scientifically discredited procedure. For example, Kenny, Clemens, and Forsythe (1988) found that those using the techniques did no better than chance in determining nutritional status using muscle testing. Finally, TFT even borrows some of its concepts from quantum physics. For instance, the idea of active information, in which small amounts of energy can affect large systems, is used to support the existence of perturbations (Bohm and Hiley 1993). There are obvious problems with the theoretical basis for TFT, not the least of which is the complete lack of scientific evidence for the existence of "thought fields."

TFT, as with other new "energy" therapies, is based on misconceptions or outright distortions of the concept of energy as it is used by scientists (Saravi 1999). In physics, energy is defined simply as the capacity to do work, and energy exchanges are observable and measurable. Energy therapists, in contrast, use the term to describe a kind of universal life force that influences health, but they provide no direct data to document the presence of such a force. Saravi concludes that "New Agers' and psychobabblers' 'energy' has only a remote relationship with its physical, scientific counterpart. For them, it is just a word conveniently invoked to explain phenomena whose very existence is far from certain" (47).

EXTRAORDINARY CLAIMS OF SUCCESS

TFT is marketed primarily through the Internet. To attract potential therapists to take TFT courses and to persuade prospective clients to pay for this therapeutic approach, amazing claims are presented on several TFT-related Web sites. For example, Callahan's primary Web site[1] claims that TFT allows individuals "to eliminate most negative emotions within minutes." In addition, Callahan asserts that TFT's effectiveness increases with higher levels of training. For example, another Web site[2] publicizes that therapists can achieve an 80 percent effectiveness rate from learning to use specific algorithms, a 90–95 percent effectiveness rate from using "Causal Diagnostic" techniques, and an over 97 percent effectiveness rate using a technique mysteriously termed "Voice Technology." Yet another Web site,[3] this one based in the United Kingdom, states that TFT is the only psychotherapy that can "genuinely claim to offer a cure." TFT claims to be able to "cure" people of a variety of psychological problems, including phobias, panic, post-traumatic stress disorder, addictions, sexual problems, pain, depression, anger, general distress, and even other less serious problems such as fingernail biting (Hooke 1998a). One noted TFT therapist even claims to have cured her dog of a fear of heights using the trauma algorithm (Danzig 1998).

Despite these miraculous assertions, no controlled studies have been published in peer-reviewed scientific journals to provide evidence for TFT's claims. Instead, testimonials and uncontrolled case studies are offered to support these astonishing declarations of success (Callahan 1995). The vast majority of these claims are made via Internet postings (Lohr, Montgomery, et al. 1999). Such anecdotes, however, do not constitute probative data on the question of TFT's efficacy. Callahan often claims that his public demonstrations of TFT on television shows such as *The Leeza Gibbons Show* (aired October 12, 1996) provide dramatic proof of success, thereby circumventing the need for empirical research. However, such vivid but uncontrolled presentations are not evidential, given the extraordinary demand characteristics (i.e., the implicit pressure engendered by the situation for clients to behave in accordance with their beliefs about what is expected of them) inherent in such settings, not to mention the lack of objective, standardized assessments of improvement in symptoms (Hooke 1998b). Given that Callahan claims to have been using his techniques for over twenty years, it is curious why no controlled studies have been conducted. It should be quite easy to demonstrate the effects of a treatment with a 97 percent effectiveness rate using accepted methods of clinical science.

THE LIMITED RESEARCH FINDINGS

TFT has recently attracted the attention of two Florida State University researchers. In considering their work, it is important to note that none of their findings have been published in peer-reviewed journals; instead they report their results in one of the researcher's self-published Internet "journal." Carbonell and Figley (1999) tested four controversial treatments for trauma, including TFT. Thirty-nine individuals who reported distress from having experienced a traumatic event were given one of the four treatments for up to one week. Overall, Carbonell and Figley reported that participants demonstrated some improvement in self-rated distress and on questionnaire measures from pre-treatment to six-month follow-up. This study is so seriously flawed, however, that the results are completely uninterpretable. The most critical flaw is the absence of any control for the passage of time. In the absence of a no-treatment or a placebo control group, there is no way to know if any observed improvement was a function of factors such as the natural remission of symptoms over time, statistical regression to the mean (i.e., the tendency for extreme scores on a measure to be less extreme upon retest), or placebo effects. This concern is heightened by the absence of measures taken immediately following treatment, as the only outcome measures were reported six months following treatment. Also, subjects were not diagnosed with post-traumatic stress disorder using standard diagnostic criteria, and it is not clear how much subjects were impaired by their traumatic experiences. Moreover, daily diaries and recordings of distress revealed that subjects appeared to have difficulty distinguishing distress associated with the normal ups and downs of life from distress associated with their trauma. For example, a participant who had suffered childhood abuse reported high distress, but upon query disclosed that this distress was due to her car getting a flat tire rather than her trauma, raising questions about the reliability of these subjective distress ratings (Huber 1997).

Furthermore, the authors did not report subjecting their data to statistical analysis, instead relying on their visual inspection of the data for interpretation. Interestingly, even these data do not support the large effect sizes claimed by TFT supporters. On the contrary, mean scores on the self-report questionnaires showed only relatively paltry changes in symptoms, far below the claims of miraculous improvement that Callahan and others have consistently claimed. Thus, Carbonell and Figley's (1999) study, which is the most serious research attempt to date, does not support the effectiveness of TFT. Nevertheless, the results of this study, originally presented at a 1995 symposium, are frequently cited by Callahan and others as providing evidence of TFT's efficacy (Callahan and Callahan 1997). The only other "research" on TFT is either presented in internally circulated publications such as Callahan's newsletter *The Thought Field,* nonscientific magazine reports (e.g., Shamis 1996), or on Web sites (e.g., Carbonell 1996; see Swenson 1999 for a review).

ALTERNATE EXPLANATIONS

Occam's Razor is a principle often applied in science indicating that, all things being equal, the most parsimonious explanation for a phenomenon is the preferred one. Applying this principle to TFT, there is little need for concepts such as energy fields and perturbations to explain any effects that TFT might show. TFT highlights specific tapping sequences as its proposed mechanism of action; however, other components of the treatment protocol may be responsible for any observed benefits. In addition to the absence of controls for spontaneous remission, no research has ruled out factors that are common—to greater or lesser degrees—in all psychotherapies. These include placebo effects resulting from the mere expectation for improvement, demand characteristics, therapist enthusiasm and support, therapist-client alliance, and effort justification (i.e., the tendency to report positive changes in order to justify the effort exerted; Lohr, Lilienfeld, Tolin, and Herbert 1999). Thus, despite the absence of empirical evidence to support TFT's claims of tremendous effectiveness, it would not be surprising to find that the procedure sometimes produces benefits for some individuals owing to these common mechanisms shared by all forms of psychotherapy. Serious psychotherapy innovators go to great lengths to conduct studies to demonstrate that the hypothesized active ingredients of their procedures outperform these so-called "nonspecific" effects. No such effort has been made by the promoters of TFT.

Callahan, however, dismisses the possibility that TFT could be explained by such mechanisms. He asserts that "clinical evidence" has ruled out the possibility of nonspecific or placebo effects accounting for TFT's results, but fails to support this claim (Callahan and Callahan 1997). He frequently states that placebo effects cannot be operative in TFT because some clients express skepticism that the tapping will work (Hooke 1998a). This argument demonstrates a misunderstanding of the placebo concept, which does not necessarily require the individual to fully believe in the practitioner's explanation for why a procedure works (Bootzin 1985; Dodes 1997). Callahan (1999) also reports case studies in which he claims to have observed a "re-balancing" of the autonomic nervous system after treatment with TFT, and that this somehow refutes the placebo explanation. In fact, it is well accepted that the autonomic nervous system, including phenomena such as pulse, blood pressure, and electrocardiogram changes, can be influenced by various psychological events, including placebos (Ross and Buckalew 1985).

In addition to nonspecific and placebo effects, TFT appears to incorporate procedures from existing, well-established therapies. TFT therapists instruct clients to focus repeatedly on distressing thoughts and images during the tapping sequences. Such repeated exposure to distressing cognitions is a well-known behavior therapy technique called imagery exposure (Foa and Meadows 1997). Furthermore, TFT therapists utilize cognitive coping statements throughout treatment (e.g., "I accept and forgive them for what they did"), which represent another established cognitive therapy technique. In short, any effects that TFT might show can be readily explained by known mechanisms, without invoking unfounded concepts such as "perturbations" and "thought fields" (Hooke 1998a).

TFT AND EFT

Since the emergence of TFT, several therapists have recently developed offshoot therapies based on treating the body's energy fields. The most successful of these TFT derivatives was developed by Gary Craig. Craig (1997), who has a degree in engineering and formerly studied under Callahan, created what he calls Emotional Freedom Techniques (EFT). EFT is very similar to TFT, except that it employs one simplified and ubiquitous tapping procedure instead of applying different algorithms to treat different problems. On his Web site[4], Craig asserts that Callahan's reliance on differing algorithms is unnecessary because he has witnessed TFT therapists tap in the wrong order or apply the wrong algorithm to the particular problem and still obtain improvements. Craig's anecdotal evidence appears to contradict Callahan's anecdotal evidence. Furthermore, Craig extends his tapping therapy far beyond the realm of mental health, reporting testimonials from individuals who claim to have successfully used EFT to treat everything from autism to warts and various other medical problems with positive results. In the latest developments, Craig has reported on the positive effects of "surrogate tapping," in which therapists tap on themselves to treat the problems of others.

A scientifically minded investigator would have then taken Craig's observations a step further and tested a completely "placebo" algorithm which did not tap on any supposed energy meridians to see if it produced similar results. However, Craig reports that he has never carried out his simple experiment nor does he know of anyone who has (Craig, personal communication, January 14, 2000). Furthermore, Craig speculates that a placebo algorithm may be impossible because tapping anywhere on the body will affect the body's energy meridians. This position conveniently renders Craig's theory unfalsifiable and therefore outside the realm of science.

PSEUDOSCIENCE IN PSYCHOTHERAPY

Lilienfeld (1998) argues that the proliferation of pseudoscience in psychotherapy is threatening the public welfare and damaging the reputation of psychology. Lohr, Montgomery et al. (1999) assert that the contemporary commercial promotion of treatments for the sequelae of trauma, such as EMDR and TFT, are commonly characterized by a host of pseudoscientific practices. In general, pseudoscience can be identified as consisting of "claims presented so that they appear scientific even though they lack supporting evidence and plausibility" (Shermer 1997, 33). For example, TFT incorporates scientific-sounding terminology by speaking of "bioenergies" and taking concepts from quantum physics out of context in an attempt to gain credibility. No empirical evidence is provided for the existence of central concepts such thought fields or perturbations, which are instead inferred through ad hoc, circular reasoning. For example, Callahan and Callahan (1997) state that perturbations are ultimately demonstrated through their effects, meaning that a perturbation in the thought field must have existed because after treatment the person no longer experiences distress.

The hallmark of a science is falsifiability (Popper 1965). A scientific proposition must specify, a priori, predictions that can be refuted, at least in principle. Callahan has not provided a framework by which his theory could be brought under scientific investigation. As is characteristic of pseudoscience, only confirming evidence of TFT is sought out and presented by advocates (Lohr, Montgomery, et al. 1999). Neither Callahan nor other proponents, including Carbonell and Figley (1999), have subjected TFT to controlled evaluation using accepted scientific methods and published results in peer-reviewed journals.

The objective of a pseudoscience is often persuasion and promotion, in lieu of responsible investigation of claims (Bunge 1967). Web sites advertise courses and multilevel training in TFT techniques for thousands of dollars. The highest level of training in TFT is called Voice Technology (VT), which supposedly allows the therapist to diagnose perturbations and treat clients entirely over the telephone by analyzing their voices. The effectiveness of VT is said to approach 100 percent (Callahan 1998). Callahan sells this technique for $100,000, and trainees must sign nondisclosure contracts that forbid them from discussing or revealing any aspects of the technique. Recently, the Arizona Board of Psychologist Examiners put a psychologist on probation for refusing to provide specific information about VT to back up his assertion of its high degree of effectiveness (Foxhall 1999; Lilienfeld and Lohr 2000). Interestingly, on his Web site[5] Gary Craig, who was trained in the method, stresses that the putative "secret" behind VT is readily available "in the public domain and can be learned at a weekend workshop for a few hundred dollars." The mystery surrounding VT only has the effect of obfuscating independent examination and investigation.

Finally, pseudosciences explain away or reinterpret failures as actually providing confirmatory evidence (Lakatos 1978). Callahan proposes the existence of a phenomenon termed "psychological reversal" to explain instances in which TFT fails to work. Psychological reversal is claimed to result in self-sabotaging attitudes and behaviors and is manifested in the reversed flow of energy that blocks the effects of the treatment (Callahan 1998). The prescribed treatment for such a condition involves reciting more cognitive coping statements (e.g., "I accept myself, even though I have this problem") that may alleviate distress independent of tapping. In addition, "energy toxins" are claimed to be substances that negatively affect the thought field, even if the person is not physically allergic to these supposed pathogens. These substances are proposed to cause a previously eliminated symptom to return (Joslin 1999). Using "muscle testing" procedures and VT, the offending pathogen can allegedly be identified, then removed until the treatment works again. Both psychological reversal and energy toxins are prime examples of post hoc reasoning and attempts to ignore disconfirming evidence by creating uncorroborated explanations of TFT failures.

CONCLUSION AND IMPLICATIONS

Despite extraordinary claims to the contrary, TFT is not supported by scientific evidence. The theoretical basis of TFT is grounded in unsupported and discredited concepts including the Chinese philosophy of *chi* and Applied Kinesiology. Many of the practices of TFT proponents are much more consistent with pseudoscience than science. Controlled studies evaluating the efficacy of TFT will be required for the treatment to be taken seriously by the scientific community.

TFT is only now beginning to garner negative press, and critiques are starting to appear in the popular literature. For example, Swenson (1999) recently reviewed the extraordinary claims for TFT made by Callahan and others, and noted the absence of controlled research to support these claims. Recently in the SKEPTICAL INQUIRER, Lilienfeld and Lohr (2000) reported on the American Psychological Association's decision in late 1999 to prohibit its sponsors of continuing education programs for psychologists from offering credits for training in TFT, as well as the sanctioning of an Arizona psychologist for using TFT and Voice Technology within the practice of psychology.

Nevertheless, thousands of therapists from various professional disciplines continue to pay for TFT training courses. Much of TFT's marketing success can be attributed to the prevalence of pro-TFT Web sites that promote strong claims of its effectiveness. TFT therapists, some of whom have no traditional training in psychology or psychotherapy, appear to be satisfied with TFT's vivid anecdotal stories of success, and are not aware of or not bothered by the overwhelming lack of empirical support for the procedure. Englebretsen (1995), among others, points to the alarming rise of postmodernist attitudes currently permeating the mental health field, exemplified by the willingness of some clinicians to value compelling anecdotal stories over controlled empirical data. This postmodernist mindset promotes the notion that all truth is relative and contextual; science is only one of many modes of thinking, each of which is equally valid. Such attitudes render the mental health field fertile breeding ground for pseudoscientific therapies such as TFT and its derivatives. Healthy skepticism competes head-to-head with extraordinary claims and, as is often the case, many mental health clinicians choose to ignore the facts in favor of miraculous possibilities.

NOTES

1. http://www.tftrx.com
2. http://www.thoughtfield.com
3. http://homepages.enterprise.net/ig/
4. http://www.emofree.com/scien-i.htm
5. http://www.emofree.com/about.htm

REFERENCES

Beyerstein, B. L., and W. Sampson. 1996. Traditional medicine and pseudoscience in China: A report of the second CSICOP delegation (part I) Skeptical Inquirer 20(4): 18–27.

Bohm, D. and B. Hiley. 1993. *The Undivided Universe: An Ontological Interpretation of Quantum Theory.* New York: Routledge.

Bootzin, R.R. 1985. The role of expectancy in behavior change. In *Placebo: Theory, Research, and Mechanisms,* edited by L. White, B. Tursky, and G. Schwartz. New York: Guilford, pp. 196–210.

Bunge, M. 1967. *Scientific Research.* New York, Springer.

Callahan, R. 1985. *Five Minute Phobia Cure.* Wilmington, DE: Enterprise.

———. 1995. Thought Field Therapy (TFT) algorithm for trauma: A reproducible experiment in psychotherapy. Paper delivered at the Annual Meeting of the American Psychological Association.

———. 1997. Thought Field Therapy: The case of Mary. Electronic Journal of Traumatology 3(1). Available: http://www.fsu.edu/-trauma/T039.html.

———. 1998. Response to Hooke's review of TFT. Electronic Journal of Traumatology 3(2). Available: http://www.fsu.edu/-trauma/v3i2art4.html.

———. 1999. TFT and Heart Rate Variability. *The Thought Field Newsletter* 5(2).

Callahan, R.J., and J. Callahan. 1997. Thought Field Therapy: Aiding the bereavement process. In *Death and Trauma: The Traumatology of Grieving,* edited by C. Figley, B. Bride, and N. Mazza. Washington, D.C.: Taylor & Francis, pp. 249–267.

Carbonell, J.L. 1996. An experimental study of TFT and acrophobia. Available: http://www.tftrx.com/ref_articles/6heights.html.

Carbonell, J.L., and C. Figley. 1999. A systematic clinical demonstration of promising PTSD treatment approaches. Electronic Journal of Traumatology 5(1). Available: http://www.fsu.edu/trauma/promising.html.

Craig, G. 1997. Six days at the VA: Using Emotional Freedom Therapy-Produced by Gary Craig. Videocassette.

Danzig, V. 1998. CT-TFT changes Karma. *The Thought Field Newsletter* 4(2).

Dodes, J.E. 1997. The mysterious placebo. Skeptical Inquirer 21(1): 44–46

Englebrersen, G. 1995. The filling of scholarly vacuums. Skeptical Inquirer 21(4): 57–59.

Foa, E.B., and E.A. Meadows. 1997. Psychosocial treatments for posttraumatic stress disorder: A critical review. *Annual Review of Psychology* 48: 449–480.

Fohall, K. 1999. Arizona board sanctions psychologist for use of Thought Field Therapy. *American Psychological Association Monitor* 30(8): 8.

Gist, R., S.J. Woodall, and L.K. Magenheimer. 1999. "And then you do the Hokey-Pokey and you turn yourself around ..." In *Response to Disaster: Psychosocial, Community, and Ecological Approaches,* edited by R. Gist and B. Lubin. Philadelphia: Brunner/Mazel, 269–290.

Herbert, J.D., S.O. Lilienfeld, J.M. Lohr, R.W. Montgomery, W.T. O'Donohue, G.M. Rosen, and D.F. Tolin. in press. Science and pseudoscience in the development of Eye Movement Desensitization and Reprocessing: Implications for clinical psychology. *Clinical Psychology Review.*

Hooke, W. 1998a. A review of Thought Field Therapy. Electronic Journal of Traumatology 3(2). Available: http://www.fsu.edu/-trauma/v3i2art3.html.

Hooke, W. 1998b. Wayne Hooke's reply to Roger Callahan. Electronic Journal of Traumatology 3(2). Available: http://www.fsu.edu/-trauma/v3i2art5.html.

Huber, C.H. 1997. PTSD: A search for "active ingredients." *Family Journal* 5(2): 144-148.

Joslin, G. 1999. A follow-up toxin treatment for a previously treated multiple personality patient. *The Thought Field Newsletter* 5(2).

Kenny J.J., R. Clemens, K.D. Forsythe. 1988. Applied Kinesiology unreliable for assessing nurrient status. *Journal of the American Dietetic Association* 88(6): 698-704.

Lakatos, I. 1978. Introduction: Science and pseudoscience. In *The Methodology of Scientific Research Programs: Philosophical Papers,* edited by J. Worrall and G. Currie. Cambridge, England: Cambridge University Press.

Leonoff, G. 1995. The successful treatment of phobias and anxiety by telephone and radio: A replication of Callahan's 1987 study, *The Thought Field Newsletter* 1(2).

Lilienfeld, S.O. 1996. EMDR treatment: Less than meets the eys? Skeptical Inquirer 20(1): 25-31.

———. 1998. Pseudoscience in contemporary clinical psychology: What it is and what we can do about it. *The Clinical Psychologist* 51(4): 3-9.

Lilienfeld, S.O. Lilienfeld, D.F. Tolin, and J.D. Herbert. 1999. Eye Movement Desensitization and Reprocessing: An analysis of specific versus nonspecific treatment factors. *Journal of Anxiety Disorders* 13(1-2): 185-207.

Lohr, J.M., R.W. Montgomery, S.O. Lilienfeld, and D.F. Tolin. 1999. Pseudoscience and the commercial promotion of trauma treatments. In *Response to Disaster: Psychosocial, Community, and Ecological Approaches* edited by R. Gist and R. Lubin. Philadelphia: Brunner/Mazel, pp. 291-326.

Popper, K. 1965. *The Logic of Scientific Disovery.* New York: Harper.

Ross, S., and L.W. Buckalew. 1985. Placebo agentry: Assesment of drug and placebo effects. In *Placebo: Theory, Research, and Mechanism,* ed. L. White, B. Tursky, and G. Schwartz. New York: Guilford, 67-82.

Sampson, W., and B.L. Beyerstein. 1996. Traditional medicine and pseudoscience in China: A report of the second CSICOP delegation (part 2). Skeptical Inquirer 20(5): 27-36.

Saravi, F.D. 1999. Energy and the brain: Facts and fantasies. In *Mind Myths: Exploring Popular Assumptions about the Mind and Brain,* edited by S. Della Saia. New York: Wiley & Sons, 43-58.

Shamis, B. 1996. Thought Field Therapy. *Visions Magazine* 8 (Nov): 8-9, 32-33.

Shermer, M. 1997. *Why People Believe Weird Things: Pseudoscience, Superstition, and other Confusions of Our Time*. New York: W.H. Freeman.

Swenson, D.X. 1999. Thought Field Therapy: Still searching for the quick fix. *Skeptic* 7(4): 60–65.

REVIEW AND CONTEMPLATE

1. What is thought field therapy (TFT)? Briefly explain how TFT is claimed to work and what disorders it is used to treat.

2. How is the concept of "energy" in energy therapies different from the concept of energy in physics?

3. Briefly describe the evidence for the effectiveness of TFT, including the study by Carbonell and Figley (1999). What are some limitations of this evidence?

4. TFT proponents claim that specific tapping sequences that affect thought fields produce any positive improvements TFT patients might exhibit. What are some alternative explanations for such improvements?

5. Which of the six characteristics of pseudoscience discussed in Chapter 1 seem most closely related to TFT?

9.3 "A Close Look at Therapeutic Touch"

IN AN ARTICLE published in *Orthopaedic Nursing*, Dr. Sherron Herdtner told the story of a man named Paul who fell 20 feet from a ladder and shattered his elbow. Paul had surgery to repair his elbow, but he was in pain and was not able to work or help his wife with their newborn baby. Although Paul wasn't sure whether therapeutic touch (TT) would help him, he gave it a try. Dr. Herdtner explained that after his first TT session, Paul "experienced greater movement in his wrist and arm and did not feel pain on movement. … That night he did yard work, helped his wife with the dishes, and took his children out for ice cream." She concluded that "Paul's experience with therapeutic touch helped him physically, emotionally, and spiritually."

Imagine that a nurse could promote the healing of wounds, relieve pain from burns, alleviate symptoms of Alzheimer's disease or AIDS, and treat cancer by simply sweeping her hands slightly above a patient's body. These are some of the extraordinary claims made about TT, a practice that has become very popular among nurses. TT practitioners believe that they can use their hands to detect problems with a person's "energy field," which they then realign or balance to promote healing.

In 1996, a 9-year-old girl named Emily Rosa designed an experiment to test TT practitioners for her fourth-grade science fair project. The entire practice of TT rests on practitioners' claims that they can detect the "human energy field" and manipulate it, so Emily decided to find out if they can actually detect such "energy." With the help of her mother and a couple of other scientists, Emily published her experiments in the prestigious *Journal of the American Medical Association*. The following reading is the famous article by Emily and her coauthors that discusses the theory behind TT, the quality of the literature that supports it, and the results of Emily's experiments. While reading this article, consider how it illustrates the difference between pseudoscientific and scientific approaches to gaining knowledge (see Chapter 1). Although a couple of decades have passed since Emily and her coauthors presented evidence suggesting that TT is a pseudoscientific practice, there are still thousands of practitioners of TT and related practices (e.g., Healing Touch and Reiki). These practitioners can be found in many hospitals and medical facilities across the country.

Reference

Rosa, L., Rosa, E., Sarner, L., & Barrett, S. (1998). A close look at therapeutic touch. *Journal of the American Medical Association, 279,* 1005–1010. NOTE: This article can be retrieved online at https://jamanetwork.com/journals/jama/fullarticle/187390.

ARTICLE 9.3

"A CLOSE LOOK AT THERAPEUTIC TOUCH"
LINDA ROSA, EMILY ROSA, LARRY SARNER, AND STEPHEN BARRETT

Therapeutic touch (TT) is a widely used nursing practice rooted in mysticism but alleged to have a scientific basis. Its practitioners claim to heal or improve many medical problems by manual manipulation of a "human energy field" (HEF) perceptible above the patient's skin. They also claim to detect illnesses and stimulate recuperative powers through their intention to heal. Therapeutic Touch practice guides[1-6] describe 3 basic steps, none of which actually requires touching the patient's body. The first step is centering, in which the practitioner focuses on his or her intent to help the patient. This step resembles meditation and is claimed to benefit the practitioner as well. The second step is assessment, in which the practitioner's hands, from a distance of 5 to 10 cm, sweep over the patient's body from head to feet, "attuning" to the patient's condition by becoming aware of "changes in sensory cues" in the hands. The third step is intervention, in which the practitioner's hands "repattern" the patient's "energy field" by removing "congestion," replenishing depleted areas, and smoothing out ill-flowing areas. The resultant "energy balance" purportedly stems disease and allows the patient's body to heal itself.[7]

Proponents of TT state that they have "seen it work."[8] In a 1995 interview, TT's founder said, "In theory, there should be no limitation on what healing can be accomplished."[9] Table 9.1 lists some claims made for TT in published reports.

BACKGROUND
Professional Recognition
Proponents state that more than 100 000 people worldwide have been trained in TT technique,[38] including at least 43 000 health care professionals,[2] and that about half of those trained actually practice it.[39] Therapeutic Touch is taught in more than 100 colleges and universities in 75 countries.[5] It is said to be the most recognized technique used by practitioners of holistic nursing.[40] Considered a nursing intervention, it is used by nurses in at least 80 hospitals in North America,[33] often without the permission or even knowledge of attending physicians.[41-43] The policies and procedures books of some institutions recognize TT,[44] and it is the only treatment for the "energy-field disturbance" diagnosis recognized by the North American Nursing Diagnosis Association.[45] *RN*, one of the nursing profession's largest periodicals, has published many articles favorable to TT.[46-52]

Linda Rosa, Emily Rosa, Larry Sarner, and Stephen Barrett, "A Close Look at Therapeutic Touch," *Journal of the American Medical Association*, vol. 279, no. 13, pp. 1005-1010. Copyright © 1998 by American Medical Association. Reprinted with permission.

TABLE 9.1: Claims Made for Therapeutic Touch

Calms colicky infants,[9] hospitalized infants,[10] women in childbirth,[11] trauma patients,[12] and hospitalized cardiovascular patients[13,14]
Promotes bonding between parents and infants[15]
Increases milk let down in breast-feeding mothers[16]
Helps children make sense of the world[17]
Protects nurses from burnout[18] and effects changes in their lifestyle[19]
Helps to evaluate situations where diagnosis is elusive[9]
Relieves acute pain,[20] especially from burns[21]
Relieves nausea,[22,23] diarrhea,[5] tension headaches,[24] migraine headaches,[21] and swelling in edematous legs and arthritic joints[7]
Decreases inflammation[25]
Breaks fever[21]
Remedies thyroid imbalances[5]
Helps skin grafts to seed[9]
Promotes healing of decubitus ulcers[7]
Alleviates psychosomatic illnesses[5]
Increases the rate of healing for wounds, bone and muscle injuries, and infections[26]
Relieves symptoms of Alzheimer disease,[27] acquired immunodeficiency syndrome,[5] menstruation,[28] and premenstrual syndrome[21]
Is an innovative means of social communication[29]
Is effective with the aged,[30,31] asthmatic or autistic children, stroke patients, and coma patients[9]
Supports people with multiple sclerosis and Raynaud disease[32]
Treats measles[33] and many different forms of cancer[34]
Comforts the dying[35-37]
Helps to bring some dead back to life[2]

Many professional nursing organizations promote TT. In 1987, the 50 000-member Order of Nurses of Quebec endorsed TT as a "bona fide" nursing skill.[32] The National League for Nursing, the credentialing agency for nursing schools in the United States, denies having an official stand on TT but has promoted it through books and videotapes,[3,53,54] and the league's executive director and a recent president are prominent advocates.[55] The American Nurses' Association holds TT workshops at its national conventions. Its official journal published the premier articles on TT[56-59] as well as a recent article designated for continuing education credits.[60] The association's immediate past president has written editorials defending TT against criticism.[61] The American Holistic Nursing Association offers certification in "healing touch," a TT variant.[62] The Nurse

Healers and Professional Associates Cooperative, which was formed to promote TT, claims about 1200 members.[39]

THE TT HYPOTHESIS

Therapeutic Touch was conceived in the early 1970s by Dolores Krieger, PhD, RN, a faculty member at New York University's Division of Nursing. Although often presented as a scientific adaptation of "laying-on of hands,"[63-68] TT is imbued with metaphysical ideas.

Krieger initially identified TT's active agent as *prana,* an ayurvedic, or traditional Indian, concept of "life force." She stated,

> Health is considered a harmonious relationship between the individual and his total environment. There is postulated a continuing interacting flow of energies from within the individual outward, and from the environment to the various levels of the individual. Healing, it is said, helps to restore this equilibrium in the ill person. Disease, within this context, is considered an indication of a disturbance in the free flow of the pranic current.[68]

Krieger further postulated that this "pranic current" can be controlled by the will of the healer.

> When an individual who is healthy touches an ill person with the intent of helping or healing him, he acts as a transference agent for the flow of prana from himself to the ill person. It was this added input of prana ... that helped the ill person to overcome his illness or to feel better, more vital.[68]

Others associate all this with the Chinese notion of *qi,* a "life energy" alleged to flow through the human body through invisible "meridians." Those inspired by mystical healers of India describe this energy as flowing in and out of sites of the body that they call *chakras.*

Soon after its conception, TT became linked with the westernized notions of the late Martha Rogers, dean of nursing at New York University. She asserted that humans do not merely possess energy fields but *are* energy fields and constantly interact with the "environmental field" around them. Rogers dubbed her approach the "Science of Unitary Man,"[69] which later became known as the more neutral "Science of Unitary Human Beings." Her nomenclature stimulated the pursuit of TT as a "scientific" practice. Almost all TT discussion today is based on Rogers' concepts, although Eastern metaphysical terms such as *chakra*[2,70] and *yin-yang*[71] are still used.

The HEF postulated by TT theorists resembles the "magnetic fluid" or "animal magnetism" postulated during the 18th century by Anton Mesmer and his followers. Mesmerism held that illnesses are caused by obstacles to the free flow of this fluid and that skilled healers ("sensitives") could remove these obstacles by making passes with their hands. Some aspects of mesmerism were revived in the 19th century by Theosophy, an occult religion that incorporated Eastern metaphysical concepts and underlies many current New Age ideas.[72] Dora Kunz, who is considered TT's codeveloper, was president of the Theosophical Society of America from 1975 to 1987. She collaborated with Krieger on the early TT studies and claims to be a fifth-generation "sensitive" and a "gifted healer."[20]

Therapeutic Touch is set apart from many other alternative healing modalities, as well as from scientific medicine, by its emphasis on the healer's intention. Whereas the testing of most therapies requires controlling for the placebo effect (often influenced by the recipient's belief about efficacy), TT theorists suggest that the placebo effect is irrelevant. According to Krieger,

> Faith on the part of the subject does not make a significant difference in the healing effect. Rather, the role of faith seems to be psychological, affecting his acceptance of his illness or consequent recovery and what this means to him. The healer, on the other hand, must have some belief system that underlies his actions, if one is to attribute rationality to his behavior.[65]

Thus, the TT hypothesis and the entire practice of TT rest on the idea that the patient's energy field can be detected and intentionally manipulated by the therapist. With this in mind, early practitioners concluded that physical contact might not be necessary.[13] The thesis that the HEF extends beyond the skin and can be influenced from several centimeters away from the body's surface is said to have been tested by Janet Quinn, PhD, and reported in her 1982 dissertation.[14] However, that study merely showed no difference between groups of patients who did or did not have actual contact during TT. Although Quinn's work has never been substantiated, nearly all TT practitioners today use only the noncontact form of TT.

As originally developed by Krieger, TT did involve touch, although clothes and other materials interposed between practitioner and patient were not considered significant.[56] It was named TT because the aboriginal term *laying-on of hands* was considered an obstacle to acceptance by "curriculum committees and other institutional bulwarks of today's society."[66] The mysticism has been downplayed, and various scientific-sounding mechanisms have been proposed. These include the therapeutic value of skin-to-skin contact, electron transfer resonance, oxygen uptake by hemoglobin, stereochemical similarities of hemoglobin and chlorophyll, electrostatic potentials influenced by healer brain activity, and unspecified concepts from quantum theory.[66, 67]

Therapeutic Touch is said to be in the vanguard of treatments that allow "healing" to take place, as opposed to the "curing" pejoratively ascribed to mainstream medical practice. Therapeutic Touch supposedly requires little training beyond refining an innate ability to focus one's intent to heal; the patient's body then does the rest.[5] Nurses who claim a unique professional emphasis on caring are said to be specially situated to help patients by using TT.[56, 69] Nonetheless, proponents also state that nearly everyone has an innate ability to learn TT, even small children and juvenile delinquents on parole.[2,17,82]

Proponents describe the HEF as real and perceptible. Reporting on a pilot study, Krieger claimed that 4 blindfolded men with transected spinal cords "could tell exactly where the nurse's hands were in their HEFs during the Therapeutic Touch interaction."[5] In ordinary TT sessions, practitioners go through motions that supposedly interact with the patient's energy field, including flicking "excess energy" from their fingertips.[3]

Therapeutic Touch is claimed to have only beneficial effects.[39] However, some proponents warn against overly lengthy sessions or overtreating certain areas of the body. This caution is based on the notion that too much energy can be imparted to a patient, especially an infant, which could lead to hyperactivity.[5,78,74]

LITERATURE ANALYSIS

Although TT proponents refer to a voluminous and growing body of valid research,[63,75,76] few studies have been well designed. Some clinical studies, mostly nursing doctoral dissertations, have reported positive results, principally with headache relief, relaxation, and wound healing.[1] However, the methods, credibility, and significance of these studies have been seriously questioned.[41,87-95] One prominent proponent questions the validity of the typical placebo control used in these studies.[96]

Two of the authors (L.R. and L.S.) have conducted extensive literature searches covering the years 1972 through 1996. Using key words such as *therapeutic touch, touch therapies, human energy field, quackery,* and *alternative medicine,* we have searched MEDLINE, *Index Medicus,* CINAHL, *Dissertation Abstracts, Masters Abstracts, Science Citation Index, Government Publications Index, Books in Print, National Union Catalog, Reader's Guide to Periodical Literature,* and *Alternative Press Index.* We attempted to obtain a full copy of each publication and every additional publication cited in the ones we subsequently collected. During 1997, we continued to monitor the journals most likely to contain material about TT.

These methods have enabled us to identify and obtain 853 reports (or abstracts), of which 609 deal specifically with TT, 224 mention it incidentally, and 20 discuss TT predecessors. Ninety-seven other cited items were either non-published or were published in obscure media we could not locate. Only 83 of the 853 reports described clinical research or other investigations by their authors. Nine of these studies were not quantitative. At most, only 1 (the study by Quinn[14]) of the 83 may have demonstrated independent confirmation of any positive study.[97] (That study was conducted by a close associate of the original researcher.) To our knowledge, no reported study attempted to test whether a TT practitioner could actually detect an HEF.

Of the 74 quantitative studies, 23 were clearly unsupportive. Eight reported no statistically significant results,[16,58,98-103] 3 admitted to having inadequate samples,[22,56,104] 2 were inconclusive,[11,105] and 6 had negative findings.[106-111] Four attempted independent repli-

---

1 References 5, 13, 14, 23, 24, 26, 28, 30, 68, 77–86

cations but failed to support the original findings.[112-115] To our knowledge, no attempt to conduct experiments to reconcile any of these unsupportive findings has been reported.

In 1994, the University of Colorado Health Sciences Center (UCHSC), Denver, empaneled a scientific jury in response to a challenge to TT in its nursing curriculum. After surveying published research, the panel concluded that "there is not a sufficient body of data, both in quality and quantity, to establish TT as a unique and efficacious healing modality."[116]

A few months later, a University of Alabama at Birmingham research team declared that their own imminent study (financed by a $335 000 federal grant) would be "the first real scientific evidence" for TT.[117,118] This project compared the effects of TT and sham TT on the perception of pain by burn patients. The final report to the funding agency noted statistically significant differences in pain and anxiety in 3 of 7 subjective measurements, but there was no difference in the amount of pain medication requested.[119]

With little clinical or quantitative research to support the practice of TT, proponents have shifted to qualitative research, which merely compiles anecdotes.[120] This approach, which involves asking subjects what they feel and drawing conclusions from their descriptions,[17,48,121-128] was sharply criticized by UCHSC's scientific panel.[116]

Both TT theory and technique require that an HEF be felt in order to impart any therapeutic benefit to a subject. Thus, the definitive test of TT is not a clinical trial of its alleged therapeutic effects, but a test of whether practitioners can perceive HEFs, which they describe, in print and in our study, with such terms as *tingling, pulling, throbbing, hot, cold, spongy,* and tactile *as taffy*. After doing its own survey, the UCHSC panel declared that no one had "even any ideas about how such research might be conducted."[115] This study fills that void.

METHODS

In 1996 and 1997, by searching for advertisements and following other leads, 2 of us (L.R. and L.S.) located 25 TT practitioners in northeastern Colorado, 21 of whom readily agreed to be tested. Of those who did not, 1 stated she was not qualified, 2 gave no reason, and 1 agreed but canceled on the day of the test.

The reported practice experience of those tested ranged from 1 to 27 years. There were 9 nurses, 7 certified massage therapists, 2 laypersons, 1 chiropractor, 1 medical assistant, and 1 phlebotomist. All but 2 were women, which reflects the sex ratio of the practitioner population. One nurse had published an article on TT in a journal for nurse practitioners.

There were 2 series of tests. In 1996, 15 practitioners were tested at their homes or offices on different days for a period of several months. In 1997, 13 practitioners, including 7 from the first series, were tested in a single day.

The test procedures were explained by 1 of the authors (E.R.), who designed the experiment herself. The first series of tests was conducted when she was 9 years old.

The participants were informed that the study would be published as her fourth-grade science-fair project and gave their consent to be tested. The decision to submit the results to a scientific journal was made several months later, after people who heard about the results encouraged publication. The second test series was done at the request of a Public Broadcasting Service television producer who had heard about the first study. Participants in the second series were informed that the test would be videotaped for possible broadcast and gave their consent.

During each test, the practitioners rested their hands, palms up, on a flat surface, approximately 25 to 30 cm apart. To prevent the experimenter's hands from being seen, a tall, opaque screen with cutouts at its base was placed over the subject's arms, and a cloth towel was attached to the screen and draped over them (Figure 9.1).

FIGURE 9.1:   Experimenter hovers hand over one of subject's hands. Draped towel prevents peeking. Drawing by Pat Linse, Skeptics Society.

Each subject underwent a set of 10 trials. Before each set, the subject was permitted to "center" or make any other mental preparations deemed necessary. The experimenter flipped a coin to determine which of the subject's hands would be the target. The experimenter then hovered her right hand, palm down, 8 to 10 cm above the target and said, "Okay." The subject then stated which of his or her hands was nearer to the experimenter's hand. Each subject was permitted to take as much or as little time as necessary to make each determination. The time spent ranged from 7 to 19 minutes per set of trials.

To examine whether air movement or body heat might be detectable by the experimental subjects, preliminary tests were performed on 7 other subjects who had no training or belief in TT. Four were children who were unaware of the purpose of the test. Those results indicated that the apparatus prevented tactile cues from reaching the subject.

The odds of getting 8 of 10 trials correct by chance alone is 45 of 1024 (P=.04), a level considered significant in many clinical trials. We decided in advance that an individual would "pass" by making 8 or more correct selections and that those passing the test would be retested, although the retest results would not be included in the group analysis. Results for the group as a whole would not be considered positive unless the average score was above 6.7 at a 90% confidence level.

RESULTS
Initial Test Results

If HEF perception through TT was possible, the experimental subjects should have each been able to detect the experimenter's hand in 10 (100%) of 10 trials. Chance alone would produce an average score of 5 (50%).

Before testing, all participants said they could use TT to significant therapeutic advantage. Each described sensory cues they used to assess and manipulate the HEF. All participants but 1 certified massage therapist expressed high confidence in their TT abilities, and even the aforementioned certified massage therapist said afterward that she felt she had passed the test to her own satisfaction.

In the initial trial, the subjects stated the correct location of the investigator's hand in 70 (47%) of 150 tries. The number of correct choices ranged from 2 to 8. Only 1 subject scored 8, and that same subject scored only 6 on the retest.

After each set of trials, the results were discussed with the participant. Because all but 1 of the trials could have been considered a failure, the participants usually chose to discuss possible explanations for failure. Their rationalizations included the following: (1) The experimenter left a "memory" of her hand behind, making it increasingly difficult in successive trials to detect the real hand from the memory. However, the first attempts (7 correct and 8 incorrect) scored no better than the rest. Moreover, practitioners should be able to tell whether a field they are sensing is "fresh." (2) The left hand is the "receiver" of energy and the right hand is the "transmitter." Therefore, it can be more difficult to detect the field when it is above the right hand. Of the 72 tests in which the hand was placed above the subjects' right hand, only 27 (88%) had correct responses. In addition, 35 (44%) of 80 incorrect answers involved the allegedly more receptive left hand—consistent with randomness. Moreover, practitioners customarily use both hands to assess. (3) Subjects should be permitted to identify the experimenter's field before beginning actual trials. Each subject could be given an example of the experimenter hovering her hand above each of theirs and told which hand it is. Since the effects of the HEF are described in unsubtle terms, such a procedure should not be necessary, but including it would remove a possible post hoc objection. Therefore, we did so in the follow-up testing. (4) The experimenter should be more proactive, centering herself and/or attempting to transmit energy through her own intentionality. This contradicts the fundamental premise of TT, since the experimenter's role is analogous to that of a patient. Only the practitioner's intentionality and preparation (centering) are theoretically necessary. If not so, the early experiments (on relatively uninvolved subjects, such as infants and barley seeds), cited frequently by TT advocates, must also be discounted. (5) Some subjects complained that their hands became so hot after a few trials that they were no longer able to sense the experimenter's HEF or they experienced difficulty doing so. This explanation clashes with TT's basic premise that practitioners can sense and manipulate the HEF with their hands during sessions that typically last 20 to 30 minutes. If practitioners become insensitive after only brief testing, the TT hypothesis is untestable. Those who made this complaint did so after they knew the results, not before. Moreover, only 7 of the 15 first trials produced correct responses.

FOLLOW-UP TEST RESULTS

The 1997 testing was completed in 1 day and videotaped by a professional film crew. Each subject was allowed to "feel" the investigator's energy field and choose which hand the investigator would use for testing. Seven subjects chose her left hand, and 6 chose her right hand.

The test results were similar to those of the first series. The subjects correctly located the investigator's hand in only 53 (41%) of 130 tries. The number of correct answers ranged from 1 to 7. After learning of their test scores, one participant said he was distracted by the towel over his hands, another said that her hands had been too dry, and several complained that the presence of the television crew had made it difficult to concentrate and/or added to the stress of the test. However, we do not believe that the situation was more stressful or distracting than the settings in which many hospital nurses practice TT (eg, intensive care units). Figure 9.2 shows the distribution of test results.

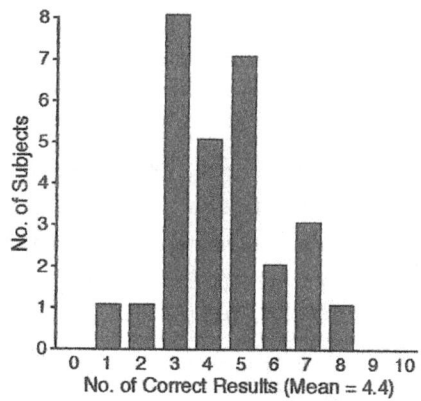

FIGURE 9.2: Distribution of test results.

Our null hypothesis was that the experimental results would be due to chance ($\mu=5$). Our alternative hypothesis was that the subjects would perform at better than chance levels. The t statistic of our data did not exceed the upper critical limit of the Student t distribution (Table 9.2). Therefore, the null hypothesis cannot be rejected at the .05 level of significance for a 1-tailed test, which means that our subjects, with only 123 of 280 correct in the 2 trials, did not perform better than chance.

TABLE 9.2: Statistical Analysis

STATISTICAL FUNCTION	INITIAL TEST (N = 15)	FOLLOW-UP TEST (N = 13)
Mean (95% confidence interval)	4.67 (3.67–5.67)	4.08 (3.17–4.99)
SD	1.74	1.44
α (1-tailed test)	.05	.05
t statistic	−0.7174	−2.222
Upper critical limit of Student t distribution	1.761	1.782
Alternative hypothesis, $\mu = 6.67$	0.9559	0.9801
Alternative hypothesis, $\mu = 7.50$	0.999644	0.999953

Our data also showed that if the practitioners could reliably detect an HEF 2 of 3 times, then the probability that either test missed such an effect would be less than .05. If the practitioners' true detection rate was 3 of 4, then the probability that our experiment missed it would be less than 3 in 10,000. However, if TT theory is correct, practitioners should always be able to sense the energy field of their patients. We would also expect accuracy to increase with experience. However, there was no significant correlation between the practitioners' scores and the length of time they had practiced TT ($r=0.23$). We conclude on both statistical and logical grounds that TT practitioners have no such ability.

COMMENT

Practitioners of TT are generally reluctant to be tested by people who are not proponents. In 1996, the James Randi Educational Foundation offered $74 2000 to anyone who could demonstrate an ability to detect an HEF under conditions similar to those of our study. Although more than 40 000 American practitioners claim to have such an ability, only 1 person attempted the demonstration. She failed, and the offer, now more than $1.1 million, has had no further volunteers despite extensive recruiting efforts.[129]

We suspect that the present authors were able to secure the cooperation of 21 practitioners because the person conducting the test was a child who displayed no skepticism.

CONCLUSION

Therapeutic touch is grounded on the concept that people have an energy field that is readily detectable (and modifiable) by TT practitioners. However, this study found that 21 experienced practitioners, when blinded, were unable to tell which of their hands was in the experimenter's energy field. The mean correct score for the 28 sets of 10 tests was 4.4, which is close to what would be expected for random guessing.

To our knowledge, no other objective, quantitative study involving more than a few TT practitioners has been published, and no well-designed study demonstrates any health benefit from TT. These facts, together with our experimental findings, suggest that TT claims are groundless and that further use of TT by health professionals is unjustified.

The television program "Scientific American Frontiers" showed excerpts from the second test series on November 19, 1997.

Lisa Feldman Barrett, PhD, Department of Psychology, Boston College, graciously helped with our statistical analyses.

REFERENCES

1. Boguslawski M. The use of Therapeutic Touch in nursing. *J Continuing Educ Nuts*. 1979;10(4):9–15.
2. Krieger D. *Therapeutic Touch Inner Workbook*. Santa Fe, NM: Bear; 1997:162.
3. Quinn JF. *Therapeutic Touch: Healing Through Human Energy Fields: Theory and Research* [videotapes and study guide]. New York, NY: National League for Nursing; 1994:42-2485–42-2487, 42-2493.
4. Krieger D. *Living the Therapeutic Touch: Healing as a Lifestyle*. New York, NY: Dodd Mead; 1987.
5. Krieger D. *Accepting Your Power to Heal: The Personal Practice of Therapeutic Touch*. Santa Fe, NM: Bear; 1993.
6. Chiappone J. *The Light Touch: An Easy Guide to Hands-on Healing*. Lake Mary, Fla: Holistic Reflections; 1989:14.
7. Quinn JF, Strelkauskas AJ. Psycho immunologic effects of Therapeutic Touch on practitioners and recently bereaved recipients: a pilot study. *ANS Adv Nurs Sci*. 1993;15(4):13–26.
8. Jarboux D. Nurse knows Therapeutic Touch "works." *Boulder Sunday Camera*. January 2, 1994:3E.
9. Putnam ZE. Using consciousness to heal. *Massage Ther J*. Fall 1995:47–48, 50, 52, 54, 56, 58, 60.
10. Leduc E. Therapeutic Touch. *Neonat Network*. 1987;5(6):46–47.
11. Krieger D. Therapeutic Touch during childbirth preparation by the Lamaze method and its relation to marital satisfaction and state anxiety of the married couple. In: Krieger D. *Living the Therapeutic Touch: Healing as a Lifestyle*. New York, NY: Dodd Mead; 1987:157–187.
12. Glazer S. The mystery of "Therapeutic Touch." *Washington Post*. December 19-26, 1995; Health section: 16–17.
13. Heidt PR. Effect of Therapeutic Touch on anxiety level of hospitalized patients. *Nurs Res*. 1981;30(1)32–37.

14. Quinn JF. *An Investigation of the Effects of Therapeutic Touch Done Without Physical Contact on State Anxiety of Hospitalized Cardiovascular Patients* [dissertation]. New York: New York University; 1982.
15. Thayer MB. Touching with intent: using Therapeutic Touch. *Pediatr Nurs.* 1990;16(l): 70–72.
16. Mersmann CA. *Therapeutic Touch and Milk Let Down in Mothers of Non-nursing Preterm Infants* [dissertation]. New York: New York University; 1993.
17. France NEM. The child's perception of the human energy field using Therapeutic Touch. *J Holistic Nurs.* 1993;11:319–331.
18. Meehan MTC. The Science of Unitary Human Beings and theory-based practice: Therapeutic Touch. In: Barrett EAM, ed. *Visions of Rogers' Science-Based Nursing*. New York, NY: National League for Nursing; 1990:67–81. Publication 15–2285.
19. Peters PJ. *The Lifestyle Changes of Selected Therapeutic Touch Practitioners: An Oral History* [dissertation]. Minneapolis, Minn: Walden University; 1992.
20. Boguslawski M. Therapeutic Touch: a facilitator of pain relief. *Top Clin Nurs.* 1980;2(1)27–37.
21. Satir F. Healing hands. *Olympian.* July 19, 1994.
22. Brown PR. *The Effects of Therapeutic Touch on Chemotherapy-induced Nausea and Vomiting: A Pilot Study* [master's thesis]. Reno: University of Nevada; 1981.
23. Sodergren KA. *The Effect of Absorption and Social Closeness on Responses to Educational and Relaxation Therapies in Patients With Anticipatory Nausea and Vomiting During Cancer Chemotherapy* [dissertation]. Minneapolis: University of Minnesota; 1993.
24. Dollar CE. *Effects of Therapeutic Touch on Perception of Pain and Physiological Measurements From Tension. Headache in Adults: A. Pilot Study* [master's thesis]. Jackson: University of Mississippi Medical Center; 1993.
25. Quinn JF. Holding sacred space: the nurse as healing environment. *Holistic Nurs Pract.* 1992;6(4):26–36.
26. Wirth DP. The effect of non-contact Therapeutic Touch on the healing rate of full thickness dermal wounds. *Subtle Energies.* 1990;1(1):1-20.
27. Woods DL. *The Effect of Therapeutic Touch on Disruptive Behaviors of Individuals With Dementia of the Alzheimer Type* [master's thesis]. Seattle: University of Washington; 1993.
28. Misra MM. *The Effects of Therapeutic Touch on Menstruation*. [master's thesis]. Long Beach: California State University; 1993.
29. Putnam ZE. The woman behind Therapeutic Touch: Dolores Krieger, PhD, RN. *Massage Ther J.* Fall 1995:50, 52.
30. Simington JA, LaingGP. Effects of Therapeutic Touch on anxiety in the institutionalized elderly. *Clin Nurs Res.* 1993;2:438–450.
31. Quinn J F. The Senior's Therapeutic Touch Education Program. *Holistic Nurs Pract.* 1992;7(1): 32–37.

32. Krieger D. Therapeutic Touch: two decades of research, teaching and clinical practice. *Imprint*. 1990;37:83, 86–88.
33. Fiely D. Field of beams. *Columbus Dispatch*. August 20, 1995:1B-2B.
34. Calvert R. Dolores Krieger, PhD, and her Therapeutic Touch. *Massage Magazine*. 1994;47:56–60.
35. Mueller Jackson ME. The use of Therapeutic Touch in the nursing care of the terminally ill person. In: Borelli MD, Heidt PR, eds. *Therapeutic Touch: A Book of Readings*. New York, NY: Springer; 1981:72–79.
36. Brunjes CAF. Therapeutic Touch: a healing modality throughout life. *TopClinNurs*. 1983;5(2):72–79.
37. Messenger TC, Roberts KT. The terminally ill: serenity nursing interventions for hospice clients. *J Gerontol Nurs*. 1994;20(11):17–22.
38. Maxwell J. Nursing's new age? *Christianity Today*. 1996;40(3):96–99.
39. Kauffold MP. TT: healing or hokum? debate over "energy medicine" runs hot. *Chicago Tribune Nursing News*. November 19, 1995:1.
40. Keegan L. Holistic nursing. *J Post Anesth Nurs*. 1989;4(1):17–21.
41. Bullough VL, Bullough B. Therapeutic Touch: why do nurses believe? *Skeptical Inquirer*. 1993:17: 169–174.
42. Dr Quinn studies Therapeutic Touch. *University of Colorado School of Nursing News*. May 1989:1.
43. Cabico LL. *A Phenomenological Study of the Experiences of Nurses Practicing Therapeutic Touch* [master's thesis]. Buffalo, NY: D'Youville College; 1992.
44. Rosa LA. When magic gets to play science. *Rocky Mountain Skeptic*. 1993;10(6): 10-12.
45. Carpenito LJ, ed. *Nursing Diagnosis: Application to Clinical Practice*. 6th ed. Philadelphia, Pa: Lippincott; 1995:355–358.
46. Sandroff R. A skeptic's guide to Therapeutic Touch. *RN*. 1980;43(l):24–30, 82–83.
47. Raucheisen ML. Therapeutic Touch: maybe there's something to it after all. *RN*. 1984;47(12):49–51.
48. Haddad A. Acute care decisions: ethics in action. *RN*. 1994;57(11):21–22, 24.
49. Swackhamer AH. It's time to broaden our practice. *RN*. 1995;58(1):49–51.
50. Schmidt CM. The basics of Therapeutic Touch. *RN*. 1995;58(6):50, 52, 54.
51. Ledwith SP. Therapeutic Touch and mastectomy: a case study. *RN*. 1995;58(7):51–53.
52. Keegan L, Cerrato PL. Nurses are embracing holistic healing. *RN*. 1996;59(4):59.
53. Moccia P, ed. *New Approaches to Theory Development*. New York, NY: National League for Nursing; 1986;15–1992.
54. Barrett EAM, ed. *Visions of Rogers' Science-Based Nursing*. New York, NY: National League for Nursing; 1990;15–2285.
55. Moccia P. Letter to the editor. *Time*. 1994;144 (24):18.
56. Krieger D. Therapeutic Touch: the imprimatur of nursing. *Am J Nurs*. 1975;75: 784–787.

57. Krieger D, Peper E, Ancoli S. Therapeutic Touch: searching for evidence of physiological change. *Am J Nurs*. 1979;79:660–662.
58. Macrae JA. Therapeutic Touch in practice. *Am J Nurs*. 1979;79:664–665.
59. Quinn JF. One nurse's evolution as a healer. *Am J Nurs*. 1979;79:662–664.
60. Mackey RB. Discover the healing power of Therapeutic Touch. *Am J Nurs*. 1995;95(4) 57-33.
61. Joel LA. Alternative solutions to health problems. *Am J Nurs*. 1995;95(7):7.
62. Hover-Kramer D. Healing Touch certificate program continues to bring the human dimension to the nation's nurses. *Beginnings*. 1992;12(2):3.
63. Cowens C, Monte T. *A Gift for Healing: How You Can Use Therapeutic Touch*. New York, NY: Crown Publishing Group; 1996.
64. Krieger D. The response of in-vivo human hemoglobin to an active healing therapy by direct laying on of hands. *Human Dimensions*. Autumn 1972: 12–15.
65. Krieger D. Therapeutic Touch and healing energies from the laying on of hands. *J Holistic Health*. 1975;1:23–30.
66. Krieger D. Therapeutic Touch: an ancient, but unorthodox nursing intervention. *J N Y State Nurs Assoc*. 1975;6(2):6–10.
67. Krieger D. Healing by the laying-on of hands as a facilitator of bio-energetic change: the response of in-vivo human hemoglobin. *Int J Psychoenergy Syst*. 1976;1(1):121–129.
68. Krieger D. The relationship of touch, with intent to help or to heal, to subjects' in-vivo hemoglobin values: a study in personalized interaction. In: *Proceedings of the Ninth ANA Nurses Research Conference*. New York, NY: American Nurses' Association; 1973:39–59.
69. Rogers ME. *An Introduction to the Theoretical Basis of Nursing*. Philadelphia, Pa: Davis; 1970.
70. Karagulla S, Kunz D. *The Chakras and the Human Energy Field: Correlations Between Medical Science & Clairvoyant Observation*. Wheaton, Ill: Theosophical Publishing House; 1989.
71. Randolph GL. The yin and yang of clinical practice. *Top Clin Nurs*. 1979;I(I):31–42.
72. Brierton TD. Employers' New Age training programs fail to alter the consciousness of the EEOC. *Lab Law J*. 1992;43:411–420.
73. Emery CE. Therapeutic Touch: healing technique or New Age rite? *Providence Sun Journal-Bulletin*. November 27, 1994:A1, A24.
74. Knaster M. Dolores Krieger's Therapeutic Touch. *East/West*. 1989;19(8):54–57, 59, 79–80.
75. Colorado State Board of Nursing. *Subcommittee to Investigate the Awarding of Continuing Education Units to Nurses for the Study of Therapeutic Touch and Other Non-traditional and Complementary Healing Modalities. Recommendations*. Denver: Colorado State Board of Nursing; 1992.

76. Mulloney SS, Wells-Federman C. Therapeutic Touch: a healing modality. *J Cardiovascul Nurs*. 1996, 10(3)57–49.
77. Brown CC, Fischer R, Wagman AMI, Horrom N, Marks P. The EEG in meditation and Therapeutic Touch healing. *J Altered States Conscious*. 1977; 3:169–180.
78. Quinn JF. Therapeutic Touch as energy exchange: testing the theory. *Adv Nurs Sci*. 1984;6(1): 4249.
79. Guerrero MA. *The Effects of Therapeutic Touch on State-Trait Anxiety Level of Oncology Patients* [master's thesis]. Galveston: University of Texas; 1985.
80. Keller EAK, Bzdek VM. Effects of Therapeutic Touch on tension headache pain. *Nurs Res*. 1986;35 (2):101–106.
81. Meehan MTC. Theory development. In: Barrett EAM, ed. *Visions of Rogers' Science-Based Nursing*. New York, NY: National League for Nursing; 1990;15–2285: 197–207.
82. Kramer NA. Comparison of Therapeutic Touch and Casual Touch in stress reduction of hospitalized children. *Pediatr Nurs*. 1990;16:483–485.
83. Shuzman E. *The Effect of Trait Anxiety and Patient Expectation of Therapeutic Touch on the Reduction in State Anxiety in Preoperative Patients Who Receive Therapeutic Touch* [dissertation]. New York: New York University; 1993.
84. Sies MM. *An Exploratory Study of Relaxation Response in Nurses Who Utilize Therapeutic Touch* [master's thesis]. East Lansing: Michigan State University; 1993.
85. Wirth DP, Richardson JT, Eidelman WS, O'Malley AC. Full thickness dermal wounds treated with Therapeutic Touch: a replication and extension. *Complementary Ther Med*. 1993;1:127–132.
86. Gagne D, Toye RC. The effects of Therapeutic Touch and relaxation therapy in reducing anxiety. *Arch Psych Nurs*. 1994;8:184–189.
87. Schlotfeldt RM. Critique of: Krieger D. The relationship of touch, with intent to help or heal, to subjects' in-vivo hemoglobin values: a study in personalized interaction. In: *Proceedings of the Ninth ANA Nurses Research Conference*. New York, NY: American Nurses' Association; 1973:59–65.
88. Walike BC, Bruno P, Donaldson S, et al. " ... [A]ttempts to embellish a totally unscientific process with the aura of science...." *Am J Nurs*. 1975; 75:1275, 1278, 1292.
89. Levine ME. "The science is spurious...." *Am J Nurs*. 1979;79:1379–1380.
90. Clark PE, Clark MJ. Therapeutic Touch: is there a scientific basis for the practice? *Nurs Res*. 1984; 33(1):3841.
91. Meehan MTC. Therapeutic Touch. In: Bulechek GM, McCloskey JC, eds. *Nursing Interventions: Essential Nursing Treatments*. 2nd ed. Philadelphia, Pa: Saunders; 1992501–212.
92. Fish S. Therapeutic Touch: can we trust the data? *J Christian Nurs*. 1993;10(3):6–8.
93. Meehan MTC. Therapeutic Touch and postoperative pain: a Rogerian research study. *Nurs Sci Q* 1993;6(2):69–78.

94. Bandman E L, Bandman B. *Critical Thinking in Nursing.* Norwalk, Conn: Appleton & Lange; 1995.
95. Meehan MTC. Quackery and pseudo-science. *Am J Nurs.* 1995;75(7):17.
96. Meehan MTC.... And still more on TT. *Res Nurs Health.* 1995;18:471–472.
97. Rosa LA. *Survey of Therapeutic Touch "Research."* Loveland, Colo: Front Range Skeptics; 1996.
98. Tharnstrom CAL. *The Effects of Non-contact Therapeutic Touch on the Parasympathetic Nervous System as Evidenced by Superficial Skin Temperature avid Perceived Stress* [master's thesis]. San Jose, Calif: San Jose State University; 1993.
99. Parkes BS. *Therapeutic Touch as an Intervention to Reduce Anxiety in Elderly Hospitalized Patients* [dissertation]. Austin: University of Texas; 1985.
100. Mueller Hinze ML. *The Effects of Therapeutic Touch and Acupressure on Experimentally-Induced Pain* [dissertation]. Austin: University of Texas; 1988.
101. Bowers DP. *The Effects of Therapeutic Touch on State Anxiety and Physiological Measurements in Preoperative Clients* [master's thesis]. San Jose, Calif: San Jose State University, 1992.
102. Ison M, Sneed NV. Anxiety and Therapeutic Touch. *Issues Ment Health Nurs.* 1995;16:97–108.
103. Fedoruk RB. *Transfer of the Relaxation Response: Therapeutic Touch as a Method for Reduction of Stress in Premature Neonates* [dissertation]. Baltimore: University of Maryland; 1984.
104. Hogg PK. *The Effects of Acupressure on the Psychological and Physiological Rehabilitation of the Stroke Patient* [dissertation]. Alameda: California School of Professional Psychology; 1985.
105. Snyder M, Egan EC, Bums KR. Interventions for decreasing agitation behaviors in persons with dementia. *J Gerontol Nurs.* 1995;21(7)34–40, 54–55.
106. Schweitzer SF. *The Effects of Therapeutic Touch on Short-term Memory Recall in the Aging Population: A Pilot Study* [master's thesis]. Reno: University of Nevada; 1980.
107. Randolph GL. Therapeutic and physical touch: physiological response to stressful stimuli. *Nurs Res.* 1984;33(l)53–36.
108. Nodine JL. *The Effects of Therapeutic Touch on Anxiety and Well-being in Third Trimester Pregnant Women* [master's thesis]. Tucson: University of Arizona; 1987.
109. Post NW. *The Effects of Therapeutic Touch on Muscle Tone* [master's thesis]. San Jose, Calif. San Jose State University; 1990.
110. Straneva JAE. *Therapeutic Touch and In Vitro Erythropoiesis* [dissertation]. Bloomington: Indiana University; 1992.
111. Bush AM, Geist CR. Testing electromagnetic explanations for a possible psychokinetic effect of Therapeutic Touch in germinating corn seed. *Psycholog Rep.* 1992;70:891–896.

112. Edge H. The effect of laying on of hands on an enzyme: an attempted replication. Paper presented at: 22nd Annual Convention of the Parapsychology Association; August 15-18, 1979; Moraga, Calif.
113. Meehan MTC. *The Effect of Therapeutic Touch on the Experience of Acute Pain in Postoperative Patients* [dissertation]. New York: New York University; 1985.
114. Hale EH. A *Study of the Relationship Between Therapeutic Touch and the Anxiety Levels of Hospitalized Adults* [dissertation], Denton: Texas Women's University; 1986.
115. Quinn JF. Therapeutic Touch as energy exchange: replication and extension. *Nurs Sci Q*. 1989; 2(2):79-87.
116. Claman HN, Freeman R, Quissel D, et al. *Report of the Chancellor's Committee on Therapeutic Touch*. Denver: University of Colorado Health Sciences Center; 1994.
117. Butgereit B. Therapeutic Touch: U AB to study controversial treatment for Pentagon. *Birmingham News*. November 17, 1994:1A, 10A.
118. Turner JG. *Tri-Service Nursing Research Grant Proposal* [revised abstract]. 1994. Grant No. MDA905-94-Z-0080.
119. Turner JG. *The Effect of Therapeutic Touch on Pain & Anxiety in Bum Patients* [grant final report]. Tri-Service Nursing Research Program; November 14, 1996. Grant No. N94020.
120. Lionbeiger HJ. Therapeutic Touch: a healing modality or a caring strategy. In: Chinn PL, ed. *Nursing Research Methodology: Issues and Implementation*. Rockville, Md: Aspen Publishers; 1986: 169-180.
121. Lionberger HJ. *An Interpretive Study of Nurses' Practice of Therapeutic Touch* [dissertation]. San Francisco: University of California; 1985.
122. Polk SH. *Client's Perceptions of Experiences Following the Intervention Modality of Therapeutic Touch* [master's thesis]. Tempe: Arizona State University; 1985.
123. Hamilton-Wyatt GK. *Therapeutic Touch: Promoting and Assessing Conceptual Change Among Health Care Professionals* [dissertation]. East Lansing: Michigan State University, 1988.
124. Heidt PR. Openness: a qualitative analysis of nurses' and patients' experiences of Therapeutic Touch. *Image J Nurs Sch*. 1990;22:180-186.
125. Thomas-Beckett J G. *Attitudes Toward Therapeutic Touch: A Pilot Study of Women With Breast Cancer* [master's thesis]. East Lansing: Michigan State University; 1991.
126. Clark AJ, Seifert P. Client perceptions of Therapeutic Touch. Paper presented at: Third Annual West Alabama Conference on Clinical Nursing Research; 1992.
127. Samarel N. The experience of receiving Therapeutic Touch. *J Adv Nurs*. 1992;17: 651-657.
128. Hughes PP. *The Experience of Therapeutic Touch as a Treatment Modality With Adolescent Psychiatric Patients* [master's thesis]. Albuquerque: University of New Mexico; 1994.
129. James Randi Educational Foundation. Available at: http://www.randi.org. Accessed March 15, 1997.

REVIEW AND CONTEMPLATE

1. What is Therapeutic Touch (TT)? What are the three basic steps in performing it?

2. Briefly describe the overall results of the 74 quantitative studies of TT identified by Rosa et al. (1998). Do they suggest that TT is an effective therapy?

3. Briefly describe the procedure used by Rosa et al. (1998) to test TT practitioners, and state the results.

4. The James Randi Educational Foundation offered $1 million to anyone who could demonstrate an ability to detect a human energy field. What was the result of this offer?

5. Which of the six characteristics of pseudoscience discussed in Chapter 1 seem most closely related to TT?

Chapter 10

SOCIAL PSYCHOLOGY

10.1 "Mass Delusions and Hysterias: Highlights From the Past Millennium"

ON THE EVENING of September 1, 1944, Mrs. Kearney went to bed with her 3-year-old daughter in Mattoon, Illinois. That evening, she detected a sweet smell in her bedroom. As the smell grew stronger, she began to feel paralysis in her legs and lower body. She suspected someone had gassed her, but a neighbor and the police could find no evidence of the mysterious gasser. Later, her husband reported seeing a prowler—dressed in dark clothes and a tight-fitting cap—near the bedroom window. Mr. Kearney chased the prowler, but the person escaped. The police were called a second time, but a thorough search of the neighborhood turned up nothing. On September 2, the local newspaper reported the story with the headline "'Anesthetic Prowler' on Loose." It wasn't long before Mattoon police received dozens of calls about similar gas attacks involving nearly 30 victims.

Today, scientists believe that the "Mad Gasser of Mattoon" never existed. Social psychologists who study social influence have known for a long time that people sometimes rely on others to help them interpret events and determine what actions to take, especially when they are unsure of themselves or when the situation is ambiguous. Thus, Mattoon residents who smelled an unusual odor or experienced ambiguous physical symptoms (e.g., nausea or a burning feeling in the throat) might have followed the lead of earlier "victims" by interpreting the event as gasser related and calling the police, even though no gasser existed.

In this article, Bartholomew and Goode (2000) discuss this event and other historical examples of mass delusions and hysterias, which illustrate the power of social forces to create widespread beliefs in paranormal or nonexistent phenomena. Thus, this article is a good illustration of how normal social processes can lead to paranormal beliefs, a point raised in Chapter 1.

Reference

Bartholomew, R. E., & Goode, E. (2000, May/June). Mass delusions and hysterias: Highlights from the past millennium. *Skeptical Inquirer, 24*, 20–28.

ARTICLE 10.1

"MASS DELUSIONS AND HYSTERIAS: HIGHLIGHTS FROM THE PAST MILLENNIUM"

ROBERT BARTHOLOMEW AND ERICH GOODE

Over the past millennium, mass delusions and hysterical outbreaks have taken many forms. Sociologists Robert Bartholomew and Erich Goode survey some of the more colorful cases.

The turn of the second millennium has brought about, in the Western world at least, an outpouring of concern about cosmic matters. A major portion of this concern has taken a delusional, even hysterical turn, specifically in imagining an end-of-the-world scenario. "The end of the world is near," predicts Karl de Nostredame, supposedly the "last living descendent" of Nostradamus; "White House knows doomsday date!" he claims (Wolfe 1999, 8). Against this backdrop, it seems an appropriate time to survey a sample of social delusions and group hysterias from the past millennium. Given the enormous volume of literature, we will limit our list to the more colorful episodes.

The study of collective delusions most commonly falls within the domain of sociologists working in the sub-field of collective behavior, and psychologists specializing in social psychology. Collective delusions are typified as the spontaneous, rapid spread of false or exaggerated beliefs within a population at large, temporarily affecting a particular region, culture, or country. Mass hysteria is most commonly studied by psychiatrists and physicians. Episodes typically affect small, tightly knit groups in enclosed settings such as schools, factories, convents and orphanages (Calmeil 1845; Hirsch 1883; Sirois 1974).

Mass hysteria is characterized by the rapid spread of conversion disorder, a condition involving the appearance of bodily complaints for which there is no organic basis. In such episodes, psychological distress is converted or channeled into physical symptoms. There are two common types: anxiety hysteria and motor hysteria. The former is of shorter duration, usually lasting a day, and is triggered by the sudden perception of a threatening agent, most commonly a strange odor. Symptoms typically include headache, dizziness, nausea, breathlessness, and general weakness. Motor hysteria is prevalent in intolerable social situations such as strict school and religious settings where discipline is excessive. Symptoms include trance-like states, melodramatic acts of rebellion known as histrionics, and what physicians term "psychomotor agitation" (whereby pent-up anxiety built up over a long period results in disruptions to the nerves or neurons that send messages to the muscles, triggering temporary bouts of twitching, spasms, and shaking). Motor hysteria appears gradually over time and usually takes weeks or months

Robert E. Bartholomew and E. Goode, "Mass Delusions and Hysterias: Highlights from the Past Millennium," *Skeptical Inquirer*, vol. 24, pp. 20-28. Copyright © 2000 by Center for Inquiry. Reprinted with permission.

to subside (Wessely 1987; Bartholomew and Sirois 1996). The term mass hysteria is often used inappropriately to describe collective delusions, as the overwhelming majority of participants are not exhibiting hysteria, except in extremely rare cases. In short, all mass hysterias are collective delusions as they involve false or exaggerated beliefs, but only rarely do collective delusions involve mass hysteria as to do so, they must report illness symptoms.

Many factors contribute to the formation and spread of collective delusions and hysterical illness: the mass media; rumors; extraordinary anxiety or excitement; cultural beliefs and stereotypes; the social and political context; and reinforcing actions by authorities such as politicians, or institutions of social control such as the police or military. Episodes are also distinguishable by the redefinition of mundane objects, events, and circumstances and reflect a rapidly spreading folk belief which contributes to an emerging definition of the situation … .

MILAN, ITALY, 1630

British journalist Charles Mackay (1852, 261–265) described a poisoning scare that terrorized Milan, Italy, in 1630, coinciding with pestilence, plague, and a prediction that the Devil would poison the city's water supply. On one April morning people awoke, and became fearful upon finding "that all the doors in the principal streets of the city were marked with a curious daub, or spot." Soon there was alarm that the sign of the awaited poisoning was at hand, and the belief spread that corn and fruit had also been poisoned. Many people were executed. One elderly man was spotted wiping a stool before sitting on it, when he was accused of smearing poison on the seat. He was seized by an angry mob of women and pulled by the hair to a judge, but died on the way. In another incident, a pharmacist and barber named Mora was found with several preparations containing unknown potions and accused of being in cahoots with the Devil to poison the city. Protesting his innocence, he eventually confessed after prolonged torture on the rack, admitting to cooperating with the Devil and foreigners to poisoning the city and anointing the doors. Under duress he named several accomplices who were eventually arrested and tortured. They were all pronounced guilty and executed. Mackay states that "The number of persons who confessed that they were employed by the Devil to distribute poison is almost incredible," noting that "day after day persons came voluntarily forward to accuse themselves" (264).

LILLE, FRANCE, 1639

Mackay (1852, 539–540) reports that in 1639 at an all-girls' school in Lille, France, fifty pupils were convinced by their overzealous teacher that they were under Satanic influence. Antoinette Bourgignon had the children believing that "little black angels" were flying about their heads, and that the Devil's imps were everywhere. Soon, each of the students confessed to witchcraft, flying on broomsticks and even eating baby flesh. The students came close to being burned at the stake but were spared when blame shifted to the headmistress, who escaped at the last minute. The episode occurred near the end of the Continental European witch mania of 1400 to 1650, when at least 200,000 people were executed following allegations of witchcraft.

SALEM, MASSACHUSETTS, 1691–1693

In 1692, Salem Village (now Danvers, Massachusetts) was the scene of a moral panic that spread throughout the region and involved witchcraft accusations which led to trials, torture, imprisonment, and executions. Others died in jail or during torture. At least twenty residents lost their lives. Social paranoia was such that two dogs were even accused and executed! All convictions were based on ambiguous evidence. The witch mania began in December 1691, when eight girls living in the vicinity of Salem exhibited strange behaviors including disordered speech, convulsive movements, and bizarre conduct. Explanations for the "fits" range from outright fakery to hysteria to ergot poisoning of the food supply. By February 1692, the affected girls had accused two elderly women and a servant from Barbados named Tibula of being witches, and they were arrested. Soon hundreds of residents were accused of witchcraft, and trials were held. In May 1693, the episode ended when Governor Phips ordered that all suspects be released (Nevins 1916; Caporael 1976; Karlsen 1989).

LONDON, ENGLAND, 1761

On February 8, 1761, a minor earthquake struck London, damaging several chimneys. When another tremor occurred on the following month on the exact day as the first (March 8), the coincidence became the subject of widespread discussion. According to Mackay (1852), a lifeguard named Bell then predicted that London would be destroyed in a third quake on April 5, "As the awful day approached, the excitement became intense, and great numbers of credulous people resorted to all the villages within a circuit of twenty miles, awaiting the doom of London" (259). People paid exorbitant fees to temporarily board with households in such places as Highgate, Hampstead, Islington, Blackheath, and Harrow. The poor stayed in London until two or three days before the predicted event before leaving to camp in fields in the countryside. When the designated time arrived, nothing happened.

LEEDS, ENGLAND, 1806

In 1806, a panic spread through Leeds and the surrounding communities that the end of the world was at hand. The "panic terror" began when a hen from a nearby village was said to begin laying eggs inscribed with the message, "Christ is coming." Large numbers flocked to the site to examine the eggs and see the "miracle" firsthand. Many were convinced that the end was near and suddenly became devoutly religious. Mackay (1852, 261) states that excitement then quickly turned to disappointment when a man "caught the poor hen in the act of laying one of her miraculous eggs" and soon determined "that the egg had been inscribed with some corrosive ink, and cruelly forced up again into the bird's body...."

BRITISH SOUTH AFRICA, 1914

In the war scare setting of British South Africa in 1914, local newspapers erroneously reported that hostile monoplanes from adjacent German South West Africa were making reconnaissance flights as a prelude to an imminent attack. The episode coincided with the start of World War I. Despite the technological impossibility of such missions (the maneuvers reported by witnesses were beyond those of airplanes of the period and their capability of staying aloft for long periods), thousands of residents misperceived ambiguous, nocturnal aerial stimuli (stars and planets) as representing enemy monoplanes (Bartholomew 1989).

ISLAND OF BANDA, INDONESIA, 1937

During March 1937, the first Indonesian Prime Minister, Soetan Sjahrir, was living on the Moluccan island of Banda, where he described a head-hunting rumor-panic which swept through his village. The episode coincided with rumors that a tjoelik (someone who engages in head-hunting for the government) was operating in the area and searching for a head to be placed near a local jetty that was being rebuilt. According to tradition, government construction projects will soon crumble without such an offering. Sjahrir (1949) said that "people have been living in fear" and were "talking and whispering about it everywhere" (162), and after 7 p.m. the streets were nearly deserted. There were many reports of strange noises and sightings. Sjahrir stated: "Every morning there are new stories, generally about footsteps or voices, or a house that was bombarded with stones, or an attack on somebody by a tjoelik with a noose, or a cowboy lasso. Naturally, the person who was attacked got away from the tjoelik in a nick of time!" (164). Sjahrir described the scare as an example of "mass psychosis."

USA, 1938

On Halloween Eve 1938, a live fictional radio drama produced by Orson Welles was broadcast across much of the United States by the CBS Mercury Theatre. It depicted an invasion by Martians who had landed in Grovers Mill, New Jersey, and soon began attacking with heat rays and poison gas. Princeton University psychologist Hadley Cantril (1940) concluded that an estimated 1.2 million listeners became excited, frightened, or disturbed. However, subsequent reviews of Cantril's findings by sociologists David Miller (1985), William Sims Bainbridge (1987), and others, concluded that there was scant evidence of substantial or widespread panic. For instance, Miller found little evidence of mobilization, an essential ingredient in a panic. Hence, it was a collective delusion and not a true panic. Cantril also exaggerated the extent of the mobilization, attributing much of the typical activity at the time to the "panic." In short, many listeners may have expressed concern but did not do anything in response, like try to flee, grab a gun for protection, or barricade themselves inside a house. Either way one looks at this episode, it qualifies as a collective delusion. If, as Cantril originally asserted, many listeners were frightened and panicked, it is a mass delusion. Conversely, if we are to accept the more recent and likely assessments that the "panic" was primarily a media creation inadvertently fueled by Cantril's flawed study, then erroneous depictions of a mass panic that have been recounted in numerous books and articles for over six decades constitute an equally remarkable social delusion.

MAD GASSER OF MATTOON, 1944

During the first two weeks of September 1944, residents of Mattoon, Illinois, were thrust into the world media spotlight after a series of imaginary gas attacks by a "phantom anesthetist." On Friday night, September 1, Mattoon police received a phone call that a woman and her daughter had been left nauseated and dizzy after being sprayed with a sweet-smelling gas by a mysterious figure lurking near their bedroom window. The woman also said she experienced slight, temporary difficulty in walking. Despite the ambiguous circumstances and lack of evidence, the following evening the incident was afforded sensational coverage in the Mattoon Daily Journal-Gazette ("Anesthetic Prowler on Loose"). After seeing the story, two other Mattoon families recounted for police similar "gas attacks" in their homes just prior to the incident.

Before the reports ceased (after September 12), police logged over two dozen separate calls involving at least twenty-nine victims, most of whom were females. University of Illinois researcher Donald Johnson (1945) investigated the episode, concluding that it was a case of mass hysteria. Their transient symptoms included nausea, vomiting, dry mouth, palpitations, difficulty walking, and in one instance, a burning sensation in the mouth. Given the influential role of the Mattoon news media, it may be that victims were redefining mundane symptoms such as a panic attack, chemical smell, one's leg "falling asleep," and the consequences of anxiety such as nausea, insomnia, shortness of breath, shakiness, dry mouth, dizziness, etc. as gasser-related.

"MIRACLE" IN PUERTO RICO, 1953

At 11 a.m. on May 25, 1953, an estimated 150,000 people converged on a well at Rincorn, Puerto Rico, to await the appearance of the Virgin Mary as predicted by seven local children. Over the next six hours, a team of sociologists led by Melvin Tumin and Arnold Feldman (1955) mingled in the crowd conducting interviews. During this period, some people reported seeing colored rings encircling the sun, and a silhouette of the Virgin in the clouds, while others experienced healings, and a general sense of well-being. Others neither saw nor experienced anything extraordinary. A media frenzy preceded the event, and a local mayor enthusiastically organized the visionaries to lead throngs of pilgrims in mass prayers and processions. Tumin and Feldman found that the majority of pilgrims believed in the authenticity of the children's claim, and were seeking cures for conditions that physicians had deemed incurable. Various ambiguous objects in the immediate surroundings (clouds, trees, etc.) mirrored the hopeful and expectant religious state of mind of many participants.

SEATTLE WINDSHIELD PITTING EPIDEMIC, 1954

On March 23, 1954, reports appeared in Seattle newspapers of damaged automobile windshields in a city eighty miles to the north. While initially suspecting vandals, the number of cases spread, causing growing concern. In time, reports of damaged windshields moved closer to Seattle. According to a study by Nahum Medalia of the Georgia Institute of Technology and Otto Larsen of the University of Washington (1958), by nightfall on April 14, the mysterious pits first reached the city, and by the end of the next day, weary police had answered 242 phone calls from concerned residents, reporting tiny pit marks on over 3,000 vehicles. In some cases, whole parking lots were reportedly affected. The reports quickly declined and ceased. On April 16 police logged forty-six pitting claims, and ten the next day, after which no more reports were received.

The most common damage report involved claims that tiny pit marks grew into dime-sized bubbles embedded within the glass, leading to a folk theory that sand-flea eggs had somehow been deposited in the glass and later hatched. The sudden presence of the "pits" created widespread anxiety as they were typically attributed to atomic fallout from hydrogen bomb tests that had been recently conducted in the Pacific and received saturation media publicity. At the height of the incident on the night of April 15, the Seattle mayor even sought emergency assistance from President Dwight Eisenhower.

In the wake of rumors of radioactive fallout and a few initial cases amplified in the media, residents began looking at, instead of through, their windshields. An analysis of the mysterious black, sooty grains that dotted many windshields was carried out at the Environmental Research Laboratory at the University of Washington. The material was identified as cenospheres—tiny particles produced by the incomplete combustion of bituminous coal. The particles had been a common feature of everyday life in Seattle, and could not pit or penetrate windshields.

Medalia and Larsen noted that because the pitting reports coincided with the H-Bomb tests, media publicity seems to have reduced tension about the possible consequences of the bomb tests—"something was bound to happen to us as a result of the H-bomb tests—windshields became pitted—it's happened—now that threat is over" (186). Secondly, the very act of phoning police and appeals by the mayor to the governor and even President of the United States "served to give people the sense that they were 'doing something' about the danger that threatened" (186).

PHANTOM SLASHER OF TAIWAN, 1956

For a two-week period in 1956, residents in the vicinity of Taipei, Taiwan, lived in fear that they would be the next victim of a crazed villain who was prowling the city and slashing people at random with a razor or similar type weapon. At least twenty-one slashing victims were reported during this period, mostly women and children of low income and education. Norman Jacobs was teaching in Taipei at the time, and conducted a survey of local press coverage of the slasher. Jacobs concluded that those affected had erroneously attributed mundane slash marks to a dastardly slasher (Jacobs 1965).

Rumors amplified by sensational press coverage treating the slasher's existence as real served to foment the scare by altering the public's outlook to include the reality of a daring slasher. Police eventually concluded that the various "slashings" had resulted from inadvertent, everyday contact in public places, that ordinarily would have gone relatively unnoticed. For instance, one man told police in detail how he had been slashed by a man carrying mysterious black bag. When a doctor determined that the wound was made by a blunt object and not a razor, the "victim" admitted that he could not recall exactly what had happened, but assumed that he had been slashed "because of all the talk going around." In another case, it was not the supposed victim but physicians who were responsible for creating an incident. An elderly man with a wrist laceration sought medical treatment but the attending doctor grew suspicious and contacted police when the man casually noted that a stranger had coincidentally touched him at about the same time when he first noticed the bleeding. A more thorough examination led to the conclusion that the "slash" was an old injury that had been re-opened after inadvertent scratching.

On May 12 police announced the results of their investigation: they concluded that the episode was entirely psychological in origin. Of the twenty-one slashing claims examined by their office, they determined that "five were innocent false reports, seven were self-inflicted cuts, eight were due to cuts other than razors, and one was a complete fantasy" (Jacobs, 1965, 324).

FIRST FLYING SAUCER WAVE, 1947

On June 24, 1947, Kenneth Arnold was piloting his private plane near the Cascade mountains in Washington state when he saw what appeared to be nine glittering objects flying in echelon-like formation near Mount Rainier. He kept the objects in sight for about three minutes before they traveled south over Mount Adams and were lost to view (Arnold 1950; Arnold and Palmer 1952; Gardner 1988; Clark 1998, 139–143).

Worried that he may have observed guided missiles from a foreign power, Arnold eventually flew to Pendleton, Oregon, where he tried reporting what he saw to the FBI office there. But the office was closed, so he went to the offices of The East Oregonian newspaper. After listening to Arnold's story, journalist Bill Bequette produced a report for the Associated Press. It is notable that at this point, Arnold had described the objects as crescent-shaped, referring only to their movement as "like a saucer would if you skipped it across the water" (Gardner 1957, 56; Story 1980, 25; Sachs 1980, 207–208). However, the Associated Press account describing Arnold's "saucers" appeared in over 150 newspapers.

The AP report filed by Bequette was the proto-article from which the term "flying saucer" was created by headline writers on June 25 and 26, 1947 (Strentz 1970). Of key import was Bequette's use of the term "saucer-like" in describing Arnold's sighting. Bequette's use of the word "saucer" provided a motif for the worldwide wave of flying saucer sightings during the summer of 1947, and other waves since. There are a few scattered historical references to disc-shaped objects, but no consistent pattern emerges until 1947, with Arnold's sighting. There have only been a handful of occasions prior to 1947 that a witness has actually used the word "saucer" to describe mysterious aerial objects. Hence, the global 1947 flying saucer wave can be regarded as a media-generated collective delusion unique to the twentieth century....

THE HISPANIC GOATSUCKER, 1975 TO PRESENT

Between February and March 1975, reports circulated in Puerto Rico of a mysterious creature attacking domestic and farm animals, draining their blood and scooping out chunks of their flesh. Residents claimed that they heard loud screeches and/or flapping wings coinciding with the attacks. Academics and police examined the carcasses, blaming everything from humans to snakes to vampire bats. Locals referred to the attacker as "The Vampire of Moca." This incident may have been spurred by the better known "cattle mutilation mystery" (Ellis 1996, 3). In November 1995, similar attacks were reported on the island. Called chupacabras or goatsucker, (named after a crepuscular bird that steals goat's milk), the bizarre being was described as a "bristly, bulge-eyed rat with the hind legs of a kangaroo, capable of escaping after its crimes in high speed sprints" (Preston 1996). It also exuded a sulfur-like stench. Stories described the bodies of animals disemboweled and drained of blood. One member of a Civil Defense team in a small city in the affected area says he spends half his time responding to chupacabras calls. Some people, he reported, have been so distraught "that they have had to be taken to the hospital" (Navarro 1996). Interest in the creature ran so high on May 1996 that a chupacabras Web site received enough hits to be ranked in the top 5 percent of all Web sites (Ellis 1996, 2). By March 1996, goatsucker stories had spread to Hispanic communities in Florida; by May, accounts of chupacabras attacks began to circulate in Mexico and soon after, to the Mexican-American community in Arizona. The chupacabras flap ended abruptly in mid-1996, and almost nothing has been reported on it since....

WEST BANK, JORDAN, 1983

Between March and April 1983, 947 mostly female residents of the Israeli-occupied Jordan West Bank reported various psychogenic symptoms: fainting, headache, abdominal pain, and dizziness (Modan et al., 1983). The episode was precipitated by poison gas rumors and a long-standing Palestinian mistrust of Jews. The medical complaints appeared during a fifteen-day period, amid rumors and intense media publicity that poison gas was being sporadically targeted at Palestinians. The episode began in, and was predominantly confined to, schools in several adjacent villages. In one incident on March 27, sixty-four residents in Jenin were rushed for local medical care after believing that they had been poisoned when thick smoke belched from an apparently faulty exhaust system on a passing car. In all, 879 females were affected. Following negative medical tests, it became evident that no gassings had occurred, the hypothesis was discredited, and the transient symptoms rapidly ceased.

MASS DELUSION BY PROXY IN GEORGIA, 1988

A rarely reported form of what could be described as mass delusion by proxy occurred at a Georgia elementary school near Atlanta in 1988. It involved the re-labelling of mundane symptoms that were instigated and maintained by erroneous beliefs among hypervigilant parents. The episode began during a routine social gathering of parents and students at the school cafeteria in early September. A student's mother commented that, ever since the term began, her child had experienced numerous minor health problems and looked pale. Other mothers at the meeting noted similar signs and symptoms in their children since the beginning of the school term: pallor, dark circles under the eyes, headaches, fatigue, nausea and occasional vomiting. They soon suspected that something in the school building was to blame, a view confirmed on October 11 when the school was evacuated after a minor natural gas leak occurred during routine maintenance. When intermittent minor gas leaks continued over the next month, concerned parents picketed the school and appealed to the local media, which highlighted their fears. After negative environmental and epidemiological studies, Philen et al. (1989) concluded that mothers had almost exclusively redefined common and everpresent childhood illnesses, while the children in question neither sought attention nor were overly concerned with their symptoms, maintaining high attendance levels throughout the term.

KOSOVO, 1990

On March 14, 1990, at least four thousand residents in the Serbian province of Kosovo, in the former Yugoslavia, were struck down by a mystery illness that persisted for some three weeks. According to Dr. Zoran Radovanovic (1995), the head of the community medicine faculty at Kuwait University, the symptoms were psychogenic in nature and prompted by ethnic Albanian mistrust of Serbs. The transient complaints were almost exclusively confined to young adolescent ethnic Albanians, and included headache, dizziness, hyperventilation, weakness, burning sensations, cramps, chest pain, nausea, and dry mouth. The episode began at a high school in Podujevo, and rapidly spread to dozens of schools within the province. An outbreak of respiratory infection within a single class appears to have triggered fears that Serbs may have dispensed poison. Influential factors included rumors, the scrutinization of mundane odors and substances, visits by health authorities that served to legitimate fears, ethnic tension between Serbs and Albanians, and mass communication. The dramatic proliferation of cases across the province on March 22 coincided with the implementation of an emergency disaster plan whereby ethnic Albanians seized control of public health services.

NIGERIAN GENITALIA VANISHING EPIDEMIC OF 1990

During 1990, an episode of "vanishing" genitalia caused widespread fear across Nigeria. Native psychiatrist Sunny Ilechukwu (1992) said that most reports of attacks involved male victims. Accusations were usually triggered by incidental body contact with a stranger in a public place, after which the "victim" would feel strange scrotum sensations and grab their genitals to confirm that they were still there. Then they would confront the person as a crowd would gather, accusing them of being a genital thief, before stripping naked to convince bystanders that their penis was really missing. Many "victims" claimed that the penis had been returned once the alarm had been raised or that, although the penis was now back, "it was shrunken and so probably a 'wrong' one or just the ghost of a penis" (95). The accused was often threatened or beaten until the penis had been "fully restored," and in some instances, the accused was beaten to death. Ilechukwu (1992, 96) described the scene in one city: Men could be seen in the streets of Lagos holding on to their genitalia either openly or discreetly with their hands in their pockets. Women were also seen holding on to their breasts directly or discreetly by crossing the hands across the chest. It was thought that inattention and a weak will facilitated the "taking" of the penis or breasts. Vigilance and anticipatory aggression were thought to be good prophylaxis.

Social and cultural traditions contributed to the outbreak as many Nigerian ethnic groups "ascribe high potency to the external genitalia as ritual and magical objects to promote fecundity or material prosperity to the unscrupulous" (Ilechukwu 1988, 313). The belief in vanishing genitalia was not only plausible but institutionalized; many influential Nigerians expressed outrage when police released suspected genital thieves. A Christian priest even claimed that a Bible passage where Jesus asked "Who touched me?" because the "power had gone out of him," referred to genital stealing (101–102).

CONCLUDING REMARKS

The next one thousands years will yield a new batch of social delusions and hysterical outbreaks that will reflect the hopes and fears of future generations. While it is not possible to know the exact nature of these episodes, we can confidently predict one of the first delusions of this period. For at the start of the second Christian millennium, we should be mindful that the millennial notion is itself a social delusion. The concept does not exist in nature but is a human creation—a product of history and circumstance. It has no significance beyond the meaning that humans attach to it. Yet, students of history know well that the consequences of beliefs can enormously influence the course of history.

REFERENCES

Arnold, K. 1950. *The Flying Saucer As I Saw It*. Boise, Idaho: Self-published.

Arnold, K., and R. A. Palmer. 1952. *The Coming of the Saucers: A Documentary Report on Sky Objects that Have Mystified the World*. Amherst, Wisconsin: Self-published.

Bainbridge, W. S. 1987. Collective behavior and social movements. Pp. 544-576. In R. Stark (ed.), *Sociology*. Belmont, California: Wadsworth.

Bartholomew, R. E. 1989. The South African monoplane hysteria; An evaluation of the usefulness of Smelser's Theory of Hysterical Beliefs. *Sociological Inquiry 59(3)*: 287-300.

Bartholomew, R. E., and F. Sirois. 1996. Epidemic hysteria in schools: An international and historical overview. *Educational Studies 22(3):* 285-311.

Barnes, R. H. 1993. Construction sacrifice, kidnapping and headhunting rumours on flores and elsewhere in Indonesia. *Oceania 64:* 146-158.

Bulgatz, J. 1992. *Ponzi Schemes, Invaders from Mars & More Extraordinary Popular Delusions and the Madness of Crowds*. New York: Harmony Books.

Calmell, L. F. 1845. *De la Folie, Consideree Sous le Point de vue Pathologigue, Philosophique, Historique et Judiciaire* [On the Crowd, Considerations on the Point of Pathology, Philosophy, History and Justice], Paris: Ballere.

Cantril, H. 1940 [1947]. *The Invasion From Mars: A Study in the Psychology of Panic*. Princeton, New Jersey: Princeton University Press.

Caporael, L. 1976. Ergotism: The Satan loosed in Salem? *Science 192:21-26*.

Clark, J. 1998. *The UFO Encyclopedia: The Phenomenon from the Beginning*. Volume One: A-K (second edition). Omnigraphics, Incorporated: Detroit, Michigan.

Darnton, R. 1984. *The Great Cat Massacre and Other Episodes in French Cultural History*. New York: Basic Books.

Drake, R. A. 1989. Construction sacrifice and kidnapping: Rumor panics in Borneo. *Oceania 59:269-278*.

Ellis, B. 1996. Chupacabras mania spreads. *Foaftale News 39:2-3*.

Forth, G. 1991. Construction sacrifice and head-hunting rumours in central Flores (Eastern Indonesia): A Comparative Note. *Oceania 61:257-266*.

Gardner, M. 1988. *The New Age: Notes of a Fringe Watcher*. Buffalo, New York: Prometheus Books.

Gardner, M. 1957. *Fads and Fallacies in the Name of Science*. New York: Dover.

Griggs, W. N. 1852. *The Celebrated 'Moon Story.'* New York: Bunnell and Price.

Hecker, J. F. C. 1844. *Epidemics of the Middle Ages* (translated from German by B. Babington) London: The Sydenham Society.

Hirsch, A. 1883. Handbook of Geographical and Historical Pathology. New Sydenham Society: London.

Ilechukwu, S. T. C. 1992. Magical penis loss in Nigeria: Report of a recent epidemic of a koro-like syndrome. Transcultural Psychiatric Research Review 29:91-108.

———. Letter from S. T. C. Ilechukwu, M. D. (Lagos, Nigeria) which describes interesting koro-like syndromes in Nigeria. Transcultural Psychiatric Research Review 25:310-314.

Jacobs, N. 1965. The phantom slasher of Taipei: Mass hysteria in a non-western society. Social Problems 12:318-328.

Johnson, D. M. 1945. The "Phantom Anesthetist" of Mattoon: A field study of mass hysteria. Journal of Abnormal and Social Psychology 40:175-186.

Johnston, F. 1980. When Millions Saw Mary. Chulmleigh, England: Augustine Publishing.

Karlsen, C. F. 1989. The Devil in the Shape of a Woman: Witchcraft in Colonial New England. New York: Vintage.

Mackay, C. 1852. Memoirs of Extraordinary Popular Delusions and the Madness of Crowds Volume 2. London: Office of the National Illustrated Library.

Madden, R. R. 1857. Phantasmata or Illusions and Fanaticisms of Protean of Protean Forms Productive of Great Evils. T. C. Newby: London.

Medalia, N. Z., and O. Larsen. 1958. Diffusion and belief in a collective delusion. Sociological Review 23:180-186.

Miller, D. 1985. Introduction to Collective Behavior. Belmont, Calif.: Wadsworth.

Modan, B., M. Tirosh, E. Weissenberg, C. Acker, T., Swartz, C. Coston, A., Donagi, M. Revach, and G. Vettorazzi. 1983. The Arjenyattah epidemic. Lancet ii:1472-1476.

Navarro, M. 1996. A monster on loose? Or is it fantasy? The New York Times, January 26, p. A10.

Nevins, W. S. 1916. Witchcraft in Salem Village. Franklin: New York.

Persinger, M., and J. Derr. 1989. Geophysical variables and behavior: LIV. Zeitoun (Egypt) Apparitions of the Virgin Mary as tectonic strain-induced luminosities. Perceptual and Motor Skills 68:123-128.

Philen, R. M., E. M. Kilbourn, and T. W. McKinley. 1989. Mass sociogenic illness by proxy: Parentally reported in an elementary school. Lancet ii: 1372-1376.

Preston, J. 1996. In the tradition of Bigfoot and Elvis, the Goatsucker. The New York Times, June, 2, p. 2E.

Radovanovic, Z. 1995. On the origin of mass casualty incidents in Kosovo, Yugoslavia, in 1990. European Journal of Epidemiology 11:1-13.

Rockney, R. M., and T. Lemke. 1992. Casualties from a junior high school during the Persian Gulf War: Toxic poisoning or mass hysteria? Journal of Developmental and Behavioral Pediatrics 13:339-342.

Sachs, M. 1980. The UFO Encyclopedia. New York: Perigee.

Sirois, F. 1974. Epidemic hysteria. Acta Psychiatrica Scandinavica Supplementum 252:7-46.

Sjahrir, S. 1949. Out of Exile (translated from Dutch by Charles Wolf). New York: Greenwood Press.

Story, R. 1980. The Encyclopedia of UFOs. New York: Doubleday.

Strentz, H. J. 1970. A Survey of Press Coverage of Unidentified Flying Objects, 1947-1966. Doctoral Dissertation, Northwestern University, Department of Journalism.

Tumin, M. M., and A. S. Feldman. 1955. The miracle at Sabana Grande. Public Opinion Quarterly 19:124-139.

Wessely, S. 1987. Mass hysteria: Two syndromes? Psychological Medicine 17:109-120.

Wolfe, R. 1999. Weekly World News, September 28:8-9.

REVIEW AND CONTEMPLATE

1. What are collective delusions and mass hysteria? Which term best characterizes the poisoning scare of Milan, Italy in 1630?

2. Describe the "miracle" in Puerto Rico in 1953 and explain how it is related to the concept of perceptual set (consult an introductory psychology textbook for information about perceptual set).

3. What evidence suggests that flying saucer sightings in 1947 were a collective delusion prompted by the media?

4. Describe two historical examples of mass hysteria.

5. Which of the two major themes of this book discussed in Chapter 1 seem most closely related to this article? Explain your answer.

10.2 "Does Venting Anger Feed or Extinguish the Flame? Catharsis, Rumination, Distraction, Anger, and Aggressive Responding"

THE WEBSITE FOR Sin City Smash explains that it is a "a recreational rage room facility in Las Vegas, NV dedicated to providing Destruction Therapy to the masses." They explain that

> stress can negatively affect you both mentally and physically ... [and] play a role in the increased suicide rates, substance abuse, depression, and violent crimes. That's why we built a rage room ... that provides a safe, fun environment for people like you and me who experience very normal feelings of sadness, depression, anxiety, and stress to release these feelings appropriately. Essentially we're encouraging you to take your anger and frustration out on us!

In their rage room, customers can enter a room full of furniture, appliances, and other objects that they can smash with sledgehammers and other tools. Destruction therapy (or destructotherapy) started in Spain in 2003, and it has inspired a number of rage rooms (also referred to as anger rooms or wrecking clubs) in cities across the United States.

Can releasing anger, stress, and aggressive impulses actually improve a person's emotions and health, as suggested by the owners of Sin City Smash? Sigmund Freud believed that human aggression results from an inborn drive within us and that if we do not release our aggressive impulses, they could build up over time, causing us psychological problems or leading us to "explode" in an aggressive rage. Freud believed in catharsis, or the idea that venting our anger should decrease our aggressive urges. Thus, he would predict that smashing objects in a rage room would have positive effects on our emotions and behavior, leading to a decrease in anger and aggressive behavior. The idea of catharsis is still popular among the general public, and I am sure it's partly responsible for the development of destructotherapy and rage rooms across the country.

A crucial question for assessing the potential of rage rooms or destructotherapy to improve our well-being is whether releasing anger actually decreases anger and aggressive behavior or has the opposite effect. In this article, social psychologist Brad Bushman describes the results of a study in which he put the catharsis hypothesis to the test.

Reference

Bushman, B. J. (2002). Does venting anger feed or extinguish the flame? Catharsis, rumination, distraction, anger, and aggressive responding. *Personality and Social Psychology Bulletin, 28,* 724–731.

ARTICLE 10.2

"DOES VENTING ANGER FEED OR EXTINGUISH THE FLAME? CATHARSIS, RUMINATION, DISTRACTION, ANGER, AND AGGRESSIVE RESPONDING"

BRAD BUSHMAN

Does distraction or rumination work better to diffuse anger? Catharsis theory predicts that rumination works best, but empirical evidence is lacking. In this study, angered participants hit a punching bag and thought about the person who had angered them (rumination group) or thought about becoming physically fit (distraction group). After hitting the punching bag, they reported how angry they felt. Next, they were given the chance to administer loud blasts of noise to the person who had angered them. There also was a no punching bag control group. People in the rumination group felt angrier than did people in the distraction or control groups. People in the rumination group were also most aggressive, followed respectively by people in the distraction and control groups. Rumination increased rather than decreased anger and aggression. Doing nothing at all was more effective than venting anger. These results directly contradict catharsis theory.

The belief in the value of venting anger has become widespread in our culture. In movies, magazine articles, and even on billboards, people are encouraged to vent their anger and "blow off steam." For example, in the movie *Analyze This*, a psychiatrist (played by Billy Crystal) tells his New York gangster client (played by Robert De Niro), "You know what I do when I'm angry? I hit a pillow. Try that." The client promptly pulls out his gun, points it at the couch, and fires several bullets into the pillow. "Feel better?" asks the psychiatrist. "Yeah, I do," says the gunman. In a *Vogue* magazine article, female model Shalom concludes that boxing helps her release pent-up anger. She said,

> I found myself looking forward to the chance to pound out the frustrations of the week against Carlos's (her trainer) mitts. Let's face it: A personal boxing trainer has advantages over a husband or lover. He won't look at you accusingly and say, "I don't know where this irritation is coming from." ... Your boxing trainer knows it's in there. And he wants you to give it to him. ("Fighting Fit," 1993, p. 179)

In a *New York Times Magazine* article about hate crimes, Andrew Sullivan writes, "Some expression of prejudice serves a useful purpose. It lets off steam; it allows natural tensions to express themselves incrementally; it can siphon off conflict through words, rather

Brad J. Bushman, "Does Venting Anger Feed or Extinguish the Flame? Catharsis, Rumination, Distraction, Anger, and Aggressive Responding," *Personality and Social Psychology Bulletin*, vol. 28, no. 6, pp. 724-731. Copyright © 2002 by SAGE Publications. Reprinted with permission.

than actions" (Sullivan, 1999, p. 113). A large billboard in Missouri states, "Hit a Pillow, Hit a Wall, But Don't Hit Your Kids!"

Catharsis Theory

The theory of catharsis is one popular and authoritative statement that venting one's anger will produce a positive improvement in one's psychological state. The word *catharsis* comes from the Greek word *katharsis*, which literally translated means a cleansing or purging. According to catharsis theory, acting aggressively or even viewing aggression is an effective way to purge angry and aggressive feelings.

Sigmund Freud believed that repressed negative emotions could build up inside an individual and cause psychological symptoms, such as hysteria (nervous outbursts). Breuer and Freud (1893–1895/1955) proposed that the treatment of hysteria required the discharge of the emotional state previously associated with trauma. They claimed that for interpersonal traumas, such as insults and threats to the ego, emotional expression could be obtained through direct aggression: "The reaction of an injured person to a trauma has really only … a 'cathartic' effect if it is expressed in an adequate reaction like revenge" (p. 5). Breuer and Freud believed that expressing anger was much better than bottling it up inside.

Freud's therapeutic ideas on emotional catharsis form the basis of the hydraulic model of anger. The hydraulic model suggests that frustrations lead to anger and that anger, in turn, builds up inside an individual, similar to hydraulic pressure inside a closed environment, until it is released in some way. If people do not let their anger out but try to keep it bottled up inside, it will eventually cause them to explode in an aggressive rage. The modern theories of catharsis are based on this model. Catharsis is seen as a way of relieving the pressure that the anger creates inside the psyche. The core idea is that it is better to let the anger out here and there in little bits as opposed to keeping it inside as it builds up to the point at which a more dangerous explosion results.

If venting really does get anger "out of your system," then venting should decrease aggression because people are less angry. Almost as soon as psychology researchers began conducting scientific tests of catharsis theory, the theory ran into trouble. In one of the first experiments on the topic (Hornberger, 1959), participants first received an insulting remark from a confederate. Next, half of the participants pounded nails for 10 minutes—an activity that resembles many of the "venting" techniques that people who believe in catharsis continue to recommend even today. The other half did not get a chance to vent their anger by pounding nails. After this, all participants had a chance to criticize the person who had insulted them. If catharsis theory is true, the act of pounding nails should reduce subsequent aggression. The results showed the opposite effect. The people who had hammered the nails were more (rather than less) hostile toward the confederate afterward than were the ones who did not get to pound any nails.

In 1973, Albert Bandura issued a statement calling for a moratorium on catharsis theory and the use of venting in therapy. Four years later, Geen and Quanty (1977) published their influential review of catharsis theory in *Advances in Experimental Social Psychology*. After reviewing the relevant data, they concluded that venting anger does not reduce aggression. If anything, they concluded, it makes people more aggressive afterward. More recent research has come to similar conclusions (e.g., Bushman, Baumeister, & Stack, 1999). Geen and Quanty also concluded that venting anger can reduce physiological arousal but people must express their anger directly against the provocateur. People also must believe that the provocateur will not retaliate. Venting against substitute targets does not reduce arousal.

Cognitive Neoassociation Theory

According to cognitive neoassociation theory (Berkowitz, 1993), aversive events (e.g., frustrations, provocations, hot temperatures) produce negative affect. Negative affect, in turn, automatically stimulates thoughts, memories, expressive motor reactions, and physiological responses associated with both fight and flight tendencies. The fight associations give rise to rudimentary feelings of anger, whereas the flight associations give rise to rudimentary feelings of fear.

Cognitive neoassociation theory posits that aggressive thoughts are linked together in memory, thereby forming an associative network. Once an aggressive thought is processed or stimulated, activation spreads out along the network links and primes or activates associated thoughts as well. Not only are associated aggressive thoughts linked together in memory, but thoughts are also linked along the same sort of associative lines to emotional reactions and action tendencies (Bower, 1981; Lang, 1979). Thus, the activation of aggressive thoughts can engender a complex of associations consisting of aggressive ideas, emotions related to violence, and the impetus for aggressive actions.

Cognitive neoassociation theory predicts that venting should increase rather than decrease angry feelings and aggressive behaviors. Venting involves behaving aggressively, often against "safe" inanimate objects. To vent, people punch pillows, wallop punching bags, beat on couches with foam baseball bats, throw dishes on the ground, kick trash cans, scream and swear into pillows, and so forth. In essence, venting is practicing how to behave aggressively. Such aggressive activity should prime aggressive thoughts, feelings, and behavioral tendencies, especially if the people think about the source of their anger while venting. Thus, venting should keep angry feelings active in memory and also should increase the likelihood of subsequent aggressive responses.

Rumination and Distraction

Most pop psychology and self-help books implicitly assume that people are ruminating about their provocateur while venting anger. Some authors, however, are more explicit.

For example, John Lee (1993) gives the following advice to angry people in his popular book *Facing the Fire: Experiencing and Expressing Anger Appropriately*:

> Punch a pillow or a punching bag. Punch with all the frenzy you can. If you are angry at a particular person, imagine his or her face on the pillow or punching bag, and vent your rage physically and verbally. You will be doing violence to a pillow or punching bag so that you can stop doing violence to yourself by holding in poisonous anger. (p. 96)

Some devices for venting anger make it easy for people to ruminate about their provocateur. For example, consider the following advertisement from a toy catalog:

> WHEN YOU NEED SOMETHING THAT WON'T HIT BACK. *Wham-It* stands 42″ tall and takes abuse from kids and adults alike. When you feel like you just have to strike out, *Wham-It* is always on call. New clear vinyl pocket lets you insert a photo or drawing.

Rumination is defined as "self-focused attention," or directing attention inward on the self, and particularly on one's negative mood (Lyubomirsky & Nolen-Hoeksema, 1995). Any process that serves to exacerbate a negative mood, such as rumination, should increase anger and aggression. In contrast, any process that distracts attention away from an angry mood should reduce anger and aggression. If provoked individuals are induced to think about how they feel, they will maintain, or exacerbate, their angry mood. If they are induced to think about something else, however, the anger will dissipate in time.

Previous research has shown that rumination increases angry feelings. In one study (Rusting & Nolen-Hoeksema, 1998), college students were angered by reading a story about a professor who treated a student unfairly and were told to imagine themselves in a similar situation. Some students ruminated by writing about emotion-focused and self-focused topics (i.e., "Why do you think the way you do"), whereas others were distracted by writing about nonemotional, irrelevant topics (i.e., "the layout of the local post office"). Participants who ruminated for 20 minutes reported being angrier than did participants who were distracted. Another study found that aggression toward an insulting confederate was decreased by having people solve distracting math problems (Konecni, 1974). Solving the math problems presumably distracted people from the source of their anger. Two other studies found that rumination increased displaced aggression after a minor triggering event (Bushman, Pedersen, Vasquez, Bonacci, & Miller, 2001). In Study 1, provoked participants focused attention on or away from their negative mood and later engaged in displaced aggression against a competent or fumbling confederate. Provoked participants who ruminated engaged in more displaced aggression against the fumbling confederate than did participants who were distracted. Study 2 replicated the findings from Study 1 using different operational definitions and a substantially longer (8-hour) rumination period.

To date, no research has examined the effects of rumination and distraction in the effects of venting activities on anger and subsequent aggression. According to cognitive neoassociation theory, ruminating while venting should prime aggressive thoughts, feelings, and behavioral tendencies.

Overview

In the present study, 600 college students (300 men, 300 women) were first angered by another participant who criticized an essay they had written. In fact, there was no other participant. Next, participants were randomly assigned to rumination, distraction, or control groups. Participants in the rumination group hit a punching bag as long, as hard, and as many times as they wanted to. While they hit the bag, they were told to think about the other participant who had criticized their essay. For a visual aid, they were shown a photo ID of a same-sex college student described as the "other participant" on a 15-inch computer monitor. Participants in the distraction group also hit a punching bag as long, as hard, and as many times as they wanted to. While they hit the bag, they were told to think about becoming physically fit. As a visual aid, they were shown a photo ID of a same-sex athlete from a health magazine on a 15-inch computer monitor. Participants in the control group did not hit the punching bag. Instead, they sat quietly for a couple minutes while the experimenter supposedly worked on the other participant's computer. No attempt was made to reduce the anger of participants in the control group. Anger was measured using a mood form. Aggression was measured by allowing participants to blast their provocateur with loud and long noises through a pair of headphones on a competitive reaction time task. Catharsis theory would predict the lowest levels of anger and aggression among participants in the rumination condition. Cognitive neoassociation theory would predict the exact opposite results.

METHOD

Participants

Participants were 602 undergraduate college students (300 men and 302 women) enrolled in introductory psychology courses.[1] Students received extra course credit in exchange for their voluntary participation. The data from 2 women were discarded because they refused to hit the punching bag. The final sample consisted of 300 men and 300 women. There were 100 men and 100 women in each of the three experimental conditions (i.e., rumination, distraction, control).

Procedure

Participants were tested individually, but each was led to believe that he or she would be interacting with another participant of the same sex. They were told that the researchers were studying first impressions.

After giving informed consent, each participant wrote a one-paragraph essay on abortion, either pro-choice or pro-life (whichever the participant supported). After finishing, the participant's essay was taken away to be shown to the other participant (who was in fact nonexistent) for evaluation. Meanwhile, the participant was permitted to evaluate the partner's essay, which expressed the opposite view on abortion (e.g., if the participant's essay was pro-choice, the partner's essay was pro-life).

A short time later, the experimenter brought the participant's own essay back with comments ostensibly made by the other participant. All participants received bad evaluations consisting of negative ratings on organization, originality, writing style, clarity of expression, persuasiveness of arguments, and overall quality. The ratings ranged from –10 to –8 on a 21-point scale ranging from –10 (*very bad*) to +10 (*very good*). There was also a handwritten comment stating "This is one of the worst essays I have read!" Previous research has shown that this procedure makes people quite angry (e.g., Bushman & Baumeister, 1998; Bushman, Baumeister, & Phillips, 2001; Bushman et al., 1999).

After reading the evaluation, the participants rated how much they wanted to perform each of 10 activities on a list. Included in this list of activities was "hitting a punching bag." Other activities included playing solitaire, reading a short story, watching a comedy, and playing a computer game. Ratings were made on a 10-point scale ranging from 1 (*not at all*) to 10 (*extremely*).

The punching bag manipulation came next. Two thirds of participants received the punching bag procedure. If the participant did not rank the punching bag activity first, the experimenter asked if the participant would be willing to hit the punching bag, explaining that ratings were needed for each activity on the list and that more ratings were needed for the punching bag activity. By requesting the participant to agree, we were able to ensure that the punching bag activity was the result of choice by all participants, including those who had not originally listed it as their top choice.

Participants who received the punching bag procedure were told that because physical appearance could influence their impression of their partner, a coin would be tossed to determine whether they would know what their partner looked like. On the basis of the coin toss, participants were assigned to rumination or distraction conditions. Participants in the rumination condition were told that they would know what their partner looked like. On a 15-inch computer monitor, participants were shown a photo ID of another Iowa State University student of the same sex. The experimenter actually rolled a die to determine which of six photo IDs to show. The names and identification numbers were removed from all IDs. The experimenter then gave the participant some boxing gloves and demonstrated how to hit the 70-pound punching bag (Everlast, Model 4820). Participants were told that they should think about their partner while hitting the bag.[2]

Participants in the distraction condition were told that they would not know what their partner looked like. Instead of thinking about their partner while hitting the bag, they were told to think about becoming physically fit. Instead of seeing a photo ID of their partner on the computer screen, they saw a photo of someone of the same sex exercising. The photos were taken from fitness magazines and the experimenter rolled a die to determine which photo to show.

Participants in both the rumination and distraction condition were told that their partner would not see them (due to the coin toss). The participant was left alone to hit the punching bag. They were told they could hit it as long and as many times as they wanted to. Because there was an intercom system in the participant's room, the experimenter was able to time how long the participant hit the bag and count the number of times the participant hit the bag. The experimenter also rated how hard the participant hit the bag on a 10-point scale ranging from 1 (*very soft*) to 10 (*very hard*). The experimenter also asked the participant how hard he or she hit the bag (using the same 10-point scale). Participants then indicated how much they enjoyed hitting the punching bag on a 10-point scale ranging from 1 (*not at all*) to 10 (*extremely*).

Participants in the control condition did not hit the punching bag. Instead, they sat quietly for 2 minutes. The justification for the delay was that the experimenter was fixing their partner's computer. No attempt was made to reduce participant's anger during the 2-minute delay. Instead, participants in the no punching bag group did nothing at all. This allowed a test of the hypothesis that angry people are better off doing nothing at all than engaging in cathartic activities.

Next, participants completed a mood form that measured anger and positive affect. The anger measure consisted of 15 adjectives (e.g., *angry, annoyed, furious*) from the hostility subscale of the revised Multiple Affect Adjective Checklist (Zuckerman & Lubin, 1985). The positive affect measure consisted of 10 adjectives (e.g., *alert, determined, enthusiastic*) from the positive affect subscale of the Positive and Negative Affect Schedule (Watson, Clarke, & Tellegen, 1988). Watson and his colleagues define positive affect as a state of "high energy, full concentration, and pleasurable engagement" (p. 1063). All adjectives were rated along a 5-point Likerttype scale, where 1 = *very slightly or not at all*, 2 = *a little*, 3 = *moderately*, 4 = *quite a bit*, and 5 = *extremely*. Participants were told to "indicate to what extent you feel this way right now, that is, at the present moment." The alpha coefficients for the measures of anger and positive affect were .88 and .89, respectively.

The next part of the procedure was presented as a competitive reaction time task, based on a paradigm developed by Taylor (1967). Previous studies have established the construct validity of this paradigm (e.g., Bernstein, Richardson, & Hammock, 1987; Giancola & Zeichner, 1995). The participant was told that he or she and the partner would have to press a button as fast as possible on each trial and whoever was slower would receive a blast of noise. The participant was permitted to set in advance the intensity of the noise that the other person would receive between 60 decibels (level 1) and 105 decibels (level 10) if the other lost. A nonaggressive no-noise setting (level 0) also was offered. In addition to deciding the intensity, the winner decided the duration of the loser's suffering because the duration of the noise depended on how long the winner held the button pressed down. In effect, each participant controlled a weapon that could be used to blast the other person if the participant won the competition to react faster.

The reaction time task consisted of 25 trials. After the initial (no provocation) trial, the remaining 24 trials were divided into three blocks with eight trials in each block. Within each block of trials, the other participant set random noise levels (ranging from 65 decibels to 100 decibels) and random noise durations (ranging from 0.25 seconds to 2.5 seconds). The participant heard noise on half of the trials within each block (randomly determined). An iMac computer controlled the events in the reaction time task and recorded the noise levels and noise durations the participant set for the other person. The white noise was delivered through a pair of Telephonics TDH-39P headphones.

Half of participants completed the mood form first, followed by the competitive reaction time task. The other half of the participants completed the competitive reaction time task first, followed by the mood checklist. A full oral debriefing (with probe for suspicion) followed. Because none of the participants expressed any suspicion, all 600 were included in the data analyses.

RESULTS

Primary Analyses

Positive Mood

There was no significant effect for experimental condition on positive mood, $F(2, 594) = 0.24$, $p > .05$ (see Table 10.1). Regardless of the condition they were in, men were in a more positive mood than were women, $M = 31.51$, $SD = 7.85$, and $M = 28.12$, $SD = 7.40$, $F(1, 594) = 29.31$, $p < .0001$, $d = 0.44$.

Anger

There was a main effect for experimental condition on anger, $F(2, 594) = 5.23$, $p < .01$ (see Table 10.1). Participants in the rumination group felt more angry than did participants in the distraction and control groups, $t(594) = 2.20$, $p < .05$, $d = 0.22$, and $t(594) = 3.15$, p

TABLE 10.1: Anger and Aggression Levels for Participants in the Control, Distraction, and Rumination Groups

MEASURE	CONTROL		DISTRACTION		RUMINATION	
Positive mood	29.61[a]	(7.34)	29.71[a]	(7.86)	30.11[a]	(8.23)
Anger	26.25[b]	(10.98)	27.32[b]	(10.88)	29.78[a]	(11.56)
Aggression	−0.21[b]	(1.27)	0.01[ab]	(1.39)	0.21[a]	(1.54)

NOTE: n = 200 in each group. Standard deviations are in parentheses. Subscripts refer to within-row comparisons. Means having the same subscript are not significantly different at the .05 significance level.

< .005, $d = 0.31$. Participants in distraction and control groups did not differ in terms of how angry they felt, $t(594) = 0.95$, $p > .05$.

Aggressive Behavior

The same pattern of results was found for the two measures of aggression—noise intensity and noise duration. Thus, the two measures were standardized and summed to form a more reliable measure of aggression. The same pattern of results also was obtained on Trial 1 and on the remaining 24 trials of the competitive reaction-time task. Thus, the responses on the 25 trials were standardized and summed.

There was a main effect for experimental condition on aggression, $F(2, 594) = 5.03$, $p < .01$ (see Table 10.1). Participants in the rumination group were more aggressive than participants in the control group, $t(594) = 3.17$, $p < .005$, $d = 0.30$. Participants in the distraction group were more aggressive than participants in the control group and were less aggressive than participants in the rumination group, although neither difference was statistically significant, $ts(594) = 1.68$ and 1.49, $ps > .05$. Men were also more aggressive than were women, $M = 0.44$, $SD = 1.62$, and $M = -0.44$, $SD = 0.99$, $F(1, 594) = 66.52$, $p < .0001$, $d = 0.33$.

Discussion

Does venting anger extinguish or feed the flame? The results from the present research show that venting to reduce anger is like using gasoline to put out a fire—it only feeds the flame. By fueling aggressive thoughts and feelings, venting also increases aggressive responding. People who walloped the punching bag while thinking about the person who had provoked them were the most angry and the most aggressive in the present experiment. Venting did not lead to a more positive mood either.

People in the distraction group were less angry than were people in the rumination group, but they were not less aggressive. Thus, performing an aggressive activity such as hitting a punching bag can increase aggression even if people are distracted while performing the activity.

In the present experiment, people were best off doing nothing at all than venting their anger. No attempt was made to reduce anger or aggressive impulses in the control group. Even so, anger and aggression levels were lowest in the control group. The results might have been more dramatic if participants in the control group actively sought to reduce their angry feelings.

Overall, the present results support cognitive neoassociation theory (Berkowitz, 1993) and directly contradict catharsis theory. Venting while ruminating about the source of provocation kept aggressive thoughts and angry feelings active in memory and only made people more angry and more aggressive. These results provide one more nail in the coffin containing catharsis theory.

Magnitude of Observed Effects

Although the effects obtained in the present study were small to moderate in size (see Cohen, 1988), they are in the opposite direction predicted by catharsis theory. In the present study, the distraction activity was an aggressive one—angered people hit a punching bag. Larger effects might have been obtained if distraction activity would have been a nonaggressive one, such as working a crossword puzzle. Similarly, larger effects might have been obtained if angered people would have engaged in a behavior incompatible with anger and aggression, such as watching a funny TV program or petting a puppy (e.g., Baron, 1976, 1983).

Can These Findings Be Due to Arousal?

One well-known finding in psychology is that arousal enhances whatever response is dominant (e.g., Cottrell & Wack, 1967; Criddle, 1971; Eysenck, 1975; Markovsky & Berger, 1983; Zajonc, Heingartner, & Herman, 1969; Zajonc & Sales, 1966). This finding is central to the drive theory of social facilitation (e.g., Geen & Bushman, 1987, 1989). Walloping a punching bag for a few minutes can certainly increase arousal levels. Because participants in the present study all were provoked, it seems likely that aggression would be a dominant response for them. Arousal cannot, however, explain the pattern of results obtained in the present study. If the results were due to arousal, people in the distraction group should have been more aggressive than people in the rumination group because they hit the punching bag a greater number of times. The results, however, were in the opposite direction.

Is Intense Physical Activity an Effective Technique for Managing Anger?

If used as a form of distraction, intense physical activity does not necessarily increase anger, even if the activity is aggressive in nature (e.g., hitting a punching bag). Physical activity should, however, increase anger if the person is provoked after engaging in the intense physical activity. According to excitation transfer theory, the arousal from the physical activity will be misattributed to the provocation and will therefore transfer to the provocation (e.g., Zillmann, 1979). Mislabeling the arousal from the physical activity as anger would therefore increase aggressive responding (e.g., Zillmann, Katcher, & Milavsky, 1972). In the present study, participants were provoked before engaging in an intense physical activity, so excitation transfer should not occur. Although it might be good for your heart, intense physical activity is probably not an effective technique for reducing anger and aggression.

Conclusion

Catharsis theory predicts that venting anger should get rid of it and should therefore reduce subsequent aggression. The present findings, as well as previous findings, directly contradict catharsis theory (e.g., Bushman et al., 1999; Geen & Quanty, 1977). For reducing anger and aggression, the worst possible advice to give people is to tell them to imagine their provocateur's face on a pillow or punching bag as they wallop it, yet this is precisely what many pop psychologists advise people to do. If followed, such advice will only make people angrier and more aggressive.

NOTES

1. According to Cohen (1988), most of the effects in the social sciences are small to moderate in size. I assumed that the effect obtained in the present study would be in this range. A power analysis (Cohen, 1988) revealed that with power = .80 and two-sided significance level = .05, 400 participants were needed in each group to detect a small effect (i.e., d = 0.20) and 64 participants were needed in each group to detect a moderate effect (i.e., d = 0.50). Thus, the present study included 200 participants in each group.
2. One man in the rumination group became so angry while hitting the punching bag that he also punched a hole in the laboratory wall.

REFERENCES

Bandura, A. (1973). *Aggression: A social learning theory analysis*. Englewood Cliffs, NJ: Prentice Hall.

Baron, R. A. (1976). The reduction of human aggression: A field study of the influence of incompatible reactions. *Journal of Applied Social Psychology, 6*, 260–274.

Baron, R. A. (1983). The control of human aggression: An optimistic perspective. *Journal of Social and Clinical Psychology, 1*, 97–119.

Berkowitz, L. (1993). *Aggression: Its causes, consequences, and control*. New York: McGraw-Hill.

Bernstein, S., Richardson, D., & Hammock, G. (1987). Convergent and discriminant validity of the Taylor and Buss measures of physical aggression. *Aggressive Behavior, 13*, 15–24.

Bower, G. (1981). Mood and memory. *American Psychologist, 36*, 129–148.

Breuer, J., & Freud, S. (1955). *Studies on hysteria* (Standard ed., Vol. II). London: Hogarth. (Original work published 1893–1895)

Bushman, B. J., & Baumeister, R. F. (1998). Threatened egotism, narcissism, self-esteem, and direct and displaced aggression: Does self-love or self-hate lead to violence? *Journal of Personality and Social Psychology, 75*, 219–229.

Bushman, B. J., Baumeister, R. F., & Phillips, C. M. (2001). Do people aggress to improve their mood? Catharsis beliefs, affect regulation opportunity, and aggressive responding. *Journal of Personality and Social Psychology, 81*, 17–32.

Bushman, B. J., Baumeister, R. F., & Stack, A. D. (1999). Catharsis, aggression, and persuasive influence: Self-fulfilling or self-defeating prophecies? *Journal of Personality and Social Psychology, 76*, 367–376.

Bushman, B. J., Pedersen, W. C., Vasquez. E. A., Bonacci, A. M., & Miller, N. (2001). *Chewing on it can chew you up: Effects of rumination on displaced aggression triggered by a minor event*. Manuscript submitted for publication.

Cohen, J. (1988). *Statistical power analysis for the behavioral sciences* (2nd ed.). New York: Academic Press.

Cottrell, N. B., & Wack, D. L. (1967). Energizing effects of cognitive dissonance upon dominant and subordinate responses. *Journal of Personality and Social Psychology, 6*, 132–138.

Criddle, W. D. (1971).The physical presence of other individuals as a factor in social facilitation. *Psychonomic Science, 22*, 229–230.

Eysenck, M. W. (1975). Effects of noise, activation level, and response dominance on retrieval from semantic memory. *Journal of Experimental Psychology: Human Learning and Memory, 1*, 143–148.

Fighting fit. (1993, July). *Vogue, 183*, 176–179.

Geen, R. G., & Bushman, B. J. (1987). Drive theory: The effects of socially engendered arousal. In B. Mullen & G. R. Goethals (Eds.), *Theories of group behavior* (pp. 89–109). New York: Springer-Verlag.

Geen, R. G., & Bushman, B. J. (1989). The arousing effects of social presence. In H. Wagner & A. Manstead (Eds.), *Handbook of psychophysiology* (pp. 261–281). New York: John Wiley.

Geen, R. G., & Quanty, M. B. (1977). The catharsis of aggression: An evaluation of a hypothesis. In L. Berkowitz (Ed.), *Advances in experimental social psychology* (Vol. 10, pp. 1–37). New York: Academic Press.

Giancola, P. R., & Zeichner, A. (1995). Construct validity of a competitive reaction-time aggression paradigm. *Aggressive Behavior, 21*, 199–204.

Hornberger, R. H. (1959). The differential reduction of aggressive responses as a function of interpolated activities. *American Psychologist, 14*, 354.

Konecni, V. J. (1974). Self-arousal, dissipation of anger, and aggression. *Personality and Social Psychology Bulletin, 1*, 192–194.

Lang, P. J. (1979). A bio-informational theory of emotional imagery. *Psychophysiology, 16*, 495–512.

Lee, J. (1993). *Facing the fire: Experiencing and expressing anger appropriately*. New York: Bantam.

Lyubomirsky, S., & Nolen-Hoeksema, S. (1995). Effects of self-focused rumination on negative thinking and interpersonal problem solving. *Journal of Personality and Social Psychology, 69*, 176–190.

Markovsky, B., & Berger, S. M. (1983). Crowd noise and mimicry. *Personality and Social Psychology Bulletin, 9*, 90–96.

Rusting, C. L., & Nolen-Hoeksema, S. (1998). Regulating responses to anger: Effects of rumination and distraction on angry mood. *Journal of Personality and Social Psychology, 74*, 790–803.

Sullivan, A. (1999, September 27). What's so bad about hate? *New York Times Magazine*, pp. 50–57, 88, 104, 112–113.

Taylor, S. P. (1967). Aggressive behavior and physiological arousal as a function of provocation and the tendency to inhibit aggression. *Journal of Personality, 35*, 297–310.

Watson, D., Clarke, L. A., & Tellegen, A. (1988). Development and validation of brief measures of positive and negative affect: The PANAS scales. *Journal of Personality and Social Psychology, 54*, 1063–1070.

Zajonc, R. B., Heingartner, A., & Herman, E. M. (1969). Social enhancement and impairment of performance in the cockroach. *Journal of Personality and Social Psychology, 13*, 83–92.

Zajonc, R. B., & Sales, S. M. (1966). Social facilitation of dominant and subordinate responses. *Journal of Experimental Social Psychology, 2*, 160–168.

Zillmann, D. (1979). *Hostility and aggression*. Hillsdale, NJ: Lawrence Erlbaum.

Zillmann, D., Katcher, A. H., & Milavsky, B. (1972). Excitation transfer from physical exercise to subsequent aggressive behavior. *Journal of Experimental Social Psychology, 8*, 247–259.

Zuckerman, M., & Lubin, B. (1985). *Manual for the MAACL-R: The Multiple Affective Adjective Checklist Revised*. San Diego, CA: Educational and Industrial Testing Service.

REVIEW AND CONTEMPLATE

1. Explain the theory of catharsis and the hydraulic model of anger.

2. Briefly describe the study conducted by Bushman (2002), including what participants did in the three different conditions and what effects those conditions had on the participants' level of anger and aggressive behavior.

3. Cognitive neoassociation theory predicts that venting (i.e., behaving aggressively) should increase rather than decrease angry feelings and aggressive behavior. Explain (a) why, according to the theory, this should happen and (b) whether the results of Bushman's (2002) study are consistent or inconsistent with this theory.

4. Chapter 1 discussed six important characteristics of pseudoscience. Find a website that promotes a rage room (or anger room) in the United States and explain whether you believe they are promoting a scientific or pseudoscientific therapy. If you believe it's pseudoscientific, state which of the six characteristics of pseudoscience seem most relevant. In your answer, include quotes from the website, and provide the URL for the website.

10.3 "False Confessions: Causes, Consequences, and Implications for Reform"

DURING THE EVENING of April 19, 1989, a 28-year-old woman was attacked and raped in New York City's Central Park. Her skull had been fractured, her body temperature had dropped to 84 degrees, and she had lost 75% of her blood. Although the woman recovered, she had no memory of the assault. Police suspected several African American and Latino teenagers who were in custody for other attacks in the park that night. Antron McCray was one of five teenagers who, after lengthy police interrogation, confessed to attacking the woman. He was convicted of rape and assault and was sentenced to 5–10 years in prison for his role in the crime. After serving 6 years in prison, Antron was released in 2002 after Matias Reyes, a convicted murderer and rapist who was not one of the five teenagers, confessed that he alone committed the crime. DNA evidence corroborated his confession.

Why would a teenager confess to a crime he did not commit? Doesn't his confession suggest that he must have played some role in the attack? Psychologists have found that although people believe that (a) confessions provide strong evidence of a person's guilt and (b) people do not confess unless they are guilty, under certain circumstances, people do confess to crimes they did not commit. In fact, researchers have found that a substantial percentage of prisoners who were later declared innocent because of DNA evidence had confessed to the crime for which they were wrongfully convicted. In this reading, Saul Kassin discusses the role of social influence and other factors in producing false confessions, and he discusses research experiments that elicited false confessions from participants. As you will see in this article, the elicitation of false confessions is also related to phenomena discussed in earlier chapters in this book, such as people's pseudoscientific beliefs about multiple personalities (or Dissociative Identity Disorder), repressed memories, and lie detection.

Reference

Kassin, S. M. (2008). False confessions: Causes, consequences, and implications for reform. *Current Directions in Psychological Science, 17,* 249–253.

"FALSE CONFESSIONS: CAUSES, CONSEQUENCES, AND IMPLICATIONS FOR REFORM"

SAUL KASSIN

In criminal law, confession evidence is highly persuasive—yet fallible. Despite the pervasive myth that people do not confess to crimes they did not commit, the pages of American history, beginning with the Salem witch trials of 1692, bear witness to all the men and women who were wrongfully convicted and imprisoned, often because of false confessions. Although the prevalence rate is unknown, recent analyses reveal that 20 to 25% of prisoners exonerated by DNA had confessed to police, that the percentage is far higher in capital murder cases (White, 2003), and that these discovered instances represent the tip of an iceberg (Drizin & Leo, 2004).

After reviewing a number of cases throughout history, and drawing on theories of social influence, Wrightsman and I proposed a taxonomy that distinguished three types of false confessions: *voluntary, compliant*, and *internalized*. Still used today, this classification scheme has provided an important framework and has since been used, critiqued, extended, and refined in subtle ways (Kassin & Wrightsman, 1985).

Voluntary false confessions are those in which people claim responsibility for crimes they did not commit without prompting from police. Often this occurs in high-profile cases. When *Black Dahlia* actress Elizabeth Short was murdered in 1947, more than 50 people confessed. In 2006, John Mark Karr confessed to the unsolved murder of young JonBenet Ramsey. There are several reasons why innocent people volunteer confessions, such as a pathological need for attention or self-punishment, feelings of guilt or delusions, the perception of tangible gain, or the desire to protect someone else.

In contrast, people are sometimes induced to confess through the processes of police interrogation. In compliant false confessions, the suspect acquiesces in order to escape from a stressful situation, avoid punishment, or gain a promised or implied reward. Like the social influence observed in Milgram's classic obedience studies, this confession is an act of public compliance by a suspect who perceives that the short-term benefits of confession outweigh the long-term costs. This phenomenon was dramatically illustrated in the 1989 Central Park jogger case, in which five New York City teenagers confessed after lengthy interrogations, each claiming he expected to go home afterward. All the boys were convicted and sent to prison, only to be exonerated in 2002 when the real rapist gave a confession that was confirmed by DNA evidence.

Lastly, internalized false confessions are those in which innocent but vulnerable suspects, exposed to highly suggestive interrogation tactics, not only confess but come

Saul M. Kassin, "False Confessions: Causes, Consequences, and Implications for Reform," *Current Directions in Psychological Science*, vol. 17, no. 4, pp. 249-253. Copyright © 2008 by SAGE Publications. Reprinted with permission.

to believe they committed the crime in question. The case of 14-year-old Michael Crowe, whose sister was stabbed to death, illustrates this phenomenon. After lengthy interrogations, during which Crowe was misled into thinking there was substantial physical evidence of his guilt, he concluded that he was a killer: "I'm not sure how I did it. All I know is I did it" (Drizin & Colgan, 2004, p. 141). Eventually, he was convinced that he had a split personality—that "bad Michael" acted out of jealous rage while "good Michael" blocked the incident from consciousness. The charges against Crowe were later dropped when a drifter from the neighborhood was found with Crowe's sister's blood on his clothing.

Inspired by tales of innocents wrongfully convicted, recent research has focused on three sets of questions: (a) Why are innocent people often misidentified for interrogation, (b) what factors put innocent suspects at risk to confess, and (c) how accurate are police, juries, and others at judging confession evidence?

WHY INNOCENT PEOPLE ARE INTERROGATED

Typically, the confrontational process of *interrogation* is preceded by an information-gathering *interview* conducted by police to determine if a suspect is guilty or innocent. In *Criminal Interrogations and Confessions* (Inbau, Reid, Buckley, & Jayne, 2001), the most influential manual on interrogation, police are thus advised on the use of verbal cues, nonverbal cues, and behavioral attitudes to detect deception—at, they claim, exceedingly high levels of accuracy.

For a person who is falsely accused, this first impression may determine whether he or she is interrogated or sent home. Yet in laboratories all over the world, research has shown that people are only about 54% accurate in judging truth and deception; that training produces little, if any, improvement compared to naive control groups; and that police, customs inspectors, and other so-called experts perform only slightly better, if at all (Bond & DePaulo, 2006).

In a study that examined performance in a criminal context, some lay participants but not others were randomly assigned to training in a popular law enforcement method of lie detection (Kassin & Fong, 1999). These students then watched videotaped interviews of suspects, some guilty and others innocent, denying their involvement in various mock crimes. As in past studies, observers could not differentiate between guilty and innocent suspects. Importantly, those who underwent training were less accurate, more confident, and more biased toward seeing deception than were those who had not received training. In a follow-up study with these same tapes, experienced detectives were tested—and they exhibited the same tendencies, making prejudgments of guilt, with confidence, that were frequently in error (Meissner & Kassin, 2002).

At present, psychological scientists are seeking ways to improve human lie-detection performance. Some studies have shown that interviewers can boost their accuracy by withholding crime details while questioning suspects, trapping those who are guilty, but not those who are innocent, in inconsistencies when these facts are disclosed (Hartwig,

Granhag, Strömwall, & Vrij, 2005). Other studies have suggested that because lying is more effortful than telling the truth, interviewers who tax a suspect's cognitive load (e.g., by distraction or by having interviewees tell their stories in reverse order) can make more accurate true/false judgments by attending to effort cues such as hesitations (Vrij, Fisher, Mann, & Leal, 2006).

WHY INNOCENT PEOPLE CONFESS

Observational studies and surveys have shown that the modern American police interrogation—in which interrogators are legally prohibited from drawing confessions through violence, physical discomfort, threats, or promises—is a psychologically oriented process (Kassin et al., 2007; Leo, 1996; see Table 10.2). In their training manual, Inbau et al. (2001) recommend a multistep approach that is essentially reducible to an interplay of three processes: *isolation*, which increases anxiety and the suspect's desire to escape; *confrontation*, in which the interrogator accuses the suspect of the crime, sometimes citing real or fictitious evidence to bolster the claim; and *minimization*, in which a sympathetic interrogator morally justifies the crime, leading the suspect to expect leniency upon confession.

TABLE 10.2: Ten Most Frequent Interrogation Practices, as Self-Reported by 631 North American Detectives (Kassin et al., 2007)

TACTIC	ESTIMATED FREQUENCY
Isolating the suspect from family and friends	4.49
Conducting interrogation in a small private room	4.23
Identifying contradictions in the suspect's story	4.23
Establishing rapport/gaining the suspect's trust	4.08
Confronting the suspect with evidence of guilt	3.90
Appealing to the suspect's self-interest	3.46
Offering sympathy, moral justifications, & excuses	3.38
Interrupting the suspect's denials and objections	3.22
Pretending to have independent evidence of guilt	3.11
Minimizing the moral seriousness of the offense	3.02

NOTE. Ratings were made on a 1-point (*never*) to 5-point (*always*) scale.

Situational Risk Factors

Anecdotal evidence from DNA exonerations suggests that certain interrogation tactics exert too much influence. One potentially problematic tactic is the presentation of false evidence. American police are permitted to bolster their accusations by telling suspects that there is incontrovertible evidence of their guilt (e.g., a hair sample, eyewitness identification, or failed lie-detector test)—even if no such evidence exists. Can such trickery trap innocent people into confession?

Over the years, basic research has shown that misinformation can alter people's perceptions, beliefs, memories, and behaviors. With regard to confession, this hypothesis was tested in a laboratory experiment (Kassin & Kiechel, 1996). College students typed on a keyboard in what they were led to believe was a reaction-time study. At one point, subjects were accused of causing the computer to crash by pressing a key they had been instructed to avoid. They were asked to sign a confession. All subjects were truly innocent and all initially denied the charge. In some sessions but not others, a confederate said she witnessed the subject hit the forbidden key. This false evidence nearly doubled the number of students who signed a written confession, from 48% to 94%. As measured moments later, this manipulation also increased the number of subjects who actually believed they were culpable. Follow-up studies have replicated the effect even when the negative consequences of confession were raised.

A second problematic tactic is minimization, the process by which interrogators minimize the crime by offering sympathy and moral justification. Interrogators thus suggest to suspects that their actions were spontaneous, accidental, provoked, peer-pressured, or otherwise justifiable. Past research has shown that minimization remarks lead observers to infer that leniency will follow from confession, even without an explicit promise. To assess the behavioral effects of this tactic, researchers paired subjects with a confederate for a problem-solving study and instructed them to work alone on some trials and jointly on others (Russano, Meissner, Narchet, & Kassin, 2005). In a guilty condition, the confederate sought help on an individual problem, inducing the subject to violate the experimental rule; in the innocent condition, the confederate did not make this request. The experimenter soon "discovered" a similarity in solutions, separated the subject and confederate, and accused the subject of cheating. Blind to guilt or innocence, the experimenter tried to get the subject to sign an admission by promising leniency, making minimizing remarks, using both tactics, or using no tactics. Compared to the no-tactics condition, minimization—as effectively as an offer of leniency—increased not only true confessions from the guilty but false confessions from the innocent (see Fig. 10.1).

Dispositional Vulnerabilities

Some people are dispositionally more malleable than others—and at greater risk for false confessions. For example, individuals whose personalities make them prone to *compliance* in social situations are especially vulnerable because of their eagerness to please others and avoid confrontation. Individuals who are prone to *suggestibility*—whose memories can be altered by misleading questions and negative feedback—are also subject to influence. People who are highly anxious, fearful, depressed, delusional, or otherwise psychologically disordered, and people who are mentally retarded, are particularly prone to confess under pressure (for a review, see Gudjonsson, 2003).

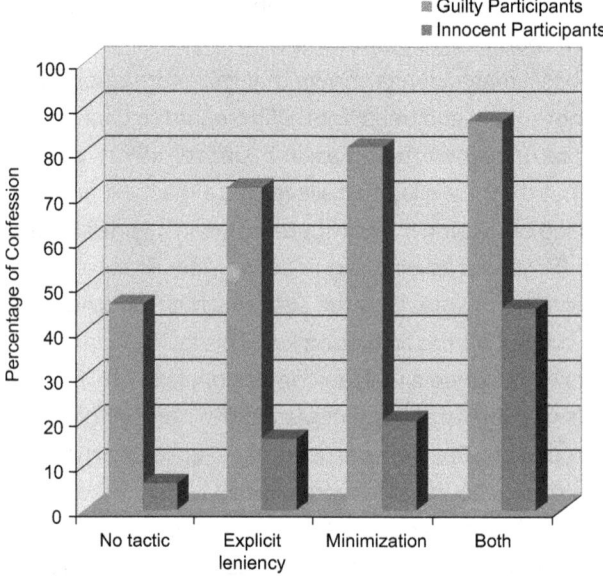

FIGURE 10.1: Percentage of guilty and innocent subjects who confessed to cheating after a promise of leniency, minimization remarks, both tactics, or no tactics (Russano, Meissner, Narchet, & Kassin, 2005).

Youth is a particularly substantial risk factor. More than 90% of juveniles whom police seek to question waive their *Miranda* rights to silence and a lawyer. In fact, the presence of a parent or other "interested adult"—which many states require, to protect young suspects—does not help, as adults often urge their youths to cooperate with police (Oberlander & Goldstein, 2001). The problem is evident in the disproportionate number of juveniles in the population of false confessors (Drizin & Leo, 2004). As to what makes juveniles so vulnerable, developmental research indicates that adolescents display an "immaturity of judgment" in their decision making—a pattern of behavior that is characterized by impulsivity, a focus on immediate gratification, and a diminished capacity for perceptions of future risk (Owen-Kostelnik, Reppucci, & Meyer, 2006). For the myopic adolescent, confession may serve as an expedient way out of a stressful situation. To make matters worse, most justice-involved youth have diagnosable psychological disorders, putting them at "double jeopardy" in the interrogation room (Redlich, 2007).

The Phenomenology of Innocence

On Sept. 20, 2006, Jeffrey Deskovic was released from prison in New York, where he had spent 15 years for a murder he had said he committed but did not. Why did he confess? "Believing in the criminal justice system and being fearful for myself, I told them what they wanted to hear," Deskovic said. Certain that DNA testing on the semen would establish his innocence, he added: "I thought it was all going to be okay in the end" (Santos, 2006, p. A1).

Anecdotal and research evidence has suggested the ironic hypothesis that innocence itself may put innocents at risk (Kassin, 2005). People who stand falsely accused believe that truth and justice will prevail and that their innocence is transparent to others. As a result, they cooperate with police, waive their rights, and speak freely, often not realizing that they are under suspicion. In a study that illustrates the point, some subjects but not others were assigned to commit a mock theft of $100, after which they were "arrested" and apprised of their rights by a security guard. As predicted, those who were innocent were more likely to sign a waiver and talk than were those who were guilty (81% vs. 36%). Afterward, most explained that they waived their rights precisely because they were innocent: "I did nothing wrong," "I had nothing to hide" (Kassin & Norwick, 2004). In short, *Miranda* warnings may not protect citizens who need it most—those accused of crimes they did not commit.

WHY INNOCENT CONFESSORS ARE CONVICTED

When a suspect retracts his or her confession, pleads not guilty, and goes to trial, a sequence of two courtroom decisions is set into motion. First, a judge determines whether the confession was voluntary and admissible as evidence. Then a jury, hearing the admissible confession, determines whether the defendant is guilty beyond a reasonable doubt. But can people distinguish between true and false confessions, or do most people believe, simply, that no one would confess to a crime he or she did not commit?

Addressing the first question, researchers videotaped male prison inmates making true confessions to their crimes and concocting false confessions to crimes they did not commit. When laypeople and police investigators later judged these statements from videotapes or audiotapes, neither group fared well, exhibiting accuracy rates that ranged from 42% to 64% (Kassin, Meissner, & Norwick, 2005). Mock-jury studies have further shown that confession is a highly potent form of evidence and that people do not fully discount confessions even when these confessions are coerced. To illustrate, mock jurors were presented with one of three versions of a murder trial—a low-pressure confession version, a high-pressure confession version, and a no-confession control version. Confronted with the high-pressure confession, subjects judged the statement to be involuntary and said it did not influence their decisions. Yet when it came to verdicts, this same confession significantly boosted the conviction rate—from 19% in the no-confession control group to 47% in the high-pressure confession condition—even when subjects were specifically asked to disregard confessions they thought were coerced (Kassin & Sukel, 1997).

Criminal justice statistics reinforce the point that people uncritically accept confessions, which invariably unleash a chain of adverse legal consequences. In one sample, a striking 81% of innocent confessors who pled not guilty and went to trial were ultimately convicted by juries. Hence, it appears that confessions are "inherently prejudicial and highly damaging to a defendant, even if it is the product of coercive interrogation, even if it is supported by no other evidence, and even if it is ultimately proven false beyond any reasonable doubt" (Drizin & Leo, 2004, p. 959).

CONCLUSIONS AND IMPLICATIONS

Recent DNA exonerations reveal three sets of problems with confession evidence: (a) Police cannot accurately distinguish between truth tellers and liars; (b) certain psychological interrogation tactics put innocents at risk to confess, especially if they are young, mentally impaired, or otherwise vulnerable; and (c) judges and juries intuitively tend to trust confessions, even if they know that these confessions were coerced.

Having identified these problems, psychological scientists now seek solutions that inform policies and practices. One goal is to improve the quality of confession evidence. Hence, researchers are working on ways to increase the accuracy with which police interviewers judge suspects, to develop methods of interrogation that get offenders but not innocents to confess, and to protect vulnerable suspect populations. A second goal is to improve the way judges and juries evaluate confessions in court. Toward this end, there are two possible mechanisms. One involves a greater use of expert witnesses to educate judges and juries about the psychology of confessions. The second is to ensure that judges and juries can observe how the confessions are produced by requiring that police videotape entire interrogations. In coming years, more research is needed to evaluate the impact of these approaches.

Recommended Reading

Gudjonsson, G.H. (2003). (See References). An encyclopedic review by a leading clinical researcher in Great Britain.

Kassin, S.M., & Gudjonsson, G.H. (2004). The psychology of confessions: A review of the literature and issues. *Psychological Science in the Public Interest, 5,* 33–67. A comprehensive overview of research and policy issues.

Lassiter, G.D. (Ed.). (2004). *Interrogations, confessions, and entrapment*. New York: Kluwer Press. An edited volume containing original chapters by leading researchers.

Leo, R.A. (2008). *Police interrogation and American justice*. Cambridge, MA: Harvard University Press. An in-depth analysis of police interrogations and the confessions they produce.

Vrij, A. (2008). *Detecting lies and deceit: Pitfalls and opportunities*. Chichester, England: Wiley. An overview of the rapidly growing science of lie detection.

REFERENCES

Bond, C.F., & DePaulo, B.M. (2006). Accuracy of deception judgments. *Personality & Social Psychology Review, 10*, 214-234.

Drizin, S.A., & Colgan, B.A. (2004). Tales from the juvenile confessions front. In G.D. Lassiter (Ed.), *Interrogations, confessions, and entrapment* (pp. 127-162). New York: Kluwer Academic.

Drizin, S.A., & Leo, R.A. (2004). The problem of false confessions in the post-DNA world. *North Carolina Law Review, 82*, 891-1007.

Gudjonsson, G.H. (2003). *The science of interrogations and confessions: A handbook.* Chichester, England: Wiley.

Hartwig, M., Granhag, P.A., Strömwall, L., & Vrij, A. (2005). Detecting deception via strategic closure of evidence. *Law and Human Behavior, 29*, 469-484.

Inbau, F.E., Reid, J.E., Buckley, J.P., & Jayne, B.C. (2001). *Criminal interrogation and confessions* (4th ed.). Gaithersburg, MD: Aspen.

Kassin, S.M. (2005). On the psychology of confessions: Does *innocence* put *innocents* at risk? *American Psychologist, 60*, 215-228.

Kassin, S.M., & Fong, C.T. (1999). "I'm innocent!" Effects of training on judgments of truth and deception in the interrogation room. *Law and Human Behavior, 23*, 499-516.

Kassin, S.M., & Kiechel, K.L. (1996). The social psychology of false confessions: Compliance, internalization, and confabulation. *Psychological Science, 7*, 125-128.

Kassin, S.M., Leo, R.A., Meissner, C.A., Richman, K.D., Colwell, L.H., Leach, A.-M., & La Fon, D. (2007). Police interviewing and interrogation: A self-report survey of police practices and beliefs. *Law and Human Behavior, 31*, 381-400.

Kassin, S.M., Meissner, C.A., & Norwick, R.J. (2005). "I'd know a false confession if I saw one": A comparative study of college students and police investigators. *Law and Human Behavior, 29*, 211-227.

Kassin, S.M., & Norwick, R.J. (2004). Why suspects waive their Miranda rights: The power of innocence. *Law and Human Behavior, 28*, 211-221.

Kassin, S.M., & Sukel, H. (1997). Coerced confessions and the jury: An experimental test of the "harmless error" rule. *Law and Human Behavior, 21*, 27-46.

Kassin, S.M., & Wrightsman, L.S. (1985). Confession evidence. In S. Kassin & L. Wrightsman (Eds.), *The psychology of evidence and trial procedure* (pp. 67-94). Beverly Hills, CA: Sage.

Leo, R.A. (1996). Inside the interrogation room. *The Journal of Criminal Law and Criminology, 86*, 266-303.

Meissner, C.A., & Kassin, S.M. (2002). "He's guilty!": Investigator bias in judgments of truth and deception. *Law and Human Behavior, 26*, 469-480.

Oberlander, L.B., & Goldstein, N.E. (2001). A review and update on the practice of evaluating Miranda comprehension. *Behavioral Sciences and the Law, 19*, 453-471.

Owen-Kostelnik, J., Reppucci, N.D., & Meyer, J.R. (2006). Testimony and interrogation of minors: Assumptions about maturity and morality. *American Psychologist, 61,* 286-304.

Redlich, A.D. (2007). Double jeopardy in the interrogation room: Young age and mental illness. *American Psychologist, 62,* 609-611.

Russano, M.B., Meissner, C.A., Narchet, F.M., & Kassin, S.M. (2005). Investigating true and false confessions within a novel experimental paradigm. *Psychological Science, 16,* 481-486.

Santos, F. (2006). DNA evidence frees a man imprisoned for half his life. *The New York Times,* September 20, 2006, p. A1.

Vrij, A., Fisher, R., Mann, S., & Leal, S. (2006). Detecting deception by manipulating cognitive load. *Trends in Cognitive Sciences, 10,* 141-142.

White, W.S. (2003). Confessions in capital cases. *University of Illinois Law Review, 2003,* 979-1036.

REVIEW AND CONTEMPLATE

1. Name and describe two "problematic tactics" sometimes used by American police during interrogations that research studies have shown can elicit false confessions from some subjects.

2. Name and describe three types of false confessions. Which of these types was elicited from Michael Crowe, who was accused of killing his sister?

3. Kassin (2008) explained that "some people are dispositionally more malleable than others—and at a greater risk for false confessions." Describe two personality traits that might make people more vulnerable to false confessions.

4. Kassin (2008) stated that "recent DNA exonerations reveal three sets of problems with confession evidence." Describe these problems.

INDEX

A

Abducted (Clancy), 151
abductions
    and aliens, 155–157
    and unidentified flying objects (UFOs), 155–157
"A Close Look at Therapeutic Touch", 289–299
Advances in Experimental Social Psychology, 324
advertising, subliminal, 121–128
age-regression, 169–170
    hypnotic, 170
    non-hypnotic, 172
    vivid and realistic experiences during, 171
aggressive behavior, 330. *See also* anger
    cognitive neoassociation theory and, 324
    experimental condition on, 330
Ainger-Clark, Julie, 87
Air, Water and Places (Hippocrates), 41
aliens, 155–157
    and abductions, 155–157
alternative therapies, 25
ambiguously specific prophecies, 182–185
American Holistic Nursing Association, 290
American Nurses' Association, 290
Analyze This, 322
anatomically correct dolls, 233
anger. *See also* aggressive behavior
    intense physical activity and, 331
    levels for participants in control, distraction, and rumination, 330
Applied Kinesiology, 278, 284
Areni, Charles, 127
Arnold, Kenneth, 314
aromatherapy, 113–118
auditory learners, 139, 140–141
auditory memories, 145
auditory representations, 141–142
Auerbach, Lloyd, 65
autism, 96–104
    and pseudoscience, 98–99
    and psychoanalytic explanations, 99–100
    etiology of, 99–104
"autistic-spectrum disorders", 97

B

Baby Einstein Company, 87
Baby Einstein video, 87, 88
"backmasking", 122
backward masking, 122
Bainbridge, William Sims, 311
Barrett, Stephen, 289
Bartholomew, Robert, 308–317
beliefs, 40
    paranormal, 40
    pseudoscientific, 40
Beloff, John, 65
Bennell, Craig, 216–222
Bensley, D. A., 63–70
Bermeitinger, Christina, 125
Beyerstein, Barry, 20–28
bibliotherapy, 174–175
Blanke, Olaf, 68
body language, 241
bogus personality interpretation, 172
brain
    and creativity, 47, 51–52
    left, 48–50
    plasticity, 52–54
    related belief, 47
    right, 48–50
    use of, 48

"brain-based" educational tools, 55
brainwashing, 126–128
Bruck, Maggie, 32–36
Burgess, Cheryl, 152–161
Burgess, Melissa Faith, 152–161
Bushman, Brad, 322–331

C

California Department of Developmental Services, 101
Callahan, Roger, 276, 277
Campbell, Don, 109–110, 112
Candida albicans, 100–101
candidiasis, 100–101
"Can Minds Leave Bodies? A Cognitive Science Perspective", 63–70
Cantril, Hadley, 311
"Can We Really Tap Our Problems Away? A Critical Analysis of Thought Field Therapy", 277–284
Capel, Charles, 130–131
catharsis theory, 323–324
"Causal Diagnostic" techniques, 279
causal judgments, 194
Ceci, Stephen, 32–37
Chapman, Jean, 226
Chapman, Loren, 226
chi (Chinese philosophy), 278, 284
child abuse, and multiple personality disorder, 158
child development
 and autism diagnosis, 96–104
 and videos for young children, 87–95
childhood
 autobiographical memory gaps in, 258
 DID in, 269
 physical and/or sexual abuse in, 259
children
 and auditory memories, 145
 and sexual abuse interviews, 31, 34–35
 and suggestive interviewing, 31–37
 and teaching modality, 145–148
 and visual memories, 145

Chiong, Cynthia, 88–95
Clancy, Susan, 151
cognition, 181–212
cognitive neoassociation theory, 324
cognitive science approach
 and out-of-body experience, 66–70
"compared to what" problem, 206
compliant false confessions, 336
conjunction fallacy, 193–194
consciousness, 47–57
Cool, Nadean, 166
Cooper, Grant, 124
Cooper, Joel, 124
Craig, Gary, 282, 283
creativity, and brain, 47, 51–52
Criminal Interrogations and Confessions (Inbau, Reid, Buckley and Jayne), 337
criminal profiling
 5 W's of, 216–218
 people believe in, 220–222
 police officers' opinions of, 218
 putting to the test, 218–220
"Criminal Profiling: Granfalloons and Gobbledygook", 216–222
Crisis Dreaming, 84
cross-cultural studies, and DID, 268–269
Crowe, Michael, 337–338
cure, vs. symptomatic relief, 25
Current Directions in Psychological Science, 96

D

Damphousse, Kelly, 248–252
dark prophecies, 186–189
deceit, patterns of, 242–244
DeLoache, Judy, 88–95
Descartes, René, 64
Deskovic, Jeffrey, 340
disease, vs. illness, 21
dispositional vulnerabilities, 339–340
"Dissociative Identity Disorder: A Contemporary Scientific Perspective", 257–270

dissociative identity disorder (DID). *See also* multiple personality disorder
   cross-cultural studies, 268–269
   distribution of cases across clinicians, 266–267
   etiology of, 258–262
   evidence for sociocognitive model of, 262–269
   in childhood, 269
   posttraumatic model, 259–260
   recommended treatment practices for, 262–264
   role-playing studies, 267–268
   sociocognitive model, 260–262
   two competing etiological models, 258–262
distortion of reality, 26–27
distraction, 324–325
"Do Babies Learn From Baby Media?", 88–95
Doctrine of Signatures, 190
"Does Venting Anger Feed or Extinguish the Flame? Catharsis, Rumination, Distraction, Anger, and Aggressive Responding", 322–331
"Do Visual, Auditory, and Kinesthetic Learners Need Visual, Auditory, and Kinesthetic Instruction?", 140–149
Dowd, Will, 109–112
Draw-a-Person Test (DAP), 226
dream interpretation, 173
"Dream Interpretation and False Beliefs", 75–85
dualistic paranormal beliefs
   cognitive science approach, 66–70
   current belief, 64–65
   origins of, 63–64
   out-of-body experiences, 62, 65–66

E

early memories, 169–170
Edwards, Jenny, 276
Eisenhower, Dwight, 313
Emotional Freedom Techniques (EFT)
   autism and, 282
   TFT and, 282
empirically solvable problems, 6
The Empty Fortress (Bettelheim), 100

Ernst, Ezard, 113
essential oils, 117–118
Eye Movement Desensitization and Reprocessing (EMDR), 277

F

Facing the Fire: Experiencing and Expressing Anger Appropriately (Lee), 325
false confessions
   compliant, 336
   internalized, 336
   voluntary, 336
"False Confessions: Causes, Consequences, and Implications for Reform", 336–342
false interpretation study, 76–83
false memories, 167
false memory creation, hypothesized path, 174–176
Feldman, Arnold, 312
Frazer, Sir James, 63–64
Freud, Sigmund, 74, 75

G

Gamer, Matthias, 238–245
Garb, Howard, 227–235
Gaudiano, Brandon, 97–104, 277–284
Gendreau, Paul, 216–222
Gilovich, Thomas, 191–201, 205–212
Goode, Erich, 308–317
Greenwald, Anthony G., 123
guided imagery, 35, 167
Guilty Knowledge Test, 240–242

H

Halvorson, Peter, 8, 19
Hand Test, 233
Handwriting Analysis (Graphology), 233
Heath, Chip, 182–189
hemisphericity, 49–50
Herbert, James, 97–104, 277–284
Herdtner, Sherron, 288
Hippocrates, 41

Hitler, Adolph, 181
human figure drawings, 234
Hurricane Katrina, 181, 204
hypnosis, 167–168
hypnotic age-regression, 170

I

Ilechukwu, Sunny, 317
illness, vs. disease, 21
illusory correlations, 40–44
imaging on trial, 245–246
innocence, phenomenology of, 340–341
internalized false confessions, 336
interviewer bias, 32–35
    and suggestive interviews, 32–33
    techniques of convey bias, 33–34
Islam, Nadia, 88–95

J

Jacobs, Norman, 314
Jansen, Karl, 69
Jiae Choi, 113
Johnson, Donald, 312
Journal of the American Medical Association, 288

K

Karr, John Mark, 336
Kassin, Saul, 336–342
Keeping Mozart in Mind, 111, 112
Kennedy, John F., 181
ketamine, 69
Kidd, E., 47
Kim, David, 127
kinesthetic learners, 140–141
Krieger, Dolores, 291
Kunz, Dora, 292

L

Larsen, Otto, 313
learning
    auditory, 139
    visual, 139
Lee, Derrick Todd, 215
Lee, John, 325
The Leeza Gibbons Show, 279
left brain, 48–50
Life Events Inventory (LEI), 76–83
"Like Goes With Like: The Role of Representativeness in Erroneous and Pseudoscientific Beliefs", 191–201
Lilienfeld, Scott, 165–176, 227–235, 257–270
Lindell, A., 48
Lock, Timothy, 166–176
Loftus, Elizabeth, 75–85, 166–176
Lombardo, Pasquale, 75–85
lucid dreaming, 66
Lüscher Color Test, 233
Lynn, Steven Jay, 166–176, 257–270

M

Mackay, Charles, 309
Malvagia, Stefano, 75–85
"Mass Delusions and Hysterias: Highlights From the Past Millennium", 308–317
mass hysteria, 261, 308–309, 312
Maturitas, 113
Mazzoni, Giuliana, 74–85
McCray, Antron, 335
McCutcheon, Lynn, 115–118
meaning-based representations, 142–143
Medalia, Nahum, 313
medical beliefs, 195–198
Meijsing, Monica, 70
memories, 141–142
    auditory, 145
    early, 169–170
    false, 167
    visual, 145
memory errors, 167
"Memory Recovery Techniques in Psychotherapy: Problems and Pitfalls", 166–176
Mesmer, Anton, 291
Michaels, Kelly, 31

Miller, David, 311
Miller, Zell, 110
Miranda rights, 340
modality
    content's best, 148–150
    teaching, to children, 145–148
    theory, 143–144, 148–149
"Mozart Effect", 108–112
Mozart Effect for Children, 109
multiple personality disorder, 157–160. *See also* dissociative identity disorder (DID)
    and satanism, 158–160
    child abuse and, 158
mumps, measles, and rubella (MMR) vaccination, 101–103
Myeong Soo Lee, 113
"The Myth of the Mozart Effect", 109–112
myths
    and paranormal beliefs, 47
    and truth verification, 47

N

Nathan, Debbie, 255
National Association for Holistic Aromatherapy, 113
natural oils, 117
neurological development, 52–54
neuromarketing, 54–56
neuroscience, 47–57
New York Times Magazine, 322
non-invasive neuroimaging techniques, 53
Nostradamus, Michel, 181
"Nostradamus's Clever 'Clairvoyance': The Power of Ambiguous Specificity", 182–189
Nurse Healers and Professional Associates Cooperative, 290

O

O'Doherty, Katherine, 88–95
"On the Belief That Arthritis Pain Is Related to the Weather", 41–44

Order of Nurses of Quebec, 290
Orthopaedic Nursing, 288
out-of-body experience (OBE), 62, 65–66
    and cognitive science approach, 66–70
    and lucid dreaming, 66
    somatic, 67–68
    visual, 68

P

paranormal beliefs, 40. *See also* beliefs
    and myths, 47
    and out-of-body experiences, 62
    origins of dualistic, 63–64
paranormal phenomena, 10
parent-teaching condition, 91
"Past-Life Identities, UFO Abductions, and Satanic Ritual Abuse: The Social Construction of Memories", 152–161
past-life personalities, experimental creation of, 153–155
past life regression, 170–171
Penfield, Wilder, 68
perception
    and brainwashing, 126–128
    and subliminal messages, 120
Persinger, Michael, 69
personality and psychological testing, 215–252
phenomenology of innocence, 340–341
placebo effect, 23
"Portrait of a Lie", 238–245
Posadzki, Paul, 113
posttraumatic model, 259–260
Powell, Colin, 237
Power Balance wristband, and pseudoscience, 10–12
Pratkanis, Anthony R., 123
Pratt, J.G., 65
Programming the Nation, 126
pseudoscience
    and autism, 98–99
    and cognitive process, 13
    and Power Balance wristband, 10–12

and social process, 13
described, 7–10
in psychotherapy, 282–283
objective of, 283
vs. science, 5–7
pseudoscientific beliefs, 40, 197–198
"Psychic Crime Detectives: A New Test for Measuring Their Successes and Failures", 132–137
psychics, 132–137
   as crime detectives, 130–131
psychoanalysis
   representativeness heuristic and, 198–199
psychokinesis, 47
psychological disorders and therapies, 255–299
Psychological Science in the Public Interest, 139
"psychomotor agitation", 308
"psychosomatic" symptoms, 24–25
psychotherapy
   clinical features of patients with, 265–266
   pseudoscience in, 282–283
publicly verifiable knowledge, 6

Q
Quinn, Janet, 292

R
Radovanovic, Zoran, 316
Ramsey, JonBenet, 336
Redelmeier, Donald, 41–44
Reiser, Martin, 133–134
representativeness heuristic, 190, 192–193
   and causal judgments, 194
   and medical beliefs, 195–198
   and pseudoscientific beliefs, 197–198
   and psychoanalysis, 198–199
   conjunction fallacy, 193–194
Rhine, J.B., 65
right brain, 48–50
Right-brained Children in a Left-brained World (Freed and Parsons), 48
right-brain teaching, 47
role-playing studies, 267–268
Rorschach Inkblot Test, 226
Rosa, Emily, 289–299
Rosa, Linda, 289–299
Rosenzweig Picture Frustration Study, 233
rumination, 324–325

S
Sarner, Larry, 289–299
satanism, and multiple personality disorder, 158–160
Savitsky, Kenneth, 191–201
science, vs. pseudoscience, 5–7
Scientific American, 14
"seek and ye shall find" problem, 207–208
selective matching, 43
selective memory, 43
selective memory problem, 208–212
sensation
   aromatherapy, 113–118
Sentence Completion Test, 233
"Separating Fact From Fiction in the Etiology and Treatment of Autism: A Scientific Review of the Evidence", 97–104
September 11, 2001 terrorist attacks, 181–182
Seventeen magazine, 14
sexual abuse interviews, and children, 31, 34–35
Sharp, Ian, 97–104
Shaw, Gordon, 109–110
Sherman, Kathleen, 88–95
Short, Elizabeth, 336
Sjahrir, Soetan, 311
Skeptical Inquirer, 14
Snook, Brent, 216–222
social psychology, 307–342
sociocognitive model, 260–262
"Some Systematic Biases of Everyday Judgment", 205–212

Spanos, Nicholas, 152–161
"Special K", 69
Spiegel, Herbert, 255
split-brain research, 50–51
"spontaneous remissions", 22
Stemman, Roy, 132–137
stereotype induction, 34
Stroebe, Wolfgang, 120–128
Strouse, Gabrielle, 88–95
subliminal messages, 120–128
"The Subtle Power of Hidden Messages", 121–128
"The Suggestibility of Young Children", 32–37
suggestive interviewing
  and children, 31–37
    and interviewer bias, 32–35
    techniques, 32–35
Sybil Exposed (Nathan), 255
symptomatic relief, vs. cure, 25
symptom interpretation, 171–172
systematic empiricism, 6
Szondi Test, 233

T

Taylor, Paul, 216–222
Teaching for the Two-sided Mind (Williams), 48
telepathy, 47
Thalbourne, Michael, 65
Thematic Apperception Test (TAT), 226
  doubts about, 230–231
  faults in the figures, 230–232
  picture imperfect, 231
Therapeutic Touch (TT)
  claims made for, 290
  hypothesis, 291–293
  literature analysis, 293–294
  professional recognition, 289–290
The Thought Field, 280
Thought Field Therapy (TFT), 277
  alternate explanations, 281–282
  Emotional Freedom Techniques (EFT) and, 282

  extraordinary claims of success, 279
  limited research findings, 280
  origins and methods, 277–278
  pseudoscience in psychotherapy, 282–283
  theoretical underpinnings, 278–279
Troseth, Georgana, 88
Tumin, Melvin, 312
Tversky, Amos, 41–44

U

unidentified flying objects (UFOs), 155–157
  and abductions, 155–157
United Nations Security Council, 237
University of Alabama, Birmingham, 294
University of Colorado Health Sciences Center (UCHSC), Denver, 294
University of Florence, 76–83

V

Vanderborght, Mieke, 88–95
video-with-interaction condition, 90
video-with-no-interaction condition, 90
visual learners, 139
visual learning, 139
visual memories, 145
visual out-of-body experience (OBE), 68
visual representations, 142
"Voice Stress Analysis: Only 15% of Lies About Drug Use Detected in Field Test", 248–252
Voice Technology (VT), 279
voluntary false confessions, 336
VSA software programs, 249
  detecting deception, 251–252
  deter people from lying, 251–252
  out of the lab, into the field, 249–250
  to use or not use, 252

W

Walt Disney Company, 87
West, Donald, 132–137
"What's That I Smell? The Claims of Aromatherapy", 115–118

"What's wrong with this picture?", 227–235
"Why Bogus Therapies Seem to Work", 20–28
"Why Right-brain Teaching Is Half-Witted: A Critique Of The Misapplication of Neuroscience to Education", 48–57
Wilbur, Cornelia, 255
Willingham, Daniel, 140–149
Wiseman, Richard, 132–137
Wood, James, 227–235
World War I, 311

Y

Yafeh, Maziar, 182–189

Printed in the USA
CPSIA information can be obtained
at www.ICGtesting.com
LVHW080319010224
770270LV00008B/18